THE MALPRACTITIONERS

Also by the same author:

MORALISTS AND MANAGERS
PUBLIC INTEREST MOVEMENTS IN AMERICA
1976 Anchor Press

The Malpractitioners

by JOHN GUINTHER

ANCHOR PRESS / DOUBLEDAY
GARDEN CITY, NEW YORK
1978

We gratefully acknowledge the following for permission to reprint:

Chart on "Perinatal and Maternal Mortality Rates by Type of Hospital" was prepared by the American Foundation for Maternal and Child Health, Inc., based on data from the *National Study of Maternity Care: Survey of Obstetric Practice and Associated Services in Hospitals in the United States* by the Committee on Maternal Health of the American College of Obstetricians and Gynecologists, 1970, and reprinted by permission; quoted material from *A Legislator's Guide to the Medical Malpractice Issue,* copyright © 1976 by the Health Policy Center, Graduate School, Georgetown University.

ISBN: 0-385-12898-3
LIBRARY OF CONGRESS CATALOG CARD NUMBER 77-92215

PRINTED IN THE UNITED STATES OF AMERICA
FIRST EDITION

Again for Carol

Contents

Acknowledgments

The help of many people made the writing of this book possible. Their number includes doctors, nurses, insurance executives, actuaries, lawyers, government officials, as well as individuals who have been plaintiffs in malpractice suits. Several of these source people, whose employment might be jeopardized if their co-operation became known, spoke to me only on the promise they would not be named or be otherwise identifiable. From that group, I particularly want to thank "Rose Turner." More than any other person, she was responsible for awakening my interest in the medical malpractice problem, giving me my first insights into the complex and far-reaching tragedies which provide the sometimes nearly invisible webbing in which all the other issues discussed in this book are permanently cocooned.

The following people, who can be named, also gave to me freely of their time and advice. A number of them, I know, will disagree with certain conclusions I have reached and none, in any event, should be held accountable for those opinions or any errors I may have made in research. They are listed in no special order of importance but with an equal amount of gratitude. My thanks, therefore, to Eli Bernzweig whose knowledge of the malpractice problem is second to no one's; to J. Robert Hunter, Insurance Administrator of the United States; to Robert Begam and R. Bruce Gebhardt of the Association of Trial Lawyers of America; to Steven Blumenkrantz and John Herzfeld of the Insurance Services Office; to Philipp Stern, actuary of the New Jersey Insurance Department; to David Bell, M.D., and William Hewson, M.D.; and to each of the following attorneys, representing both the plaintiff and the defense bar: James Beasley, Jeffrey Stopford, S. Gerald Litvin, Elwood S. Levy, Turrey Kepler, A. Grant Sprecher, Joseph B. Erwin, David O'Brien, Frank Shields, and

David Shrager; and to these helpful friends David Cohen and Morton Jacobs. For his courtesy in providing access to important research material, I want to express especial appreciation to Edward Schwartz of the National Council for Health Services Research; and to Greg Webber and Judith Delbaum of Pennsylvania Blue Cross/Blue Shield. For some of the material on drug injuries in Chapter Ten, I am grateful to Doris Haire, president of the American Foundation for Maternal and Child Health, Inc.

A separate acknowledgment goes to two attorneys, Robert M. Fellheimer and Max R. Millman, whose explanations of the intricacies of tort law were invaluable in the writing of Chapter Three.

My thanks as always to Alan Halpern, editor of *Philadelphia Magazine*, in which some of this material appeared in a different form. For her encouragement, enthusiasm for the project, and excellent advice throughout, I want to thank Elizabeth Frost Knappman, editor, Anchor Press/Doubleday, as well as her associate, Joan Kass.

A final note: All the medical malpractice case histories narrated in this book summarize actual events. Sources are described in the Bibliography and Notes sections. An exception to attribution occurs for those instances in which confidential sources were used. In them, all the medical facts of the episode are intended to be accurately portrayed, based on information from the sources themselves and independently obtained confirming documentation. However, specific events, locations, names, descriptions of persons, and quotations have been fictionalized; none of the characters in these episodes are intended to portray any person, living or dead.

CHAPTER ONE

The Victims

I

The time was just before midnight on a Saturday evening. The place was the emergency room of a general hospital situated close to the heart of the city's black ghetto. The staff doctor in charge was a wiry and intense young man named Jack Kane. By becoming a doctor, Kane had fulfilled the only ambition in life he could ever remember having. His family was lower middle class, and he had had to work full time while attending college, an expenditure of energy that reflected itself in his grades. Six medical schools had rejected his application, but he was persistent and the seventh decided to take a chance on him and ultimately was pleased it did. Kane might never pioneer any new frontiers in medicine, but he was devoted, meticulous, and average adroit surgically.

This night, however, the average and dedicated Dr. Kane was about to make a mistake, one that would be more easily explained away by his hospital employer and its attorneys when a malpractice suit resulted than Kane would ever rationalize it to himself.

Emergency room duty at the hospital always reminded Kane of a story he had read in a college literature course, although the story had nothing to do with medicine. It told of a police captain who was in charge of conducting line-ups. Into the white glare of the line-up's platform, night after night, year after year, stepped, one after the other, the dregs of the city's society, the thieves, the hustlers, the dopers, the child molesters, the ancient children and the men and women who had never had a youth. The captain would sometimes scream at the shuffling denizens under his light, sometimes cajole them, sometimes insult them, sometimes simply read out to them their endless arrest records, until, as though he were their director and they his actors, it was hard for him to tell where they left off and he began. The captain, the author noted, had bad dreams. So did Jack Kane. One part of him was always the captain acting as captain, reading records and treating symptoms of featureless people—a kid shot by a cop; a cop shot by a kid—the bullet holes, the extra-rich blood slipping over the lips of knife wounds, the gray and visible intestines. But another part of him was the captain as director. As the captain in the story had with the numbers of the crimes and their pointlessness, so did Kane become immersed in the quantity, rather than the quality, of the agony all around him. Even as his hands worked under one order, his mind became part of the screams, of the disorientation, his hours a collage of black skin and pink wounds. The other doctors and nurses he worked with and to whom he often spoke seemed to him from a separate world, clearly his world—he was always aware of that—but a less real world than the subterranean one of the dying and the hopeless whose holes were like fingers pointing, not at him, but at some upper world they only sensed existed.

Perhaps, Kane would later think, it was the absence of horror in Tommy Manning that drew him away from the subterranean world in which, like an automaton, the doctor part of him had been performing competently. The fourteen-year-old Manning, like almost all his patients, was black, but unlike most of the black boys that Kane was used to treating, Tommy had retained his childhood vibrancy; he was interested, not just in himself, but in the things he saw around him. The trip to the hospital had a quality of adventure to him, and he asked Kane questions with the curiosity of one who expects that each event will peel away to reveal something more wonderful to come. Perhaps, therefore, it was Tommy's joy in life that put Kane off guard, although the less mystical part of him knew it was simply that the boy's wound appeared trivial. An hour before he was brought to the hospital, Tommy and his sister were walking home when the boy was struck by a bullet fired in a gang fight that mysteriously erupted around him. At first the boy was sure he had just been nicked, a scratch, but his parents were less certain and they brought him to the clinic. As he conversed with the chattering boy, Kane examined the wound; the bullet, it was clear to him, had entered the fleshy part of the upper shoulder and had not exited. It would have to be removed, but there was no hurry. (Out of the corner of his eye, Kane saw a middle-aged black man being placed on the examining table; he was clutching his bleeding stomach.) Telling his nurse to make an appointment for the boy for the following Tuesday, Kane placed a Band-Aid over the bullet's entrance point and then, because he liked Tommy, he took a precious moment to say, "Don't be frightened now, son. It's just a little flesh wound. We'll take it out and you'll have a souvenir." Tommy slid down from the table, steadied himself against it for a moment, looked up at Kane, and as if ashamed of himself said softly, "Gee, I guess I am a little scared. My legs, they feel so weak." "You'll be fine," Kane said and the boy went off with his parents.

The next morning when Tommy Manning woke up, he found himself paralyzed from the waist down. Kane had been wrong. The bullet hadn't stopped in the flesh; rather it had continued its way downward through the boy's body and had severed his spinal cord. He would spend the rest of his life in a wheelchair. Jack Kane's dreams would get worse.

II

It has always been possible in the United States for patients to sue their doctors for causing them injury during the course of their medical treatment. Such suits, however, remained extremely rare into the 1950s, and it wasn't until the mid-1960s that the amount of litigation began to rise sharply; at that time, increments in the filing of malpractice claims, which had been hovering between 2 per cent and 5 per cent each year, suddenly rose to 15 per cent per annum, a pace that has been more or less maintained ever since.[1] As a result, as long ago as the late 1960s, some medical spokesmen were already warning of a burgeoning malpractice problem which had the most serious implications not just for the doctors who were getting sued but for their patients as well. Even so, in 1972, a federal study of malpractice noted that two thirds of all Americans had no awareness that a problem of any kind existed.[2] Just three years later, however, a Gallup Poll revealed that 90 per cent of the people it sampled now "knew" the nation was facing a "malpractice crisis."[3] Quite apparently, a great deal of public education had been going on during that three-year interval.

For many people, television drama was the principal informative source. The first half of the 1970s was the time of the medical shows. Kindly Dr. Marcus Welby was then at the zenith of his infallibility, and not far behind were various stalwart and dedicated surgeons roaming the corridors of other stainless and perfect video hospitals, curing patients while in search of high ratings. During these years, virtually every one of these programs, the viewers of each numbered in the millions, devoted at least one episode to the agony the hero underwent when he was falsely accused of malpractice.

Many others first learned of the malpractice problem from their newspapers. There they read stories of multimillion-dollar verdicts for injured patients, and soon after also read of doctors who were threatening to stop treatment of their patients unless steep increases in their malpractice insurance costs were rescinded. For people living in states like New York[4] and California,[5] the threat became a reality as thousands of doctors went on strike, for a time causing medical care to virtually cease except in emergency situations. In other states, like Wisconsin,[6] a strike was averted only at the last moment.

By the mid 1970s, too, the American Medical Association (AMA) and the American Hospital Association (AHA) had already launched full blown anti-malpractice campaigns,[7] their efforts backed by the insurance companies that were paying out on the ever more frequent and costly verdicts incurred by their customers. Sometimes acting together and sometimes separately, these allies proposed new laws, many of which were passed, having as their purpose to curb the frequency of the malpractice suits and to provide emergency insurance sources in those states in which the commercial companies asserted that, no matter how much they charged, they could no longer afford to write policies. The new laws, however, seemed to do little to change the frequency of the claims, while the new state-operated insurance funds proved even more expensive for the doctors and hospitals than had been the old commercial sources.

Statistics on the problem from all sides were invariably ominous and widely publicized. The figures quoted, however, were rarely in agreement with one another. For example:

* The senior vice-president of the American Insurance Association reported that in 1975, 20,000 malpractice claims were filed, or about *one for every fifteen physicians in active practice.*[8]

* In 1975, also, St. Paul Fire & Marine Insurance Company, the nation's leading malpractice insurer, reported *claims against one*

of every ten of its doctor customers. By projection, that would be about 35,000 claims for that year.[9]

* Far gloomier were another set of statistics released by the AMA. It asserted (for 1976) 52,000 claims or about *one for every seven doctors*. By 1980, the AMA said, *one in every four doctors* could expect to be named as defendants in malpractice claims.[10]

* Sheer optimism was the view the giant Travelers Insurance Company took of the AMA statistics. In 1975, it told a United States Senate Subcommittee that already *more than one of every two* of its customers were having malpractice claims lodged against them.[11]

Estimates of the cost to the public of the crisis that had arisen varied as widely as the statistics on its frequency. For 1975, these numbers ranged from a low of $2 billion to $11 billion.[12]

Nor was there agreement about the causes of the problem. Dr. Sidney Wolfe of Ralph Nader's Public Citizen Health Research Group criticized a medical system that in his view presumes it doesn't have to account to its patients for its conduct toward them.[13] They, in turn, increasingly resent "the frequently poor technical quality of [the] health care [they receive] . . . more people are now acquainted with such problems as overprescribing of antibiotics, unnecessary surgery, preventable adverse drug reactions, needless hospital infections and the like."[14] Without the poor health care, in Wolfe's view, there'd be nothing to resent and therefore no malpractice problem. Stating the same thesis more succinctly was Robert Cartwright, past president of the Association of Trial Lawyers of America (a group whose members represent injured patients in malpractice suits): "(T)he sole cause of medical malpractice cases *is* medical malpractice."[15]

But perhaps not so. Some analysts (including those representing the AMA[16] and certain federal government spokesmen[17]) believe that many, and perhaps the majority of malpractice suits, have no legitimate basis. The miracle cures created by modern American medicine, they note, have caused people to develop unreasonable expectations of what can be accomplished by doctors, and therefore they are likely to sue "when medical results are less than perfect."[18] Since the best doctors perform the most difficult work, it is they, not the rare incompetent physician, who, according to this theory, are the most likely objects of litigation. The American insurance industry has espied a related cause. "We are living," its spokesmen point out, firmly if redundantly, "in an increasingly litigious society in which citizens are quick to sue."[19]

The insurers themselves, however, are not above attack. Although it is true, according to their critics, that malpractice claims, for a variety of reasons, have been steadily on the rise, the increment has not been sufficient to merit the response the insurance industry has made to it. Rather, it is argued, the insurers have seized on a genuine but manageable problem in claims frequency and exploited it into a crisis for purposes of their own.

During the course of this book, each of these causal theories will be discussed in some detail. Some, although not all, of the premises put forth have, through reiteration if nothing else, gained widespread public credence, despite the fact that they are based on documentation that is either false or misleading. The various solutions that emanate from these theories will also be described. Certain of them, whether we ultimately agree with their reasoning or not, represent serious and objective thinking on the part of people who are both knowledgeable and concerned. Other proposals, however, even as they protect the interests of their advocates, mount attacks, advertently or otherwise, on traditional and important citizen rights, raising questions that go well beyond the medical and legal issues involved.

Still other questions are more basic. Without the answers to them, or, in some instances, the realization that, despite what some say, there simply are at present no reliable answers, we lack the information to assess meaningfully either the theories, the motivations, or the solutions proferred. For example, what exactly is medical malpractice? Who pays for its costs? What kinds of charges do plaintiffs raise in their suits? What defenses can doctors make to the charges? Are doctors more or less likely to win a suit now than in the past? In the chapters that immediately follow this one, these questions and related ones, will be addressed.

In the balance of this chapter, we will look at some others, more of a demographic nature, such as: What, in fact, do we know about the people who do the suing? About the doctors who get sued? Under what medical circumstances are misadventures most likely to occur that will later give rise to a suit?

III

To some of these questions, we have more complete answers than for others. We do know, for example, a great deal about the *settings* in which a medical injury is most likely to occur. Three major studies are all in large-scale agreement on that, one undertaken by the Department of Health, Education and Welfare (HEW) in 1972; another, conducted in 1974 by the statistical arm of the malpractice insurers, the Insurance Services Office (ISO); and a third, completed in 1977, by the National Association of Insurance Commissioners (NAIC), the state bodies that regulate insurance company practices.

All three discovered that three quarters or more of all situations that eventually lead to malpractice claims occur in hospitals. This is hardly surprising. Hospitalized patients normally receive a greater variety and amount of medical care than do non-hospitalized ones, with any phase of that treatment capable of producing the kinds of injuries that might give the patient grounds for suit. Since the differences among the studies are insignificant, Table A is based on the detailed ISO analysis, except as noted:[20]

TABLE A

SITES OF INCIDENTS LEADING TO MALPRACTICE CLAIMS

IN HOSPITALS:	PERCENTAGE	
Operating Room	39.7	
Patient's Room	11.9	
Emergency Room	9.8	
X-ray Room	4.2	
Recovery Room	0.7	
Intensive Care Unit	0.6	
Cardiac Care Unit	0.2	
Unspecified	11.7	
TOTAL HOSPITAL		78.8%
NON-HOSPITAL SITES		
Doctor's Office	18.8	
Patient's Home	0.6	
Nursing Home	0.6*	
All Other	1.2	
NON-HOSPITAL		21.2%

* BASED ON HEW FIGURES.[21]

Table A must be interpreted carefully. The postoperative hospital patient seems to be the least likely to suffer a medical injury when most seriously ill, i.e., while in intensive care, and is in the greatest danger when in his or her own room. This may well be so, but most patients spend little or no time in intensive care and a great deal of time in their rooms, in which not only postoperative complications may set in, but the patient may fall from bed or be otherwise injured in ways that can lead to a claim but may not be directly related to the doctor's care. Noteworthy, also, is the very low percentage of malpractice allegations arising from nursing home situations, despite a considerable body of evidence[22] suggesting that malpractice is rife in many of these institutions.

The dominance of the operating room as the site in which a malpractice-type injury most often occurs leads to the conclusion that those who perform the operations, the surgeons, are the doctors most likely to be sued. That this, in fact, is the case was revealed by both the NAIC and the HEW studies, though with some statistical differentiations. In Table B, which follows, malpractice claims against general practitioners have been eliminated since some of these doctors perform surgery, while others do not, and there is no way of knowing from the studies how many of the suits against them involved surgery and how many not. Nevertheless, for comparison purposes, other specialists who rarely if ever perform surgery are included:

TABLE B

MALPRACTICE CLAIMS FILED AGAINST SELECTED MEDICAL AND SURGICAL SPECIALTIES

	% OF ALL DOCTORS IN THE SPECIALTY*	% OF ALL CLAIMS FILED AGAINST, PER HEW STUDY	% OF ALL CLAIMS FILED AGAINST, PER NAIC STUDY
NON-SURGICAL			
Internists	14.0	6.9	**
Pediatricians	6.0	2.3	**
Psychiatrists	7.1	6.0	**

* Hew figures, 1972.
** Figure not stated in survey.

SURGICAL			
Obstetricians/ Gynecologists	6.3	8.3***	13.6
Opthalmologic Surgeons	3.2	2.1	1.9
Orthopedists	3.2	8.8	8.9
Urologists	1.9	2.8	2.6
Neurosurgeons	0.5****	**	2.4
Plastic Surgeons	0.5****	**	3.2
Anesthesiologists	3.6	7.9	6.1

*** The HEW survey may have included some claims involving obstetric injury under the general surgery category which is not replicated here because of its vagueness; the NAIC figure can be considered the more accurate of the two.
**** Approximate.

Note that Table B only describes how often claims are made against doctors in various categories, not how often these claims result in payments to the plaintiffs.

One of the greatest values of the NAIC study is its detailed analysis of the *kinds of treatment* most likely to lead to a malpractice claim that does eventually result in payment to the injured person. (The NAIC study is statistically ample, based on more than 20,000 such claims resolved between July 1, 1975 and June 30, 1976.[23]) Table C summarizes the NAIC findings:[24]

TABLE C

PROCEDURE CAUSING THE INJURY IN SUCCESSFUL MALPRACTICE CLAIMS

TYPE OF PROCEDURE	% OF ALL CLAIMS
Operations on the Female Genital System (includes hysterectomies but excludes childbirth)	13
Operations on the Musculoskeletal System (includes setting of fractures, other operations on bones and muscles as well as amputations)	12
Operations on the Digestive System (includes appendectomies, hemorrhoidecto-	

TYPE OF PROCEDURE	% OF ALL CLAIMS
mies, hernia repairs, and gall-bladder operations among others)	9
Operations on the Nose, Mouth, Pharynx (includes sinus and nose operations, tonsillectomies, and dental oral surgery)	5
Operations on the Skin and Subcutaneous Tissues (includes suturing)	4
Anesthesia Accidents	4
Accidents Associated with Childbirth	2
Operations on the Male Genital System	2
Operations of the Eye	2
All Others (includes operations on the nervous system, ear, respiratory system, urinary system, breasts, etc.)	6
ALL SURGICAL PROCEDURES	59%
Diagnostic and Miscellaneous Therapeutic Procedures (includes failure to diagnose an illness properly; and all accidents arising from medical treatment other than those associated with adverse drug reactions)	23
Drug Injuries	11
Hospital Procedures, Other (includes failure to monitor illnesses properly by staff)	6
ALL NON-SURGICAL PROCEDURES	40%

(NOTE: Figures do not come to 100 per cent because of rounding.)

All three of these tables express malpractice actions in frequency terms, not in the severity of the injury suffered or the size of any eventual payment made on the claim. Thus, although operations on the female genital system are the single most likely precipitant of a successful claim and obstetrician/gynecologists are the specialists most often sued, the relatively few claims involving surgery of the nervous system or cardiac operations may create much larger payments each because of the severity of the injury that can occur when these procedures go wrong.[25]

IV

The typical malpractice claimant is a middle-aged, middle-class white woman who has a high school education or better.

Once that is said, however, it is immediately necessary to hedge the description, partly because of serious gaps in the information available, and partly because the description would otherwise be misleading. Let us, therefore, look at what we actually do know about plaintiff characteristics:

Age: The average American citizen is 24 years old;[26] the average malpractice claimant, 34.[27] The *median* age of a malpractice claimant, however, appears to be somewhat older, perhaps in the early forties,[28] with (depending on whose statistics we use) anywhere from 14 per cent to 17 per cent of them 65 and older.[29] This compares to something less than 10 per cent of the total population that has reached that age.[30]

Logically malpractice claimants should be older than the general population. The older people become, the more prey they are to illnesses, both of the chronic[31] and the acute[32] variety. As a result, they see doctors more often[33] and are hospitalized far more often. As an example, 350 of every 1,000 people who are 65 or older require hospitalization each year, yet that is true of only 158 of each 1,000 people between 15 and 44.[34] Moreover, the older the patient is, the greater the average length of hospital stay and, hence, the greater exposure to the possibility of a malpractice injury: People under the age of 45 have average hospital stays of about five days; those 45 and older, ten days.[35] At the other end of the age scale, people of 18 and younger are much less likely than any other age group to become plaintiffs. They make up about 30 per cent of the total population,[36] but no more than 14 per cent of the claimants.[37]

However (and it's a big "however"), in terms of *size* of payment, the younger the claimant the larger the payout is likely to be. According to definitions set up by the NAIC, 37 per cent of all claims involving the most serious injuries occurred to patients 18 and younger, including babies. Moreover, 19 per cent of all claims in which it is asserted that the patient died because of malpractice involved those 18 and younger, more than quintuple the death rate in that age group.[38]

Sex: 51 per cent of the American population is female,[39] yet between 57 per cent and 58 per cent of all malpractice claimants are women or girls.[40] (*For this reason, during the course of this book, when it is necessary to refer to malpractice claimants by sex, feminine pronouns will be used. By the same token, since 91 per cent*[41] *of all doctors are men, as are 97 per cent of all lawyers,*[42] *generically they will be referred to by masculine pronouns.*)

For several reasons women are more likely than men to become malpractice claimants. First is the large number of injuries they receive as a result of operations on their genital system. (See Table C.) Second, partly due to pregnancy factors and partly due to the fact that they live longer than men, women see doctors more often than do men and, consequently, are more frequently exposed to the likelihood of a malpractice-type incident.

Boys, however, are more likely to be malpractice complainants than girls (20 per cent to 13 per cent).[43] This differential probably reflects sex-role stereotyping. Because boys are encouraged to be more physically active than girls, they are more likely to suffer broken bones and related injuries requiring hospitalization than are girls, again making them more exposed than girls to malpractice-type injuries. (A boy under 18 has a 23 per cent chance of being hospitalized, a girl 13 per cent.[44])

Race: Neither the NAIC nor the ISO studies covered this subject, and it appears that most insurance companies and state insurance commissions do not keep statistics by race. However, a 1970 study by HEW found that whites made up 88.9 per cent of all complainants, blacks, 9.6 per cent, all other races, less than 1 per cent.[45] That year, blacks were 11.6 per cent of the American population,[46] which suggests (if the same ratios hold true today) that blacks are about 20 per cent less likely than whites to pursue a medical injury claim.

Income, Occupation, Education. Very little research has been done on any of these subjects. NAIC ignored them entirely, while HEW and ISO dealt with income and occupation only sketchily; education not at all. We do know that somewhere between 60 per cent[47] and 67 per cent[48] of all claimants are unemployed, but since this figure includes housewives, retirees, and minors, the statistic is meaningless. Similarly, an occupational study by ISO was so poorly defined by category as to have no value.[49]

It can, nevertheless, be hypothesized that the prototypical malpractice claimant is reasonably well-educated and probably of the middle class. First, the under representation of blacks, most of whom earn lower incomes than whites and are less well-educated, suggests a middle-class bias among malpractice complainants. Second, in order to sue a doctor for malpractice, it is necessary to know it is possible to do so and then know how to find a lawyer, factors which may indicate at least average educational and economic attainments. Third, interviews with lawyers who handle malpractice cases revealed that they find most claimants to be middle-class and of average or better educational attainment.[50] Finally, people from the lowest income and lowest educational attainment section of the nation, the South, file significantly fewer suits than any other region. This pattern could, of course, also mean that Southern doctors are the least likely to commit malpractice, but to believe that we also have to believe they are superior to the doctors in the major urban centers of the northern half of the country, an illogical conclusion to accept.

In any event, wherever he may practice, whatever his specialty may be, fear of a malpractice suit is the doctor's constant companion as he goes about his medical rounds.

CHAPTER TWO

Dr. Schneider Is Unhappy

I

The operation seemed to have gone well. The patient, a forty-five-year-old man named Robert Phillips had suffered multiple fractures of the right shoulder when he fell stepping off a subway car that was in motion. Performing the surgery on him was Dr. William Schneider, an orthopedist, who had been called in on the case by the patient's family physician. A member of the teaching staff at the university hospital at which the operation took place, Schneider was, like the patient, middle-aged. Possessor of a tiny brush mustache, watery blue eyes and thinning hair, Schneider's manner was cold; the distance he established between everyone and himself emphasized by the erect, almost Teutonic manner in which he carried his slight frame. In speaking, he seemed to measure out his words as if each were a coin he was reluctant to pay out. When he did choose to spend them, however, those words could be cutting. Nurses and most of the doctors training under him lived in terror of him, and he could even be sharp-tongued with his patients, particularly, as one resident noted, when they disappointed him by refusing to make the progress he thought was proper. He was also considered one of the three or four best men in his field in the city in which he practiced.

At times, Schneider appeared aware of his personal problems with patients, but seemed to have long ago decided there was nothing he could or should do about it. He often commented to his students—it was the closest he ever came to a joke—that he had chosen surgery as a specialty because a patient on an operating table was the only one in no position to talk back to his doctor. At another time, he told a colleague he was amazed that anyone would choose psychiatry as a specialty. It seemed to him, he said, an occupation fit only for a priest, and for his part he didn't want his mind cluttered with other people's dirty secrets.

Fortunately for Schneider, he had someone to do his listening for him. This man was Dr. John Robinson, the hospital's chief resident in surgery. Twenty years Schneider's junior, Robinson, unlike his chief, had an easy way with people that made them readily trust him, and it was he, therefore, who was seen most often by Schneider's hospitalized patients, particularly for the preoperative interviews when they were at their most frightened. Robinson was happy to allow himself to be used this way; it not only gave him good experience but permitted him to remain in close contact with Schneider whose high opinion of him would count when it came time to establish his own position in the city's medical community.

On this day, Robinson had assisted Schneider in the Phillips surgery and then gone ahead to Schneider's office where the two men were to meet to discuss several other patients. Upon arriving, Robinson, as he later recalled it, noticed three pink message slips on Schneider's desk, the top one from a Mr. Madison who, Robinson knew, was the attorney representing Schneider in a malpractice case involving a fourteen-year-old girl, Anita Hadley, who suffered brain damage during an operation on which Schneider was the chief surgeon. Robinson, who had assisted at that operation also, had not been named as a defendant in the suit, but the hospital, along with Schneider and the anesthesiologist, had been. Some months before, Robinson had been interviewed by Madison about the case, and he didn't like the man: "He's one of those country club types with a buttery voice and a red face. He either drinks too much or plays golf too much, and either is bad." Schneider had played no role in selecting Madison; he, rather, had been retained by Schneider's insurance company which had the right to do so since it was their money, not Schneider's, that would have to be paid out if the case were lost.

Schneider, Robinson knew, wanted to go to trial on the case. "He considered his professional reputation at stake, or maybe it was his dignity," Robinson analyzed it. "It was as if he were walking down the street and a policeman had suddenly arrested him as a vagrant; it wasn't so much that the arrest was unjust as it was that any policeman would think a Dr. Schneider could be a vagrant." In fact, from a medical view, Robinson had no doubt that Schneider was right. If there were any fault, it was the anesthesiologist's. However, neither

Schneider nor Robinson really believed that either: "It was just one of those medical tragedies," according to Robinson. "Unforeseeable. An unforeseeable reaction to the anesthesia."

When Schneider finally arrived at the office, he examined the message slips, placed the top one in his shirt pocket and answered the other two. When he finished his calls, he swiveled his desk chair so that his back was to Robinson. Robinson said, "It went well."

Schneider did not respond.

Robinson, who wasn't sure whether he was baiting his chief at that moment or was simply curious about the unanswered call, went on, "Well, at least, he's one we won't have to worry about."

Schneider, still facing the window, "How so?"

"It won't be us he'll sue."

Schneider now swung around to face the younger man. "I don't believe I follow you, doctor."

Robinson wished he'd never started the conversation. "Well, when I spoke to him before the operation, he said the subway started up just as he was getting off. A subway shouldn't start up while the doors are open. He has a hell of a case. He's got a case there that's worth thousands of dollars. He'll sue them, and better them than us."

Schneider cogitated on that for a moment and then crisply, "Perhaps. If that's the way it happened. But keep in mind, doctor, that one way or another, should that shoulder not heal to his perfect satisfaction, it may be us as well as they whom he sues. That is, if," and Schneider's voice curled around his final word with loathing, ". . . if he's litigious."

Robinson felt a trickle of fear at Schneider's words; it came to rest at the pit of his stomach. He knew he had been fortunate not to be named a defendant in the Hadley case. Even though he had no financial responsibility—as a staff member, he was covered by the hospital's insurance—he very much didn't want it on his record he had ever been named a defendant in a malpractice action. Within the next year, he hoped to open his own office, and he might have done so already, except it meant borrowing money, not for equipment—that he could handle—but the $20,000 he needed to pay in advance for his first year's malpractice insurance. Making a bank loan for that amount was worrisome enough in itself, but if he'd already been a defendant in a suit, Robinson had heard, there would be an automatic surcharge of another thousand dollars. That a defendant might be exonerated made no difference; it was the fact the accusation had been made that cost the extra money. Worse yet, he'd heard, that the commercial insurance companies in his state didn't like to cover anybody who'd ever had a claim made against them, which meant that such unlucky doctors had to get their coverage from the new state-operated emergency malpractice insurance fund, and its rates were 25 per cent higher than even the highest rate from a private company. Thinking quickly back over the events of the operation just completed, he said, sounding weak to himself, "Everything did go well. There were no mistakes made."

"That," said Schneider, "is not, I believe, a legal consideration."

Robinson knew what he meant. Schneider and he had done nothing wrong in the Hadley case, yet Schneider was a defendant there. For a moment, Robinson couldn't even recall the shoulder patient's name or what he looked like. He was well-spoken though, he remembered that, well-educated, the kind of man who would have a lawyer, who would think about a lawyer. He had been scared when Robinson interviewed him. In pain. He wanted help. He and Schneider had given that to him. Would he sue? "This is a hell of a way to practice medicine," Robinson said.

Schneider smiled, thinly.

Three weeks later, Robinson learned that Schneider and the other defendants in the Hadley case had agreed to a pre-trial settlement by which the Hadley family received, it was rumored, more than $200,000. Robinson was shocked. It had, he believed, something to do with that message from Madison that Schneider hadn't returned while he was in the room. But he never asked Schneider about it, and Schneider never mentioned the Hadley case to him again either.

II

The nation's doctors and hospitals in 1976 paid between $1.5 billion and $1.75 billion for their malpractice insurance premiums.[1] This compares to $61.6 *million* paid in 1960.[2] (Doctors in private practice accounted for $1 billion of the 1976 total.[3] Those who work for hospitals, private or governmental, have their premiums included as part of the hospital's insurance payment.)

Thus, with approximately 350,000 doctors in private practice,[4] the *average* malpractice premium per doctor in 1976 was a little over

$3,000, or 6 per cent of the *average* doctor's gross income of $53,600.[5] The AMA, it should be noted, has estimated that the average doctor paid $4,500 for malpractice insurance in 1975, a figure which, however, is incredible if other insurance and government estimates are accepted.[6]

No matter who is right, because of the range in premium costs created by a complex rating system—see Chapter Eleven—average rates have little meaning. Using a 1975 AMA study,[7] we find that in Mississippi, a general practitioner (who doesn't perform surgery) paid only $145 for his coverage that year while even the highest rated surgeons paid less than $1,000. On the other hand, in New York, the general practitioner paid $1,763 and some surgeons, $21,584. Many paid more, both in New York and elsewhere, since these figures are based on policies that pay up to $100,000 per claim. For policies offering $1 million in protection, rates run as high as $36,000 for some surgeons.[8]

In many respects and for many reasons, which will be discussed in later chapters, 1975 was the watershed year for malpractice increases. Rates went up for all medical customers at that time—for many, spectacularly so. For example, a hospital in Long Beach, California, had its premium raised from $340,000 in 1974 to $850,000 in 1975,[9] and it, comparatively speaking, got off lucky. A Buffalo hospital reported that in the same twelve months, its insurance went up from $64,000 to $500,000, a 758 per cent increase.[10] At the same time, a medium-sized New York City hospital found its rate jumped from about $40,000 to more than $558,000,[11] while a major teaching hospital in Philadelphia was hit with an increase from $245,000 to $1,500,000.[12]

Meanwhile, on the doctor front, malpractice rates in Pennsylvania for most doctors rose 400 per cent between 1974 and 1976,[13] while in California they rose on an average of 300 per cent in 1975 alone and by the beginning of 1976, in some cases by 600 per cent.[14] When taken over a somewhat longer period, the rate picture is even more inconsistent though no less extraordinary in growth terms. In 1965, for example, a general practitioner in Tennessee paid $117 for malpractice insurance, and ten years later only $383, an increment that barely covered inflationary factors, yet a neurosurgeon in the same state saw his rate go up from $422 to $3,128. In Connecticut, during that decade, GP rates increased from $62 a year to $455; neurosurgeons from $222 to $3,712. In Michigan, GP's were paying $101 in 1965, $1,471 in 1975; neurosurgeons, $364 in the earlier year, $12,002 in the latter.[15] So it went across the nation, with the rates for non-surgeons rising during the decade by 540 per cent on the average, for surgeons by 950 per cent.[16]

The zooming rates, allocated unequally across the land, inevitably had varying impacts. The Mississippi orthopedist needed perform only one or two additional operations a year to cover the cost of his malpractice increase, but the one in New York might now be performing operations for three or fours months a year before he was finally producing income for himself and not for the insurance company.

Almost all doctors pass on their malpractice insurance fees to their patients, just as any businessman adds his insurance costs to the prices he charges.[17] Nevertheless, as rates go up, the doctor's perception that he is working more and more for his insurance company is not incorrect. Typically, he pays his premium in full at the beginning of a year, which means he has less disposable income at that time to pay his bills or invest. He only recoups as he goes along. Moreover, as a self-employed businessman, in order to determine how much he should raise his fees each year because of insurance costs, he must estimate at the beginning of the year how much he expects to earn by its end. If he overestimates (e.g., he becomes sick during the course of the year and loses time from practice), he will not have passed on 100 per cent of his costs. On the other hand, if he underestimates his probable income, he will have passed-on more than 100 per cent and have made a profit from his insurance. No doubt that occasionally happens, with some greedy doctors using the publicity about high costs of malpractice insurance to raise their fees exorbitantly. The best statistical evidence, however, suggests that most doctors do not use insurance rate increases exploitively, and are content to pass-on only 100 per cent.[18] Yet even at 100 per cent, they may be hurting themselves financially. Because of an increased insurance pass-on, the doctor is simultaneously inhibited from raising his rates to cover other increased costs he had from inflationary factors. At the same time, he knows that as his fees go up, his patients become less able to use his services, or at least won't use them as frequently. The result is that the higher the pass-ons become, the greater the likelihood that the doctor's total annual income will decrease rather than increase both in terms of income dollars and spendable ones.[19]

Hospitals similarly pass on their malpractice charges to their patients. In their case, however, the large volume of business they do each year makes accessible to them highly reliable predictors of upward and downward trends in the number of beds they fill each year, so they usually are able to gauge their pass-ons more accurately than the average doctor who may simply pick a figure out of the air.

As Dr. Robinson understood, the greatest pass-on problem is the one faced by the high-rated surgeon just starting out in practice; in the early years, his income may not even cover the malpractice premium he pays. Only somewhat less sharply hit are doctors nearing retirement age; they may wish to reduce their patient load, but to do so ordinarily does not result in a comparable decrease in their insurance rates.[20] As a result, many of these older doctors retire early rather than see 25–50 per cent of their reduced annual income go to the insurance company.[21]

For all these reasons, from about 1975 on, a small number of doctors—most of them surgeons—have simply dropped their malpractice insurance. To protect themselves from paying out on suits, they have put their assets in their spouses' names or in secret bank accounts in Switzerland or the Bahamas, and woe betide any patient they injure who then tries to collect from them. However, the number of doctors going bare in an insurance sense remain a tiny percentage of the whole, and it is far from clear that their various money manipulating devices will work if they have a malpractice verdict placed against them. Their spouses' assets might be attached anyway, and clearly their future earnings could be.

For the doctor who is hit by a malpractice suit, the financial loss can be significant. Not only is there always the possibility that a verdict against him will be larger than the value of his insurance policy, but even if he wins the suit, the chances are good, as Robinson believed, that his insurer will increase his premium anyway, and will almost certainly do so if he loses. But even should none of these eventualities arise, he still faces loss of income because of the suit. As a defendant, he will be required to spend long hours in conferences with his attorney, appear at one or more depositions at which he will be questioned by the lawyer for the plaintiff, and if the case goes to trial, spend a week or two sitting in a courtroom. All this is time which the doctor otherwise would have used to produce income for himself by treating patients.

For a doctor, however, the financial impact of a malpractice suit may be less significant than the psychic one. The very word "malpractice" has an ugly, perjorative ring to it, reminiscent of malfeasance and other misdoings of the tawdry corrupt. It also seems to the doctor to be one applied selectively to him; after all, the automobile driver whose incompetence or carelessness causes injury or death to someone isn't accused of "malpractice," though that, in fact, may be what he is guilty of.

Worse yet, emotionally the malpractice suit strikes at the very heart of the doctor's life. His entire training has been dedicated to saving people's lives or, at the very least, alleviating their pain, yet, by the malpractice suit, he stands accused of the most fundamental violation of that purpose. Instead of saving, he is said to have killed; instead of alleviating, he is said to have maimed. Nor is exoneration from the charge likely to relieve the humiliation, the anger, and the frustration which he feels when the suit papers are first served on him, or, if he ends up at trial, the blows to his reputation when he hears the plaintiff's lawyer and her expert witnesses describe him as a butcher. And with some justification, he believes that regardless of the outcome of the case, it is the accusation that will always stand in the minds of his colleagues, and in his own mind as well.

III

Because of the pass-ons, it is the public that ultimately pays the nation's annual malpractice bill. Nor are payments limited only to those who use doctor and hospital services. For example, all medical providers bill not just their patients but also various patient insurance plans. Into these bills are tucked a malpractice pass-on percentage, with the patient insurer, in turn, forwarding the charges on to their subscribers. In this fashion, a Blue Cross/Blue Shield member who never uses a doctor or hospital in the course of a year still helps pay the annual malpractice bill to the extent the pass-on has been incorporated in his or her subscription fee. In the same way, doctors and hospitals bill government agencies for treating Medicare and Medicaid patients, again with the malpractice percentage included; since such programs are publicly supported, every taxpayer, ill or not, helps pay the national malpractice cost.

Cost per citizen for all these pass-ons can be depicted several ways. If the aim is to frighten the public about the annual malpractice burden, an AMA comparison can be used which shows that each time a patient visited a doctor in 1975, she paid $1.24 toward that doctor's malpractice bill, while just two years earlier she only paid $.30.[22] If, however, the intent is to show that the problem is not one about which consumers should agitate themselves, then one need only divide the 1976 malpractice insurance bill by the national population and find the cost per person to be $7.00 a year, hardly a bankrupting figure.

The malpractice bill, however, is not just limited to insurance costs. For one thing, there's the malpractice legal system. It is paid for by taxpayers in the form of judges' salaries, juror fees, courtroom costs, and payments to arbitration panels in some jurisdictions. In addition, those states that, like Dr. Robinson's, have their own malpractice insurance systems will contract some administrative costs that are borne by taxpayers. Taken together, the governmental and judicial costs of maintaining the malpractice legal system minimally run into the upper hundreds of millions of dollars annually.

According to some analysts, the largest malpractice cost to the public, far exceeding any insurance pass-ons, is caused by a phenomenon known as *defensive medicine.* Essentially, a doctor practices defensive medicine when he orders tests for a patient, not in the belief they are required to diagnose an illness, but solely in order to create a medical track record of diligence should the patient subsequently sue him.

Defensive medicine is the delight of any statistics monger. The cost of it to the public has been given as $1 billion a year, $3 billion a year, $5 billion a year, and $7 billion a year.[23] The beauty of these figures is that they all emanated in the same year, 1975, from the same federal agency, the Department of Health, Education and Welfare. Thus, it is possible to accurately quote HEW as saying that defensive medicine is a relatively minor problem ($1 billion a year comes to about $5 per citizen) or a horrendous problem ($7 billion comes to $35 a year, or as it can be put more dramatically, $140 annually for a family of four.) Since these are 1975 figures, it is also possible to project the chosen figure upward at almost any pace desired for a later year.

One problem with all these figures is that none of them, high or low, are statistically supportable. When, for example, does defensive medicine actually occur? Some doctors, by nature and training, are extremely careful and will normally order tests that others do not.

Therefore, is it *not* defensive medicine when a careful doctor orders tests, but is defensive when a normally careless one does? Perhaps, but then we are still left with the problem of establishing in some statistical fashion which of these test-ordering doctors are the "careful" ones and which the "careless."

Assuming we can overcome the definition hurdle, we are still left with the difficulty of measuring impact. On some occasions, for example, defensive medicine itself will cause a malpractice suit; excessive exposure to X rays due to unnecessary testing may cause cancer in a patient, providing the grounds for a malpractice claims that may well be viable. But some "unnecessary" tests will also reveal to the doctor a condition he wasn't aware of after his preliminary diagnosis; not only is the patient thereby helped but the doctor has also become less likely to embark on a course of treatment that might lead to a suit.

Consequently, it is possible to come to two diametrically opposed conclusions about the impact of defensive medicine. We can say, for instance, as did Professor Marnie Mueller of Wesleyan University in a paper presented to the American Economic Association in September 1976,[24] that statistical analyses of the fees doctors charge their patients reveal "striking evidence that a portion of the X rays, lab tests, and consultations ordered by a doctor are a reflection of anxiety about a malpractice suit." (Professor Mueller also discovered a complex but apparently positive ratio between the amount of defensive medicine practiced in a state and the size of the malpractice insurance rates paid by doctors in that state.[25]) However, as Dr. Mueller also pointed out in the same paper: "It is . . . reassuring to find that defensive medicine affects claims negatively,"[26] i.e., the more testing that is done, defensive or otherwise, the less the likelihood of suit.

All this may very well be true, but it must be kept in mind that when the medical profession blames unnecessary testing on doctors' fear of malpractice suits, the profession is managing to ignore the fact that all this testing is highly profitable to doctors, laboratories, and hospitals. A CBS documentary in 1976, for example, revealed evidence of arrangements between testing laboratories and some doctors, by which the doctors received a kickback from the laboratory for each patient tested. Federally supported programs like Medicare and Medicaid have been scandal-ridden throughout their existence by similar allegations, with Medicare patients much more likely than others to be hospitalized for routine testing as well as prolonged and unnecessary stays in order that the hospital and the doctors can feed lengthily at the government trough which pays the patients' bills.[27] It appears, therefore, that although some unnecessary testing is the result of a doctor's fear of suit, the real multibillion dollar question to be answered is how much of all unnecessary testing is done exclusively to line the pockets of those who do it. Until that question is answered (and no one in the medical profession or elsewhere seems particularly eager to embark on a study that would do so), it is improper to place any financial value on the cost of "defensive" medicine as a part of the nation's annual malpractice bill. To do so distorts and exaggerates a problem that is serious enough without such gratuitous additions.

There are, however, two other forms of defensive medicine which, while they have little or no economic impact, may have adverse health effects. For many illnesses, alternate forms of treatment are available. Some are more dangerous than others, but, in many instances, the risky procedure is the one that is called for medically by the nature of the patient's symptoms. Should a doctor choose against the risky procedure because he fears a malpractice suit if he fails, then he is, in fact, practicing real defensive medicine and perhaps harming his patient.[28] The second negative form of defensive medicine was pointed out by HEW as long ago as 1973: "There appears to be a reluctance," HEW noted, "on the part of some physicians to publish in medical journals case reports describing in detail noted adverse effects of diagnostic and therapeutic procedures. The fear is that material will be picked up and used as evidence in a lawsuit . . . [To the extent] this fear does exist, it could be a major deterrent to the dissemination of important medical knowledge."[29]

CHAPTER THREE

A Standard of Care

I

Although it may come as a surprise to the doctors who think they have been sued for it, technically there is no such legal offense as "medical malpractice." Rather, each defendant to such a suit is said—as though he were a midnight prowler apprehended inside a building—to have committed a trespass.

In some senses, the distinction between malpractice and trespass as it affects doctors is one of those semantic niceties that only lawyers find pleasure in discussing. In the world of reality, the accused doctor knows that the true charge against him is malpractice—the wrongful injury of a patient—as does the lawyer who filed the suit, as does his client, as does the lawyer who will defend the doctor, and the judge and jury that may eventually hear the case, to say nothing of the company that sold the doctor his "professional liability" insurance policy.

Nevertheless, to understand—from the legal view—the rationale for the kind of action that is popularly known as a malpractice suit, to understand not only why such cases can be brought but how they can be successfully prosecuted and defended, it's necessary first to consider the law's general ideas about wrongful injury and the role that strictures against it play in the operation of an orderly society.

The driving force in American jurisprudence, based on concepts developed by the English Common Law, is that of equity. Stated rudimentarily, this means that while it is the function of the governors of a society (its legislators and other elected officials) to suggest and pass laws that will provide justice for the governed, it is for the courts to interpret those laws and apply them evenhandedly, i.e., with equity. Sometimes courts do that and sometimes they don't.

However, a court can refuse to apply a law only when it determines it is violative of the society's ideas about equitable government as embodied in its constitutional acts. For example, when the United States Supreme Court declared segregated schools unconstitutional, it was ruling that such schools, by their nature, violated some citizens' rights to the educational opportunities that others enjoyed; their right to equity (or equal protection under the law), therefore, had been abridged. When the federal government subsequently legislated into existence various affirmative action programs, the quota systems that were established had as their purpose to assure justice to those who had been long denied it, even if, at the same time, these programs meant that other people were treated less than equitably in their educational and employment endeavors. At times, concepts of equity and justice can come into clash, as occurred in the famous Bakke case which reached the United States Supreme Court in 1977. In it, Bakke alleged that medical school admissions programs under the justice concepts of the affirmative action programs violated his personal right to equitable consideration for admission to the school.

Despite the occasions when ideas of equity and justice move into opposition with one another, philosophically it remains the goal of the total society to provide both. Before either can be achieved, however, it is recognized that various restrictions on human activity must be enforced. These strictures take their form in the various trespass laws which are the fundament of both civil and criminal jurisprudence. By definition, a trespass occurs whenever one person takes or attempts to take, without permission, another person's property, rights, or attempts or does harm to another person's body.[1]

The definition sounds simple enough, but as with all legalisms, it can be tricky in its application. For example, the word "person" in the definition requires its own definition. In the United States, slaves were not considered "persons," and therefore could not be trespassed against, although their owners suffered trespass if their slaves were harmed. Therefore, at that time, not all human beings were persons, nor, for that matter, today are all persons human beings. Corporations legally are persons, based on the legislative assumption that they are an "entity," a state of existence synonymous with that of each individual. Corporations, as a result, enjoy protection against trespass and are not themselves permitted to trespass, hence, the theoretical basis for the American antitrust laws which punish them, either civilly or criminally, when they art judged to have committed a trespass. Government, however, is not a legal person, except in the sense that it is the embodiment of all persons within it. This means that government can take actions on its people's behalf against trespassers, but because it lacks persona, it cannot have a criminal trespass action brought against it (only against its employees), while civil trespass actions against it are possible only with its permission. (Many states maintain what is known as sovereign immunity forbidding such civil actions.)

Although the same definitions govern each, the punishments for criminal and civil trespasses differ. Acts that lawmakers define as criminal permit the society to imprison the offender, otherwise restrict his freedom, or force him to pay the government money in the form of fines, in the expectation that the punishment will deter him from repeating the offense. Capital punishment is one sure way of doing that. Hopefully, the punishment of the criminal deters not just him, but others from committing the same offense. Capital punishment may or may not accomplish that.

Criminal trespass penalties, therefore, exist basically to protect the safety of the whole society not an offended individual. Civil trespass laws, while performing the same societal function, simultaneously offer redress to an injured person that he does not obtain when a criminal penalty is assessed against someone who has harmed him. Under civil law, the harmed person is compensated by payment of money directly from the offender not in the form of fines to the state. In legal terminology, the civil trespass is known as a *tort*.

(Not all civil law, however, is concerned with adjudicating tortious offenses. Much of it, rather, is aimed at arriving at equitable solutions to problems in order to prevent one person from trespassing on the rights of another in the future. Divorce laws, bankruptcy laws, adoption and custody laws, and most contract law including labor union agreements with employers fall into the non-tortious category.)

A simple example shows how the tort system works parallel to the criminal system: Two neighbors, Brown and Jones, quarrel with one another. During the altercation, Brown punches Jones and breaks his jaw, requiring Jones to be hospitalized and lose time from work. As a result, Jones is out two thousand dollars in medical bills and lost wages. Because Brown punched Jones, the police arrest him and charge him with the criminal trespass of assault. Brown is convicted and required to pay a fine of $500 and put on probation for six months. Jones, however, is still lacking his $2,000, but under civil equity concepts can sue Brown to regain the money he has lost and perhaps some additional amount for his pain and suffering. The money (or "damages") which is paid Jones not only makes him financially whole from the injury but (just as does the criminal case), hopefully, prevents Brown, and those who would otherwise follow his example, from committing such violent actions in the future. Because his trespass was both criminal and civil, Brown, in this fashion, has been "deterred" by both systems.

By the same theory, a person who has been robbed can sue the robber in civil court; the family of a murdered person can sue the murderer. Since robbers rarely have money to pay if they lose a civil suit—most of them rob because they don't have money—such suits are usually futile. However, murder suits (or "wrongful death" actions as they are called legally) in some instances are worthwhile for a plaintiff to bring, e.g., a policeman who kills a civilian can sometimes be successfully sued by the surviving family with the payment coming, not from the cop, but from the municipality that employed him or put him in a position where he could kill someone.

Not all civil torts, however, are intentional or malicious in nature. People are very frequently injured, not by a gun or a punch in the nose, but as the result of an unintentional mistake by someone other than themselves. When the unintentional injury is caused by a careless or incompetent act on the part of the injuring party, that person is said to have committed a *negligent* trespass or tort. Well over 90 per cent of all so-called "medical malpractice" cases fall into the negligence tort category.

II

Dr. Schneider's patient, Robert Phillips, apparently had a negligent tort committed against him. A subway train, as Dr. Robinson observed, isn't supposed to be able to start up while its doors are still open, yet that is what happened when Phillips stepped out, causing him to fall and fracture his shoulder.

When Phillips sues to force the company to pay for his injuries, it will do the company no good in its defense to prove that this is the first time its workers were either careless or incompetent in the way they inspected the subway car doors. As far as the law is concerned, past records of carefulness mean nothing, and that's as true for a doctor who is sued as for a subway company. The law is interested only in what caused *this* accident to *this* plaintiff.

Key to the tort system is the finding of fault. When it is absent, the plaintiff cannot win. To require payment without fault not only harms the innocent defendant but also undermines the deterrence theory, which is at the heart of all trespass law. Let us suppose, for example, that Phillips cannot prove the transit company's negligence brought about his injury. To require it to pay Phillips under those circumstances presumably will discourage the company from future vigilance about the care of its equipment because it now knows it will have to pay for every injury that occurs on its premises, no matter who is at fault. The result will be more rather than fewer accidents, an anti-social consequence. (That's the legal theory anyway; whether or not that, in fact, would happen is another matter. Arguably, if the company knows it is going to be responsible for all accidents, that might cause it to become more rather than less careful.)

As can be seen from this description, tort laws do not have as their purpose to pay damages to every injured person as do no-fault or Workmen's Compensation systems. As a consequence, in the tort system, unlike the no-fault system, some alike injuries will be compensated and others will not. For example, two pedestrians slip on icy sidewalks and injure themselves; each sues the owner of the premise on which he fell. At trial, the first pedestrian proves that the owner allowed the sidewalk to remain iced after he had had a chance to clear it; the owner, therefore, is negligent and the plaintiff wins. The second pedestrian, however, falls immediately after the sidewalk became icy and before the owner could clear it; that owner, therefore, is not negligent and the plaintiff loses. If a no-fault system were applied to injuries on icy sidewalks, both plaintiffs would be compensated.

Sometimes in a tort action a defendant will win even if he is undeniably negligent. Suppose, for instance, that the person who fell on the icy sidewalk claims he suffered a back injury as a result, and produces medical testimony to back his contention; the owner of the house, however, proves that the plaintiff was being treated for the back injury before he fell. In that event, the fall on the ice was not the *proximate* (or precipitating) cause of the injury, and the plaintiff loses because he cannot show the negligence caused his injury. (He can recover, however, if he can prove that the fall aggravated a pre-existing injury or medical problem.) The same holds true if there is no injury. Had Phillips maintained his balance when he plunged out of the subway car, he has no cause for action against the transit company because no matter how egregious its negligence, it did not harm him.

The negligent householder with the icy sidewalk sometimes can win on another basis. In this instance, he denies neither his negligence nor the plaintiff's injury that resulted from it but produces a witness who testifies that he saw the plaintiff running across the ice just before he fell. Under those circumstances, the court might well decide the plaintiff brought about or contributed to his own injury and award him nothing. Similarly, if witnesses testify that Phillips forced the subway door open, perhaps because he was fearful of missing his stop, he too might be found contributorily negligent, even though the subway still shouldn't have started while the door was open.

The significance of contributory negligence on awards varies from jurisdiction to jurisdiction. In some places, when it can be shown the victim was responsible for his injury in any way whatsoever, he cannot collect. However, in the majority of jurisdictions, including the federal courts, a theory known as *comparative* negligence applies. By it, should a judge or jury decide that both the plaintiff and the defendant were at fault, then the award to the plaintiff is reduced by the degree of his contribution. For example, if it is decided that a plaintiff suffered $10,000 worth of injury but was 20 per cent negligent, he gets $8,000 rather than the full amount. Exactly how judges or juries come up with these neat percentage divisions remains one of the abiding mysteries of the law.

Some classes of defendants in tort cases are held to a higher standard of performance than other defendants. A transit company, for instance, implicitly guarantees a high degree of expertise when it asks people to pay a fare to ride its vehicles. In return for its payment, the public has a right to expect that the equipment will be carefully kept and that only competent drivers will be hired. Therefore, in the Phillips case, even if the transit company proves that the car door was flawed when it bought it, that may not be sufficient grounds for it to win, since transit companies are supposed to have personnel who can recognize flaws before they buy equipment or before it does any damage. An ordinary motorist is not held to the same degree of expertise. Should his steering wheel go out of control through no fault of his own and as a result someone is injured, the court probably will say that the motorist had a right to believe when he bought the car that the steering wheel worked, and he had no particular duty to test it further when it seemed to work. The automobile's manufacturer, who has a presumed ability to make safe steering wheels, will probably be held at fault in that case, not the motorist.

Another example illustrates the same principle in different circumstances. There are two men, Mr. Wise and Mr. Foolish, both of whom have accumulated a tidy fortune during their lives. Both men die, leaving minor children. In his will, Mr. Wise names the trust department of the largest bank in his city to administer his estate until the children come of age. Mr. Foolish names his brother, a retail merchant, as executor of his estate. Over the years, Mr. Foolish's executor invests the children's money in stocks and bonds, all of which goes sour and the children are left with nothing. Mr. Wise's bank does the same thing with the same sorry results. Mr. Foolish's children sue their uncle for his alleged negligent care of their money; Mr. Wise's children sue the bank. The Foolish children will have a difficult time winning. Since their uncle never purported to be an expert in finance, and since his brother knew that when he appointed him, the courts will not hold the uncle to a very high standard of performance. As long as he used reasonable care in investments as measured by layman's knowledge, he will not be held accountable. Wise's bank on the other hand, by operating a trust department, holds itself out as having special expertise in investment matters, and the courts will likely hold that Wise properly relied on that presumed expertise when he named the bank as administrator. Therefore, the Wise children are in a good position to recover all or at least part of the money the bank's trust department lost for them.[2]

The same higher-than-ordinary standard of care that is required of a transit company or of Wise's bank also is applied in tort cases to professional people. A professional person can be defined as anyone who, following a course of training, is licensed by the government to practice a special skill. Professionals, in this sense, include (but are not limited to) doctors, lawyers, registered nurses, architects, engineers, pharmacists, and accountants. Just as a bank implicitly guarantees investment expertise by operating a trust department, so does the professional's license act as his implicit public guarantor that he will perform his special services competently for those who come to him for help. When he doesn't do that and as a result injures his clients, he has trespassed against their rights as citizens and can be held accountable for the mis-(mal-)practice of his profession.

It is this element of "failure to practice properly" that has caused medical negligence torts to become universally known as *malpractice* cases.

The following examples, concerning professions other than medicine, illustrate some of the basic legal principles of professional malpractice: Mr. Smart, a businessman, owns land on which he wishes to erect an office building. He hires an architect to design and supervise the construction of it. Six months after it is completed, the building develops cracks along the outside walls. Mr. Smart sues the architect. The court rules in Smart's favor observing that he had a right to expect that any architect, by virtue of his education and licensure, should be able to design a building that doesn't begin to fall apart in six months.

The second case involves a malpractice allegation against an accountancy firm. One of its clients was a company we'll call Respectable Auto Insurance, Inc. Respectable sold its stock on the open market and each year published for its shareholders a statement of condition, the accuracy of which was attested to by an auditing firm, one with a national reputation for expertise. Respectable's 1976 statement, like the ones for all the years before it, showed the company to be in sound financial condition, and the statement, as usual, was made available to prospective investors. Six months after the statement was issued, the insurance commissioner of Respectable's home state forced the company out of business when his auditors discovered that the firm had written policies in amounts that exceeded its ability to pay. Moreover, the state's auditors discovered that the practice had been going on for at least two years previous. After Respectable's bankruptcy, a group of investors who had purchased stock during the two-year period got together and sued—not Respectable, which had no assets left—but the outside accountancy firm, charging it with malpractice. In their suit, the investors claimed that they had relied on the accountancy firm's imprimatur in deciding to purchase Respectable stock. Following a lengthy appeals process, the accountancy firm was required to make a multimillion-dollar payment to the investors, only part of which was covered by the firm's malpractice insurance. Evidence at the trial revealed that the accounting firm, in fact, was aware of what was going on and had several times *privately* warned Respectable's owners that they were heading for severe financial difficulties. Apparently, however, the accountants agreed to keep quiet, knowing that, if they reported the truth, Respectable would be out of business and they would lose a customer. In so doing, they may have acted to protect Respectable's owners, but they injured the innocent investors, a tort that was probably both intentional and negligent and contrary to the standards of performance of the accountancy profession.

The Respectable case is significant not only as an example of professional liability but also in pointing up one important respect in which tort cases differ from criminal ones. In it, the lower court found in favor of the accountancy firm, apparently accepting its argument that its confidential relationship to Respectable's owners was primal and the company, therefore, could not be held accountable to the investors when their interest was adverse to Respectable's. The investor plaintiffs appealed that decision and it was the higher court that reversed the verdict. Thus, as the Respectable case shows, *in tort suits, unlike criminal prosecutions, not only the defendants but the plaintiffs can appeal the verdict.* The legal reasoning is that the defendant in criminal cases has aligned against him the might of the state and hence must be protected against double jeopardy by providing only him with access to the appeals process upon conviction. In civil cases, however, which are more of a disputatious than a prosecutorial nature, both plaintiffs and defendants are seen as holding equitable positions toward one another, and therefore each are given access to the appeals courts.

The next group of cases involves malpractice actions against lawyers. The first one involves the law firm of Slither & Delay and one of their clients, a Mr. Homeowner. Being of an improvident nature, Homeowner carried no insurance on his property, and sure enough one winter's day a pedestrian slipped on his icy sidewalk, broke his kneecap, and sued Homeowner. Luckily for him, he—as in one of the examples given earlier—was legally in the clear; he had been at work when the ice formed and had no reasonable chance to clear the sidewalk prior to the accident. Upon hearing that, attorney Delay told Homeowner not to worry about a thing, and while Homeowner was present called the pedestrian's attorney and explained the circumstances. The pedestrian, however, wasn't satisfied with the explanation and a suit was filed. Lawyer Delay never got around to answering it with the result that a default judgment was entered against Homeowner for $2,000. Infuriated, Homeowner hired another attorney to sue Delay for his negligence, and Delay's insurance company was forced to pay Homeowner the $2,000 as well as his second attorney's fee. At least half and probably the majority of all malpractice cases against attorneys occur as this one did when a client's case is lost only because his attorney failed to respond in time to a legal paper.[3]

Other malpractice cases against lawyers arise much more rarely, but when they do they can be far more expensive. Take, for example, the events that befell the firm of Blueblood, Jot & Tittle (or rather befell their malpractice insurer). A firm that specialized in securities law, Blueblood *et al.*, was hired by a corporation that had decided to float a stock issue. Writing stock prospectuses is highly skilled legal work since the wording of them is tightly regulated by the federal Securities and Exchange Commission. The Blueblood firm produced the prospectus prior to the company's deadline but made a technical error, leading to the rejection of it by the SEC. Because the stock offer couldn't be made when the corporation needed it, it lost millions of dollars and the corporate officers sued the Blueblood firm citing their error as a negligent one. The court agreed. It pointed out that if the corporation had foolishly hired a law firm that didn't have expertise in the field of stock-prospectus writing, it would have had only itself to blame for the error. Blueblood, however (like Wise's bank), held itself to be expert in this field and charged accordingly. It, therefore, was to be held to the highest standard of performance, so that what might have been excusable error on the part of the lesser firm became negligent error when Blueblood made it. By analogy, in medical cases a specialist will sometimes be held to a higher standard of performance in attempting a certain procedure than will a general practitioner.

Blueblood's malpractice insurer, as a result of this verdict, was forced to pay $4 million to the corporation. Giant verdicts such as this one have made it nearly impossible for law firms specializing in stock and bond work to obtain malpractice insurance; and when they are able to obtain it, they are required to pay premiums that dwarf those charged to the highest risk doctors.[4]

The final malpractice case involving lawyers concerns the firm of Sterling, Dull, and Maunder. They had a client, Mr. Litigious, who was involved in a property dispute. The case was a complex one, and attorney Maunder did his best to research the issues adequately and to present Litigious's case in the most favorable way he could devise. Even so, Litigious lost, and feeling he shouldn't have, he hired another attorney to sue the Sterling firm for malpractice on the grounds that Maunder's handling of the case was incompetent. By way of proof, the new lawyer alleged that Maunder had made several errors that hurt Litigious's case. At trial, he offered as witnesses two attorneys who testified to that effect. Maunder, however, also produced his own attorney witnesses who didn't deny his errors but stated that, even so, his conduct of the case was well within the bounds of competence as defined by the legal profession. Principally on the basis of this testimony, the judge dismissed the case against Maunder. When last heard from, Litigious was seeking a third lawyer to sue the second one for malpractice.

III

When the judge found in favor of Maunder, he may have been expressing a natural sympathy toward a fellow lawyer; from his own years as a practicing attorney, the judge would know how easy it is to make an error in interpretation of statutes, and how some motions that are clearly error in hindsight seemed perfectly appropriate when they were made. But it is not just the sued lawyers who benefit from judges' reluctance to interpret error as negligent error. So do doctors.

Whatever the motivations of some individual judges may be, the reluctance has its true basis in public policy. The law recognizes that the successful operation of the nation's justice system and its health care depends in large part on the ability of the legal and medical professions to aid—without interference—those who come to them for help. Thus, should attorneys generally become fearful that they can be sued for *any* error they may make in interpretation of laws, they will soon become reluctant to give any client advice, and when that happens, the entire purpose of the advocacy system is lost. The same holds true for doctors. Interpreting disease can be a difficult enterprise; a patient's backache may mean anything from a muscle spasm to cancer. Doctors, therefore, like lawyers, as a matter of public policy should not have to fear that every time they don't recognize a symptom or fail to cure an illness they can be sued.

(Many doctors, of course, believe that this is the very effect that malpractice suits are having on them.)

The law, however, also recognizes that a special inferior/superior relationship exists between the client and the lawyer; between the patient and the doctor. In deciding one medical malpractice case, a California judge defined the relationship this way: ". . . the patient, being unlearned in medical sciences, has an abject dependence upon and trust in his physician . . . thus raising an obligation in the physician that transcends arm's length transactions,"[5] or as a District of Columbia judge put it: "*Caveat emptor* is not the norm for the consumer of medical services."[6] By this reasoning, because the patient cannot be expected to recognize shoddy medical treatment the same way he might be expected to recognize shoddy goods, and because he can be harmed by shoddy medical treatment to a degree he likely won't be harmed by buying inferior products, the doctor's obligation to provide quality care is a high one.

Consequently, in professional negligence cases, courts are in a constant search to define standards of acceptable care that simultaneously protect the abjectly dependent patient (or client) and yet do not have a chilling effect on the profession's ability to perform its socially important services. The demarcation line is a fine one; however, should negligence be determined—i.e., the professional's actions did not meet an acceptable standard of care—he cannot be excused on the grounds that his misbehavior furthered some philosophic goal of the society.

One way of determining the standard of care is to listen to the testimony of expert witnesses, such as those who appeared in the Maunder case. The impression these witnesses make can often be very influential on a jury's or a judge's decision. Attorneys for both sides, however, also present for a court's consideration, at the trial level and in the appeals process, decisions (such as those quoted above) that were rendered in earlier cases in which the issues were similar to the one at hand. These prior decisions (or precedents, as they are sometimes called) are not necessarily binding on a judge,[7] but they can determine the direction his rulings will take and, at the trial level, the instructions on the law that are given to the jury. Taken together, this vast accumulation of prior judicial interpretations, is known as the "common" law. It won't be found in any statute books but represents the judicial system's total knowledge of what the law means.

Therefore, the acceptable standard of care of a profession is not everything that members of the profession say it is—expert witnesses, as in the Maunder case, often disagree with one another—but rather the totality of decisions concerning care within that profession. The more frequently cases are brought against the members of a certain profession, the more precedents there will be established and the more fully the standard of care for that profession is defined. Since more than 90 per cent of all medical malpractice cases in American history have been brought since 1965,[8] acceptable standards of competent medical care are much better known today than a decade or two ago, but the definitions are also ones very much in flux as new cases and new decisions are added to the total pool of knowledge.

Although the presence of expert witnesses doesn't necessarily determine the outcome of a case, the absence of them can be harmful when one litigant has access to them and the other doesn't. Yet this, for many years, was a commonplace in malpractice litigation, with plaintiffs having great difficulty obtaining medical experts to testify in their behalf, a handicap the doctor defendants rarely had to face. Since plaintiff lawyers in negligence cases work on a contingency fee basis,[9] which means they get paid only if their client wins, the result was that many cases in which the prima-facie evidence of negligence was great went begging for a lawyer because all attorneys knew their chances of winning were slim unless they had experts to counter those the defense would produce.

Undoubtedly, in their reluctance to testify, doctors were largely propelled by a "There-but-for-the-Grace-of-God" reasoning. No matter how grossly negligent a colleague's performance might have been, to testify against him, it was believed, simply encouraged further suits. If any disciplining were necessary, let it be done quietly by the doctors themselves and out of the glare of public attention. As one prominent surgeon has put it: "Doctors distrust the judicial system, particularly the trial by jury. They honestly feel that medical cases are too complex to be fairly evaluated by non-medical people.[10]

But perhaps the greatest single stumbling block to obtaining expert witnesses for the malpractice plaintiff was the so-called *locality* rule, which, until recent years, held sway in most jurisdictions in the United States. According to it, only doctors who practiced in the place in which the alleged negligent act took place were qualified to testify as to the acceptable standard of care of that community.

In theory, the locality rule made some sense. Let us suppose a person suffers a heart attack in a rural community in which there is only one doctor, a general practitioner, who has neither the special knowledge nor the equipment to save the patient. This doctor should not be held to the same standard of care as the big-city cardiologist with his access to sophisticated life-saving equipment. Similarly, a small rural hospital cannot reasonably be expected to have either the same quantity or quality of facilities, or access to them, as would the metropolitan one, and neither it nor the doctors on its staff should be held to the metropolitan standards.

For the medically injured plaintiff, however, the locality rule was legally crippling. Faced as she was with the medical "wall of silence,"[11] she was going to have trouble getting witnesses under the best of circumstances; to further limit her to doctors in the community in which the accident occurred made her task virtually impossible. Even if she found a local physician who had no ethical qualms about testifying against a colleague or who was not lacking in faith in the jury system, this doctor, even so, would think many times before volunteering his services. A surgeon, for instance, would know that if he testified against another surgeon in the same community, he would immediately be accused of trying to destroy the reputation of a competitor. He also knew he might suddenly find himself without hospital privileges, and discover that his fellow doctors were now unwilling to take over for him when he needed help in treating his patients. In fact, he might no longer have any medical friends at all. The role of Serpico is always a difficult one.

The locality rule also had another adverse effect societally. As long as only the doctors who lived in a community were permitted to dictate its acceptable standards of care, the law, in effect, was saying that if that community standard was a poor one, then it was permissible for it to remain so.

For both these reasons—the assumption that incompetent medical care was competent when incompetent doctors said it was, and the inability of plaintiffs to get witnesses when defendants had no such difficulties—a series of legal challenges were raised to the locality rule, beginning in the 1950s but becoming increasingly frequent during the 1960s and 1970s. Gradually, courts began to respond favorably to these allegations, and today, although the locality rule remains in effect in some jurisdictions (in the South more than anywhere else), in most places a plaintiff is permitted to engage an expert witness from outside the community in which the accident occurred. History was also on the side of change; as the nation became increasingly urbanized and modes of transportation more available to carry patients to whichever facility they needed, there was less and less excuse for different standards of medical care to be practiced in different parts of the country.

As the locality rule began to crumble, the era of the medical carpetbagger dawned. These were doctors knowledgeable in various specialties who were willing to travel great distances, for a fee, to testify for plaintiffs, and the fees were often hefty ones, with $2,000 for a day's work on the witness stand not uncommon.[12] The advent of the carpetbaggers soon sprang leaks in the local wall of silence. Realizing the plaintiffs were now going to get witnesses in their behalf in any event, the local doctors became less reluctant to testify themselves. There was no reason why, as they now saw it, they shouldn't get the $2,000. This choice came the easiest for the doctors in the big cities where the most suits were filed; the size of the medical community in these places made retribution against them difficult.

For the plaintiff, the growing availability of local witnesses was a great boon. The carpetbaggers could be attacked as outsiders who'd say anything for a dollar; not so the locals whose associations with the area's hospitals and medical schools made them immediately recognizable to jurors as witnesses with impeccable credentials.

The breaching of the locality rule also affected malpractice insurers. No longer buttressed by the expectation that the plaintiff would not be able to obtain expert witnesses, they now became increasingly amenable to settling malpractice cases prior to an expensive trial. This shift in strategy by the insurers, in turn, made malpractice cases more attractive to plaintiff lawyers; rather than facing the prospect of a trial, which they might well lose, each time they took a case, they now knew that in the large majority a cash offer would be made which, if accepted by the plaintiff, guaranteed they would earn at least some fee.

One other development, which had nothing to do with witness availability, also served to make medical cases increasingly attractive to lawyers. Throughout most of American history, hospitals enjoyed immunity from suit because they were considered charitable institutions.[13] During the post-World War II period, however, in state after state,[14] immunity was rescinded by legislative fiat or court decision, as the society became generally aware that the hospital was essentially a corporate entity and, therefore, like other such "persons," should be responsible for the trespasses of its employees. (Some state-operated hospitals still can't be sued because of sovereign immunity, but only in a couple states[15] do privately operated hospitals still enjoy charitable immunity.) For a person injured by a hospital employee (such as a resident, nurse, technician, or orderly), the hospital's loss of immunity was important. As long as it had existed, only the employee who committed the injury could be sued, which was usually a waste of time since these employees ordinarily didn't carry insurance and lacked the personal wherewithall to pay for the damage they did. Hospitals, however, were highly attractive as defendants. Not only could they afford to pay, either directly or through their insurers, but jurors, it was believed, were more likely to find against them—impersonal institutions—than they would against a nurse or a struggling young resident.

By the 1970s, the medically injured patient, therefore, was no longer the pariah she had once been, but a welcome visitor to the negligence attorney's office.

CHAPTER FOUR

The Unhappiness of Rose Turner

I

"For some reason, my memory of it always begins with Saturday afternoon," Rose Turner said. "I was about to go off duty, but I was still standing by her bed. Her face was pale from all the blood she'd lost, and for a long time she'd just been staring up at the ceiling. But, as I started away from her, she gripped my wrist with her hand and looked up at me. 'They're not going to let me die, are they?' she asked. I said, no, of course, 'they' weren't going to let her die."

Rose Turner, still in her late twenties, was a tall and angular woman with surprisingly soft features and dark sad eyes. Throughout her interview, she spoke mostly in a monotone that seemed unnatural to the reporter; he knew, however, that the voice a person adopts can be like a finger in a dike; some months earlier, he'd interviewed a survivor of an airplane crash and observed the same monotone; the survivor later had a nervous breakdown. Now Rose Turner interrupted herself, "I've gone back to college," she said. "I'm taking courses. I don't know what I'm going to do yet, but I've got to get out of nursing, and it won't be anything like social work either." She smiled. "Maybe computers. Too many bad things happen to people. Too many. We kill people, you know."

As she said this, the reporter was reminded of his own stay in a hospital a year or so earlier. A woman doctor he knew socially, although she wasn't a close friend, had called him almost every evening during his stay, and once stopped by to see him although she wasn't on the hospital's staff. A month or two after his recovery, he ran into her on the street, and she seemed a little embarrassed. "You must have been wondering why I kept bugging you," she said. "But, you see, I was a resident there, and I've heard other things since. I was worried about your safety."

"I guess I'd best begin at the beginning," Rose Turner said. The real beginning, the patient herself, however, remained vague. Her name was Lillian Lazzeri, twenty-two years old, short-statured, heavy-breasted, and not an especially pretty girl as nurse Turner described her; she was, Turner said, "very sweet and very passive." Later the reporter would try to find out more about Lillian but with little success; he got a chronology, not a person. He did learn she had been born in the city's Italian community, educated in the parochial schools there, and save for an occasional summertime weekend at the shore, never spent a night away from her parents' row house until she married Ralph Lazzeri, a garage mechanic, a month before her nineteenth birthday. About a year after her marriage, Lillian became pregnant but lost the child, apparently sometime during the first trimester. Then, shortly after her twenty-second birthday, she became pregnant again. She carried the child with no evident complications into the seventh month when, on a Wednesday, vaginal bleeding began. Her physician ordered her hospitalized the next day in the community hospital at which he was a staff member.

Although small, the hospital was adequately equipped to handle pregnancy problems; the staff was considered good, with most of the residents and interns on loan from a large nearby teaching hospital. Shortly after she was admitted, Mrs. Lazzeri was examined by her physician, who correctly diagnosed her bleeding as caused by placenta praevia, a condition in which the placenta enveloping the fetus is carried unduly low with the result that the patient's cervical opening is wholly or partly obstructed by it. The problem occurs once in every 214 pregnancies,[1] with maternal death in no more than 1 per cent of all cases.[2] The danger to the fetus, however, is considerably greater, the mortality rate there approaching 25 per cent in a seventh-month baby.[3] The proper course of treatment for placenta praevia is described in standard medical textbooks.

Late Thursday morning, intravenous feeding was begun for Mrs. Lazzeri, and at the same time instruments attached to her to monitor the fetal heartbeat and the strength of prelabor contractions. At the same time, her blood was cross-matched and a supply reserved for her in her type to be immediately available in case she should begin to hemorrhage, a common, and the most dangerous, consequence of her condition. Up to this point, as Rose Turner pointed out to the reporter and as he later confirmed with physicians to whom he spoke, the care Mrs. Lazzeri was receiving was proper.

The bleeding never stopped. Beginning Thursday afternoon and continuing to Saturday afternoon, according to notes made by the nurses on duty, she soaked about three hospital pads every eight hours. At any time during this period, the physician in charge might have elected to deliver the child by Caesarian section but chose not to do so. Since the fetal heart beat was stable and labor hadn't begun, the doctor's choice, while questionable, was also arguably correct, since the longer a fetus remains inside its mother, generally speaking, the better its chance for survival.

The first really untoward event occurred at three o'clock Saturday afternoon, when Mrs. Lazzeri passed a fist-sized clot of blood. The resident in charge, however, took no action and there is no record to show he reported the clot to the obstetrician. About this time, too, the matched blood which had been reserved was released. Such blood is not kept for more than forty-eight hours, so that the release itself was not exceptional. What didn't happen was: No one ordered new blood to replace it.

After the passage of the blood clot, Mrs. Lazzeri's bleeding continued at its previous rate, and her condition remained unchanged the rest of that day and through the night until 5:15 Sunday morning. Then, she began to hemorrhage.

As Rose Turner described it: "The blood was coming out of her like pouring cream into a cup of coffee." Nurses and the resident on duty rushed to her aid. A call was placed to clear an operating room, and at the same time the hospital's blood supply center was told to rush up blood for her. "It was only then," Turner recalled, "that we found out that nobody had reordered blood for her the day before. The technician who answered the phone said it would take two hours or more to get a cross match. I screamed at him to get blood, any kind of goddamned blood up there immediately." By now, it was 5:30 and in the fifteen minutes, Mrs. Lazzeri had already saturated three pads with her hemorrhaging. About this time, either the resident or the head nurse called Mrs. Lazzeri's physician at home, and he said he would be there as soon as he could.

In the meanwhile, as Mrs. Lazzeri, fully conscious and terrified, was being prepared for surgery, the resident called the Intensive Care Nursery at the uptown teaching hospital. He asked for instructions on how to resuscitate the baby when it was born, but did not order an ambulance to take the child to the nursery where its chances of survival would be improved.

At six o'clock, with the patient still bleeding uncontrollably, the unmatched blood arrived and the nurses began to pump it into her at a rate they hoped would equal her loss. "I kept talking to her, assuring her we wouldn't let any harm come to her," said Rose Turner. At no time does there appear to have been an attempt made to reach another obstetrician, who was on duty, and who could have operated on her immediately.

At 6:30, seventy-five minutes after the onset of the uncontrollable hemorrhaging, with her doctor now on the scene, Mrs. Lazzeri was taken into the operating room. Ten minutes later, she gave birth to a live daughter. Her bleeding, however, became more massive than ever. More blood was called for, but somehow only a single unit was produced, far less than she needed. The hospital laboratory called back to say they could not provide more blood for the patient until 8:00, unless the doctor in charge was willing to sign the necessary papers. "I emphasized to them," said nurse Turner, "that this was no time to worry about signing papers," and soon after, two more units arrived. At this time, it wasn't known that during the delivery of the child, the surgeon, unable to see his way through the mass of blood, had ruptured Mrs. Lazzeri's bladder, thereby causing the increased flow of blood. Soon after the child's birth, Mrs. Lazzeri's pressure dropped to 40/0, and she was administered an ampule of soda bicarbonate, an acidotic that is administered in only dire emergency conditions.

An hour later, Mrs. Lazzeri was returned to the hospital's intensive care unit, but by 10:00 she was back in the operating room when the torn bladder condition was finally evident to those in charge. The repair work on the bladder, nurse Turner said, was done without use of anesthesia because by then the woman was so deeply in shock she didn't need it. According to a physician who examined records presented him by the reporter: "The patient was essentially dead by then."

However, with the strength of youth and basic good health, Lillian Lazzeri lingered through the afternoon, although twice her heart stopped. By the end of the afternoon, she had received seventeen units of blood, almost one-and-one-half times her own supply. She died at 7 P.M. Her infant daughter expired the following morning.

"I don't know what they told her husband about why she died,"

Rose Turner said. "I saw him there several times during the course of the day, sitting and waiting. I tried to comfort him while he was waiting, giving out false hope. I knew she couldn't live. What could I say? No, I didn't tell him what happened. Not then or later."

She had the opportunity later. She and two other nurses who were on duty throughout most of Mrs. Lazzeri's ordeal went to the viewing held at a funeral home on the same block in which Lillian Lazzeri was born. In the open coffin, the infant lay in its mother's arms. "Her husband was distraught. How do you tell him then that you think his wife was killed by people who waited too long to help her and by a hospital that was so incompetent it couldn't even keep blood available for her? You don't. You offer condolences, that's what you do. But, at one point, I guess I could have said something. His brother, I think it was the husband's brother, not hers, he took us aside and said, 'I'm not satisfied with what we were told. I don't understand why she died. Is there something we should know?' And I—I guess this is why I'm here talking to you now—I didn't answer him the way I should have. I think I said, 'It was such a tragedy,' and that's all. That family to this day doesn't know she should still be alive, and maybe her baby should be, too. But I have nightmares. When I'm awake. Something should be done about these people."

"Why do you think you didn't do anything till now?" asked the reporter.

"That's obvious. If I told the family what really happened, I'd be done as a nurse. The hospital would get rid of me, and I wouldn't be able to get another job. The word would get around about me. You aren't suppose to talk you know, it's sort of like a Mafia oath of silence." She smile. "What they say is true. Doctors bury their mistakes, and the mourners are all mutes."

II

More than one defendant is named in half of all malpractice suits; in approximately 15 per cent, three or more, with a dozen defendants to a single suit not unknown.[4] Multiple-defendant cases, as a rule, involve not only private physicians but hospitals and their personnel and, frequently, manufacturers and suppliers of medical equipment,[5] any one or all of whom may have been responsible for the allegedly negligent accident that occurred to the plaintiff. In these cases, in fact, the question of negligence may not be so much disputed as who is responsible for it. When that happens, defendants tend to attack one another, in the process often revealing information helpful to the plaintiff, one good reason that plaintiff attorneys like to get as many defendants as possible into a case.

No matter how complex a case is legally or medically, it is almost invariably instigated by the events surrounding a single medical maloccurrence. Nearly 70 per cent of the time,[6] the patient is alleged to have received improper medical or surgical care; such cases are technically, if euphemistically, called "misadventure in procedure." Another 20 per cent of claims are based on the charge that the doctor negligently or incompetently misdiagnosed an illness, with the remaining 10 per cent arising from a variety of other negligence assertions.[7] It's a rare suit, however, that contains only one allegation. Very often, it will be claimed that the first presumed act of negligence led to another, i.e., because the diagnosis was improper so was the treatment that flowed from it. In other instances, different charges will be levied at different defendants even though the suit rises from a single event. For example, in the Lazzeri death, some defendants might have been sued for failure to provide the young woman with proper care, with the hospital itself open to a negligence tort for its failure to have matched blood available when it was needed.

Despite the greater frequency of the misadventure in procedure suits, the first group of case histories that will be discussed are those involving misdiagnosis, since they involve events typically occurring at the beginning of the treatment process. In many of them, the legal question to be answered is: What should the doctor have known and when should he have known it?

CASE ONE: THE ATHLETE WITH THE HEAD COLD.[8] A member of the varsity basketball team at a midwestern university, while training for the upcoming season, developed what appeared to be a common head cold. The team physician gave him some tablets to provide symptomatic relief, and the player continued to practice. The cold, however, hung on, and about two weeks after its inception, the young man also developed a toothache, accompanied by a severe headache. He was taken to the university's oral surgery department where two decayed teeth were discovered and extracted. That night his headache worsened, and he returned to the dentist who gave him Demerol to relieve his pain. Nevertheless, over the weekend, not only did the headache persist but it was now accompanied by feelings of nausea. On Monday, the team's physician took another look at him. By this time, new symptoms had manifested themselves, including dizziness, lethargy, and loss of appetite as well as inflamed eyelids. The doctor ordered fluids and Bufferin, but they didn't help either. Soon after, the young man, who by now had been hospitalized, began to vomit. He was again visited by the team physician who noted the redness of the eyelids on his chart and also the appearance of petechia, small marks on the membrane of the mouth. The doctor ordered a blood count, a urinalysis, and a test for mononucleosis. That night the youth's temperature rose to 104.4 degrees, and the nurse noted that his eyelids had become so swollen that his eyes gave a slitted appearance. She called the doctor; he ordered Seconal. By the next morning, the basketball player could no longer touch his chin to his chest without great pain, and the doctor also noted that his eyes had begun to bulge. At that point, the doctor called in a neurologist who immediately ordered massive doses of heparin and ampicillin, both heavy-duty antibiotics. That afternoon, the youth was rushed to surgery where his ethnoid sinuses (located in the upper nasal cavity) were removed. This operation saved his life. However, by that time a massive blood clot had so blocked the arteries leading to the eyes that it caused the retinas to die, leaving the young man permanently blind. His illness was finally diagnosed as septicemia, or as it is more commonly known, blood poisoning.

CASE TWO: STOMACH-ACHE IN A WELFARE CHILD.[9] One night, the three-year-old daughter of a North Carolina woman awoke complaining that her stomach hurt. She vomited, and her mother observed that the child's belly was swollen and her navel had turned purple. The mother, who was on welfare, took the child's temperature rectally and discovered it to be 105 degrees. Frightened, she immediately took the child to a hospital emergency room where, according to her subsequent testimony, the doctor "mashed" the child on the stomach, but took no X rays, blood, or urine samples. The child continued to vomit; the doctor gave the mother some "red looking medicine" and told her to take the child home. (This doctor died before the case came to trial, but his examination notes indicate he had diagnosed an upper respiratory infection, gastroenteritis, and possible measles.) The child's condition worsened, and the next day, the frantic mother took her back to the hospital. This time another doctor took X rays but offered no treatment, reminding the mother that welfare patients had to be treated at the hospital's clinic which wasn't open until the next day. Unable to get help, the mother took her desperately ill daughter back home. The child's vomiting continued, now accompanied by diarrhea. The following day the mother took the child to the welfare clinic where the first doctor she had seen was on duty. Thirty minutes later, the child died. At autopsy, the cause of death was established as acute peritonitis resulting from a perforated appendix.

CASE THREE: THE EYE-POPPING BABY.[10] In this California case, a mother took her five-month-old infant to her doctor when it appeared the child was suffering from a cold. According to the mother, the doctor did not take the baby's temperature or make any other tests; even so, he diagnosed the condition as tonsillitis and prescribed a liquid antibiotic. Two days later, the mother brought the baby back to the doctor, telling him the child had been "thrashing about" and that his eyes seemed to be "popping out." At that point, she claimed, the doctor still didn't take the baby's temperature but after examining the nose and throat, assured her the tonsillitis was clearing up. The following day, when the same symptoms persisted, the mother says the doctor refused to see the baby. The day after that she took the baby to a hospital emergency room where spinal meningitis was immediately diagnosed. By that time, however, the baby had suffered brain inflammation, fluid on the brain, profound mental retardation, partial deafness, total blindness, and convulsive spasms of all four extremities. Life expectancy was estimated at one to two years, assuming twenty-four-hour medical care.

Each of these cases illustrates the legal principle that a doctor's mistake by itself is not grounds for a malpractice suit, but that persistence in the mistake is when symptoms develop that cannot be explained by the original diagnosis.

The team physician in the basketball player case, for example, could not be faulted for originally assuming that the patient was suffering from nothing worse than a cold. Neither could the dentist be considered negligent for assuming that the tooth pains and the accompanying headache were anything more than symptoms that would be relieved by the extractions that were performed. Even the persistence of the headache, the nausea, and the loss of appetite that followed the oral surgery could have been only side effects. By Monday, however, the team physician's conduct of the case had become questionable. Dizziness and lethargy accompanied by inflamed eyelids is not an aftereffect normally associated with either oral surgery or a cold. Even more ominous was the appearance of the petechia which are recognized medically as symptoms of internal hemorrhaging. When these symptoms appeared, according to the testimony of expert witnesses at the trial, the physician should have ordered a spinal tap, a brain scan, and had X rays taken rather than, as he did, order tests for mononucleosis. Had such steps been taken, the witnesses concurred, the septicemia would have been discovered and the young man's sight probably saved. By continuing to wait in the face of these symptoms, the mistaken diagnosis had become a negligent one. A jury agreed with the expert witnesses and found for the plaintiff in the sum of $750,000, a verdict which was subsequently upheld by the state's Supreme Court.

In Case Two, the misdiagnosis occurred at an earlier stage. The issue here, however, was not the doctor's immediate failure to recognize appendicitis. That occurs rarely in a three-year-old, and a competent doctor might well not consider it *initially*. Significant, however, are the doctor's examination notes; his multiple diagnoses show he was puzzled by the symptoms the child manifested, and as a consequence, at that point, he should have undertaken laboratory testing or minimally consulted with another physician. When he did neither and only treated the child symptomatically (apparently for gastroenteritis or a cold), he had performed negligently. The subsequent treatment of the child is simply appalling, and her death can be largely attributed to the callous refusal to treat her on the second day because she was a welfare patient.

The case was tried before a jury which found against the deceased doctor, with the verdict upheld on appeal. Like the hospital, however, the jurors apparently didn't feel the life of the daughter of a welfare mother was worth much, awarding only $65,000. The verdict might have been larger had the negligence of the hospital been considered, but that couldn't be done because the case occurred in North Carolina, a state in which hospitals enjoy "charitable" immunity from suit.

More similar to Case One was Three in which the doctor diagnosed tonsillitis in a patient suffering from meningitis. Even if the symptoms masked themselves at the time of the first visit, by the second the doctor should have been warned by the "eye popping" syndrome (just as the doctor in Case One should have been warned by the petechia) that he was dealing with something other than a minor ailment. The immediacy with which the second doctor diagnosed the meningitis further suggests negligence in diagnosis on the part of the first doctor.

There are, however, puzzling elements to this case. It was settled prior to trial with a payment of $140,000 to the plaintiff, an amount considerably less than the average in other cases in which the injuries were as severe as this one. Since, in such settlements, no court records exist of evidence that might have been offered by the defense had the case gone to trial, we have available to us only the mother's version. It may be, however, that the doctor was prepared to assert that he had been aware all along of the possibility of meningitis and just didn't tell the mother for fear of alarming her. Had that been his defense, at trial the jury would have had to decide who to believe, the mother or the doctor, a prospect both sides may well have wanted to avoid. For his part, the mother's lawyer may have feared that the jury would be more likely to believe a doctor about his ability to perceive symptoms than it would a distraught mother's medically uninformed narrative. The defense, however, had to consider the possible effects that the horrible and permanent injuries suffered by the child might have on a jury, which might make a large award out of sympathy even though the legal facts didn't merit it. Assuming that kind of reasoning, it made good sense to both sides to settle as they did. Therefore, although Case Three illustrates negligent misdiagnosis—assuming the mother's allegations are correct—the fact that defendants make a payment to settle a suit prior to trial cannot be construed, in this or any other case, as a legal admission of culpability on their part.

In the next history, not one but several doctors misdiagnosed a patient's symptoms:

CASE FOUR: HOSPITAL CARE FOR A DIABETIC.[11] A twenty-nine-year-old man, not known to be diabetic, entered a California hospital with undefined symptoms of illness. A number of tests were ordered for him, but they did not include a urinalysis. Subsequently, the patient was examined by doctors on the hospital staff, each of whom arrived at a different but equally mistaken diagnosis of his problem. Several days later, the patient lapsed into a diabetic coma and died.

As with Case Three, this one resulted in a pre-trial settlement with the widow receiving $250,000 for herself and her two children, a larger-than-average settlement in a "wrongful death" suit, a strong indication, that the attorneys for the defendant hospital realized they would have a hard time prevailing at trial.

Their legal problem, however, may not have been directly caused by the failure of the staff physicians to recognize diabetes; it rarely manifests itself for the first time in a young adult, much more commonly striking either small children or the elderly. What was negligent (or, at the very least, extraordinarily difficult to explain away) was the failure of the hospital to run a urinalysis. Had it been taken, the patient's blood-sugar problem would have become immediately evident and his life almost certainly saved. While it is unclear whether the test was ordered and not done, or if no one thought to order it at all, in any event, none of the attending physicians noticed from the patient's chart that the test hadn't been taken. Therefore, it appears that the misdiagnosis occurred, not because symptoms were ignored, but because a routine diagnostic tool was not employed, viz., the urinalysis.

The failure to diagnose here, however, would *not* have been negligent had the patient's illness been one that could not have been unmasked by undertaking tests which the symptoms suggested. In the masked illnesses, an attending physician can persist in misdiagnosis throughout the entire course of treatment yet not be negligent in the care offered. Certain cancers fall into this category. Another example is provided by the so-called Legionnaires' Disease which killed a number of American Legion conventioneers in 1976. The doctors who treated patients stricken by this illness usually diagnosed it as an acute viral pneumonia, which, in fact, its symptoms suggested it to be. Since the illness, as it turned out, was caused by a bacteria, the viral treatment was of no use to the patients and conceivably could have hastened the demise of some. Negligence, nevertheless, was not involved both because the illness was unknown and because of the cunning way in which it hid its genesis. With the etiology and treatment of the disease now identified, however, a doctor who would fail to consider it in a patient exhibiting its symptoms might well be open to a malpractice suit. The more successful medicine is in identifying the cause and treatment of illnesses, therefore, to that extent do physicians become more exposed to negligence suits when they fail to be aware of or apply the knowledge gained.

III

In some misdiagnosis suits, the doctor defendants do not deny they erred, but rather base their defense, as did attorney Maunder when sued by Litigious, on the assertion that other doctors would have made the same mistake they did:

> CASE FIVE: THE GONORRHEA DIAGNOSIS.[12] In this California case, a woman complained to her doctor of pain in her side. He diagnosed appendicitis and had the woman hospitalized preparatory to surgery. While there, she was examined by an internist who decided her pains were caused, not by appendicitis, but from gonorrhea. The woman's doctor, convinced by the internist that he was wrong, abandoned the appendicitis operation and put her on a course of treatment for the venereal disease. Three days later the patient's appendix burst, her condition complicated by peritonitis. She eventually recovered and sued the internist for malpractice by reason of his faulty diagnosis.

At trial, the internist produced several doctors as witnesses who testified that pains associated with gonorrhea and appendicitis can be mistaken for one another. Since the diagnostic mistake was one that any competent doctor might make, the internist's error was not negligent, said the witnesses. A jury agreed. A similar case in which the verdict was much more questionable occurred in Louisiana.[13] In it, the broken neck suffered by a patient in an accident went undiagnosed because his doctor never had the neck X-rayed. The severely injured patient sued the doctor for malpractice and produced on his behalf two expert witnesses who testified that failure to X-ray a neck injury is negligent on the face of it. The defendant, however, got himself three other doctors who testified they might not have X-rayed under those circumstances either. The defendant won. Whether he would have won anywhere else than in Louisiana is another matter.

In many malpractice cases involving misdiagnosis, the defendant denies that the plaintiff's injury resulted from the diagnosis. This is the proximate cause argument successfully used by the homeowner in Chapter Three who showed that the pedestrian's back injury predated his fall on the ice. It is an argument that sometimes prevails and sometimes doesn't as the following two histories show:

CASE SIX: THE PSYCHOSOMATIC FATALITY.[14] For three years, a young woman complained of a variety of ill-defined pains. Her first doctor, a neurosurgeon, could find no physical basis for her ailments and sent her to a psychiatrist who diagnosed her symptoms as the manifestations of a hysterical personality. Not long after, the woman moved and the psychiatrist referred her to a second psychiatrist who also concluded her pains were psychosomatic in origin. When they worsened, he ordered her hospitalized; a staff neurosurgeon examined her and again concluded she had no physical disorder. The woman's emotional condition continued to deteriorate and she was admitted to another hospital where, before undergoing further psychiatric treatment, a staff surgeon ordered a myelogram. It revealed evidence of a cancerous tumor on her spine. She was operated upon, but died fifteen days later; she was then twenty-seven years old. Her husband sued the various doctors except the last one—for malpractice by reason of their failure to diagnose her cancer in time to treat her.

CASE SEVEN: THE FRACTURED SUICIDE.[15] In this California case, a teen-age girl with a history of emotional problems was in an automobile accident and taken to a group health clinic where several doctors failed to diagnose that she was suffering from a broken clavicle. The girl repeatedly complained of great pain, but was told by her doctors that she was imagining it and that her assertions that she couldn't use her arm were psychosomatic in origin. Five years later, the girl who, by then, was a user of both marijuana and LSD, committed suicide. Somehow, about this time, perhaps through an autopsy, her parents for the first time became aware that their daughter's shoulder had, in fact, been broken at the time of the automobile accident. They sued the clinic for causing her "wrongful death" by suicide.

Although his case seemed the stronger of the two, the husband in Case Six lost his suit; the parents in Case Seven won theirs.

In Case Six, there appears to have been no denial on the part of any of the defendants that they had made mistaken diagnoses. Nor could they very well have done so, since the final diagnosis proved that the woman's suffering all along had been real and was caused by the cancer. Nor does there appear to have been any denial on their part that if the myelogram had been taken three years earlier, the cancer would have been revealed then. To win his case, however, the husband found he had a real problem; he could locate no expert witness willing to testify that his wife's life might have been saved or even prolonged had her condition been discovered when she first felt pain. The medical evidence, rather, went in the direction that by the time the pain manifested itself, her condition was already hopeless. Based on this evidence, the judge dismissed the case with his ruling subsequently upheld by an appeals court.

In Case Seven, the doctors also argued there was no casual relationship between their admitted failure to diagnose the fracture and the girl's subsequent suicide. In their defense, they observed that the suicide was more likely related to the patient's subsequent use of drugs. The attorney hired by the girl's family, however, made his own proximate cause argument. He claimed that, given the girl's known emotional difficulties, the doctors' insistence that she didn't feel pain when she did and that she should be able to use an arm she couldn't use, heightened her feeling of rejection, and this, in turn, led directly to her use of drugs and eventually the taking of her own life. The jury apparently agreed with him and awarded the parents $35,000. This, however, is a remarkably small verdict in a wrongful-death action, and may reflect a compromise decision by the jury. On the one hand, they may have been dismayed by the inability of several doctors to diagnose something as obvious as a fractured shoulder and even more upset by their refusal to treat seriously the girl's complaints of pain. On the other hand, however, they may have been less than convinced by the plaintiffs' argument that the broken shoulder precipitated suicide five years later; hence, the small size of the verdict.

In any event, whether or not they were right or wrong in the decision they reached, the jury's verdict was within well-established legal principles for malpractice cases. In order to prove malpractice, by misdiagnosis or for any other reason, the plaintiff need not show the compensable injury (in this case, the patient's death) occurred immediately following the mistake; on the contrary, if the patient can prove to the satisfaction of a judge or jury, as happened here, that *an unbroken chain of events* led directly from the negligent event to the adverse result, the plaintiff must be compensated.

IV

These first seven case histories all involve instances in which the doctor failed to diagnose correctly the medical problem for which the patient sought treatment. Occasionally, however, a suit occurs when a doctor diagnoses one illness properly but fails to diagnose a second illness from which the patient is also suffering:

> CASE EIGHT: HELP FOR A HEART CONDITION.[16] This patient's evident symptoms were correctly diagnosed by his doctor as indicative of a heart involvement. As a result, the patient was hospitalized, treated successfully, and released. During the course of his treatment, as part of routine testing, X rays were taken which revealed "densities of unknown origin" in the patient's pelvic area. Although the doctors in charge of his case apparently were aware of these X-ray results, they ignored them. Some time after his release, the man began to suffer severe abdominal pains. He went to a doctor who discovered he was suffering from widespread inoperable cancer of the pelvis. He died soon after.

In this case, the surviving family sued the first doctor and the hospital alleging that if the cancer had been diagnosed while the man was being treated for the heart condition, his life might have been saved. Although the widow appears to have produced expert medical testimony to back this view, the defendants successfully argued that their only duty to the patient had been to treat him for the heart problem and they had no reason to look for other unrelated illnesses, especially since the patient, at that point, was making no complaints about abdominal pains. The verdict in this case indicates that doctors cannot be held liable for failing to diagnose one illness when they are treating another. The law on this, however, is far from clear. In another case,[17] which, like Case Eight, occurred in California, a patient was injured at work, hospitalized, and treated only for that injury. During the course of treatment, the attending physicians failed to diagnose that the man was also suffering from cancer of the mouth and throat. Their failure to do so, it was argued in the subsequent malpractice suit, hastened his death. A jury agreed and made an award of $90,000. The difference here perhaps lay in the visibility of the illness: "densities of unknown origin" in an X ray can mean many things, not all of them ominous. It is, however, extremely difficult for a reasonably competent doctor to manage not to observe cancer of the mouth.

In the misdiagnosis cases discussed to this point, the alleged negligence either occurred before treatment began or had the effect of preventing treatment from being offered. Occasionally, however, a misdiagnosis occurs while treatment is underway, usually in a postoperative situation:

> CASE NINE: THE FRACTURED ELBOW FATALITY.[18] (This case never went to trial so that the events narrated are based solely on the allegations made in the plaintiff's brief.) A twenty-two-year-old man was hospitalized to have fractures of his left elbow reduced (i.e., set). The operation was successful. During the postsurgical recuperative period, however, the man developed symptoms that were diagnosed variously by the attending physicians as pneumonia and an embolism (obstruction of a blood vessel). Based on these diagnoses, antibiotics were administered along with oxygen therapy. Subsequently, as the patient's condition worsened, a tracheotomy was performed, after which the patient developed both emphysema and pneumothorax (essentially a gathering of gas in the membraneous sac of the lung). He was then placed on a high concentration of oxygen. He died.

In this case, suit was based on the assertion that both of the postoperative diagnoses were incompetently negligent. The cause of the patient's death, it was alleged, was neither pneumonia nor an embolism, but rather pulmonary insufficiency, caused by the patient's reaction to anesthesia. As a result of their failure to diagnose properly, the patient, the suit stated, not only didn't get the treatment he should have gotten but instead received a course of therapy that was harmful to his condition and hastened his demise. According to the plaintiff's attorney, the case was settled prior to trial for an amount "in excess of $100,000." There is some indication that in this case the defendants denied the accusation, and it may be the settlement, as in an earlier case, was less an admission of culpability than an expression of fear on the part of the defense attorneys that they would have a hard time explaining to any jury why a person should die following an operation to set a broken bone. Moreover, their defense was complicated by the fact that the plaintiff was ready to produce expert medical testimony to the effect that anesthesia-induced pulmonary insufficiency is a well-recognized clinical symptom, and therefore was not one of those masked reactions that an ordinarily competent doctor would not discover.

Although most misdiagnosis malpractice cases occur when the physician fails to recognize a serious illness, thereby preventing timely proper care for it, sometimes he is sued because he has diagnosed a serious illness that doesn't exist:

CASE TEN: THE MAN WHO PUT HIS AFFAIRS IN ORDER.[19] A middle-aged man had not been feeling well for some time and went to see his doctor. After a thorough examination, he was given the grim news that he was suffering from advanced carcinoma and had only twelve to eighteen months to live. The man quit his job, put his worldly concerns in order, and prepared to die. But he didn't die. The twelve to eighteen months passed and rather than his condition worsening, it clearly had improved. He went to a second doctor and was advised that the reason he was not dying from cancer was because he never had it in the first place. Despite these joyful tidings, the man sued his first doctor for malpractice, alleging he had lost income and suffered great mental anguish because of the misdiagnosis.

CASE ELEVEN: THE MAN WHO HAD THREE DAYS TO LIVE.[20] In this California case, the news was also grim. A patient, suffering from severe jaw pains, was told by his physician that he was suffering from cancer of the jaw "close to the brain," and that he would be dead in three or four days. The doctor subsequently denied he ever told the patient that, but, in any event, he was immediately admitted to a hospital. There, a plastic surgeon saw him, had an X ray taken, after which he told the patient he should have his jaw removed to prevent further spread of the cancer. The patient, for reasons which are unclear, refused; perhaps he felt that since he only had a few days to live, he might as well live them with a jaw. He did, however, permit the physician to remove a gum tissue for examination. Soon after, according to the patient's story, he was discharged from the hospital, unable to find out from anyone how long he still had to live. This allegation by the patient seems hard to believe, as does most of what happened to him, but at the subsequent trial evidence was brought forth showing that someone at the hospital had altered his medical records, apparently including the information about the diagnosis. Now out of the hospital but with his terrible jaw pains persisting, the man finally did what he probably should have done at the beginning; he went to see a dentist who discovered a decayed molar and extracted it. That, as it turned out, was all that had ever been wrong with the man. He sued the physician, the plastic surgeon, and the hospital for malpractice by misdiagnosis, mistreatment, and causing him mental anguish.

The man who put his affairs in order found his malpractice suit came to an abrupt termination when a judge dismissed the charges prior to trial. This can be done when a judge rules that, even if everything the plaintiff alleges to be true is true, there are still no legal grounds for recovery. Although the judge's reasoning in this case isn't known, he probably decided that the cancer diagnosis, by itself, did not force the man to quit his job—that was a voluntary action on his part—so that any financial loss that resulted from it was not the doctor's responsibility. The judge may have also felt that the man did not react reasonably to the dire news he received and that he should have obtained a second opinion before reconciling himself to his fate. The judge, however, may have come to his decision solely on the issue of injury. Without injury, as we have seen, there is no malpractice, and while the plaintiff undoubtedly underwent an unpleasant experience as a result of the misdiagnosis, he was not physically harmed by it. Had the man undergone chemotherapy or an operation for the cancer he didn't have, his grounds for suit would have been much stronger. He could then at least have recovered his medical expenses, any associated loss of wages, and an amount for the pain and suffering the treatment may have caused him.

The patient whose decayed tooth was diagnosed as cancer of the jaw didn't suffer any physical injury either, but he did get his case to a jury which awarded him an amount slightly in excess of $60,000. In making its award, the jury may have been impressed by a number of factors: the extraordinary nature of the misdiagnosis itself, the resultant unnecessary biopsy, the evidence that the medical records were altered, and the apparent failure of the hospital to tell the man he didn't have cancer. However, what may have weighed most on the jurors' minds was the thought that if the patient hadn't refused the operation, he would have gone through the rest of his life without a jaw, a remedy for a toothache they may have considered to be on the extreme side.

V

As society changes its view of permissible conduct, new kinds of malpractice issues are raised, as in the following misdiagnosis suits:

CASE TWELVE: THE BRAIN-DAMAGED CHILD.[21] While pregnant, a Texas woman contracted rubella (German measles), which her doctor failed to diagnose. Some months later, her child was born suffering from massive brain damage and other handicaps associated with infants whose mothers have been exposed to rubella. The mother sued the doctor, charging that he should have diagnosed her illness, in which case she would have had an abortion performed. In his defense, the doctor pointed out that abortion wasn't legal in Texas at the time of the woman's pregnancy, so that even if he had diagnosed the rubella, she couldn't have been aborted. His argument appeared a strong one since it is an absolute defense against a malpractice charge when the defendant can show that in order to forefend the adverse result, it was necessary to commit a criminal act. But his defense was irrelevant, according to the woman; not only should he have been capable of diagnosing her condition, but he should have informed her of it so that she could have gone to a state in which abortions were legal. The court upheld the woman's argument and ordered the doctor to pay all medical expenses associated with the care of the injured child.

CASE THIRTEEN: THE MISSED CYCLE.[22] A thirty-four-year-old unmarried woman who had not menstruated for three months consulted a physician. Believing she was pregnant, she told him she wanted him to perform an abortion which, in her state, was legal. The doctor instead gave her an injection to induce her period. When that failed, he had her undergo a pregnancy test, which, he told her, was negative. He then continued the injections but still to no avail. At that point, he told the young woman she was undergoing change of life. Five months later, she gave birth to a baby boy. The woman thereupon entered a malpractice suit, claiming the doctor's failure to diagnose her pregnancy led to the wrongful birth of the child. Therefore, she asserted, it was the doctor not she who was responsible for the financial support of the child. The doctor sought a court order to force the woman to name the father of the child, alleging that any financial responsibility was his. The court denied the doctor's motion, observing that the two-year statute of limitations for determining paternity had passed, and that in any case the father's role had no bearing on the doctor's failure to diagnose the pregnancy and perform the requested abortion. The case was remanded for trial on the mother's charges; the result of the case is unknown. It may have been settled out of court.

Neither of these cases, it is evident, could have been sustained even a relatively few years ago when abortion was not a legally permissible option for a woman to adopt. Not all wrongful birth cases, however, have resulted from the liberalization of abortion laws. For example, in a recent New York case,[23] a couple wanted to have a child, but were fearful to do so because their first child was born with a kidney defect and died soon after. Two obstetricians advised the wife that she should have no compunctions about becoming pregnant again since the first child's death was not due to hereditary factors. She took their advice, became pregnant, and the second child was born with the same defect, dying when it was two-and-one-half years old. The mother sued the two doctors for $4.5 million in damages because of their failure to diagnose a now-evident congenital condition.

This case as well as a similar one filed in Pennsylvania (neither of which were yet resolved at the time of the writing of this book) represent, as do the abortion cases, wrongful birth suits which, not long ago, probably would not have even been litigated. To some extent, both kinds of cases reflect the society's changing view about the desirability of women giving birth regardless of the circumstances of the pregnancy. Legally, however, congenital deformity cases differ somewhat from abortion ones. As long as completely effective contraceptive devices did not exist, it was assumed by the American society (and by American judges) that pregnancies were the inevitable consequence of the conjugal relationship. Failure of a doctor to diagnose a congenital defect, therefore, legally was mitigated by the probability that the injured child might be born anyway. For this reason, failure to diagnose was arguably not the proximate cause of

the birth of the child. The development of the effective female contraceptive pill has changed that. Because of it, when a doctor now tells a woman there's no medical reason she couldn't have a child, he is talking to a patient capable of deciding whether or not she should become pregnant. As a consequence, he has a greater legal responsibility than in the past to inform her accurately of risks. This doesn't necessarily mean that doctors will now lose suits based on failure to diagnose congenital abnormalities—they always, theoretically, had that exposure—but rather that such suits have become more frequent and the doctor's likelihood of losing them is greater because of the newfound freedom of choice about pregnancy.

Another recent medical advance related to birth control has also caused a growing number of malpractice suits. This is the vasectomy operation. Suits concerning it arise when it has been performed unsuccessfully and the husband impregnates his wife leading to the birth of an unwanted child. These cases, however, do not fall into the misdiagnosis category but rather the improper procedure cases which are the subject of the next chapter.

CHAPTER FIVE

The Screaming Child

I

By the time she reached the age of seventy-eight, the few people who knew Martha Anderson saw her as a lonely old lady whom life had largely passed by. The elder of two sisters, she had never married. Her father died when she was thirty, and for the next twenty years she lived with her mother in a small apartment in a decent neighborhood in the Midwestern city in which she had been born. When her mother died, Martha retained the apartment and lived there alone, continuing to work, as she had since she got out of high school, as a secretary in the trust department of a bank. Retiring at the age of sixty-five, the bank's choice not hers, she numbered, for a while, a small circle of women friends, most of whom had also worked at the bank. But by the time she reaced her mid-seventies, all these contemporaries had either died, were in nursing homes, or had moved in with their children and she never saw them again. A few years earlier, her childless sister had also died, leaving Martha with only one living relative, a niece. A kind-hearted woman of middle years, the niece visited her aunt at least once a month and more frequently when her own family duties did not prevent her. "Oddly enough, when you think about it," she would recall later, "Aunt Martha, in her quiet way, enjoyed life. Or maybe I should say she enjoyed her habits. She set so much time aside each day for her ablutions, for her meals, for her housework, a time for knitting, a time for reading. She went to the library twice each week, always on Tuesday and Friday, I don't why. She went to a matinee movie once each week, and the orchestra once a month. She didn't talk about the past the way old people so often do; maybe that's because there hadn't been much in her life to reminisce about, and I guess that's so, but I don't think it's fair to say. The thing is she seemed so very concerned about trying to live in the present. She talked a lot about the books she read, and although it got tiresome she'd tell me the plots of the movies." The woman smiled. "Some of them must have shocked her, but I think, vicariously anyway, she enjoyed the shock. And then she had the cat. She was sensitive about that, and would joke about old ladies and their cats. Now I have the cat. That's him over there. I guess you might say he's my legacy." The niece punched out a cigarette; she was given to irony, her listener noticed. "But it's such a damn shame," she blurted out. "My aunt wasn't doing any harm to anybody. She could have kept living. They say her life was almost over, but I don't think she thought of it that way. I mean, I don't think that just because you're old or lonely, you don't value yourself any more. Like a table. What do they call them? Actuarial tables? That's the only place she didn't have value."

In April of the year she would have been seventy-nine, Martha Anderson, indomitably healthy until then, began to suffer gas pains. When they persisted, she went to a doctor. His symptomatic treatment failed to help and he order her into a hospital for observation. The hospital, which had associations with a major medical college, was generally considered a good one.

The tests the hospital ordered for Miss Anderson were routine, even for a person of her advanced age. The first, an intravenous pylogram to check her kidney functions, was completed without incident and showed a normal result. The second, a barium enema, it was hoped would illuminate on X-ray screens the cause of her problem. Administering the enema was a young graduate of a medical school in India who had come to the United States to complete his training. At 11:30 A.M., the resident noted on Miss Andcrson's chart: "Studies in progress; no problems."

As nearly as the events of the next half hour can be reconstructed, prior to the enema, Miss Anderson was feeling comfortable and chatting with the resident and nurses administering to her. Within moments of the insertion of the syringe, however, her face convoluted in agony, her body jumped, and within a few minutes more she had suffered a stoppage of heart action. A "Code 9" was called. Doctors rushed to her aid, pounded her chest, revived her quickly, and by noon had her in close supervision in the hospital's intensive care unit. The physician in charge of the X-ray room would later state under oath: "Just before she went into arrest, the resident reported to me he was having difficulty inserting the nozzle into her rectum," but this information was not given then or subsequently to the doctors who revived her.

Although they had achieved a satisfactory revival of her heartbeat, the physicians in charge of Miss Anderson were still having their problems. They discovered she was bleeding vaginally, and rushed her to an operating room where a laceration of the vaginal wall was discovered and sutured. But that solved only one problem. Each time a needle was injected in her, bubbles of blood rose from the entry point. As one witness put it, by 6 P.M., "blood was oozing from all sites." A few minutes afterward, Martha Anderson died.

By that time, her cousin had been located and rushed to the hospital. She remembers a physician sitting her down in a waiting room and explaining to her that heart attacks sometimes occur without warning in a woman of Miss Anderson's advanced years, and that the hospital had done all it could to save her. This explanation seemed reasonable to the cousin even though, as far as she knew, her aunt had no previous history of heart disease.

Less sure was the doctor who was in charge of Miss Anderson during her last hours. She ordered an autopsy done by the city's medical examiner. The report came back listing the cause of death as "therapeutic misadventure" rather than cardiac arrest. The autopsy also observed that no traces of barium had been found in the rectum.

To a layman, the autopsy report was difficult to follow but was suspicious on the face of it. The attorney who read it first was employed by the bank that had been Miss Anderson's lifetime employer and which she had named as executor of her estate. The bank attorney turned the report over to another lawyer who specialized in negligence work. This attorney soon entered a medical malpractice suit against the hospital and against all the doctors who had treated Miss Anderson, including the physician who had seen her first and had her admitted to the hospital for tests.

Despite the ambiguous autopsy report, despite a near paucity of hospital records concerning the incident, and despite the fact that the name of the doctor who performed the procedure wasn't made available to him by the hospital, the lawyer proceeded with the case. One by one, he interviewed the available witnesses under oath at pretrial depositions. Under those circumstances, and only then, did the physician in charge of the laboratory reveal what had occurred. The

Indian doctor had made a mistake. Instead of inserting the enema in the rectum, he had placed it in the vagina. When the wall burst, the barium sulphate entered into her veins, destroying the blood's ability to coagulate. This explained why each time Miss Anderson was given a presumably life-saving injection for her heart problem, the needle's entrance caused the debilitating oozing described by the witness. Under questioning, the doctor who had ordered the autopsy was asked whether it was true to say, if indeed there had ever been medical reason to say, to the cousin that Miss Anderson had died of cardiac arrest. "No," said the doctor, "that's not true." Well, then, asked the lawyer, what was the cause of her death? "She strangled," replied the doctor. "She choked to death on her own blood."

II

A "misadventure in procedure" can occur to a patient under an almost unlimited number of medical circumstances. For example, a doctor may correctly diagnose a patient's illness, then prescribe a drug for it, to which the patient has a violent reaction, resulting in hospitalization. Or, a patient, whose illness is also correctly diagnosed, receives a blood transfusion, sickens from it, and dies. Another patient, while on the operating table, has an artery severed when the surgeon cuts in the wrong place. Still another, postoperatively groggy, climbs out of his hospital bed, falls and breaks a leg. In each case, a misadventure has occurred during treatment, sometimes the result of negligence, other times not.

Statistically, there seems no way of knowing the degree of frequency with which various procedural misadventures occur. The authors of them (hospitals and doctors) have no interest in compiling that kind of record of mistake, nor do any governmental agencies require them to do so. However, of every five "misadventures" that give rise to malpractice claims, four are associated with surgery.[1] In many of these, the surgeon's actions, however, are either not in question or else were not the instigating factor in the injury; the injury, rather, was caused by an anesthesia mishap:

CASE FOURTEEN: THE UNLUCKY YOUTH.[2] A thirteen-year-old boy was admitted to a hospital for a routine appendectomy. Prior to the surgery, attendants failed to drain the contents of his stomach. Even so, he was taken into the operating amphitheatre where the anesthesiologist had difficulty inserting a tube into his throat, apparently because his head hadn't been placed in the proper position. Immediately afterward, the boy's breathing became labored, and the anesthesiologist injected him with Prostigmin, evidently in an effort to counteract what he believed was an adverse reaction from the first drug he'd used, curare. After receiving the second injection, the boy vomited and his heart stopped. Following an unknown period of time, he was resuscitated and taken to the recovery room. There, the nurse in charge wasn't informed of the heart stoppage during the surgery, with the result the boy wasn't closely monitored; while the nurse was absent, he suffered a second seizure and by the time someone noticed it and resuscitated him, he had suffered irreversible brain damage, assuming that hadn't already occurred as a consequence of the first seizure.

CASE FIFTEEN: THE SCREAMING CHILD.[3] A five-year-old boy was admitted to a Pennsylvania hospital for a tonsillectomy. While the surgeon in charge was performing the same operation on another patient in another room, the boy was anesthetized by a nurse acting under the supervision of an anesthesiologist. Once the child was under, the anesthesiologist left to attend to a seriously ill patient. Meanwhile, the nurse continued to administer gas to the boy even though she was by now no longer using her stethoscope to monitor the heartbeat. When the surgeon entered to begin the operation, he saw, from across the room, that the child's skin had taken on a bluish cast; he immediately began emergency resuscitation, and the child's heartbeat returned to normal. He had, however, suffered irreversible brain damage, and after seven weeks in a coma, some of the time marked by thrashing and screaming, he died.

Case Fourteen was resolved by a pre-trial settlement in which the parents received $1,237,500 for the future medical care of their son, who, though now a vegetable, might live for another fifty years. In Case Fifteen, a jury awarded $455,000 to the parents of the dead child. (This award, very large for a wrongful-death case, was subsequently set aside on appeal; the case was ordered reargued, not on the issue of negligence, but solely on appropriate damages. The final result of this case is not known.)

In both these anesthesia-related cases, the evidence of negligence appears overwhelming. Nevertheless, anesthesia accidents, with consequences every bit as grievous as those in Fourteen and Fifteen, can happen with no negligence involved on anyone's part. By their nature, anesthetics, capable of rendering a person immediately unconscious, are powerful drugs which means they are dangerous drugs with often unpredictable effects that can vary from person to person. Of them all, probably halothane is the safest and therefore one of the most commonly used. Yet even it, in a tiny percentage of administrations (perhaps no more than one in ten thousand[4]) can cause severe liver damage. Since there is no way to predict which patients will have that reaction, halothane-caused injury is ordinarily not grounds for a malpractice suit. There can, however, be exceptions, as in a 1971 California case[5] in which a patient was administered halothane during a routine hysterectomy. Shortly after her release from the hospital, complications developed which were consistent with liver damage but which could also have meant postsurgical complications. The woman was readmitted to the hospital for corrective surgery, and again administered halothane. She died two days later. In the ensuing suit, it was argued that the presence of symptoms that *might* be indicative of liver damage should have been a sufficient warning to the anesthesiologist not to use halothane a second time. A jury agreed and awarded $150,000 to the woman's survivors.

In this case, as in Fourteen and Fifteen, the anesthesia accidents had in common that they occurred during minor surgery. Twenty-one anesthesia malpractice cases in which a plaintiff pursued a negligence claim successfully were studied in connection with this book. Of them, sixteen occurred during surgery of a routine nature; in the remaining five, three case summaries failed to define the surgery sufficiently to classify it, while in the other two, the surgery was major. Discounting the three unidentifiable cases, we see that only 11 per cent of the successful suits involved major surgery even though such procedures comprise 23 per cent of all operations performed annually.[6] Why there should be this apparent correlation between anesthesia malpractice and minor surgery is unclear; however, it may be that psychological factors play a role. Minor operations are ones in which nobody on the surgical team—doctors or nurses—expect anything to go wrong. Nothing ever has during the hundreds of times they've gone through the same routine in the past, so they aren't geared to thinking in terms of possible mishaps. Nor is their concentration at the high level it would be for an operation of known danger and complexity. In the tonsillectomy case, for example, the anesthesiologist left the boy to anesthetize a patient in another room, something she would hardly have done had the child been undergoing heart surgery. As a result, there was no doctor with the child while he was being anesthetized, again something that wouldn't have happened during major surgery, and the nurse who was left in charge not only stopped monitoring the child with her stethoscope—what could go wrong in a tonsillectomy?—but may also have been chatting with other attendants. In still another case,[7] the anesthesiologist unhooked his monitoring equipment after a benign cyst was removed from a patient, unaware that a second cyst was to be excised. While that was going on, the unmonitored patient suffered heart stoppage; no one noticed and he died. Lapses of concentration, of course, hardly explain all anesthesia malpractice cases; in Fourteen, for example, almost everyone who had a crack at the boy harmed him. Nevertheless, the strong relationship between preventable anesthesia mishaps and minor surgery should be the subject of medical study.

Some errors by surgeons may also be related to attention-span factors. When a doctor performs a number of operations consecutively —as often happens, frequently to fit the hospital's convenience in scheduling operating room use—it is quite likely that at some point, perhaps when weariness has momentarily reduced his ability to concentrate, he will make an error that would not have occurred had he been performing only one or two operations that day. The exhaustion factor in surgical error has never been thoroughly studied; it should be.

III

The next three histories are of the type that most people probably first think of when they hear the word "malpractice," accidents caused when the surgeon's knife slips. As we shall see, however, it is not always a knife that causes the damage:

CASE SIXTEEN: THE DISFIGURED GIRL.[8] A seventeen-year-old girl underwent surgery for the removal of a tumor of the parotid glands.

(They are saliva producers located below and in front of each ear.) The surgeon in charge was a board-certified ear, nose, and throat specialist. During the course of the operation, his knife severed a facial nerve. As a result, the girl permanently lost partial muscular control of the left side of her face. She asked for damages both for disfigurement and the pain and suffering she had been caused.

CASE SEVENTEEN: THE MAN WITH THE EYE PATCH.[9] This patient was operated upon by a specialist for mastoiditis and chronic infection of the right ear. Following the operation, the infection continued, and a year later a second procedure was attempted. This operation not only didn't solve the patient's problem but also caused pain and dizziness to develop. Soon after, a second surgeon attempted still another operation, this one to remove additional tissue and bone from the ear. Still the patient's condition did not improve, and the surgeon took the procedure one step further, performing a highly delicate operation on the inner ear. During the course of it, the drill he was using slipped, lacerating the facial nerve which controls the eye muscles. As a result, the patient could no longer blink nor close his right eye, and was forced to wear a patch over it; he also suffered other adverse nerval effects.

CASE EIGHTEEN: LOSE A SON, GAIN A DAUGHTER.[10] The three-year-old boy of an army officer was admitted to a federal hospital for a circumcision. Somehow, during the course of the operation, cauterizing fluid was spilled on the child's penis and scrotum, so severely damaging the organs that it was necessary to completely remove them. The child subsequently was required to undergo corrective surgery to give it female genitalia so that it would be capable of some kind of future sexual life. The child, now a girl, will require additional surgery as she matures, and it remains unclear to what degree sexual adjustment and other social problems will arise. The parents, who had been content to have a son, sued the United States government for giving them a daughter.

Two of these three cases resulted in sizable awards for the plaintiff. The parents of the boy-turned-girl received $850,000 as a result of their child's bizarre misadventure, while the girl with the gland problem got $425,000. The man with the ear problem, however, lost his case.

The two cases that are most nearly comparable are the gland case and the ear case. In both, the surgeon's instrument slipped, causing permanent disfigurement. In the first, despite the undeniable high qualifications of the surgeon involved (or perhaps because of them), the jury decided that most surgeons engaged in that kind of work would not have made that kind of error and the accident, therefore, was a negligent one. In Case Seventeen, however, the surgery was of a much more delicate nature, and juries (though they will not hesitate to find negligence when an appendectomy patient is maimed or killed) are usually reluctant to brand as incompetent a doctor who fails in a procedure that many of his fellow doctors would not even attempt. It is this kind of understandable—and perhaps quite proper—jury bias which, for many years, meant that hardly any malpractice cases involving heart by-pass or advanced eye surgery cases were litigated, or at least not litigated successfully by the plaintiff. However, as more surgeons have begun to attempt this kind of work, so have the number of malpractice allegations increased. They will also tend to become more winnable because the skilled pioneering surgeons established a high standard of performance that becomes the measure by which lesser surgeons, who fail, are judged. In this configuration, it can be seen that as the best surgeons create the kind of advances that help people who could not have been helped before, they also set the stage for more rather than fewer malpractice cases.

Nevertheless, the knife-slip cases are not nearly as prevalent in malpractice literature as one might suppose given the considerable frequency with which (as most surgeons will admit) such events occur. There are a number of reasons why this is so. To begin with, most knife-slip errors are correctable while the operation is still in progress. An accidentally severed artery or vein, for example, not only must be immediately repaired but when it is, the patient's recovery often won't be impeded, which means the patient has not received a compensable injury. Other surgical injuries, however, such as those that damage internal organs, cause a considerable delay even though repair was made during the surgery. When that happens, the patient, who was anesthetized when the accident happens, often has no way of learning of the damage because the only ones who can tell her won't do so for fear of a malpractice suit. As a result, such a patient may spend many extra days or weeks in the hospital, at the cost of thousands of dollars in medical bills, believing that her delay in recovery is natural and not the result of a surgical accident. Consequently, most knife-slip or other surgical errors leading to malpractice suits are those in which it is impossible to hide the mistake from the patient, e.g., severed nerves (as in Cases Sixteen and Seventeen) and external mutilations (as in Case Eighteen.)

Not all surgical errors, however, are of the knife-slip variety. The setting of broken bones can sometimes lead to hideous complications for the patients and large claims payments by the insurance companies:

> CASE NINETEEN: A CASTING PROBLEM.[11] A man was admitted to a California hospital suffering from fractures of both bones of his right forearm. He waited for several hours before anyone saw him. When he was finally attended to, no pulse could be discerned in the wounded area which also contained a jagged laceration. The doctor cleaned the wound, performed a reduction of the fractures and applied a long-arm cast. A vial of gas gangrene antitoxin was also administered. The next day, the patient complained of severe pain in the arm; the cast was split and the pain subsided. Two days later, the patient was transferred to another hospital where a "crackling" sound was noted in the arm area, leading the doctors in that hospital to discover that gangrene had set in. Within a few days, it was necessary to amputate the arm above the elbow to save the man's life.

In this case, the first hospital and the original attending physician were sued, with the case resolved by a pretrial settlement of $267,500 to the victim. Another casting problem, typical of the rather extensive literature in this area of injury, involved Dr. Samuel Sheppard of murder-case fame. After acquittal at his second trial, he resumed practice as an osteopathic surgeon. Among his patients was a fourteen-year-old boy with an arm fracture. Sheppard placed the cast too tightly and the resultant loss of circulation left the boy's arm permanently crippled. The jury verdict in this case was $250,000, larger than average in casting cases that don't require amputation, leading to the suspicion that Sheppard's notoriety may have been a factor in the size of the award.

Case Nineteen, however, represents more than a casting problem. The patient might not have developed gangrene had he been treated immediately upon arrival at the hospital. A number of misadventure-in-procedure cases are similar, arising not from surgical error but from a failure to offer treatment in a timely fashion:

CASE TWENTY: HELP DELAYED IS HELP DENIED.[12] A twenty-eight-year-old woman suffered a complete and spontaneous abortion, as diagnosed by her surgeon, an osteopath. Two days later, complaining of severe abdominal pains she went back to her doctor who ordered her hospitalized. At 3 P.M., her blood pressure and pulse were taken at the hospital, found to be normal, and she was tentatively diagnosed as exhibiting signs of anemia and a pelvic inflammation. Sometime later in the afternoon, the resident in charge began to lose confidence in that diagnosis and attempted to reach the surgeon, leaving a call in with his answering service. The resident then left the hospital. Fifteen minutes later, at 7 P.M., the woman's vital signs were taken for the first time since her admission, and it was now discovered that her blood pressure was down to 60/30 and her pulse was racing at 140 beats a minute, indicating she was in clinical shock. An intern finally located the surgeon who arrived at the hospital around 7:30. The surgeon now noted that the abortion had not been complete and that the woman was suffering instead from a ruptured ectopic pregnancy, i.e., the fetus was in an abnormal position in the uterus leading to heavy bleeding. Although the surgeon seemingly recognized that the condition required immediate surgery, he waited an additional forty-five minutes for the arrival of his partner. Next, for reasons that are unclear, another delay occurred with the result that anesthesia was not administered to the woman until 9:55 with surgery not beginning until 10:20. The woman died.

CASE TWENTY-ONE: THE INTERFERING CLERK.[13] A boy suffered a head injury when he fell on the playground at his school. His father called the family physician who told him to take the child immediately to a nearby hospital. There, the boy was turned over to an intern who commenced an examination of him. At that point, the intern received a phone call from a clerk in the hospital's administrative office who told him he was not permitted to treat the boy because the referring physician was not on the hospital staff. Obediently, the intern stopped the examination and told the father to take the boy home and "observe" him for any signs of "physical distress." Shortly after arriving home, the boy's condition visibly worsened. At that point, the family physician arrived and rushed the boy back to the hospital where, this time, he was admitted. It was, however, too late. The intracranial bleeding the boy was suffering had left him mute and permanently paralyzed from the neck down.

In many respects, Case Twenty resembles the Lillian Lazzeri case. When a patient is suffering from 60/30 blood pressure, doctors shouldn't wait for more than three hours to offer help, anymore than they should have waited for seventy-five minutes, as they did in the Lazzeri case, when the patient is bleeding uncontrollably. A jury awarded the dead woman's husband $175,000. (A dead wife, unless she is a wage earner, is usually considered to have less cash worth in a wrongful-death case than a provider husband.) In the Lazzeri case, there was no award because the husband never sued; he accepted the hospital's prevarication that his wife's death was due to cardiac arrest.

In Case Twenty-one, delay of treatment occurred solely because a clerk took it upon herself to tell a doctor he shouldn't treat a patient. This monstrous bureaucratic interference with a doctor's fundamental duty to provide medical care to the sick and injured and the doctor's docile compliance with the clerk's order apparently so infuriated the jury that they made one of the largest awards in malpractice history, $4,025,000. (The $25,000 was assessed, against the city's school system, which was a codefendant in the trespass action because of its negligent failure to have supervision at the playground where the accident occurred.)

Sometimes, however, a malpractice suit is entered, not because treatment was delayed, but because it was offered when it shouldn't have been:

CASE TWENTY-TWO: THE HERNIATED BABY.[14] A thirteen-month-old child was admitted to a hospital for a hernia operation. At the time of admission, the baby, who had a history of numerous head colds and two attacks of bronchitis, was carrying a temperature of 100.2 degrees. Despite the fever, the doctors went ahead with the surgery, and following administration of general anesthesia, the child went into cardiac arrest but was revived by closed heart massage. Despite this setback, the doctors decided to go ahead with the surgery; more anesthesia was administered and the operation commenced. Shortly afterward, the child again went into cardiac arrest, and this time closed heart massage failed to revive him, necessitating an incision to open the heart for external massage. Resuscitation came too late. The child suffered permanent brain damage, cerebral palsy, and blindness.

The issue in this case was the propriety of operating on a patient who is running a fever. Undoubtedly, there are medical circumstances in which this is a necessity; however, performing a hernia repair on any feverish patient, must less a year-old baby, is not one of them. The persistence in continuing the surgery after the first cardiac arrest is also, at the least, remarkable. The case was settled pre-trial with an award of $450,000 to the child's parents.

IV

Earlier, we described the impact of the proximate-cause doctrine on misdiagnosis cases. The same issue is frequently raised in procedural cases:

CASE TWENTY-THREE: DEATH IN THE DOCTOR'S OFFICE.[15] A man suffering from severe chest pains was taken by his wife to a hospital. The physician in charge ordered an electrocardiogram taken. The machine malfunctioned, and the doctor told an attendant to get the hospital's second machine and use it; at that point, the doctor left the hospital. Meanwhile, a search of the hospital's premises failed to locate the second machine, and the wife, by now desperate, took her husband in their car to the office of a private physician four miles away. While this doctor was taking a cardiogram, the husband died.

CASE TWENTY-FOUR: THE LEG THAT WOULDN'T HEAL.[16] In December 1970, a woman fell, fracturing her right leg in two places. An orthopedic surgeon reduced the fractures and placed the leg in a cast. Over the next three months, he saw the patient regularly, at which time the cast was removed. Two months later, the orthopedist noted in his records that the patient was still suffering pain; she, however, would later maintain that by this time the doctor had told her the leg was healed and she needed no further treatment. In any event, the doctor set up another appointment for the woman which she did not keep, allegedly because she was by then dissatisfied with the quality of care she was receiving. During the next several months, she consulted three other orthopedists, all of whom told her the leg had not healed properly and that she required corrective bone-graft surgery. The woman waited for two years and then had the surgery performed. It was not successful. Finally, in August 1974, she had a second bone-graft procedure; this one was successful and her leg finally healed. She sued the first orthopedist for his alleged negligent care of her.

CASE TWENTY-FIVE: THE PARALYZED VETERAN.[17] In 1957 a man was admitted to a Veterans Administration Hospital for a chest operation known as a thoracic laminectomy. The surgery appeared uneventful, but shortly afterward the man suffered severe distress in the chest area. He was given pain killers. His discomfort continued and finally internal bleeding was diagnosed, a condition ordinarily readily correctable. Unfortunately for this patient, help came too late. He was already permanently paralyzed with accompanying pain that was to last the rest of his life. Twelve years after the operation, he died of bronchial pneumonia.

From a defense view, the proximate-cause doctrine is raised most succinctly in Twenty-three. On the face of it, the widow's case appeared a strong one. A hospital that can manage to break one cardiogram machine and lose a second one has made a notable contribution to the history of administrative incompetence. Moreover, at the trial, the widow produced expert testimony to the effect that her husband would have had a 75 per cent chance of survival had his impending heart attack been diagnosed via the cardiogram while he was still at the hospital. The defense, however, contended that the projected 75 per cent chance was only speculation and could not, in any case, be interpreted as meaning that the failure to take the cardiogram at the hospital was the proximate cause of the death. The man, it was observed, might have died anyway. Or, alternatively, had the wife not subjected the husband to the four-mile trip to the doctor and had instead allowed him to remain in hospital care, he might have been saved by the attending physicians when the attack occurred. The absence of the machine, therefore, while regrettable and probably negligent, was not the cause of the man's death. A jury agreed.

In Case Twenty-four, the proximate-cause argument by the

plaintiff was rejected by the defense. The attorney for the orthopedist noted that the evidence failed to prove that the original surgery on the woman's leg directly related to the length of time it took to heal. When the woman failed to keep her appointment with the orthopedist, it was argued, she broke a chain of treatment he was offering which, had it been completed, might well have resulted in an earlier recovery for her than she finally obtained. Moreover, the defense contended, when the woman delayed two years in having the bone-graft surgery performed, she further contributed to her own delay in recovery. Consequently, her actions obviated any possibility of tracing negligence to the orthopedist. A jury agreed. (On appeal, this case was remanded for a new trial on a technical ground; the result of it is not known.)

A proximate-cause argument was also raised by the defense in the Tommy Manning case. In their response to the suit filed on Tommy's behalf by his parents, the defense attorneys made no attempt to deny that Dr. Kane had been negligent when he failed to have the bullet wound X-rayed; that, they agreed, is a medically imperative procedure when there is no bullet exit site. However, the attorneys argued, their stance backed by a corps of medical experts, Kane's negligence did not cause Tommy's paralysis. That had become inevitable the moment the bullet struck the spinal cord, so that even if the X ray had been taken, Tommy was already beyond surgical help and it was only a matter of hours before he became permanently paralyzed. Or, at least that was the defense's contention, one which, for reasons that will be discussed later, was never successfully countered by the Mannings' attorney.

The family of the dead veteran in Case Twenty-five had to overcome a statute of limitations problem before they could get their case to trial. In federal court, which was where their case was docketed because it involved a Veterans Hospital as defendant,[18] most injury cases must be instituted within two years of their occurrence, with a one-year limitation on a wrongful-death action such as theirs.[19] In most state courts, a two-year limitation also generally applies, although in some states the period is one year for all injuries, in others as long as five years.[20] Whatever the deadline imposed, the limitation is based on the theory that the older the cause for an action is, the more dim become the witnesses' memories and the greater the likelihood that records which might exonerate the defendant will have been lost or destroyed.

The attorney for the dead veteran's family, however, was able to overcome the statutory limitation. He pointed out that the veteran had been under continuous care by the hospital from the time of his operation until his death twelve years later. In continuous-care cases, he argued, the legal presumption is that records are kept in detail from the inception of the event, and if a defendant, in this case a Veterans Hospital, failed to do so, the fault is its. The court agreed and the case was admitted for trial. At that point, the attorney hadn't won his case but he was well on his way. After establishing that the hospital's original care for the internal bleeding had been negligent and led directly to the man's paralysis, he next produced medical evidence which showed that paralyzed patients are particularly susceptible to pneumonia. It was reasonable, therefore, he asserted, to conclude that the real or proximate cause of the man's demise was not pneumonia, as appeared on the death certificate, but the negligence-induced paralysis. His argument proved successful. The man's family received an award of $300,000, including $175,000 to cover the pain and suffering undergone by the man during his long ordeal.

In most tort situations, however, the normal statute of limitations offers no serious litigation problem for the plaintiff. The victim in an automobile accident knows immediately that he has been injured as does the person who falls on the icy sidewalk, and neither has any legal reason for delay in bringing suit. There are, however, in addition to continuous-care cases, some other exceptions. For example, in a medical case, the patient may be a minor when the negligent injury occurred, and should her parents fail to file suit on her behalf, her own right to do so has been violated. As a consequence, in most states, an adult is permitted to bring an action for an event that occurred when she was a child. This means that if she was injured medically at birth and the legal age of majority in her state is twenty-one and the statute of limitations is five years, she has until the age of twenty-six to file suit. (This rule, however, varies considerably from state to state, and to some extent from tort action to tort action.) The statute of limitations may also be waived or extended when the putative plaintiff had no way of knowing of the existence of the injury during the statutory period. This can often occur in custodial situations in which a patient or an inmate dies as the result of staff negligence which is then covered up. In such instances, the statute only begins to run when the surviving family knew or should have known of the true circumstances of the death. There are other reasons also that patients may not know they have been injured for a considerable period of time after the event:

> CASE TWENTY-SIX: THE LOST SCISSORS.[21] An Arkansas man underwent surgery for removal of half his colon. For six years following the operation, he suffered a variety of internal problems but did not seek medical care. Eventually, however, he consulted a physician who ordered X rays; they revealed the presence of a 6-inch pair of surgical scissors in the man's abdomen, left over from the colon operation. Although the statute of limitations for bringing a malpractice action in Arkansas is two years, the man sued the original doctor on the theory that his negligence—sewing the scissors into his stomach—had continued until the instrument was discovered and removed.

In this case, the plaintiff lost when the court ruled that the continuance of unexplained pain after the surgery should have caused him to seek medical help within the two-year statutory period. Presumably, had the scissors not caused him pain but many years later created an infection, he could then have recovered because only at the time of the infection would he first have had a way of learning of the presence of the foreign body. Such, in fact, has been the holding in a number of cases.[22] As a general legal rule, therefore, it can be said that the statute of limitations in a malpractice case only begins to run at the time the patient *should* have known of the injury, not necessarily at the time she did learn.

V

Up to this point, since they account for about 80 per cent of the total, we have been concerned only with misadventure in procedure cases involving surgery, or, as in the case of the boy in Case Twenty-one who was paralyzed, interference that prevented the timely performance of surgery. Malpractice literature, nevertheless, is well-populated with cases like the Martha Anderson one involving non-surgeons. Although some of these suits relate to testing, most involve negligent drug prescription. There's also the occasional case in which a doctor (or a nurse) gives a patient an injection in the wrong site, hitting a nerve and causing paralysis.[23] Because of the dangerous nature of the work they do, another category of non-surgeons, radiologists, become defendants in a fair number of cases:

CASE TWENTY-SEVEN: THE BURNED VETERAN.[24] A patient suffering from cancer of the rectum was admitted to a VA hospital. His condition was diagnosed as critical, the tumor having grown so large that it was impossible to remove it surgically. To reduce its size, radiation therapy was determined upon and over the next five days, 2,999 rads were administered, about triple the generally acceptable maximal exposure. Unlike in most other radiation malpractice cases, in which overexposure is accidental, in this one, the doctors made a conscious choice to administer the extreme dosage because of the immediate peril to the patient's life. As hoped, the radiation sufficiently reduced the size of the tumor that it could be removed. Complications developed, however; the patient's groin became scarred and thickened; bone and muscle had to be removed from his right buttock area; he required skin grafts; removal of vertebrae at the base of his spine, and eventually amputation of his testicles.

The malpractice suit brought by the patient was heard by a judge sitting without a jury. Upon listening to expert medical testimony that the radiation dosage was excessive regardless of the patient's existent condition, the judge awarded him $150,000, his verdict confirmed by an appeals court. To many doctors, it is decisions such as this one which make them shy away from extraordinary (but hopefully life-saving) procedures for fear their failure will cause a malpractice suit. The verdict, therefore, tends to encourage the kind of cautious, negative defensive medicine that was described in Chapter Two.

VI

The blood bank has been the locus of a number of malpractice suits involving misadventures in procedure. Occasionally at issue, as in the Lazzeri death, is the failure of the blood supplier to make his product available when needed. More often, however, it is the quality of the blood that causes the lawsuit:

CASE TWENTY-EIGHT: DANGEROUS BLOOD.[25] A forty-five-year-old woman was admitted to a hospital for a hysterectomy. It was performed without complications. During the course of the surgery, the patient received a transfusion of blood obtained from a community blood bank. Shortly afterward, the woman developed serum hepatitis as a direct result of that virus in the blood given her. Three months after the operation, she died. Her husband sued the hospital, the blood bank, and several of the attending physicians, charging negligence by failure to assure the purity of the blood before it was given her.

As an illness, serum hepatitis has been increasing at epidemic proportions in the United States. In 1950, for example, only 2,820 cases were reported. By the early 1970s, the annual incidence was in excess of 63,000 cases,[26] the increase directly related to the growth of drug addiction in the United States.[27] When a drug addict becomes a blood donor, as many of them do to raise cash, the illness can be transmitted through the blood directly to the patient receiving it as occurred in Twenty-eight and other cases like it.

Malpractice suits involving hepatitis transmission, however, have proven very difficult for patients to win. In six decisions in recent years,[28] three occurring in California, one in Illinois, one in Georgia, and one in Louisiana, as well as in Twenty-eight, the courts have ruled that neither hospitals nor blood banks can ordinarily be held liable for the use of the diseased blood. The judicial reasoning has varied somewhat from decision to decision, but essentially the courts have held that blood banks are vital to society and, hence, are properly immune from any negligence action arising from the way they gather their supplies. In Twenty-eight, for example, the court commented: ". . . blood donors and suppliers [are shielded] from strict liability for injuries from blood transfusions . . . The legislature [which passed the immunity statute] properly weighed the vital importance of a continuous blood supply against the relatively small risk of hepatitis and concluded that patients must accept that risk . . ." Since acting as a gatherer or transmitter of diseased blood is not in itself negligent on the part of a hospital or an outside blood bank, it is apparent from these decisions that the only way a plaintiff can recover in a serum hepatitis case is to show that the blood source *knowingly* accepted donations from addicts, a nearly impossible charge to prove.

Some errors in blood transfusion procedures, however, are considered medically negligent. In an Indiana case,[29] a patient died after receiving blood type "A" instead of her own blood type "C"; a $191,000 settlement offer was accepted by her survivors. Similarly, a $695,000 agreement was reached in a California case in which a hospital negligently failed in its performance of an exchange transfusion on a baby suffering from an Rh-blood factor problem.[30]

VII

Accidents to patients in their rooms or elsewhere on the hospital premises also cause a sizable number of misadventure in procedure malpractice cases; in them, doctors are often not involved as defendants but nurses, orderlies, and other attendants are:

> CASE TWENTY-NINE: THE WOMAN WHO WAS WILD AS A MARCH HARE.[31] A sixty-one-year-old woman was admitted to a hospital suffering from an infected burn and a condition diagnosed as "alcoholic psychosis." She was placed on a high-protein diet and administered a number of tranquillizers, including Thorazine, a highly potent one. Nurses' notes described her as "very confused and upset" with the examining physician at one point describing her in his notes as "wild as a March hare." Nine days after this notation, while left alone and without restraints, the woman climbed over the guard rails of her bed and fell, receiving multiple fractures to her right thigh and hip. She and her husband sued the hospital for its alleged negligent failure to exercise care in her behalf.

In its defense, the hospital maintained that the raised sides of the bed offered the patient adequate protection, and that her climbing over them was an unforeseeable and therefore non-negligent event. The hospital won its case at trial, but an appeals court reversed the verdict, stating that the judge should have taken into consideration the hospital's own notes about the woman's condition. Had they acted accordingly, they would have taken additional precautions (e.g., the use of restraints) to prevent her from harming herself.

A number of other cases, often involving disoriented patients, have followed the same principle. In one,[32] a lower court judge was again reversed on appeal. In this case, a seventy-five-year-old woman was admitted to the hospital for testing, was administered castor oil, and subsequently a sleeping pill. In the middle of the night, she attempted to get up to go to the bathroom, fell and broke her hip.

The hospital bed rails were not raised at the time. The appeals court commented that "a reasonably prudent person [viz., a trained hospital nurse] could foresee that a patient who had been administered castor oil and sleeping pills would have to go to the bathroom in less than alert condition and that bed rails are not only designed to keep patients in bed but to serve as an obstruction to alert her that she should ring for assistance." In still another case,[33] a patient attempted to wash his hands in his bathroom about six hours after surgery, but apparently because he was still disoriented by pain killers and tranquillizers, allowed his hands to stay under scalding hot water with the result that four fingers had to be amputated. The hospital was found negligent, and the patient received a jury verdict of $225,000.

Such accidents, however, don't always result in plaintiff verdicts. In a Texas case,[34] a woman fell out of bed in circumstances quite similar to the "Marsh hare" woman and received nothing. In a Louisiana case,[35] hospital attendants several times warned an aged man not to get out of bed without assistance; he did so anyway, fell, broke a hip, and later died when pneumonia developed. There, the court held the man was the author of his own injury, and that the hospital personnel had met an acceptable standard of conduct even though their custodial care did not extend beyond verbal warnings.

Many other hospital accidents occur outside the patient's room, and some of these can bring a finding of negligence, too. In a California case[36] a man was awarded $25,000 by a jury when an X-ray platform on which he was standing collapsed, aggravating his already degenerative arthritic condition. In still another case,[37] an elderly woman, paralyzed from the waist down, was left alone in a wheelchair at the top of a ramp. The wheelchair slid down the ramp, pitched the woman out against a concrete wall, fracturing her skull. Before she could be resuscitated, she had suffered permanent brain damage.

An X-ray technician in another case[38] somehow reversed the photos of a woman's kidneys. As a result, the surgeon mistakenly removed the woman's healthy kidney, leaving intact one which was cancerous. The woman was doomed to an early death by that mistake.

In a Delaware case,[39] a woman was admitted to the hospital for a biopsy to ascertain whether or not she had cancer of the breast. The laboratory correctly diagnosed the section as benign, and the pathoogist sent back a verbal message to that effect. However, by the time the messenger got there, he managed to get the diagnosis reversed and told the surgeon the finding was malignancy. The woman needlessly lost her breast. At trial, hospital officials were asked why they gave operating room messages verbally. They replied that was the way they had always done it. The woman received a jury award in excess of $100,000.

Occasionally a hospital will be sued for negligence because an attendant has caused the wrong patient to be operated upon. In a case decided in 1976,[40] a woman was admitted to a hospital for minor surgery of the cervix. On the day of the operation, an attendant mistakenly took her into the wrong amphitheatre where a surgeon was waiting for a patient who required removal of her thyroid gland. Without checking the identity of the patient, the surgeon began slicing away. Happily, another attendant discovered the mistake before the operation was complete, but not before a four-inch incision had been made in the woman's neck. It subsequently became infected and eventually cosmetic surgery was required. The woman's horror when she discovered what had happened to her apparently also aggravated pre-existing emotional problems. A jury awarded her $100,000. In a California case,[41] a man was hospitalized to have his leg removed. He was delivered to the operating room in place of another patient due to undergo an orchiectomy. This time nobody noticed that the wrong person was under the knife. When the man subsequently awoke in his hospital room, he discovered he still had his leg but that his testicles had been amputated. He did not consider his hospital stay a successful one.

CHAPTER SIX

The Man Whose Children Couldn't Touch Him

I

In addition to misadventures in procedure and diagnosis, a medical provider can be charged with a variety of other acts in a malpractice trespass action. They include: *patient abandonment* (refusal to continue a treatment that has been begun, perhaps because the patient has not paid a bill), *false imprisonment* (committing a patient to a mental hospital against her will and/or without sufficient grounds to do so), *failure to consult* (proceeding with a treatment without acceding to the patient's wish that another doctor be called into the case), *failure to have proper equipment or facilities* (to carry out the proposed treatment), and *premature release* (discharging a patient from treatment prior to cure.) Although any of these charges can be the principal allegation in a suit, they—along with a dozen or so others[1]—most often occur as subsidiary allegations.

Another type of malpractice suit occurs only occasionally, but when it does, it produces a maximum of embarrassment for the medical profession. In these suits, the patient alleges her doctor trespassed against her sexually:

CASE THIRTY: THE INTERNAL EXAMINATION.[2] A woman filed a malpractice suit against her physician alleging sexual misconduct on his part. While the civil suit was pending, the physician was arrested and charged with the crime of deviate sexual assault on the woman. At the criminal trial, the woman testified that during an office visit, the physician gave her an injection and told her to undress for an internal examination. As she lay on the table, she found her face and neck were becoming hot, her vision impaired, and that she felt drugged, dizzy, and too weak to get off the table. During the examination, she stated, the physician manipulated her vagina with his fingers and then performed oral sex upon her. In his defense, the doctor maintained the woman had severe emotional problems, suggesting she may have imagined what happened to her. The prosecution, however, produced six other witnesses who testified they had similar encounters with the doctor. He was found guilty of the charges and sentenced to five to ten years imprisonment. The result of the patient's malpractice suit is unknown.

CASE THIRTY-ONE: ASTHMA THERAPY.[3] A Pennsylvania woman went to an osteopathic physician, who also practiced psychiatry, for treatment of her bronchial asthma. During the course of her therapy, she later alleged, the doctor treated her with addictive and hallucinogenic drugs; required her to have sexual relationships with him; and subsequently assaulted her, fracturing her skull. A jury awarded her $665,000. (In a somewhat similar, though less violent, case in New York, a patient alleged that her psychiatrist forced her to have sex with him as therapy to cure her of homosexuality. A jury awarded her $150,000.[4])

While it may be hoped that sexual assaults upon patients by their doctors occur in reality with the same infrequency as their presence in malpractice literature would suggest, it is, nevertheless, disturbing to observe that in Case Thirty, it was only after one woman finally charged the doctor with unpermitted carnal knowledge that six other women then came forward to testify the same thing had happened to them.

Regardless of their rarity, when they occur, sex cases represent deliberate trespasses of the Brown punching Jones variety, rather than the unintentional ones, which were the subject of the case histories in Chapters Four and Five. As such, they come under the legal categorization of *batteries* or "beatings" of the patient. The technical difference between an assault and a battery is too fine to get into here, but for our purposes we can consider a *battery* as any legally impermissible touching of a patient, whether or not the threat or fact of overt violence is involved. A medical malpractice battery can occur, therefore, when a doctor improperly influences a patient to accept a course of treatment (a legal touching) that is to the doctor's and not the patient's advantage. Although the exploitation that ensues may be sexual, often it is not, as in the following history:

> CASE THIRTY-TWO: THE MAN WHOSE CHILDREN COULDN'T TOUCH HIM.[5] A twenty-five-year-old California man with a back pain was referred to an orthopedic surgeon who told him that his trouble was caused by a slipped disc and that an operation was required to cure him. Surgery in this case, in fact, was neither necessary nor desirable, but the patient had no way of knowing that and agreed to it. The surgeon then went ahead with the procedure, a relatively minor one, but botched it so badly that the patient's pains became permanent and excruciating, extending from his back to his legs. Virtually unable to work, he became a heavy drinker and was forced to refuse to let his children near him lest they touch him and exacerbate his perpetual agony. Three years after the operation, the patient developed cancer, but because of his existent injury was unable to tolerate any drug therapy for it. Doctors gave him a life expectancy of two to three years, although, had he been able to accept chemotherapy, he would have had about a 50 per cent chance of recovery. The man sued the doctor and the hospital in which the operation was performed, alleging battery by reason of unnecessary surgery, medical incompetence, and a host of other charges. The same doctor and hospital were also sued by at least one other patient, charging virtually identical injuries. Moreover, evidence at trial suggested that the surgeon had talked thirty-seven other patients into unnecessary back operations. The surgeon testified he performed them to obtain money to support his drug habit.

In the non-jury trial that followed, the judge, in rendering his decision, examined in detail the circumstances of thirteen of the thirty-seven operations. He noted that in one a "diagnosis of the necessity [for the operation] was made in an examination of the patient fully clothed [who has required hospitalization] six times since the original surgery."[6] Describing the defendant's conduct as "beyond depravity,"[7] the judge went on to conclude: "I am . . . satisfied from the evidence that [the defendant] successfully engaged in a deliberate and purposeful course of conduct intentionally designed to deceive . . . his patients."[8] Based on this reasoning, he awarded the plaintiff $1,700,000 to cover his pain, suffering, medical expenses, loss of earnings, and then tacked on an additional $2,000,000 in punitive damages. The hospital in which the doctor practiced was also found liable for its negligent failure to monitor his performance and was assessed $500,000 in damages. (In 1976, a new trial was ordered for the doctor on a technical ground. The second trial had not taken place at the time of the writing of this book.)[9]

Battery by reason of unnecessary surgery is always a grounds for a malpractice suit. However, since the patient has no way of knowing in advance that the operation is unnecessary, such events ordinarily, as in Thirty-two, only lead to a suit when the procedure is also unsuccessful, in which case the principal allegation is usually improper treatment.

II

An impermissible touching of a patient also occurs when she accepts a form of treatment proffered by her doctor without having been adequately informed of dangers inherent to it. In such instances, because the patient's *informed consent* is lacking, any subsequent harm to her person (either by reason of medication or surgery) is a trespass *even if the medical service is properly performed:*

> CASE THIRTY-THREE: THE TREMBLING WOMAN.[10] A right-handed woman saw a physician about an annoying tremor in her left arm. Although it didn't seriously handicap her, it made her self-conscious about her appearance, and she wondered if anything could be done to help her. The doctor recommended an operation which he said would stop the tremor. It did. It also stopped all movement in her left arm, which was left permanently paralyzed. She sued the doctor.

In pursuing her suit, this plaintiff never contended the operation was marked by surgical incompetence. Instead, she produced expert medical witnesses who testified that the type of surgery she had undergone, performed properly, causes paralysis in 15 per cent of all patients. The plaintiff then testified in her own behalf, asserting that the doctor had never told her of the risk of paralysis, and that if he had, she would never have agreed to the surgery, particularly since the tremor, which would have seriously impaired her had it been in her right arm, was only a minor inconvenience in her left. In his defense, the doctor told the jury he had informed the woman of the risk but that she had insisted on the operation anyway for cosmetic reasons. At the trial's close, the judge instructed the jury that, in deciding who was telling the truth, they could invoke the so-called "reasonable man" doctrine, i.e., would a reasonable person have accepted this kind of surgery had she known of the approximate one chance in six of paralysis? The jury apparently decided the woman was a "reasonable man" and awarded her $65,000.

In this case, as in a number of informed consent suits, the only real issue was a determination of fact: Had the woman been informed or hadn't she? Other informed consent allegations, however, raise thornier issues, both legally and medically:

CASE THIRTY-FOUR: THE SUCCESSFUL HEART SURGERY.[11] A patient suffered a blockage of an artery to the heart. His physician, an internist, recommended an aortic by-pass operation. While describing the procedure, the physician told the patient that the operation was dangerous and that there was a 10 per cent chance he might not survive it. The patient even so, agreed to the surgery, and it was successfully performed as far as his heart was concerned. However, the operation also resulted in damage to the patient's vision, left him with impaired speech, and paralysis of his left side. He sued.

In this case, certain facts were not in dispute. The plaintiff agreed the operation had been performed not only competently but successfully in the sense that the by-pass had meaningfully prolonged his life. On its part, the defense admitted that paralysis, partial loss of vision, and the other adverse effects the patient suffered were known risks of this form of surgery, and that the patient had not been informed of them. The sole question in dispute, therefore, was whether or not he should have been informed.

The patient said yes. Through his attorney, he maintained that had he known a by-pass operation opened him to such crippling consequences, he might well have foregone it, even though by refusing he could have been pronouncing a death sentence on himself. As his attorney observed, life, under some circumstances, is not worth living, and paralysis and loss of vision may be one of them. In any event, the attorney asserted, his client had the right to be informed of *all* risks associated with the surgery, and when he hadn't been, he was illegally prevented from making an informed decision about his health and his life.

Not so, said the defendants through their attorney. He cited a body of case law holding that doctors need inform their patients only of *usual* risks associated with a course of treatment. Having developed that theory, the attorney then produced expert witnesses who testified that the ill-effects suffered by this particular patient occur in only 1 per cent of all by-pass operations. Clearly, said the defense lawyer, this was such a miniscule risk factor that his clients had no legal obligation to inform the patient of it.

The defense, however, did not rest its case there, but went on to raise a question of medical ethics. The attorney pointed out to the jury that a doctor's duty, the entire thrust of his life's training, is to find ways to save lives not to suggest to patients ways to end them. Yet that, by the patient's own allegations, is what would have happened in this case had he been informed of the 1 per cent risk. This particular patient, the defense attorney agreed, may indeed have seen death as an acceptable alternative to paralysis, but society should not be bound by his idiosyncrasy. To find for the plaintiff, the jury was told, meant that in the future all doctors would be required to inform all patients of all risks, no matter how remote. This, he argued, could have devastating consequences. Many patients, upon hearing of an ominous but remote danger, would be frightened away from accepting the course of treatment that was most likely to help them—and lose their lives as a result. If jurors found for the plantiff, they were, the defense attorney thundered in conclusion, in effect sentencing thousands of people to death in the future.

With this burden placed on them, the jury found for the defendants, and their verdict was upheld on appeal. Nor was their decision an exceptional one. "Usual" risk has been a criterion accepted by many courts in determining how much a doctor is obligated to tell a patient in advance about a course of treatment.[12] But many doesn't mean all, and some judges, agreeing with the reasoning expressed by the plaintiff in this case, have ruled that every patient has a right to expect "full disclosure" of risk, or as another judge with a taste for redundancy put it, "full and complete disclosure."[13] Because of these clashing judicial opinions, doctors, by and large, remain in the dark about how much they are legally obliged to tell their patients about risk if they don't want later to find themselves as defendants in a malpractice suit.

Yet even if the view adopted by this jury—namely, that rare risks need not be explained to a patient—is eventually to be adopted as the legal standard, we are still left with the problem of defining when a risk is "rare." In Case Thirty-three, a 15 per cent paralysis risk was described by the plaintiff's witnesses as a "substantial one," while in this case, the internist did tell the patient of the 10 per cent possibility of death from the by-pass, suggesting that a 10 per cent risk must always be explained. However, the verdict seems to say that a doctor need not tell a patient of a 1 per cent risk. Then, what of 5 per cent? Of 9 per cent? How, in fact, are these percentages determined? To these questions, there appear to be no answers.

But even were it possible to resolve the percentage difficulty, other problems remain. For example, in what way should the disclosure be made? Generally, judges have ruled that the doctor must explain risk in lay terms if the consent is to be an "informed" one.[14] That sounds forthright enough, but it will be difficult for a judge or jury to know retrospectively whether the explanation was simple enough for a layperson to understand, or indeed whether the patient was capable of understanding the explanation *at the time* it was given. For instance, Dr. Schneider's patient, Mr. Phillips, was in great pain when he arrived at the hospital and was given sedatives which made him drowsy. It was while he was under the influence of them that Dr. Robinson explained to him the risks of the surgery and got Phillips' consent to perform it; under those circumstances, was Phillips sufficiently alert to give an informed consent? The case law on this subject is scant and contradictory.

A few elements of informed consent, however, are relatively clear. First of all, it is a *positive* duty. A doctor must voluntarily explain risk in a procedure and not wait for the patient to ask.[15]

At the same time, the law recognizes that situations can arise in which it is impossible or unwise for the attending physician to obtain the patient's consent before beginning treatment. An accident victim brought unconscious into a hospital emergency room will often need immediate help if her life is to be saved. When no member of the family is available to give consent, the doctor should not delay treatment until someone can be found. Indeed, as we have seen in Chapter Four, unnecessary delay in providing medical care can itself be grounds for a malpractice suit.

There is at least one other situation in which a battery allegation based on the informed-consent issue[16] can be raised:

CASE THIRTY-FIVE: THEY HAVE TO LEARN ON SOMEBODY DON'T THEY?[17] A young woman was admitted to the hospital for a routine hysterectomy which she assumed was going to be performed by the doctor she had engaged for that purpose. The operation, however, was undertaken by a resident, with the woman's surgeon assisting. After surgery, the woman complained of nausea, began to vomit, and suffered a distension in the pelvic area. She was subsequently transferred to the care of a specialist but died forty-five days later.

In the subsequent wrongful-death suit, the resident (and his hospital employer) were named as defendants, based on the resident's unpermitted touching of the woman by performing the hysterectomy on her. A jury agreed with the charge and found for the plaintiff.

The practice of having one surgeon perform an operation for which another was hired, without the patient's consent, is known as "ghost" surgery. Questioned about its prevalence by "CBS News,"[18] a spokesman for a New York hospital admitted that it took place, but said it was a proper exercise of medical discretion since it is the only way residents can gain the experience necessary to make them competent surgeons. The spokesman noted that, in his hospital, the surgeon engaged by the patient was always present during the operation and could take over if any difficulty arose, a defense that proved unsuccessful in Case Thirty-five. In an interview, Dr. Robinson admitted that he sometimes performed surgery for which Schneider received the fee, but he likewise maintained that Schneider was always present when the surgery took place.

The same CBS investigation, however, also produced evidence that the surgeon the patient has hired is not invariably in the operating room; that, indeed, he may well be in another room sawing away on another patient at the same time his "ghost" is performing his duties in the first room. In this fashion, some surgeons collect fees for performing two operations simultaneously. Robinson admitted he had "heard" of this going on in "other hospitals" but denied it occurred in his.[19]

Undoubtedly, the public depends on the availability of qualified surgeons to help them when they need it, and equally undoubtedly to become qualified these surgeons have to hone their skills by performing operations, not just by watching or assisting at them. While much of this experience is gained by performing procedures, under supervision, on patients who do not have a doctor of their own, there will be situations in which the surgeon can only learn important skills by operating on a patient who has hired another doctor to do the work. To carry out this learning experience deceptively, however, by not asking the patient's consent, does constitute malpractice by reason of battery. Legally it remains unclear whether the presence of the engaged surgeon in the operating room is a viable defense against the malpractice assertion. Although Case Thirty-five suggests not, there is simply not enough case precedence on the subject to be certain. However, it is clear that when the hired surgeon isn't even present for the surgery, he has condoned or caused a battery and is also open to a charge of patient abandonment, and perhaps civil and criminal fraud charges as well.

III

Doctors and hospitals can also sometimes be sued for malpractice by people who were not their patients. These cases are usually referred to as *third-party suits*; in them, it is asserted that treatment given one patient directly caused harm to someone else.

In a sense, wrongful-death suits fall into this category since the plaintiffs, the dead person's surviving family, were not themselves physically harmed by the alleged negligent event. A surviving spouse, for example, sometimes successfully seeks compensation for loss of consortium and occasionally for the mental anguish suffered when the person died at the hands of a negligent doctor. Since these suits, however, primarily seek damages based on the dead person's pain and suffering, they are not purely third-party actions.

Allegations of mental anguish suffered by someone other than the patient crop up with some regularity in malpractice literature, as witness the following:

> CASE THIRTY-SIX: THE DAUGHTER.[20] A mentally deficient girl was a permanent resident in a state mental hospital. One day she wandered from the cottage in which she was living, and the hospital officials could not find her. Eleven days later, her body was found in a wooded area just fifty feet from the edge of the parking lot of

a building adjacent to the one in which she lived. The father's suit against the hospital sought damages for his daughter's pain and suffering prior to her death, the wrongful death itself caused by the hospital's failure to conduct a careful search for her, and a separate allegation seeking payment for his own mental anguish caused by the circumstances of her death.

Remarkably enough, the wrongful death as well as the pain and suffering charges concerning the daughter were dismissed; the father, however, was awarded $5,000 for his suffering. This, in itself, is unusual. Mental-anguish cases, whether asserted by the injured plaintiff or by a third party, are only infrequently sustained by courts. Although juries often enough are sympathetic to such allegations (as in the case of the man whose jaw was almost removed), judges are not and tend to dismiss them before a jury can get hold of them, as occurred in Case Ten. In so doing, judges are expressing an unwillingness to create a chilling effect on the practice of medicine. As they see it, a physical injury allegedly caused by negligence ordinarily can be established by medical evidence, while assertions of mental anguish ordinarily cannot. Rather, they are analogous to whiplash in automobile accidents, easy to assert and nearly impossible for a defendant to disprove. As a consequence, for a mental-anguish charge even to get to trial, it is usually necessary for the plaintiff to prove specific injury, e.g., a nervous breakdown immediately following the negligent event, causing the plaintiff prolonged and costly treatment.

Nevertheless, occasionally a person who has not herself been injured by medical care can be subjected to such trauma that a mental-anguish suit based on the event will prove victorious:

CASE THIRTY-SEVEN: A DECENT AND FITTING BURIAL.[21] A Tennessee woman, somewhat past mid-term in pregnancy, was admitted to a hospital where she underwent a miscarriage. The hospital officials offered to bury the fetus, and the grief-stricken woman agreed. As the months went by, however, she became increasingly less sure she had done the right thing in accepting the hospital's offer, and she spoke to her family physician about her concern. He suggested she go to the hospital and ask to see the place in which the baby had been interred. Armed with his introduction, she returned to the hospital and spoke to an administrator. He turned her over to an attendant who was instructed to take her to the site. After a considerable travel through the lower depths of the hospital, they arrived at a large room. The attendant took the woman inside and plucked a gallon jar from a refrigerator. In it, the woman could see the infant floating, pickled in formaldehyde. (It was apparently used for medical student training.) The horrified woman suffered a near nervous collapse at the sight and later sued the hospital for the anguish the event had caused her. The judge found the hospital culpable of "outrageous conduct" and awarded the woman $175,000.

In the wording of his decision, the judge may have been expressing his personal feelings, but he was also applying a recognized legal theory by which a defendant in a trespass action can be found liable if his conduct meets the tests for a "tort of outrage." Outrage occurs when the defendant either has the specific intent of bestowing harm or acts with such reckless disregard of the feelings and welfare of the person who has sued that the act "offends against the generally accepted standards of decency and morality" in the community in which it occurred.[22] Although community standards of "decency and morality" are hard to define, as pornography prosecutors have found out, it would be a callous community indeed that would not be offended by the circumstances in which the unusual funeral urn was displayed to the Tennessee woman.

A tort of outrage, however, does not occur simply because a doctor or a hospital official exhibits bad manners toward a patient, and in that sense acts in callous disregard of her feelings. Confrontation by the ill-mannered, the patronizing, and the arrogant is one of the unfortunate hazards of life that everyone faces and is not grounds for a suit against a doctor or anyone else.

The very large majority of third-party suits, however, do not incorporate mental anguish charges. Rather, they are predicated upon showing an uninterrupted chain of events traceable to a mistake made by the medical provider in the care of someone other than the plaintiff. Third-party malpractice cases of this sort are analogous to those in which an automobile driver hits a pedestrian, throwing that pedestrian against a second person who is injured by the impact. This person has no tort action against the pedestrian, since it wasn't his fault he was thrown, but he does have a case against the driver whose negligence knocked the pedestrian into him.

Medical cases of this nature are growing in frequency[23] and can occur in a number of ways. Sometimes, as in the following histories, a lawsuit against one defendant leads directly to a second suit against another:

CASE THIRTY-EIGHT: THE NEGLIGENT DRIVER.[24] A car ran through a stop sign and hit a passer-by who suffered a broken leg. The pedestrian sued the driver of the car who eventually settled the suit for $25,000. The driver then sued the pedestrian's doctor, charging him with malpractice. At trial, the driver introduced evidence that revealed that after twenty-two treatments, the pedestrian had recovered only 55 per cent use of his leg, but that when he consulted a second doctor, he regained 80 per cent use. (Allegedly the first doctor had permitted the cast to remain on the leg too long, resulting in improper delay in inaugurating physical therapy for the patient.) A jury agreed with the driver's contention that the doctor had committed malpractice and required him to pay the driver $18,500 of the original $25,000 settlement.

CASE THIRTY-NINE: THE DOCTOR WHO SUED A DOCTOR.[25] A man went to a podiatrist (a non-MD who treats foot problems) to have a corn removed from his toe. Immediately afterward, an infection developed in his bone marrow, and he went to a medical doctor for the treatment of that. The infection worsened, gangrene threatened, and the toe had to be amputated. The patient sued the podiatrist for malpractice and won. The podiatrist, in turn, sued the medical doctor, alleging he had been negligent in the way he treated the resultant infection. A jury agreed, and the podiatrist (i.e., his insurer) recovered the amount that had to be paid out to the patient.

In each of these cases, the injured person apparently could have also sued the medical doctor for malpractice but chose not to do so, the pedestrian electing to concentrate on the driver who had injured him, the toe patient on the foot doctor. As these two cases show, however, that did not end the physicians' liability. Both were subject to collection by others who had been harmed financially through their negligence. Dr. Schneider, therefore, was wiser than perhaps he knew in fearing a malpractice suit in the Phillips operation. Phillips himself might only sue the transit company and collect damages from it, but the transit company might get some of its money back from Schneider if it could show that the extensiveness of Phillips's injury was caused by any negligence in the medical treatment he received.

Negligent *failure to warn* is probably the most common grounds on which a third-party malpractice action is brought:

CASE FORTY: THE ROOMMATE.[26] A doctor admitted a patient suffering from a contagious disease to a hospital. Soon afterward, the patient of a second doctor was placed in the same room and contracted the disease. This patient sued the contagious patient's doctor and the hospital for negligently failing to warn either himself or his physician that he was sharing a room with a person suffering from an infectious ailment.

CASE FORTY-ONE: THE BATTERED CHILD.[27] Following a divorce, the custody of an infant was given to its mother who was living with her paramour. On three occasions, this man so severely beat the child that it required medical care. In total, four doctors saw the child, but none reported evidence of the beatings either to local health authorities or to the district attorney. The final beating caused permanent brain damage in the baby, as a result of which the father, for the first time, learned what had been happening. He sued all four doctors for their failure to report the evidence of the child abuse to proper authorities or to warn him of the danger his child faced by continuing to live with its mother.

CASE FORTY-TWO: ASLEEP AT THE WHEEL.[28] A man saw his doctor, complaining of an allergy. The doctor, who knew the man was employed as a bus driver, prescribed an antihistamine, which produces drowsiness in many patients. This side effect was described in the manufacturer's literature, in its advertising, and in the Physicians Desk Reference, a book, which almost all doctors have, that lists adverse effects of all prescription drugs. Despite this ample opportunity to know of the drug's propensities, the doctor did not warn his patient not to use it while driving. The patient did and fell asleep at the wheel of his bus; it crashed, injuring a number of passengers. They sued the driver's doctor for malpractice.

In each of these cases, plaintiffs who had never met the doctors they sued won malpractice suits against them. In each, the doctor's *medical* treatment of his own patient was proper enough. The man with the infectious disease had no complaint about the way his doctor treated his illness; the antihistamine did help the driver's allergy; and even the doctors who saw the battered child competently treated the injuries she received. Each doctor, however, by failing to take an additional step, caused harm to others. The battered baby's doctors by not adhering to their legal duty to report suspected cases of child abuse not only set in motion terrible damage to the child herself but also placed on the father (who gained custody of the child) lifelong medical bills for his daughter which he had to sue to recover. The contagious patient's doctor may not have even known that another patient was placed in the same room with his patient, but because he failed to take positive action to see that that didn't happen, he was liable; the hospital was equally, if not more, negligent since it had to know the first patient was contagious at the time it placed the second patient in with him. Finally, the bus driver's doctor was under no legal obligation to prevent his patient from driving, but he was medically negligent when he didn't warn him of the possible side effects of the antihistamine, and could have been sued by the patient himself if he had fallen asleep while driving his own car and injured himself.

Finally, third-party cases can also occur when a patient is prematurely or improperly discharged from care and then harms someone. Such cases often involve injuries committed by mental patients:

CASE FORTY-THREE: THE FEARFUL WIFE.[29] A psychiatric patient was permitted to leave a Veterans Hospital to join a work-release program despite a history of threats to the life of his ex-wife. Learning of his release, the woman protested to hospital officials, expressing fear that her former husband was still homicidal and would try to kill her. The hospital ignored her pleas. The man's employer was not informed of his mental problems nor does there appear to have been any effort by the hospital to supervise him psychiatrically. While on release, the man wrote several letters to his therapist at the hospital, the contents of which revealed continuing delusional psychosis. The hospital did nothing. Soon afterward, the man murdered his former wife. Her estate sued the government as the party responsible for her death, citing the federal hospital's negligence in failing to keep the man confined and then failing to reconfine him when it gained evidence he was still psychotic. A jury awarded the wife's estate $90,000.

CHAPTER SEVEN

The Murderous Student

I

Whenever a society moves from a period of passivity to one of activism, the courts find themselves inundated with cases requiring them to consider new questions of equity. In the United States, this happened, beginning in the 1950s, as issues raised by the early civil rights movement began to find their way into the litigation process. Since, by its nature, the activist society tends to stretch itself permissively, one issue suggesting another, civil rights cases were soon followed on the court dockets by others, those concerning rights of women, homosexuals, victims of pollution, defendants in criminal cases, and so on. It was during this permissive period that courts also began to hear growing numbers of malpractice suits with medical providers.

Not all judges responded favorably to patient-rights cases anymore than all had to black rights. However, just as had occurred in the civil rights arena, quantification played an important role: Because enough cases were litigated, enough found their way to judges who were sympathetic to the equity issues raised. As a result, landmark decisions were rendered that significantly altered the provider/patient relationship. Some of them have been discussed in previous chapters. The decision in the case of the boy who was paralyzed because a hospital refused him treatment established, for the future, that no hospital may deny emergency care to a patient. Informed consent cases, although they have not led to a consensus definition of how much a doctor must reveal about risk in treatment, have established that the doctor must *voluntarily* inform the patient in language an average layperson can understand. Similarly, a number of recent third-party cases have broadened the duty of the doctor to consider the safety of others, not just his patient, in considering the treatment he prescribes. Before these decisions were rendered, the medical profession generally didn't believe it had such obligations. (In theory, it probably always did, but as long as the courts hadn't ruled, medical providers could assume otherwise.)

Definitions of required or permissible conduct, however, do not reveal themselves in any stately, undeniable progression, or even with permanence. As Sir Henry Maine observed years ago: "Social necessities and social opinions are always more or less in advance of Law. We may come indefinitely near to the closing of the gap between them, but it has a perpetual tendency to re-open."[1] This chasm between the administrators of the law and the priorities of the society create relationships of great complexity for the litigants who come before the courts. Because of it they find illiberal decisions still occurring in an era of permissiveness and permissive ones in an era of dawning conservatism. Thus, we find that many of the most important pro-patient decisions in medical cases have been handed down in the 1970s, a period in which the society has moved sharply away from the civil rights posture dominant in the 1960s.

Based on Sir Henry's insight, we can, therefore, speculate that the next step for the courts will be to discard their patient's rights orientation and render decisions more favorable to the doctor, the sort of authority figure that always fares well in conservative times. The same courts that recently told doctors they must inform their patients of risk may now so hedge that dictate as to make it virtually meaningless. The courts that struck down the locality rule may re-establish it. But even here there are crosscurrents. Either by bent of personality or by legal training, most judges are not adventurous; presented with a knotty legal problem, they prefer to take refuge in precedents already established rather than create new ones. Hence, the pro-patient decisions that were so slowly established on the heels of the permissive period, will change equally slowly and perhaps insignificantly if society, at the next swing of its ideological pendulum, moves quickly back to liberalism.

Shifts in social climate, however, do not just affect the directions that new legal precedents take. They also lead to reinterpretation of established ones. For example, a ruling clearly intended to extend protection of the rights of individuals when issued in response to a judicially perceived social liberalism may be applied in opposite ways by later judges who are now responding to the needs of public order rather than those of individual rights. The following history is illustrative:

CASE FORTY-FOUR: A COMPULSION TO MURDER.[2] A University of California student asked to see a psychotherapist on the university hospital staff. During a course of interviews, he revealed to the therapist that he sometimes felt compelled to murder the young woman he had been dating and who was out of town at the time the interviews took place. Alarmed, the therapist discussed the case with his superiors, and it was decided the student should be committed to a mental hospital. Campus police were dispatched to detail him, but somehow he managed to convince them he was rational and they let him go on his way. Nothing further was done by the hospital staff to attempt to institutionalize him. Shortly after the visit from the police, the student murdered the young woman. At no time had university authorities warned either her or her parents that the student might be dangerous. The parents sued the university for malpractice on the part of its hospital and psychiatric staff by reason of their failure to protect their daughter from the murderous student.

At trial, the university contended that its employees, the psychiatrists, had at all times acted within accepted definitions of proper medical care. They had diagnosed the young man's problem correctly and offered him treatment that would likely have helped him and protected society if the student had permitted it to be carried out. Most importantly, the defendants claimed, they were bound by their professional code of ethics to keep confidential the student's revelations to them. For that reason, to warn the young woman or her parents would itself have been malpractice against the student. (It is unclear in this case why the psychiatric staff didn't follow-up on its decision to have the student committed once the campus police let him go; they may have been intending to wait until the student's next appointment with the therapist, but the student, following his encounter with the police, never kept that meeting.) At trial, the judge accepted the university's defense. The California Supreme Court, however, reversed the verdict,[3] ruling that the university employees did have a duty to warn the potential victim and her family, which superseded any confidential relationship with the patient.

To understand the implications of this decision, let us first examine the circumstances in which doctor/patient confidentiality has previously been ruled breachable. Under some circumstances doctors know they must report "dangerous" patients to authorities. In most states, for example, as we have seen, evidence of child abuse falls under that stricture; the doctor cannot rely legally on his confidential relationship with the child's "dangerous" parent as an excuse not to report his suspicions of battering. Similarly, in a number of states a doctor must breach his confidential relationship with a patient who suffers seizures in order to see to it that the patient doesn't endanger others by driving a car. Neither could a doctor keep confidential the contagious illness of his patient if that meant exposing someone else to the illness whether that's a hospital roommate or someone else. Readers of a certain age, for instance, will remember from their childhood seeing homes in their neighborhoods plastered with pink signs bearing in bold black letters the warning: QUARANTINED, and below that the name of the dread disease, SCARLET FEVER, WHOOPING COUGH, MEASLES, and so on. By causing these signs to go up, doctors were revealing the nature of their patients' illnesses for everyone to see.

In all these instances, the right of the society in general and of individuals who might be affected in particular is considered more important than the right of any patient to secrecy, and few would question that the public interest is not served by these revelations.

Similarly, it has long been acknowledged (by the medical profession and the law) that when a doctor receives confidences from a patient which indicate to him the patient's mental condition is such that he is a danger to himself or others, the doctor should take steps to confine him. The failure of the University of California doctors to do so might well have been ruled negligent and the case ended there.

The California decision, however, went beyond that well-recognized legal principle. Under its dictates, therapists (in California anyway) now appear to have the duty to reveal confidences to others who *might* be endangered by the patient. The judicial intent in the ruling, no doubt, was laudable. The tragedy, presumably, would have been averted had the warning been given, although, on reflection, that is far from clear: If the student was capable of talking his way out of the clutches of the campus police, he might also have been capable of convincing the young woman and her parents that the doctors' warnings, had they been given, were false, that they "had it in for him," or were "twisting his words."

Be that as it may, the precedent established in this case seems to say that, in the future, no psychiatric patient may rely on the belief that information given his therapist will be used solely for his benefit, even if that benefit means institutionalizing him. For example, let us suppose a woman reveals to her therapist that she belongs to a radical political movement, believed by those in authority to advocate the violent overthrow of the government. Under the California decision, the therapist may have a duty to warn police about her membership since it prospectively presents the same danger to society as did the deranged student. To require psychiatrists to become police informants was certainly not intended by this decision, yet that can well be its practical effect, particularly as a pro-authoritarian climate develops.

Privacy violations of this kind, however, don't have to occur for the California ruling to have a destructive effect on the therapist/patient relationship. If a therapist now tells a patient in advance of treatment that he is legally obliged to reveal to "others" any information which marks him as "dangerous," the patient will likely back away from treatment, or at best become inhibited, worrying about the uses to which his personal revelations may be put. As a result, the whole purpose of the therapy is lost. Yet if the therapist doesn't tell the patient in advance of the limits to confidentiality and later does reveal information detrimental to the patient, the patient then can sue him for malpractice on the grounds his informed consent wasn't obtained before beginning treatment. As a result of the California decision, therefore, the therapist has taken on additional legal responsibility as an informer, a contrary obligation to inform the patient he may become an informer, and the patient is left with no certitude he can confide in anyone at all. Using the litigational process to dictate medical conduct would seem to have its drawbacks.

II

The decision in another recent case has alarmed the medical profession in ways not unlike the California one:

CASE FORTY-FIVE: THE DOCTOR WHO TRIED TO DO TOO MUCH.[4] A Minnesota man suffered severely splintered fractures of his right wrist and went to his family physician. After viewing X rays, the doctor placed a conventional circular cast of plaster on the wrist. Severe swelling followed, and to alleviate it, the doctor split the cast, first on one side and then on the other. As a result, bone fragments slipped and the man's wrist became permanently deformed. He sued the doctor on the grounds that he had negligently failed to refer him to an orthopedist.

At trial, the judge permitted an orthopedist to testify as an expert witness for the plaintiff. He stated it was customary for general practitioners to refer patients with complicated fractures to orthopedists who have available to them special pins to be used in such cases and have the skill to apply non-circular casts that reduce the likelihood of swelling. Despite this testimony, the judge ordered a verdict of acquittal, presumably on the grounds that the specialist's testimony failed to prove that the general practitioner had violated an acceptable standard of care in terms of his own medical training. An appeals court, however, reversed the dismissal, holding that since the general practitioner took it upon himself to attempt a procedure that required orthopedic skill, he should be held to the same standard of care that would apply to an orthopedist, and ordered the case re-tried on that basis.

The Minnesota court's rule in this case sets forth a high standard for medical conduct in referral of cases. By its terms, any time a doctor has reason to believe his skills are not adequate to treat a patient, he has the obligation (except, presumably, in emergency situations) to send the patient to a doctor with the requisite ability. The intent of this ruling is to discourage a doctor from hanging onto a patient, either because the patient produces income or because the doctor doesn't want to admit his inability to help. The patient, the court is saying, has the right to the best care medicine can provide, not just the best care his physician can provide. Denial of best care by failure to refer, therefore, is malpractice.

To the medical profession, this is an onerous ruling, not because doctors don't generally refer patients they can't help—the overwhelming majority do—but because as a legal dictate it removes from the doctor a judgmental right that has traditionally been his and when it is taken away from him, will (in the view of many physicians) inhibit his treatment practices. He may, for example, for fear of suit, now refer too many cases, inadvertently placing patients in the hands of high-priced specialists whose services they don't need. To the extent this happens, the doctor improperly loses income unless he works out an unethical kickback arrangement on his referrals. Perhaps more importantly, since it is the general practitioner who is most likely to be affected by this referral rule, it tends to discourage medical students from entering that specialty, both because the referral rule identifies them as inferior doctors and because it reduces their income potential. Yet, according to most studies,[5] from a public health view, general practice is the medical specialty in which the most doctors are needed, and therefore one that medical students should be most encouraged to enter.

This is not to say that the Minnesota ruling was not a proper one, nor to conclude that doctors are necessarily correct in their prognostications about its consequences. It does, nevertheless, like the California ruling, though in a different way, suggest that pro-patient decisions won't uniformly have pro-patient consequences. (At this point, it is useful to recall that although rulings by an appeals court are not binding outside its own state, such rulings are frequently influential as cited precedents when like cases are decided in other jurisdictions.

III

A different extension of the physician's responsibility to the patient was revealed by the following history:

CASE FORTY-SIX: THE DOCTOR WHO WAS NOT INFORMED.[6] As in the Minnesota case, a wrist fracture was involved, this time to a Colorado man who was admitted to a hospital to have it set. Prior to the surgery, the man told a nurse employed by the hospital that he felt nauseous. The nurse failed to inform the surgeon. Had she done so, he would have postponed the operation. As it was, he went ahead and while under anesthesia, the patient regurgitated four liters of fluid, at the same time inadvertently sucking an additional unknown amount into his lungs. He died ten days later. The surviving family sued both the hospital and the doctor for malpractice.

The hospital apparently reached a settlement agreement with the plaintiffs prior to trial.[7] The doctor, however, fought the charge. His first defense, as might be expected, was that the nurse was the salaried employee of the hospital and it, therefore, was exclusively responsible for any negligence on her part. But the doctor also had a second argument. He pointed out that he had relied on the nurse as a professionally trained person to inform him of any patient symptoms, and she had not, so he had a right to assume there were none.

A jury agreed with the doctor, but its verdict was set aside as contrary to law by an appeals court on the basis that a doctor has a *positive* duty to keep himself informed at all times of a patient's condition.

That such a duty exists wasn't denied by the defendant nor would it be denied by any doctor. The question here is: When has the duty been complied with? Let us suppose, for example, that just prior to the operation, the doctor had asked the patient how he was feeling and the patient, assuming the nurse had told the doctor about his nausea, simply remarked that his wrist hurt. Was the doctor then negligent? According to the Colorado decision, he may have been. It seems to say that he had an additional duty to check with nurses, residents, interns, and everyone else with whom the patient had contact about any symptoms he may have revealed to them. This, many doctors will argue, places an insuperable liability burden on the attending physician and one which, prior to the Colorado decision, the medical profession generally thought was the proper responsibility of the trained staff the hospital provided. Decisions in other jurisdictions on issues similar to this case have, in fact, placed the liability solely on the hospital, so that the definition of positive duty, as with informed consent, remains unresolved.

IV

During the course of their medical training, doctors are taught certain procedures they should always perform, others that should sometimes be performed, and still others that should be performed on some patients and not on others. By following these guidelines, doctors assume they are meeting the standard of care of their specialty. Sometimes they are, and sometimes not:

CASE FORTY-SEVEN: THE PATIENT WHO HAD DEVELOPED A DISEASE TOO YOUNG.[8] In 1959, a twenty-three-year-old woman who lived in the state of Washington visited her ophthalmologist to have her eyes examined. Myopia was diagnosed and she was fitted with corrective contact lenses. Four years later, complaining of irritation in both eyes, she returned to the ophthalmologist, one of two in a partnership, who decided her difficulties were caused by the contact lenses and prescribed adjustments in them. Her problem, however, continued. She returned for one more appointment in 1963, three times in 1967 and five times in 1968. By the final 1968 visit, she was noticing loss of vision which, for the first time, caused the doctor to believe something other than lens-adjustment problems were involved. He decided to test her eye pressure, using the Schiotz tonometry method. The test revealed the woman was suffering from glaucoma in an advanced state. Then thirty-two-years-old, the woman sued both ophthalmologists—partners in a medical enterprise can be found legally responsible for each other's negligence—on the grounds that if they had given her the test when she first complained of irritation, her vision would have been saved.

At trial, the doctor who attended her admitted that glaucoma had been in existence for at least ten years. However, the defendants produced expert witnesses who testified that the incidence of glaucoma in patients under the age of forty is so rare—one in 25,000—that it is contrary to the standard of the ophthalmologic specialty to test for it until patients have passed forty. Failure to test then, it was admitted, would be negligent since from that age onward, glaucoma incidence rises to a dangerous 2.5 patients per 100. Finding this definition of the recognized standard of care persuasive, the trial judge ruled in favor of the defendants, his verdict upheld by an appellate court.

By 1974, the case finally had reached the Washington Supreme Court. It reversed both lower courts and directed a verdict in favor of the plaintiff,[9] ordering a new trial be held only on the basis of how much money should be awarded her. In its ruling, the Supreme Court granted that the standard of care for detecting glaucoma was as the expert witnesses said. However, the court added, that *shouldn't* be the standard. "The incidence of glaucoma in one out of 25,000 persons under the age of 40 may appear quite minimal," the court's opinion observed. "However, that one person, the plaintiff in this instance, is entitled to the same protection as afforded persons over 40 . . . The precaution of giving this [Schiotz] test to patients under 40 years of age is so imperative that irrespective of its disregard by the standards of the ophthalmology profession, it is the duty of the courts to say what is requisite to protect patients under 40 from the damaging effects of glaucoma. We therefore hold, as a matter of law, that the reasonable standard of care that should have been followed under the undisputed facts of this case was the timely giving of this simple, harmless pressure test to this plaintiff and that, in failing to do so, the defendants were negligent, which proximately resulted in the blindness sustained by the plaintiff for which the defendants are liable."[10]

On the face of it, the Washington decision appears a proper one. Patients can go blind from many causes not under the control of their physicians, but they should not lose their vision due to glaucoma simply because they're the wrong age when the symptoms appear. Were the Schiotz test a dangerous one, then its use might properly be limited only to those patients who, regardless of age, exhibited glaucoma symptoms, but that, as the court pointed out, is not the case; the test not only is harmless but also takes only a moment to perform, using an instrument that is standard office equipment for every ophthalmologist.

The Washington decision, nevertheless, in its implications is one that has frightened the medical profession. When the court, *ex post facto*, determined that one professionally accepted standard of treatment wasn't proper, it was also calling into question all similar standards by which doctors, whatever their specialty, make their judgments about a patient's condition. Now no longer able to rely on standards taught in medical school, the doctor's liability has correspondingly risen, and he must assume he can be sued for failure to unearth exceedingly rare causes of illness. As a consequence, some medical spokesmen believe, the tendency will be to subject patients to usually needless, expensive, and sometimes dangerous tests of the "defensive" variety, rather than immediately treat the patient for what appears to be the cause of the illness and most often is.

While this gloomy breast beating on the part of the medical profession no doubt overstates the dangers of the precedent established by the Washington case (after all, a very important factor in that decision was the simplicity, reliability, and non-dangerous nature of one specific test), the ruling in the case nevertheless exemplifies the perception widely held by doctors that judges—in their gap-closing effort to protect patients' rights—are moving in a direction that defines all mistakes as negligent ones and denies to the profession its ability to judge, based on its own scientific training, how best to help the ill.

To doctors, too, there is an exquisite irony to this mounting attention the courts have paid to the rights of patients. It has come about, as they see it, exactly at a time in which they, as a profession, are giving those same patients a quality of medical care unrivaled anywhere in the world, and far superior to that offered American patients even ten or twenty years earlier. Yet, the better the care provided, the more frequent become the malpractice suits and the higher and the more mysterious the standards of treatment to which they are held.

CHAPTER EIGHT

The Vise of History

I

The doctors may be right. They may be caught in a vise of history in which forces beyond their control have placed them in a dilemma from which they cannot, on their own, extricate themselves. As they point out, during the course of the twentieth century, major changes have occurred in the way people live, in their goals, and in their expectations about life. Medical science, by its advances, has brought about some of these changes and been affected by all of them. As a result, the amount of medical care offered has grown both in complexity and in size, and the amount of doctor error has inevitably grown along with it. In that sense, the growth in malpractice suits can be seen as the by-product of medical progress.

Assuming this analysis is correct, then attempts to solve the malpractice crisis by improving the performance of doctors will have little effect, since the claims rate is principally determined by social phenomena with which the profession interacts but does not control. Therefore, reduction of the claims rate can be accomplished only by undoing the historic process that brought it about (an impermissible solution since that requires reduction in the socially desired quantity and quality of medical services) or, alternatively, by adopting legal steps that have a deterrent effect on claims frequency, the latter the position generally espoused by the AMA and other spokesmen for the profession.

To assess the validity of the vise of history theory, perhaps the best place to start is with medical science's achievements over the past seventy-five years or so. These can be divided into four major categories:

First, techniques have been developed to treat once untreatable illnesses, with surgical advances the most dramatic. New forms of heart surgery, nervous system surgery, tumor removals, and transplants, among others, now save thousands of lives annually and improve the quality of life for tens of thousands more.

Second, keeping pace with the new techniques, has been the invention of sophisticated medical tools, some of which monitor the condition of patients and warn of adverse developments, others acting as diagnostic aids, still others as instruments of surgical implementation.

Third, the discovery and development of the so-called "miracle" drugs has, among other accomplishments, nearly eliminated tuberculosis (the nation's number one killer at the turn of the century) as a cause of death,[1] and similarly significantly reduced the fatality rate of pneumonia and influenza,[2] along with other infections caused by viruses or bacteria.

Fourth, breakthroughs in vaccine research have eliminated or sizably reduced the frequency of other illnesses, including diphtheria, poliomyelitis, measles, whooping cough, and rubella.[3]

Taken together, these achievements have helped bring about a 300 per cent growth in the American population since 1900,[4] a period during which the average person's life expectancy has increased by about twenty-five years.[5] Women have been the principal beneficiaries. As medicine has gained in its understanding of pregnancy complications and eliminated puerperal fever, maternal fatalities have become increasingly rare. The result is that women, whose life span was almost the same as that of men in 1920 (about fifty-four years each),[6] now outlive men by about a dozen years on the average.[7] At the same time, the infant mortality rate (deaths during the first year of life) have precipitately declined because of these and other medical advances, further adding to the numbers of the population and its longevity. For example, when Martha Anderson was born around the turn of the century, she had less than an even chance of surviving her first year;[8] by 1954, the year of Lillian Lazzeri's birth, the infant death rate was down to 25 per 1,000 live births; and by 1976, the year Lillian's daughter was born, the death rate had been reduced even further, now standing at 13 per 1,000 live births.[9]

As the population grew, so did the amount of medical care offered, heightening—as the vise of history theory points out—the likelihood of accidents that could become the basis for suits. Confirming evidence for this analysis can be found in the malpractice history of professions other than medicine. During the first half of the 1960s, when medical claims were rising by no more than 5 per cent per year,[10] suits against architects and engineers suddenly leaped forward at a 10 per cent rate annually.[11] The "malpractice crisis" for these two professions coincided with the zenith of the post-war building boom. When, in the early 1970s, the amount of construction work requiring the services of architects and engineers declined precipitately, so did the number of suits against them, suggesting that, all along, suit frequency was related to the growing quantity of work performed, not some mysterious decline in its overall quality. If the insurance companies are to be believed, the number of malpractice suits against architects—although not engineers—began to rise again in the second half of the 1970s. The number of lawyers in the United States also began to increase sharply in the 1960s[12] in response to the greater amounts of work available to them. (The construction boom, with its accompanying expansion in real estate sales, proved as much a benefit for lawyers as for architects and engineers, and a much more long-lasting one.) Even so, malpractice suits against attorneys did not begin to appear in significant numbers until the middle of the 1970s.[13] The suit lag here reflects the existence of an attorney "wall of silence" which was much more effective for a longer period of time than had been the medical one. Lawyers who had never been reluctant in theory to sue doctors—their only hesitation rose from the difficulty in getting witnesses—generally believed it was violative of the unspoken club rules of their profession to sue one another. It was only when it became evident to some attorneys, their insight based on the success of other malpractice suits, that sizable fees could be earned by suing their fellow lawyers that the wall was breached.

Because of the improvements that have occurred in illness prevention, however, the quantitative need for medical care in the United States has been less than the population growth rate. Nor has the need proceeded at an even pace across the age spectrum. Since most of the diseases eliminated or controlled during the twentieth century are those that preyed on the young (polio, measles, diphtheria, diabetes, and to a lesser but still substantial degree tuberculosis, influenza, and pneumonia) the need for pediatric care, in a disease-treatment sense, has lessened over the years, with recent declines in birth rates[14] a further decelerating factor. Yet, precisely because children and young mothers no longer die at the rate they once did, the necessity to treat illnesses of mature years has risen sharply. (The American population, in fact, has been aging rapidly. In 1930, people over the age of sixty-five made up only 5 per cent of the total,[15] a figure that has since doubled,[16] and is expected to double again by the middle of the next century.[17])

The large-scale survival of people into mature years meant that the frequency of difficult chronic ailments of aging (arthritis, rheumatism, arteriosclerosis, some heart problems,[18]) as well as acute ones (cancer, myocardial infarctions, strokes, and the like,[19]) became the ones doctors increasingly faced. For none of these diseases, however, was there developed the vaccines or other drugs that solved many of the diseases of childhood and youth. As a consequence, not only is the population prone to the difficult illnesses of the aging process, but such advances as have been made in the treatment of them, by prolonging life, have exposed the affected patients to increased amounts of medical care, some of which will be legally negligent. In one significant malpractice case,[20] a man's life was saved when he underwent a new form of heart surgery. Twelve months later he developed cancer which his doctor failed to recognize, leading to a malpractice suit that resulted in a pre-trial settlement in excess of $200,000. Had it not been for the "miracle" heart operation, the patient wouldn't have lived long enough to be malpracticed against for the cancer.

But the medical profession has not only created new problems for itself by its success in causing people to live longer, it has also found itself facing changing incidences of illnesses and accidents related to alterations in the way people live. One of the most serious is also the most obvious: The rabbitlike multiplication in the use of the automobile since the early years of the twentieth century has led to a like multiplication in injury from automobile accidents. Conversely, as the number of people employed in factories and on farms has declined, so has the number of accidents associated with these occupations.[21]

Perhaps the most factor in changing the pattern of illness, however, has been the urbanization of the population. As recently as 1940, almost half of all Americans lived rurally, yet by 1974, the last year for which statistics are available, three of every four people lived in cities or suburbs,[22] marking a 40 per cent swing in population domicile in a single generation. One of the serious medical complications caused by urbanization has been the increased exposure of people to various forms of pollution—most notably that of the air—so that acute respiratory infections, rare when population was largely rural, became major American disease factors, presently accounting for 5 per cent of all hospital admissions compared to less than 1 per cent thirty years ago.[23] Related is the rising incidence of fatalities from bronchitis, emphysema, and asthma. In 1950, they were so infrequently the cause of death they were listed among "all others" in mortality rates; by 1975, they had risen to tenth among killers. (See Table D, below, for changes in leading causes of death since 1950.)

TABLE D

TEN LEADING CAUSES OF DEATH IN THE UNITED STATES, 1950–75[24]

CAUSE OF DEATH	RANK: 1975	DEATHS PER 100,000 POP.	RANK: 1950	DEATHS PER 100,000 POP.
Heart Disease	1	349.2	1	356.8
Cancer	2	170.5	2	139.8
Cerebrovascular Accidents (Strokes)	3	98.1	3	104.0
Accidents (Auto, etc.)	4	49.5	4	60.6
Influenza and Pneumonia	5	25.9	6	31.3
Diabetes Mellitus	6	17.7	10	16.2
Cirrhosis	7	15.8	13	9.2
Arteriosclerosis	8	15.3	8	20.4
Diseases of Early Infancy	9	13.6	5	40.5
Bronchitis, Emphysema & Asthma	10	12.7	*	*

* Grouped with "all other causes" in 1950. The two diseases that have dropped from the top-ten list since 1950 are tuberculosis, ranked seven in 1950, with 22.1 deaths per 100,000, presently 1.7; and nephritis and nephrosis, ranked nine in 1950, with 18.7 deaths per 100,000, presently 3.8.

During the same period of urbanization, streptococcic sore throats have also increased at epidemic proportions; in 1950, 64,500 cases were reported; in 1975, more than 400,000.[25] (Some analysts also associate the rise in frequency of cancer with the polluted environment, but the evidence here is less convincing: Lung cancer occurs with the greatest frequency in the Gulf Coast states, which are not highly urbanized, with stomach cancer centered in such northern tier states as North Dakota, Minnesota, and Wisconsin. Bladder cancer, equally inexplicably, preys with particular venom on the residents of New Jersey.[26])

The new problems faced by medicine are also associated with the great number of white-collar jobs associated with the urbanized economy. As recently as 1955 only slightly more than one third of all Americans earned their living that way (blue-collar labor was the principal employer), yet by the end of the next twenty years, one of every two Americans was employed in some form of white-collar job.[27] Partly because of the sedentary nature of these occupations, those who hold them are more likely than those engaged in physical work to suffer heart attacks and arteriosclerosis.[28] Moreover, many white-collar jobs, particularly those in the professions and in sales and managerial areas, are highly stressful, thereby contributing in their own way to heart attacks and probably to the extraordinary rise in recent years in alcoholism; note in Table D, for example, the percentage of deaths caused by cirrhosis of the liver, a disease almost always the consequence of heavy drinking. Urban stress, no doubt, further accounts for some of the increment in people seeking care from mental health facilities, a figure that stood about 1.5 million people a year in the 1950s, but became more than 5 million annually by the 1970s.[29] (This statistic *does not* include visits to private psychiatrists.) The growing prevalence of these illnesses as well as others (including high blood pressure, hypertension, and infectious hepatitis in its relation to drug addiction) are also reflective of the frustrations of those mired in the poverty of the ghetto life of the big cities.

The impact of socially influenced disease trends on the malpractice problem is in part quantitative (more treatments, more mistakes) but not purely so and perhaps not most seriously so.

For example, insurance companies have statistically observed that doctors in rural areas are less likely to be sued for malpractice than those who practice in big cities and suburbs, supposedly because people who live in small towns and on farms have close relationships with their doctors which make them unwilling to sue them, or perhaps because it doesn't make any sense to sue the only doctor around since you're going to need him the next time you're sick. Whatever the reason, malpractice claims first became a serious problem in the United States exactly at the time the nation was undergoing large-scale urbanization. The population shift, therefore can hardly be discounted as a causative agent in the malpractice problem. It may, nevertheless, in the fashion of some diseases, mask a more serious symptom. Concomitant with the urbanization, though not caused by it, was the growth in the number of medical specialists, and it is they, and particularly the surgeons among them who are sued the most often and have the largest verdicts entered against them.

Ironically, it was the advances medicine made during the first half of the twentieth century that created the need for specialization. The virulent diseases that had long plagued the population either ran their course, in which case the victims recovered, or else they died. When faced with killers like pneumonia and tuberculosis, cripplers like polio, or the infectious diseases of childhood, all doctors therefore stood equal before them, capable only of offering palliatives, there was no need for specialization in a disease for which there was no cure. That, however, was not the case with the illnesses that were left over when the virulent ones were conquered. Degenerative and complex, the cure (or the alleviation) of them required doctors who focused their entire training upon understanding and treating their symptoms.

The relationship between specialization and litigation is even more dramatic than that between litigation and urbanization. In the 1950s, prior to the onslaught of malpractice claims but at a time when urbanization was already in full swing, specialists were still relatively rare, with general practitioners then making up more than 60 per cent of all doctors. During the 1960s and 1970s, as the number of specialists rose so did the number of claims. By the mid-1970s, the general practitioner's presence in the medical population had declined to less than 25 per cent, with surgical specialists up from a fifth to a third, the remaining doctors those who specialized in non-surgical areas.[30]

While suits against specialists may reflect the fact that they do more daring work than non-specialists and, hence, are more likely to make the kinds of errors that lead to claims situations, the nature of their relationship to their patients may be a close link to their suit proneness. Unlike general practitioners and pediatricians, specialists don't have a permanent roster of clients. Rather, their relationship with patients is transitory, so much so that in many instances the surgical patient doesn't even know the name of one of his most important doctors, the anesthesiologist, until he gets a bill from him.

As a result, when something goes wrong with a specialist's patient, she doesn't have the compunctions against suing that she would if the same thing occurred with the doctor who had served her and her family well over the years.

But there is a second and perhaps even more important reason for the specialist's suit proneness, and that is the expectation level he creates in his clients. A patient comes to him because he is reputed to be an expert in handling the medical problem from which the patient is suffering. When he fails to succeed, the patient will judge his performance more critically than that of the doctor with whom the patient started out, since that doctor admitted his inability to help when he made the referral. That the patient has the legal right to expect a high level of specialist competence has, as we have seen, been recognized in all forms of professional liability cases, with the courts almost invariably holding the expert to a higher level of accomplishment than the non-expert.

The malpractice problem, as it relates to specialization, is one more exemplification of the vise of history in which the medical profession is enmeshed: Because of specialization most people are aided, but also because of it those who aren't aided are likely to sue. (Specialization, however, also causes other problems relating to malpractice that aren't explainable by the vise of history theory. They will be discussed later.)

II

Certain evolvements in social priorities, unrelated to medicine itself, have caused doctors to increase the numbers of services they offer.

One of the most notable of these changes came about as a governmental response to the emerging power of the American labor union movement during the 1930s and 1940s. Its lobbying powers were persuasive in forcing the enactment of Workmen's Compensation laws, one version or another of which had been passed in every state of the union by 1948.[31] Under them, insurance systems were established guaranteeing payment of medical care to employees suffering work-related injuries. As a result, the accessibility to doctors' services was importantly increased, with many workers now getting treatment for injuries they might have had to ignore as long as they were required to pay for them out of their own pockets. Increasingly liberally administered, these laws have opened the way to large amounts of new income for the medical profession. In 1950, compensation insurance provided $20 *million* worth of payments to doctors; in 1974, $1.7 *billion.*[32]

The second great quantification occurred when the society decided —during the activist days of the 1960s—to do something to allow the poor and the elderly in its midst to obtain adequate medical care. The result was the Social Security Act of 1965 which established Medicare (for any person sixty-five or older) and Medicaid (for the poor, including the aged poor).

The impact of Medicare and Medicaid can be assessed in three ways: (1) the amount and quality of care the two programs provided to those they were supposed to help; (2) the income they produced for the medical profession; and, for our purposes, (3) the effect they may have had on the growth of the malpractice claims problem.

In terms of reaching its beneficiaries, Medicare has been much the more successful of the two programs. About 95 per cent of those eligible to join have done so[33] compared to slightly more than 50 per cent of the eligible poor who have ever received a penny's worth of help from Medicaid.[34] Medicare subscribers, however, hardly get a free medical ride (as Medicaid patients do) as a result of their enrollment. Only about 35 per cent of their health-care costs are paid for by Medicare,[35] which means that the majority of subscribers are required to pay most of the remainder of their costs either out of the checks they receive from the same Social Security Administration, which operates the program, or else from Medicaid and welfare payments. The result is that government, one way or another, pays most of the elderly's medical bills but by maintaining control over the sources of the money, it is also able to sustain job-providing bureaucracies for the non-elderly and the non-poor that could not exist if the recipients had control over their funds by a single-payment system.

Since Medicare covers only a little more than a third of all health costs, thus having a depressant effect on doctor utilization, the total amount of medical care received by the elderly since the passage of the Act has increased by only 25 per cent.[36] Nevertheless, the amounts paid to doctors and hospitals as reimbursements for Medicare services increased by 50 per cent between 1968 and 1973 alone.[37] For each $1.00 of care the elderly receive through Medicare, the medical profession receives $2.00. There is, in fact, little control over the extent to which medical providers can exploit the program. A key provision of the 1965 Act allows doctors to charge Medicare patients whatever the "customary fee"[38] in the community may be, a codicil apparently intended to encourage doctors to accept Medicare patients but which, in reality, allows them to decide what is "customary" and then charge it—sometimes billing the government at one rate and the patient at another lower rate. Medicare patients are also more likely to be hospitalized than others, regardless of health, and kept hospitalized longer than other patients, in this way allowing the hospitals to use their bodies to get money from the government.[39]

The Medicare program, however, has been a model of probity and efficiency compared to Medicaid which has, since its inception, been riddled by the bilking of taxpayers, with impoverished patients literally becoming money-making machines for unscrupulous providers. Bills are submitted for unnecessary tests or tests not performed; prescriptions are written for which the doctor gets a kickback from the pharmacist or other provider, such as an orthopedic shoe store; reimbursements are made for unrequired surgery which, if the patient is lucky, has not been performed at all, and so on. Annual incomes from Medicaid of $100,000 to $300,000 for doctors running clinics in poverty areas are far from uncommon, and criminal prosecutions have resulted when the fraud has been particularly blatant. While all this has been going on, the medical profession has not even seen to it that minimal standards of performance established by the legislation were met. For example, in 1969 Congress mandated that health-screening and treatment programs for poor children be established in every state. Six years later, of thirteen million children eligible for the program, one which would not be a big money maker for the doctors, only three million had actually been touched by it.[40]

The single greatest beneficiary of Medicare and Medicaid, however, has been the nation's nursing home industry. Prior to the passage of the original Social Security Act in 1935, nursing homes, or "old age" homes as they were then generally known, played an insignificant role on the health scene, such few as there were usually state or church operated. By 1940, as the first Social Security checks were beginning to go out, the commercial nursing home was also starting to manifest itself, encouraging the children of the elderly to stow their parents in them with the check part of the ransom paid. (Old-age homes also, typically, required the new inmate to sign over personal property holdings to be paid the home upon death, which was, consequently, sometimes hastened.) Even so, as recently as 1960, nursing homes still accounted for only $492 million or 1.9 per cent of the nation's health budget.[41] The Social Security Act of 1965 changed all that. It provided for Medicare payments to nursing homes for up to 100 days after hospital discharge, and then Medicaid payments, in many instances, for unlimited periods afterward. Since many nursing home inmates were also on welfare, the number of government checks a home could garner grew by leaps and bounds, with profits limited only by the amounts paid out for the care of the residents. As a result, by 1970, the nursing home industry was a $3.8 billion business, and by 1975 it had again doubled its income to $7.4 billion or about 7 per cent of the health-care budget for that year,[42] *with 50 per cent of all income coming from Medicaid payments.*[43]

Since some nursing homes are owned by doctors, others administered by a doctor, and all of them have, at least *pro forma,* doctors available to serve their residents, they have become a major source of income for the medical profession. While a number of these institutions are well and humanely run, many and perhaps most are not. As a 1975 HEW survey reported: "Recent federal and state studies in fourteen states found that a majority of nursing homes are unsafe, inadequately staffed, and neglectful of patients, and many operators engage in fraud, kickbacks, and profiteering."[44] The profiteering is done on the residents, sometimes with staff doctors participating and sometimes not,[45] the operators charging the government for doctor care billed but not given, medications not provided, nursing care that's non-existent, and food that is not given. Because of the dependent and indigent nature of the people who are exploited in this way, the doctors who participate in these schemes are rarely criminally prosecuted and even more rarely sued for the malpractice which is rife.

If the warehousing of the aged in nursing homes has decreased, the number of negligence suits with which the medical profession is beleagured, Medicare and Medicaid have accelerated the amount of litigation. Because, like Workmen's Compensation, the two programs have increased exposure to medical care, using our quantitative theory, they have also increased the likelihood of instances of negligent care. More importantly, since the aged and the impoverished are more prone to serious illnesses than the younger and more affluent members of the society,[46] the aged because of their years and the poor because of malnutrition and inadequate prenatal care, they are also the population segments most likely to require the complex forms of medical treatment, including surgery, which are fecund in malpractice-producing incidents.

Malpractice claims suddenly began their increase at a 10–15 per cent annual rate in 1966,[47] the year Medicare and Medicaid went into effect, and although this hardly suggests the two programs were responsible for the differential, evidence of an impact can be inferred. Moreover, as recently as 1970 only 0.1 per cent[48] of all malpractice claims incidents occurred in hospital out-patient clinics, which at that time were still in the developmental stage as the site at which most Medicaid and some Medicare patients were treated. By 1976, out-patient clinics had become responsible for 2.0 per cent of all claims,[49] a rate increase greater than the growth in their usage. Further, the HEW study found that people over the age of sixty-five accounted for almost twice the number of malpractice claims as their presence in the population, and about equal to their presence in the hospital population,[50] from which it can be presumed that to the extent Medicare and Medicaid encourage hospitalization of the elderly, to that degree do they set up malpractice situations. Finally, the state of Florida, which has the oldest population in the country[51] also has one of the highest malpractice claims rates in the country, suggestive of at least a Medicare impact.[52]

There is other evidence, however, that moves in the opposite direction. The Florida example is contrasted with that of California, which has a far higher percentage of malpractice claims than any other state but has only an average number of people who are sixty-five and older.[53] Further, studies by ISO[54] and NAIC,[55] both more recent than HEW's, each found that people covered by Medicare were only slightly more likely than their percentage in the total population to become claimants, and only about half as likely as their presence in the hospital population. As for Medicaid, while we can do some informed guessing, statistically its malpractice impact is impossible to measure. Not only do no agencies keep records of plaintiff income in malpractice litigation, but Medicaid itself has a much more fluctuating influence than has Medicare, since it is state (not federal) administered with budgets and patient outreaches varying widely from state to state and year to year.

Therefore, although we can assume that the Social Security Act of 1965 has played some role in the escalation of claims frequency, it is far from clear that the number of claims have risen in proportion to the amount of new services offered.

III

If the social activism, which brought about Workmen's Compensation and the Social Security Act of 1965, created one of the vises of history, albeit a profitable one, by which the medical profession has been forced to quantify its services and, consequently, its exposure to suit, medicine has also been affected by (and profited from) other characteristics of the "pro-rights," "litigious" population it serves. Better educated than any previous generation, it has knowledge of the importance of good medical care, and looks for it; more affluent, it can afford to obtain it, and does so. The statistics on both points are revelatory. In terms of educational attainment, the average American has now more than twelve years of schooling compared to about eight at the time of the Second World War, with the number of people who have completed college rising some 400 per cent during the same period.[56] In terms of affluence, since 1960 alone the average income per citizen has almost doubled in terms of constant, non-inflated dollars.[57]

The resultant growth in health-care expenditure has been nothing short of staggering. In 1940, the nation spent under $4 billion for medical and health care services; by 1950, $12 billion; by 1960, $25 billion; by 1970, $70 billion; by 1980, an estimated $175 billion.[58] Even when the declining purchasing power of the dollar is incorporated, from 1950 on, the health budget has increased by more than 300 per cent[59] or from 4.6 per cent of the gross national product to almost 8 per cent at present.[60]

The national affluence, however, has not been spread equally among the medical providers. Hospitals have been getting an ever-larger bite, starting at $.18 of every health dollar in 1930, $.25 by 1940, $.33 by 1960, and about $.40 at present.[61] The doctors' share of the pie has dropped from $.28 to $.18 in the same period.[62] In terms of actual dollars, payments to hospitals rose from $650 million in 1930 to $8.5 billion in 1960 to more than $40 billion by 1970, and should hit $50 billion by 1980. Meanwhile, physician income rose only from $1 billion to $18 billion between 1930 and the mid-1970s.[63] (The remainder of the health-care dollar is taken up by such items as dental bills, drug bills for both prescription and nonprescription remedies, medical research, construction of medical facilities, physical therapy, and so on, to say nothing of the burgeoning share going to the nursing home proprietors.)

The amount of the health-care budget engorged by hospitals is mainly due to the runaway rates they charge patients. For example, during the decade beginning in 1967, the Consumer Price Index rose about 70 per cent as did the fees doctors charge patients; yet, during the same period, the cost of a semiprivate hospital room rose by more than 230 per cent.[64]

Nevertheless, hospitals have also meaningfully increased the total services they offer, thereby providing one more clue to the cause of the malpractice problem. When we recall that 80 per cent of all malpractice incidents occur in hospitals and then note that the hospital admissions have risen from 18 million a year at the beginning of the 1960s to double that amount by the mid-1970s,[65] we are facing a quantitative factor of no mean proportions. To it can be added hospital care to outpatients, which also doubled in roughly the same period, from 85 million to 170 million contacts a year.[66]

When all these factors are taken together, we see the vise of history theory expressed at its most distinguished. On the one side, we have a medical profession that, because of its success in fighting certain illnesses, is now confronted with complex ones requiring specialization; in turn, setting up patient/doctor relationships that lack continuity but contain high expectations which often can't be met. On the other, we have a changing society that not only develops new serious medical problems because of its changes, but also becomes increasingly affluent, well-educated, and activist, so that it demands not only more health services for those who can afford it but also passes legislation providing it to illness-prone population segments, which previously were kept away from meaningful care almost entirely. The conclusion is inevitable: The medical system falters in a malpractice sense, not because it hasn't met these demands but because it has done so. Had it responded less well, had it attempted less, the errors it makes would be fewer and so would the number of suits instituted against it.

IV

Unfortunately for the sake of this theory, there are some facts that cannot be explained by it. For example, were it an adequate answer, then a statistical congruence should exist between access to medical care and claims frequency. This, however, is not so.

The following chart, comparing the number of doctors in a state with that state's malpractice claims rate, is revelatory:

TABLE E

	MALPRACTICE CLAIMS RATE PER 100 PHYSICIANS*	
United States		6.21
States with an Oversupply of Doctors:†		
California	9.64	
Maryland	4.64	
New York	4.50	
Connecticut	4.18	
Massachusetts	2.73	
AVERAGE		5.14
States with the Most Severe Shortage of Doctors:†		
Alaska	2.51	
North Dakota	2.89	
Mississippi	3.97	
South Dakota	5.71	
Arkansas	6.64	
Alabama	11.69	
AVERAGE		5.23

* National Association of Insurance Commissioners Claims Survey, 1977.[67]
† American Medical Association, 1973.[68]

As Table E shows, the five highly urbanized states with the largest supply of doctors (and presumably because of their metropolitan character the largest number of specialists) have a slightly *lower* claims rate than the six largely rural states with the most serious undersupply of physicians (and presumably the lowest number of specialists). Under the vise of history theory, we should expect the high supply, high specialist states to have by far the highest claims rates.

Neither is there any discernible relationship between hospital bed availability and the malpractice rate. Theoretically, the more beds, the more accidents, assuming, as is usually true, that bed availability can be equated with patient admission rates. There is one state, Michigan, that comes close to proving the theory. It is just about on the national average in numbers of hospital beds, numbers of doctors, and in its malpractice claims rate.[69] However, its neighboring state, Minnesota, has a much higher than average number of hospital beds, an adequate physician supply, yet a malpractice rate that is lower than average.[70] Particularly disturbing to the theory is California. While it has both a large supply of physicians and a large supply of malpractice suits, at the same time its hospital bed supply is well below the national average (3.7 per 1,000 population compared to the national average of 4.3[71]).

Another factor, however, raises the most serious questions about the theory. If malpractice claims relate primarily to quantification of services and growth in specialization, then the number of claims should rise at a rate comparable to the impetus factors. But that hasn't happened either. The claims rate instead has far outstripped the integers. Between 1960 and 1978, for example, both the number of hospital admissions and the number of surgical specialists doubled;[72] the claims rate, however, tripled.[73] (Nor did other doctors take up the slack; the total number of physicians offering services of any kind during the same period increased by only 50 per cent.[74])

Useful as it may be, therefore, as an analysis of some causes of the malpractice problem, the vise of history theory appears, finally, to be an insufficient one. This suggests that certain practices of the medical profession, which are unaffected by outside forces, play an important causative role of their own, a thesis that will be examined in the next two chapters.

CHAPTER NINE

Unnecessary Surgery and Other Dilemmas

I

In 1977 well over 40,000 doctors were named in malpractice claims,[1] or about one of every nine in active practice.[2] The figure, although duly alarming to the medical profession and to malpractice insurers, can be analyzed as insignificant statistically when we consider that nearly 40 million patients were treated in hospitals that year, that 175 million or so were served by outpatient clinics, and that 900 million or more contacts took place between patients and doctors by way of office visits or house calls.[3] Situations that led to malpractice claims, therefore, occurred in only about one of every 30,000 patient/provider contacts.

While it is of value in estimating the likelihood of a malpractice claim in 1977, this analysis does not provide us with an integer of the frequency with which malpractice actually occurred. As we have seen from our case histories, doctors frequently win the actions brought against them, which means the courts, in those suits, decided no malpractice took place; such cases must be eliminated from any picture drawn of medical negligence. To be added to that picture, however, must be the other medical misadventures that were marked by malpractice but that, for one reason or another, never led to the filing of a claim.

Consequently, to assess the true dimensions of the malpractice problem, we must look to evidence more reliable than the claims rate. One step in that direction was taken in 1972 when the HEW Malpractice Commission, recognizing that the number of claims filed each year represented only what was currently occurring in terms of litigation, not what *could* occur, made a study of the medical chart records of two urban hospitals that had patient admission, treatment, and discharge patterns typical of the nation as a whole.[4] Working in co-operation with staff physicians, the HEW investigators discovered that *more than seven of every one hundred persons who are admitted to a hospital can expect to be injured by the treatment they receive while patients.*[5]

Any time a patient is so harmed, she is said to have incurred an *iatrogenic* (literally, physician-induced) injury. These iatrogenic incidents can range from the most trivial (e.g., a skin rash caused by a reaction to a drug) to the most severe (e.g., the adverse reaction to an anesthesia). Some iatrogenic injuries are completely unpreventable or else they develop from one of the acceptable risks entailed in most medical and surgical procedures. (The patient who was partly blinded and paralyzed following by-pass surgery is just one example of the latter.) Nevertheless, the HEW discovery of a high number of iatrogenic injuries was significant since the existence of injury is the prerequisite for the filing of a malpractice suit. Having determined the iatrogenic rate, HEW experts then restudied each incident to determine how it came about. This second study concluded that *29 per cent of all medical accidents are caused by negligent care on the part of a doctor or attendant.*[6]

Three years after the HEW Malpractice Commission went out of business, its executive director, attorney Eli Bernzweig, analyzed the findings this way: "It means," he said, "[that] in the normal course of events, one could expect [the 1975 rate of] 35 million hospital admissions to give rise to 2.6 million treatment-related injuries, with 770,000 of them attributable to some form of negligent conduct. These figures assumed [the] 7.6% injury rate and [the] 29% negligence rate [found by the HEW survey], but even if we were to halve both the injury rate and the negligence rate (i.e., from 7.6% to 3.8% for injury, and from 29% to 14.5% for negligent injury) the net result is still a very substantial 1.3 million injuries, with 193,000 of them probably attributable to negligent treatment."[7]

A 1977 study published by the California Hospital Association[8] disagreed with the HEW findings. It identified the iatrogenic injury risk rate for a hospital patient at 4.65 per 100 admissions and the negligence rate at about 20 per cent of that. Thus, its findings were lower than the HEW's but still considerably higher than Bernzweig's when he arbitrarily halved the HEW rate.

By striking a balance among these various hypotheses, we can assume that by the late 1970s (when hospital admissions were closer to 40 million than the 35 million Bernzweig used for 1975) upward of two million iatrogenic injuries were occurring in hospitals annually, with about 400,000 of them caused by negligence.

However, since both studies confined themselves to injury rates discoverable from medical charts, the actual hospital injury rate must be far higher than that, since hospital charts only show injuries associated with treatment and do not reveal adverse results caused by misdiagnosis, itself the precipitant of about 20 per cent of all malpractice suits.[9] Moreover, neither the California nor the HEW study depicted injuries that occur during hospitalization but which only come to light after the patient is discharged. (For example, mistakes in setting fractures won't be revealed until the cast is removed, usually long after the patient has left the hospital. Similarly, the presence of medical instruments left in a patient's body often aren't discovered till years afterward.)

Finally, neither study had any way of considering the amount of injury that occurs in doctors' offices and other non-hospital settings, yet 20 per cent of all malpractice claims name such sites as the place where the allegedly negligent injury was received.

Since these factors have never been statistically studied, we can only guess at their impact. However, projecting injury from the hospital studies and from known litigation rates, we can reasonably (and conservatively) assume that more than 5 million patients are harmed by iatrogenic injury and more than 1 million by negligent injury each year.

In view of the vast amount of medical treatment that is offered, this figure still may not seem very high. It begins to become so, however, when we consider that the overwhelming majority of doctor/patient contacts involve care for the most routine illnesses (colds, respiratory infections) and those of the chronic variety (rheumatism, for example) during the course of which it is nearly impossible for the worst doctor to harm a patient. Further, the 900 million contacts mentioned at the office level don't mean that is the number of illnesses treated there. Many of the contacts are repeated treatments by a doctor for the same illness, so that if the doctor initially misdiagnoses the illness and then gives the patient the wrong care over and over again, the incidence of negligent events is multiplied by the number of the improper treatments. Furthermore, many people who are *not* sick get doctor care; that number includes adults undergoing annual physical checkups, babies and small children under routine pediatric care, to say nothing of the tens of millions of visits each year by pregnant women to their obstetricians.

Therefore, given the number of situations in which it is realistically possible for medical injury to occur, an ominous amount of it does. Assuming, minimally, that 70 per cent of all treatment is of a routine nature, in the remaining 30 per cent of the contacts, the injury rate is as high as one in four and the negligent rate about one in twelve, not a very comforting thought for anyone with a complex illness requiring intensive or surgical care.

However, from the doctor's point of view, no matter how much he bewails the growth in the claims rate, these same statistics show that the likelihood of his being called to account when he causes a negligent injury is remote. If, for example, we posit 40,000 claims against 5 million injuries, there is a better than 99 per cent chance the injury will not result in a malpractice claim. Or, if we posit the claims rate against the negligence rate (keeping in mind that not all claims by any means actually reflect negligence on the part of the doctor), even then the doctor still has a better than 95 per cent chance of not getting sued. Nor, for that matter, as we shall see, do all, or even the majority, of claims filed result in a suit.

The malpractice claims frequency rate is low for many reasons. To begin with, some people, no matter how clearly they have been injured by malpractice, won't pursue a claim simply because they don't want to get involved in the legal system; if their private insurance covers the cost of the injury, they let it go at that. Others are ignorant. An HEW study, for example, found that only 5 per cent of all people could define the legal meaning of malpractice, while another 20 per cent didn't even attempt a definition.[10] Ignorance of the law, of course, has never been any bar to suit. However, the same study found that about half of all respondents also believed that if they engaged a lawyer, they would have to pay him some form of fee even if they lost.[11] This ignorance of the contingency fee system, no doubt, discourages many suits, particularly on the part of low and moderate income patients. Still others won't sue because they like the doctor who has injured them, or else they have moved from the jurisdiction in which the injury occurred and therefore don't find it feasible to pursue a legal action.

Nor are all medical injuries of the degree of seriousness that makes it likely that they will become the basis for a suit. For example, a doctor improperly sets a broken toe with the result that it becomes permanently crooked. Malpractice has occurred and with it a winnable case. However, the amount of damages that will be awarded for a crooked toe is miniscule, and few patients will bother to raise such a claim. And even if they want to, it won't be easy for them to find a lawyer who will waste his time litigating such a charge. The contrary, however, is also true. As former HEW Malpractice Commission executive director, Bernzweig has observed: "The more severe the damages, the greater the likelihood of a malpractice claim, particularly if the patient lacks other forms of financial relief."[12] Presumably, therefore, if hospitals didn't bill patients for the extra medical costs associated with an iatrogenic injury, claims frequency would be comparably reduced, and some evidence indicates that the handful of hospitals that have adopted such a fair-minded policy have indeed been rewarded with lower claims rates.[13]

Finally, in order to pursue a malpractice claim, the patient must be able to perceive that an injury has occurred. This is often a difficult knowledge to acquire. Unlike the victim of an automobile accident who was healthy before the car hit her, the medical victim is almost always already ill when visited by an iatrogenic event, negligent or not.[14] For her, it is difficult to know that some of her symptoms may be caused by a misprescribed drug and are not just the natural consequences of her sickness. Moreover, again unlike the auto accident victim who was conscious at the point of impact and knows who hurt her, the medical victim is typically under anesthesia or disoriented in a postoperative condition when her mal-event happens. As a result, only those who caused her injury are ordinarily in a position to tell her about it, and fearful of suit they will not voluntarily do so and instead will often lie to her when she (or her surviving family) ask questions. While certain gross injuries can't be hidden in this fashion, many other events, such as the negligence involved in Lillian Lazzeri's death, can be, and they routinely are.[15]

II

While a substantial portion of the iatrogenic injury that occurs each year is both non-negligent and non-preventable, there are, nevertheless, flaws in the medical delivery system which increase the probability of all medical injury. These flaws are not explicable by any vise of history theorizing, but rather are principally associated with inadequate monitoring by the profession of the medical activities of some of its members.

One such activity is surgery. Approximately 18 million Americans —one in every twelve persons—is operated upon each year.[16] *Requisite* procedures, those without which the patient would die or suffer devastating injury, account for about 3.5 million[17] of the total. The remaining 77 per cent are *elective*. Of these elective operations, at least several million, and perhaps many more than that, are unnecessary, motivated in most instances by the surgeon's desire to enrich himself.

The line between an elective and an unnecessary operation can be a fine one; medical experts of equal knowledge will disagree on definition both in generality and in specific cases. However, essentially a *proper* elective procedure is one for which there are substantial medical indications that the patient will benefit from it; in the *unnecessary* operation, there are no medical indications that the operation should be performed and there may be indications that it should not be performed.

Hemorrhoids are an example of an ailment for which surgery is always elective. It is a condition which is non-life threatening and for which medical as well as surgical treatment is available. Since, however, surgery offers more rapid relief from hemorrhoids than the alternative treatment, it is often the correct choice to adopt in terms of the patient's comfort and return to well-being. In some instances, however, the hemorrhoidal condition is of such a nature or degree of development that the prudent treatment is medical, and when surgery is undertaken in those instances it is definably unnecessary. Tonsillitis, gall bladder problems, many disturbances of the female genital system, among others, can fall into the same category.

Elective surgery is also sometimes recommended properly for the relief of psychic rather than physical distress. Plastic surgery is the most common example of that, although some nerve operations for the relief of tremors and tics, as well as some eye operations are also of a cosmetic nature, indicated principally to increase the patient's sense of self-esteem.

Elective surgery is often associated with cancer treatment. An internist may recommend chemotherapy, a surgeon surgery. Should the patient elect chemotherapy and it works, it cannot, for that reason, be inferred that the surgical choice would have meant an "unnecessary" operation, assuming the surgeon had sound medical reasons for his choice.

Other proper elective choices frequently arise when patient symptoms are confusing. For example, a patient develops signs that may mean the presence of appendicitis. Some doctors, under those circumstances, won't operate unless the symptoms define themselves more clearly. Other doctors, however, fearing the possibility of peritonitis if the patient actually has appendicitis, will operate immediately. In the latter event, should it turn out that the patient's appendix is healthy, the surgery may have been technically unnecessary, but it can't be defined as one that shouldn't have been performed.

A number of studies have been undertaken to gauge the frequency of true unnecessary surgery. Hearings in 1975 by a United States House of Representatives Subcommittee on Health brought forth testimony from researchers at Stanford, Cornell, and Harvard universities[18] that 17.6 per cent of all elective procedures recommended by one surgeon were abandoned when the patient got a second opinion.[19] From this, it was assumed that each abandoned procedure was contraindicated, suggesting that a like percentage holds true when there is no consultation. But this may not be so. The desirability of surgery in non-consultation situations will sometimes be more self-evident than in the more complex cases in which consultation is likely. If that is so, the percentage of unnecessary non-consultive operations may be lower than the study suggests. (This study was attacked by the American Medical Association, not on that ground, but based on an inadequate sampling and too broad an interpretation of the word "unnecessary."[20])

A 1976 study of unnecessary surgery published by the New York *Times*,[21] partly relying on the Congressional figures but also on studies by the Cornell University Medical College and other expert sources, analyzed the frequency of contraindicated operations in various elective situations and determined that 70 per cent of the 724,000 tonsillectomies performed annually are unnecessary, as are 14 per cent of the 472,000 gall bladder removals, 22 per cent of the 787,000 hysterectomies, 22 per cent of the 223,000 prostatectomies, and 17 per cent of the 200,000 hemorrhoidectomies. In total, these unnecessary procedures resulted in 12,500 fatalities, or more than one sixth of the 70,000 deaths[22] that occur each year following surgery which is elective. The number of non-fatal iatrogenic injuries was not estimated, nor was the number of the unnecessary procedures which were also negligently performed.

However, another study, this one published in 1977 by the American College of Surgeons, suggests that few of these fatalities could have occurred without negligence. Surveyed were postoperation deaths in a selection of hospitals in Connecticut, Maryland, Michigan, North Carolina, Ohio, Washington, and Pennsylvania.[23] The investigators found that 85 of 245 deaths in these institutions were preventable, the result of surgeon error. Included were fatalities from hernia repairs, gall bladder removals, hysterectomies, and appendix removals. "About these," said the College, "a primary assumption was made: After one of these surgical procedures *no patient should die* or suffer a life-threatening complication."[24] (Italics added.)

The incidence of unnecessary surgery, in fact, may be much higher than that estimated at the Congressional hearing or projected by the New York *Times*. The possibility arises when comparisons are made between surgeons who work on a fee basis, as most American surgeons do, with those who are salaried. The theory here is that the fee surgeon will perform unnecessary work to bolster his income while the salaried surgeon won't because he earns the same amount of money whether he operates or not.

In England, for example, where doctors are salaried under a national health plan, the surgery rate is about half that of the United States, while for some procedures, including hysterectomies, the British frequency is only 40 per cent of the American.[25] (The latter point is of particular interest when we recall that operations on the female genital tract are the single most frequent cause of malpractice claims.) Comparisons between English and American surgical rates, nevertheless, must be treated with caution. In England there are far fewer hospital beds per capita than in the United States, which may mean that, lacking hospital space for patient recuperation, English doctors are more likely than Americans to lean toward non-surgical treatment in elective situations. It is also possible that fewer operations are required in England than in the United States because the English people, on the whole, appear somewhat less exposed to the debilitating illnesses typical of American life. Other analysts point out, chauvinistically, that less surgery is performed in England than here because their doctors aren't as adept at it as are ours.[26]

Perhaps. It is instructive, therefore, to see what happens when we compare surgery rates between American doctors who work on a salary with those who work on a fee. Three such studies are available, and all use as their base the surgery rates in health maintenance organizations (HMO's). People who belong to an HMO—the most famous is the Kaiser Plan—pay one annual subscription fee, in return for which they receive an unlimited amount of medical care. In a few of the small HMO's, doctors work on a fee basis.[27] However, in most of the sizable ones the doctors are salaried.

The first of the three studies was undertaken in 1960[28] and revealed that 49 of every 1,000 HMO subscribers underwent surgery that year compared to 69 of every 1,000 who used a fee doctor, a 39 per cent differential. The veracity of this study was attacked on several grounds, most substantively on the basis that HMO members, because of the high cost at the time of the subscription fee,[29] tended to be middle class and, hence, members of the most well-educated segment of the population who are aware of the importance of preventive care and are less likely as a result to fall prey to illnesses that require surgery.[30] Some critics from the medical sector have also charged[31] that HMO doctors are under orders by their employers to hold back on surgery in order to reduce wear and tear on the equipment in the hospitals owned by the HMO, simultaneously making unnecessary the hiring of large numbers of hospital staff. This accusation does not appear to have been substantiated.

The second and third studies were both undertaken by the federal government and both published in 1975. In one,[32] the United States Civil Service Commission took a cross-section of federal employees, some of whom were covered by private hospitalization plans like Blue Cross, and others who were members of an HMO, thus removing the objection to the first study that it was comparing unlike groups. The study found that the HMO members were 50 *per cent less likely to be hospitalized and 50 per cent less likely to undergo surgery than were those who went to private doctors,* thus arriving at the same differential that the British/American study had uncovered. The final study, published by the Social Security Administration,[33] even more convincingly undermined the criticism of the 1960 study, since it concerned itself solely with surgical rates for poor people covered by Medicaid. The results were identical to the Civil Service and the British/American study: Poor people served by salaried HMO doctors were only half as likely to be operated upon as those who were served by fee-earning doctors.

While these three studies shouldn't be accepted as proof that one of every two operations taking place in the United States are medically unnecessary since there are too many variables to assume that, the consistency of their findings is impressive and seems to remove any doubt that the surgeon's desire to earn a fee is the most important motive behind unnecessary operations. (Some unnecessary surgery is also undertaken to provide bodies for surgical residents to practice on; and some is the consequence of misdiagnosis of the patient's condition.)

Whether the unnecessary surgery percentage in the United States is 17 per cent or 50 per cent or some figure higher or lower than either, the likelihood is the situation will worsen rather than improve in the future, or at least it will as long as surgeons continue to have the capacity to earn so much more money than non-surgeons. For example, the median income net (i.e., income after payment of tax-deductible expenses) for a general practitioner in the United States is $37,600; a general surgeon, however, averages $51,180; an orthopedic surgeon, $62,410.[34] Because of that financial incentive, the nation has become surgically over-populated. A 1970 study by the American College of Surgeons, in which the American Surgical Association joined, concluded that at that time the United States already had 22,000 more surgeons than were required, and American medical schools were training *eight times* the number of surgeons that were needed,[35] this despite the fact that the same medical schools were turning out a woefully insufficient number of general practitioners. Another study, published at about the same time,[36] was in its way even more disturbing. It revealed that the amount of surgery that occurs in a community rises in proportion to the number of surgeons available to perform it, suggesting that as the competition among surgeons increases, the more likely each is to take up the knife in defense of his income.

It would appear, therefore, that the unnecessary surgery problem in the United States would disappear, and along with it much of the iatrogenic and negligent injury rate, if all American doctors worked on a salaried rather than a piece-work basis. While such might, indeed, be the happy consequence of such a remedy, it is not one which, given the American medical profession's devotion to the free enterprise system, is hardly likely of accomplishment.

More realistic is a proposal advocated by some surgeons, though only tentatively because it sounds so self-interested. Under it, surgical practice would be limited to doctors who pass the rigorous qualifying examinations of such certifying bodies as the American Board of Surgery. (There would be some exceptions: A non-certified doctor could perform surgery in emergency situations or in areas in which a certified surgeon is not available.) At present, about one third of all doctors who practice surgery are not Board-certified, or a total of approximately 40,000 doctors who either have never attempted to gain a certification or who tried and failed.[37] Some of these doctors may be every bit as adept as the certified (and should be given an opportunity to qualify) and some of the certified ones may be past their prime (and should be weeded out). Nevertheless, it is the non-certified ones who, as a general rule, are the ones who perform the majority of the procedures that are most often unnecessary and cause most of the associated injuries and deaths.[38] The higher level of the performance of the certified surgeon is also attested to by the NAIC malpractice claims study which found that *board-certified surgeons are significantly less likely to be successfully sued for negligence than the non-certified.*[39] This was true despite the fact that the certified surgeons were uniformly more likely than the others to undertake the difficult procedures that can cause grave injury when they fail.[40]

Such impressive statistics cannot be taken to mean that Board-certified surgeons have cornered the market on medical ethics when it comes to eschewing improper surgery. Rather, because of the competition from the non-certified, they too dabble in it in order to keep up their income. However, as one analyst has put it, if the non-certified surgeons were driven from the flock, the consequent limitation of surgery to the certified ones "would give [them] so much legitimate work to do that there would be neither time nor temptation to do unnecessary surgery."[41]

While it is unclear how this plan could be implemented without stirring up lawsuits from non-certified surgeons claiming they were being deprived of a livelihood, it at least represents a recognition on the part of some members of the medical profession of the seriousness of the unnecessary surgery problem, and the desirability of the profession to take steps to do something about it.

III

Drug therapy, in terms of patient injury, appears to present a problem even more serious in medical-care delivery than surgery, necessary or otherwise. It is not, however, nearly as productive of law suits as is surgery, partly because the effects of drug injury are more difficult to perceive than surgical injury, and partly because drug injury more often occurs from an unpredictable and therefore nonnegligent cause than does the surgical misadventure.

The rise in drug-related patient injury is closely associated with advancements in chemotherapy. Because of these advances, millions of patients each year now enjoy a rapid and uncomplicated recovery from illnesses that were once either crippling, long-term, or fatal. Because they are powerful enough to cure, however, the new drugs are also capable of causing great harm. For example, a study compiled by Dr. Herschel Jick of the Boston University Medical Center[42] discovered that each year 300,000 patients suffer drug reactions of such severity that they must be hospitalized, making drug reaction one of the ten leading causes of hospitalization in the United States.[43] Nor is the patient who is already in the hospital immune from the ill effects of drugs. Jick's study found that one of every eighteen hospital-originated prescriptions also cause an adverse reaction, 10 per cent of them serious, 1.2 per cent fatal. Another contemporaneous study, also done in Boston by the Lemuel Shattuck Hospital and Tufts University Medical School,[44] traced 6,199 consecutive drug reactions and discovered 27 fatalities, all but 5 of them in patients who were not terminally ill. Statistics such as these have led Dr. Wolfe of the Nader Health Research Group to assert that 30,000 patients are killed annually by drugs prescribed to help them while they are hospitalized.[45]

Antibiotics, the class of drugs capable of the most dramatic help to the sick, are also the most dangerous. Although they do not seem to cause adverse reactions more frequently than other drugs,[46] when they occur their effects are 50 per cent more likely to be severe. (When a reaction occurs from an antibiotic it is severe 15 per cent of the time, compared to 10 per cent with non-antibiotics.) The fatality rate is high. A study done in Florida[47] can be interpreted as showing at least 25,000 deaths annually from antibiotics, while other estimates place the figure as high as 100,000 annually.[48]

Contributing to that total are antibiotic reactions that weaken the body's natural defenses. Ordinarily, the human system contains many bacteria that prey on one another, keeping the numbers of each in check and preventing disease. When, however, a broad spectrum antibiotic is administered to combat a dangerous infection, it may not only kill off the target bacteria but many others as well. The result is that one or two resistant species are able to proliferate at will leading to the so-called "super infection" which has a mortality rate, depending on which statistics are used, of 30–50 per cent.[49] Antibiotics may also be associated with the onslaught of another complex and often fatal infection known as the Gram negative reaction, although some experts believe it is principally associated with advanced age and debility.

As onerous as their effects can be, drug reactions usually are a consequence of acceptable medical risk taking. No doctor should or will hold back on administering a drug necessary to the patient's health on the remote chance that the drug will prove harmful; it is far better to treat the patient's adverse reaction than to no longer have a patient to treat.

Nevertheless, sometimes drugs are misprescribed. Often the result is of no harm to the patient, though of no help either. Other times, however, the misused drug causes a reaction, leading to countless numbers of unnecessary injuries each year, with one in every 100 to 200, if the Jick and similar studies are correct,[50] having fatal consequences.

Two case histories are illustrative. In one,[51] a man was hospitalized with a kidney infection. His doctor prescribed neomycin, a powerful and frequently very effective antibiotic but one that under no circumstances should be used on a patient with a kidney involvement. The man's doctor didn't know this, however, or had forgotten it, nor did he, apparently, bother to read the manufacturer's warning to that effect on the drug's package. As a result, for a complex series of medical reasons, the patient was rendered totally and permanently deaf. In the second case,[52] a woman went to her physician for treatment of a mild sore throat. The doctor administered a shot of penicillin and within a few minutes the woman lay dead at his feet. He hadn't bothered to inquire if she was allergic to the drug or administer a simple test that would have shown that she was. Part of the tragedy in this case is that many doctors would consider the choice of penicillin to treat a sore throat wrong in the first place.

Overprescription (i.e., administering a drug stronger than necessary to treat the patient's symptoms) is probably the single greatest cause of improper drug therapy. One study of prescription practices in the United States[53] revealed that between 1967 and 1971 the number of prescriptions written for the most powerful of all drugs—

the antibiotics—doubled despite the fact that no medical evidence existed to suggest that the frequency of bacterial infection—the only reason for prescribing an antibiotic—was on the increase. A somewhat more recent study,[54] although it made no distinctions in drug potencies, was also suggestive; it compared prescriptions written in the United States with those in Scotland and found that the thrifty Scots took only half as many drugs as Americans yet appear every bit as healthy and perhaps more so than their American cousins.

The drug that perhaps most vividly illustrates the American physician's propensity to overprescribe is chloramphenicol, better known by one of its trade names, Chloromycetin. This drug is truly one of the great wonder antibiotics. Developed after the Second World War, it is effective in treating a wide range of illnesses, both serious and minor. Unfortunately, chloramphenicol, in a statistically significant number of cases, also causes a fatal form of cancer known as aplastic anemia, a fact that was unknown to the medical profession until it was revealed during the course of a malpractice suit.[55] Since then chloramphenicol has carried on its label the warning that it is the drug of choice only for such virulent but rare diseases as typhoid and Rocky Mountain spotted fever. However, despite the few medical situations in which it is worth taking the chance of using chloramphenicol, the drug continues to be manufactured in sizable amounts because doctors continue to prescribe it improperly and legally negligently. As recently as the 1970s, for example, the drug was prescribed 161,000 times for illnesses which, as the Health Research Group's Dr. Wolfe put it: ". . . no competent physician could reasonably argue chloramphenicol is indicated."[56] Included in that total were 12,000 prescriptions for the common cold and another 24,000 for upper respiratory infections, which, as it happens, are two of the few ailments for which the drug is not even helpful.

Chloramphenicol, however, is not the only drug with known dangerous propensities which is frequently prescribed when other equally effective but safer drugs are available. Thorazine is a case in point; a highly effective but powerful tranquillizer, it is properly indicated only for the treatment of profoundly psychotic patients.[57] In normal or moderately distressed patients, it can have unpredictable and occasionally dangerous side effects;[58] in some, it appears to cause the development of Parkinson's disease-type syndrome, and it can have pernicious effects on asthmatics.[59] Nevertheless, Thorazine continues to be prescribed for patients whose needs could be adequately treated by milder tranquillizers, and it seems to be particularly favored by prisons and other custodial institutions solely to keep their populations passive.[60] One Pennsylvania institution for delinquent girls, for example, administered Thorazine orally *every* day to *every* child, and injected it intravenously (its most potent and dangerous form) to girls who caused minor disciplinary problems. The drug was dispensed with a physician's permission.[61]

While proper prescription techniques are taught in medical school, afterward the vast majority of doctors are forced to rely on the drug industry itself for new information about prescription practices. The industry is more than willing to provide it, spending in excess of a billion dollars a year[62] to tell doctors how to prescribe via advertisements in medical journals, package descriptions, and through salesmen's visits to doctors' offices. Although much of the information conveyed is accurate and important, as are the descriptions published by the companies in the Physicians Desk Reference, the fact remains that these companies are in the business of selling drugs not discouraging their customers from using them. Dependent as he is on the drug companies for his prescription knowledge, it is little wonder that the doctor often becomes lost in the Madison Avenue phrasing of the advertising (the merits always in big type, the dangers in discreet small type with the information conveyed often less than fully informative) or that he is often vague in his own mind about which of the more than 1,200 drugs on the market[63] he should choose for a particular patient, especially since many of the drugs treat the same symptoms yet differ in their adverse effects from patient to patient. Objective information, theoretically anyway, is available to him in the form of articles published by independent researchers in medical journals. However, the busiest doctors, typically also the ones longest away from medical school, are the ones with the least time for such reading. The result is that they are the ones who not only write the most prescriptions but also the largest percentage of the wrong ones.[64]

Improper use of drugs may also be the principal reason that the United States, despite great strides in the past fifty years, continues to have an alarmingly high infant mortality rate. In all, fifteen nations with populations of 2.5 million or more[65] have better records than the American one. When only the somewhat larger nations are included, the American position is still poor:

TABLE F

INFANT MORTALITY RATES (DEATHS TO AGE OF ONE YEAR)[66]

NATION	RATE PER 1,000 LIVE BIRTHS (1973)
Sweden	9.6
Japan	10.0
Netherlands	11.5
France	15.5
Canada	15.6
West Germany	16.0
United Kingdom	16.9
United States	17.7
Soviet Union	26.3

Among the array of drugs to which American pregnant women are exposed are: nausea remedies, diuretics, laxatives, appetite suppressants, antacids, antispasmatics, uterine stimulants, sedatives, tranquillizers, muscle relaxants, amnesiacs, narcotics, analgesics, and regional and inhalation anesthesia at the time of childbirth.[67] The medical effect of this bizarre army of chemical intervention has never been adequately studied scientifically,[68] either as to the effects of the drugs singly or in combination. Although American doctors in increasing numbers have begun to question the efficacy of this persistent drugging of expectant mothers and that women themselves, harboring the same worry, are in growing numbers opting for relatively drug-free pregnancies, routine administration of these drugs mains widespread.[69]

Statistically, at the time of birth, the mother and her child appear to be in the greatest danger if they are patients at the nation's best hospitals, those operated by medical colleges or affiliated with them. (See Table G below.) To some extent, the poor record of the teaching hospitals can be explained by the fact that they are the ones most likely to care for low-income women who, in their pregnancies and deliveries, may be suffering from the medical aftereffects of malnutrition and inadequate pregnancy care. However, these institutions also are the ones most likely to interfere with the normal progress of labor and birth solely to provide learning experiences for the medical students they are training. The safest place for a woman to give birth, assuming a physician or trained midwife is in attendance, may,

TABLE G

PERINATAL AND MATERNAL MORTALITY RATES BY TYPE OF HOSPITAL

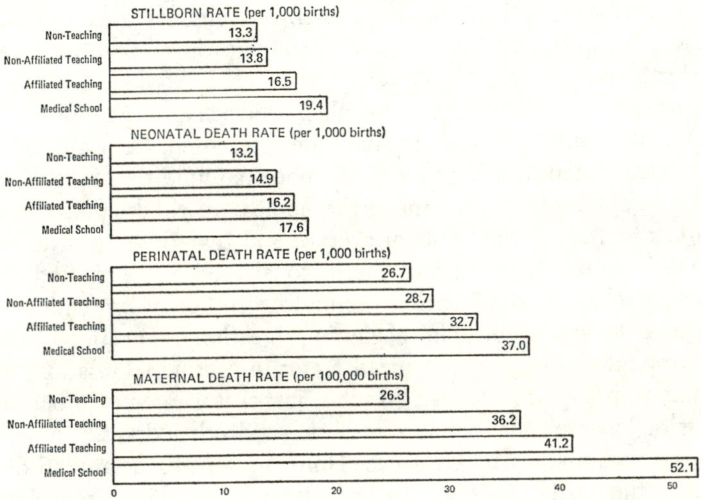

DEFINITIONS:

Stillborn—Fetus weighing 500 grams or more and born dead.

Neonatal Death—Death of a liveborn infant within the first 28 days of life.

Perinatal Death—Stillbirths plus Neonatal Deaths.

SOURCE:

National Study of Maternity Care: Survey of Obstetric Practice and Associated Services in Hospitals in the United States by the Committee on Maternal Health of the American College of Obstetricians and Gynecologists, 1970.

in fact, be at home, because chemical use in the form of anesthetics and other drugs, as well as such mechanical interventions as forceps delivery, are much more rarely employed in the home setting than in hospitals. Relevant is a study of birth difficulties undertaken by the medical schools of Stanford and Wisconsin universities which compared two groups of mothers, each identified medically as "low-risk," some of whom gave birth at home and some in hospitals. The analysis discovered that "the hospital group experienced significantly more birth injuries, neonatal infections . . . more respiratory diseases . . . and more total non-congenital neonatal complications" than did the home-birth group.[70]

By using drugs sparingly if at all in delivery, a considerable amount of mental retardation may be prevented. A California Health Department Study[71] of low-risk mothers found that "the incidence of mental retardation among the home-born children . . . was one-fifteenth that of the national average and that the rate of cerebral palsy was one-tenth that of the national average." This finding apparently relates to the fact that the undrugged home-born children experience little difficulty in beginning breathing. On the other hand, respiratory delay, a recognized factor in causing retardation, is relatively common in American hospitals just as it is rare in European ones with low-use reliance on anesthetics and other drugs.[72] Along this same line, a study by Dr. M. S. Hoffman, a pediatrician and director of the Dallas Academy, a school for learning-impaired children, found that youngsters with difficult birth histories were sixteen times as likely to fail in school as those with rapid- and normal-birth histories, and that children born following chemically induced labor were 2.5 times as likely to fail as the normal-delivery children.[73]

Although the sample in Dr. Hoffman's investigation may have been too small to be statistically reliable, her study is part of the fabric of evidence which suggests that convenience rather than health is still the principal American emphasis in childbirth. It is convenient for the mother to have a comfortable, drug-lulled pregnancy. It is even more convenient for the doctor to keep her that way and then send her for birth to a hospital where attendants, also using drugs, can take care of most of the work, so that the doctor need not arrive until the last moment instead (as in the case of home birth) being required to be present throughout labor and delivery.

The problems raised by prescriptive chemotherapy, whether they relate to the conscious choices of the drugged pregnancy or the accidental administration of the wrong nostrum to the wrong patient at the wrong time, are complex, but like those associated with unnecessary surgery are ones which are resolvable within the research capacity of the medical profession and within its ability to monitor its own members. Yet these problems not only continue but appear to be moving on an upward spiral, despite the malpractice suits they have left in their wake. Neither are they the only problems that the medical profession, while under the onslaught of litigation, has failed to take any meaningful action to allay.

CHAPTER TEN

The Best of Care

A young woman with a backache went to her family physician who, unable to diagnose the cause of her problem, referred her to a surgeon. He told the woman her trouble stemmed from a "misplaced" uterus and that a "simple" operation would affect a cure. The woman agreed to the procedure and during the course of it, the surgeon not only moved her uterus but one of her ovaries as well. At the same time, he ripped her bladder, necessitating a second operation. When the woman was finally patched back together, she found she was still suffering from the backache. Soon after, she went to see an orthopedic surgeon who immediately recognized that one of her legs was slightly shorter than the other; he placed a lift in one shoe and the backache disappeared.[1]

A surgeon in a southwestern state performed a gall bladder operation, tied off the wrong duct and the patient died. A hospital autopsy uncovered the cause of the patient's death, but no one at the hospital bothered to tell the surgeon about it. A few months later, he performed a second gall bladder removal, again tied off the wrong duct, again the patient died. Again the hospital knew what had caused the death but still did nothing about it. Then, within six months of the first operation, the surgeon—possibly thinking his luck was about to turn—tried a third gall bladder removal, tied off the wrong duct, and killed his third patient. It was only then the hospital took its first step to have his license revoked, apparently working on the theory that a doctor, unlike a dog, should have at least two free bites. No steps were taken to discipline the hospital.[2]

A surgeon in a western state caused two patient deaths, probably caused two others, and apparently permanently injured at least two more. He wrought all this devastation, not over his entire career, but in a period of a few months during which he was allowed to continue his practice while fighting charges by his state medical board that he was unfit to be a doctor. In the interim, no one warned his patients they were taking their lives in their hands by permitting him to touch them.[3]

Unfortunately, doctors like these are no great rarity on the American medical scene. According to Dr. Robert C. Derbyshire, past president of the National Federation of State Medical Boards,[4] 5 per cent of all physicians and surgeons in active practice in the United States are definably incompetent.[5] (The estimate is based on studies of hospital records and on known incidences of alcoholism, drug addiction, and mental illness among doctors.[6]) While some sources place the incompetency rate as low as 3 per cent,[7] Roger O. Egeberg, M.D., a top HEW official,[8] is in agreement with Derbyshire, and doubtlessly an argument could also be made that 5 per cent errs on the low side. In any event, accepting the Derbyshire analysis, we can assume that 20,000 of the nation's 400,000 active doctors[9] are incompetent. This group sees 10 million individual patients annually,[10] or a total of 45 million patient contacts based on the 4.5 times a year that the average American visits a doctor.[11]

Alarming as the statistics appear to be, they don't mean that every patient with an incompetent doctor is always harmed by him. Happily, most illnesses, including some of the very serious ones, will cure themselves eventually, no matter how inadequately they are treated. Nevertheless, the incompetent doctor is always a danger, as the examples just given have shown, and the chances that patients will be protected by anyone from medical incompetence are dim indeed. For example, in a New York *Times* interview in January 1976, Dr. Derbyshire noted that when a hospital learns of habitual bad performance by a staff member, typically "the hospital says to him, 'If you resign from the staff, we won't hold this against you.'" The doctor then obligingly quits, Derbyshire says, and goes to another city or state and sets up practice there; or he may simply affiliate himself with another hospital in the same city. Holding up its part of the bargain, the first hospital provides the incompetent doctor with good references when the second hospital asks about him. "This is pretty hard on patients," comments Dr. Derbyshire.[12]

The failure of doctors and hospitals to take action against the incompetents appears, in part, to be due to fear that the accused doctor will sue his accusers for libel. Evidence to back this belief developed a few years ago when Arizona passed a law granting immunity from a libel action to any doctor who reported another. Immediately afterward, the reporting of unfit doctors in that state quadrupled.[13]

Something of the "old boy" syndrome may be involved, too. Just as policemen rarely if ever report their fellow cops to the authorities for brutalizing a prisoner, many doctors seem to consider it violative of club rules to report a doctor who brutalizes his patients with bad treatment, even though theoretically they are obligated to do so; says the AMA's Principles of Ethics: "A physician should expose, without fear or favor, incompetent or corrupt, dishonest or unethical conduct on the part of members of the profession."[14]

Another reason little reporting occurs is because many doctors believe, cynically but usually with good reason, that even if they do finger a colleague nothing will be done about him. Between 1963 and 1975, a period in which the medical population contained an average 15,000 incompetents, just sixty-six license revocations occurred in a typical year,[15] and relatively few of these revocations were based on incompetency allegations. A selection of 291 consecutive disciplinary actions against doctors during the first half of the 1970s[16] reveals that in 169 of them the doctor lost his license because of violations of narcotics laws, conviction of a crime, or "unprofessional" conduct, which can cover many a medical sin of which incompetency is only one. In another 110 cases, no reason was given for the revocation, a figure that includes some doctors who resigned their licenses while under investigation of charges that remain secret. Of the remaining twelve cases, three lost their licenses because of alcoholism, three others for mental illness, while the remaining six had theirs revoked for "extreme" incompetency, a choice of adjective that speaks for itself.

Assuming, which it may not be proper to do, that state medical licensure boards have a zealous interest in protecting the public from incompetent doctors, many of them are hamstrung because of the restrictive nature of the statutes they administer, laws which, in many instances, were written under the direction of their state's Medical Society. For example, at the beginning of 1976, incompetence, negligence, or malpractice was a grounds for revocation or even suspension of license in only twenty-three states,[17] so that, throughout most of the country, no matter how inept he is, a doctor has no worry that he will lose his license for those reasons, even temporarily.

Because of the rise in malpractice suits, a few states, but only a few, have stiffened their medical disciplinary procedures. One is California. Until very recently, the only grounds for revocation or suspension of a doctor's license in that malpractice-plagued state was "immoral, unprofessional, or dishonest conduct" with "discipline" the only action provided for "gross negligence."[18] The new California malpractice law, however, has set up an investigative unit, which may[19] be taking seriously its mandated task to discover and discipline medical incompetence through license revocation.

If the California investigative unit does, in fact, do its job, it will be something of an exception. In many states in which the wording of the law is equally praiseworthy in the protection it provides patients, the office that is supposed to do the protecting is either so underfinanced or understaffed that little or no meaningful activity ever takes place. In New York, for example, a state with 55,000 doctors—2,750 of whom are incompetent by Derbyshire's yardstick—the Board for Professional Medical Conduct has only seven investigators to uphold the law, none of them doctors, few of them professionally trained, and each of whom spends almost all his time looking into minor matters like excessive medical charges or errors in billing.[20]

Taking the nation as a whole, just 430 doctors of 400,000 each year receive notification *of any kind* from a state licensure board about the way they practice medicine, and the overwhelming majority of these communications cite the doctor for advertising his services or misprescribing narcotics, not for any negligence in his practice.[21]

II

The growing number of foreign trained doctors practicing in the United States may be adding to the medical incompetency problem.

Foreign medical school graduates (or FMG's as they are called in medical shorthand) first became a significant presence on the American scene in the 1960s. At the beginning of that decade, they numbered less than 10 per cent of all doctors, by its end, 18 per cent; by 1975, 24 per cent, by 1980, a projected 30 per cent.[22] So great was the influx that by the latter half of the 1960s, their admission rate each year had begun to exceed the number of doctors graduated from American medical schools, with more than two of every five doctors licensed to practice medicine in the United States each year an FMG.[23]

The way to America for the FMG's was opened by the Immigration Act of 1965 which abolished long-standing quota systems against Asians becoming American citizens. Since that time about 70 per cent of the entering FMG's have been Asiatics with Indians, Filipinos, and South Koreans the nationalities most frequently represented;[24] after completing their residencies, about three of every four remain here.[25]

They are needed, too. Since the doctor supply in the United States is just about adequate to the nation's requirements,[26] it is evident that if the FMG's didn't fill one in every four slots, a significant shortage would exist. (The picture, even so, is not good; because of the maldistribution of the medical population, thirty of the fifty states suffer from moderate to severe shortages of doctors, and only five—California, New York, Connecticut, Massachusetts, and Maryland—appear to have a surplus.[27])

The vacuum in medical services the FMG's filled was one created and maintained by the American medical schools under policies established by the AMA.[28] While it is true that the number of American-trained doctors has increased by about 30 per cent since 1960, during the same period medical schools were also turning down far more applicants than ever before, with the admission percentage down from 53 per cent in 1958 to 33 per cent in 1978.[29] Even were we to assume that the higher rejection rate means that more unqualified students are applying for admission than ever before, the percentage decline remains startling and the reason for it unclear. The AMA maintains[30] that enrollment limitation has been beneficial, that because of it the United States enjoys a "superlative medical system."[31] Restrictive enrollment, the AMA observes, has permitted medical schools to develop a ratio of 1.4 students to each professor,[32] thereby creating a maximal learning situation. Admissions policies in American medical schools, therefore, are based on teacher availability, not on the desire to exclude anyone. Competitive reasons, however, are probably dominant. The restrictive admissions policy was adopted by the AMA in the 1930s when physician income had declined precipitately due to the Depression.[33] At that time doctors reasoned that if enrollments were held back, there'd be more patient money to go around for those already in practice, and there seemed no reason to abandon this attractive thesis when the post-War boom years arrived. Around that time a new economic motive evidenced itself as increasing numbers of medical students began to specialize in surgery, where their incomes would be 25–50 per cent higher than in general practice. Since too many surgeons meant too small a slice of the pie for everyone, the answer again was to keep enrollments down. That didn't quite work out, however. In the 1960s, the federal government, in an effort to force American medical schools to accept more students, initiated a capitation system under which a medical school received cash grants for each student it accepted; the amount has varied from year to year but has averaged about $800 to the school for each student.[34] It has been this federal bribery, not any desire on the part of American schools to produce enough doctors to meet American medical needs, that instigated the recent increase in American medical school enrollment.

The FMG's were never the economic threat to practicing American doctors that newly licensed American-trained doctors were. Only about one of every six of the FMG's[35] have entered private practice compared to more than three of every five American-trained doctors,[36] with most of the remaining FMG's, upon completing residencies, joining hospitals as full-time staff physicians. Had the percentage of American students accepted to American medical schools remained at the 1958 level, approximately three of every four positions obtained by the FMG's would have gone to Americans. Had that happened, the FMG's, not finding well-paid posts in the United States upon completion of their residencies, would have been likely to return to their native lands, usually in Asia, where their skills were badly needed.

What occurred then in the United States, beginning in the mid-1960s, was a trade-off of one form of bigotry (against Asians) for another (American medical schools against American students). From a societal view, if not the American student view, the trade-off is acceptable if each of two premises is correct: First, that the restrictive policies of the American schools has resulted in weeding out students who, if they were trained, would prove incompetent as doctors; and, second, that the FMG's who take the place of the students the American schools don't graduate are themselves as competent—or more so—than the rejected Americans would have been.

Since the truth of each premise depends on something that doesn't occur—liberal admissions policies by American medical schools—neither is susceptible to completely objective proof. There is, however, no evidence that the stiffened admissions requirements for the American schools has reduced the American-trained physician incompetency rate since the 1950s, and there is some evidence that it has caused these schools to reject many candidates ideally suited to become general practitioners,[37] a group which, as we have seen, is in woefully short supply in the United States. The FMG's don't help solve this problem either since the vast majority of them also specialize.

In order for the second premise to be true—namely, that the FMG's have as high a level of competency as the American-trained doctors—we have to assume that they were graduated from medical schools that had training and admissions standards as rigorous as the American ones. Conceivably this is so, but the test performances of FMG's suggest otherwise.

For example, in order to obtain either an internship or a residency in an American hospital, every FMG must first pass a qualifying examination set up by the Educational Council for Foreign Medical Graduates (ECFMG). According to a study published by HEW in 1975: "Passing this examination . . . is . . . regarded as an indication that the FMG is competent to provide patient care in a supervised setting. However, the average passing rate for FMG's taking a single ECFMG exam is only 39%. FMG's repeatedly retake the exam, and 67% of all those who take it ultimately pass. Since the ECFMG is administered abroad as well as here, it would be reassuring to think that the failures were all FMG's not yet working in this country. However, an ECFMG survey of FMG's taking the examination in this country in January 1973 found that *the pass rate was only 15% for FMG's already working in the health field here.*"[38] (Italics added.)

In point of fact, many FMG's who are not licensed to practice medicine in the United States and who have failed to pass the qualifying test, nevertheless, are involved in care of patients. According to the *New England Journal of Medicine*,[39] some are hired by hospitals as low-paid laboratory assistants and then permitted to treat patients, giving hospitals a cheap labor pool and probably causing some of them to wonder why their patients complain about the quality of care they get in return for their $200-or-more-a-day in room rent. The same article further revealed that (as of 1974) eleven other states permitted the hiring of non-supervised, non-licensed FMG's to offer physical and psychiatric care in state-operated hospitals.

Psychiatry, in fact, is a favored line of endeavor for FMG's; at present, *one of every four* licensed American psychiatrists is an FMG,[40] and they are particularly prevalent in state mental hospitals, holding 60 per cent of all positions in them, as noted in a study by the American Psychiatric Association.[41] In West Virginia, for example, in 1974 all staff physicians in that state's five mental hospitals and its one institution for the retarded were staffed by FMG's.[42] (Such hospitals, depressing and offering low pay and little prestige, are unattractive to American psychiatric graduates.) Undoubtedly, many of the FMG psychiatrists are sensitive and highly able practitioners. Nevertheless, the statistics mean that at least 25 per cent of the mentally disturbed people in the United States communicate their problems to doctors for almost all of whom English is a second language and who, at best, have limited knowledge of the types of stress endemic to the American culture.

Regardless of what their potential as doctors may be when they come to the United States, once they get here FMG's are likely to get a lesser quality of training than will American graduates. It is the policy of a number of hospitals[43] to place FMG's primarily on night duty, a time when specialists and other staff physicians who could teach them aren't available. Moreover, FMG's are less likely than American graduates to land the plum training positions in hospitals affiliated with medical schools. The FMG's occupy only 28 per cent of these residencies, while in non-affiliated hospitals they comprise 59 per cent.[44] Their most likely employer is the metropolitan hospital serving inner-city neighborhoods.[45] In such hospitals in Newark and Jersey City, FMG's make up 77 per cent of all residents; in New York City, more than half.[46] When an FMG's medical associates during his training are largely other FMG's, his chances are poor of assimilating American medical methods, the English language, or absorbing American cultural patterns that will be helpful to him in his subsequent career in the United States whether that be as a general practitioner, a surgeon, a psychiatrist, or a staff physician.

A true test of medical competence is board certification in a specialty, and most FMG's attempt to obtain it. Their record is not good. In 1972, the latest year for which figures are available, American medical school graduates passed specialty board examinations 73 per cent of the time; only 37 per cent of the FMG's did.[47]

Still another test of the competency of the FMG is his proneness to malpractice suits. On this subject, the information is scant. Although insurers do keep FMG suit statistics, their figures are confined to the 15 per cent in private practice not the 85 per cent on hospital staffs. Therefore, any payments caused by the latter show up only in the hospital statistics and can't be separated by doctor. Theoretically, however, the FMG's should have a much lower than average claims frequency because of the sizable number of them in psychiatry and pathology, two specialties in which suits are rare regardless of where the doctor hails from. (One figure from the NAIC study[48] seems to give confirmation to this theory, but the NAIC's ability to define terms, tenuous at best, is at its most opaque here, and since the commissioners don't answer any questions about their study,[49] it is impossible to know what they mean.) Whatever the percentages may be, attorneys representing plaintiffs and defendants clearly consider that FMG's in surgery and other high-risk fields are especially claims prone because of lack of competence; of a dozen lawyers interviewed, eleven described the FMG's as a "significant," "major," or "substantive" factor in the malpractice problem.[50]

In late 1976, the medical-care problems created by the FMG's were recognized when Congress passed Public Law 94-484, which had as its principal sponsor Senator Edward Kennedy of Massachusetts. This legislation established new, tough examinations that an FMG must pass before he can be granted an entrance visa to the United States, and required the deportation of thousands of FMG's already studying or practicing in this country who could not pass the test. The law, however, has been watered down by a number of amendments, largely in response to the panicked demands of inner-city hospitals that would be stripped of 80 per cent of their staffs if deportations were carried out. The ultimate impact of the law on the FMG problem, therefore, remains unclear.

III

The language barrier that exists between some FMG's and their patients points up another problem in medical performance—in the view of some, it is a major underlying cause of malpractice litigation. According to this argument, communications between patient and doctor in the United States has become generally poor and is deteriorating rapidly. Not only do the growing number of FMG's often not know how to communicate, and the growing number of specialists often not have the time to do so, but doctors in general, it is said, alienate their patients with impersonal care, often failing to take the time to explain illnesses to them or respond sympathetically to their questions. The consequence is a series of misunderstandings between doctor and patient that become the fertile ground for subsequent lawsuits. If this is true, then the malpractice-prone doctor is not the one who fails to offer proper treatment but the one who, for whatever reasons, doesn't establish rapport with his patients.

The theory is one that enjoys wide credence among doctors themselves when they are asked to explain the growing frequency of malpractice litigation. Useful on this point is a survey by the magazine *Medical Opinion.*[51] A questionnaire on malpractice was mailed to 3,000 physicians and surgeons across the country, and almost 1,000 replies were received, with a surprisingly high 47 per cent from doctors who had either been sued or threatened with suit. (Perhaps doctors who have felt the breath of a malpractice allegation on their necks are more likely to answer questions about it than those who have not.) The respondents were asked to select from a list of nine choices the one they believed was the "single most common cause of malpractice suits today." The first choice was "poor communication between physician and patient," named by 37 per cent of the suit-threatened doctors and 44 per cent of the non-threatened. Other choices and amalgamated percentages of response were: Aggressive lawyers, 26 per cent; declining public regard for doctors (which could be related to poor communications), 12.5 per cent; increasing complexity of medical practice, 8.5 per cent; increased public education about medicine (the more they know, the more likely they are to sue), 3.5 per cent; "bad" medicine, 2 per cent; current system of patient care, 1.5 per cent; poorly trained physicians, 0.5 per cent; other not specified reasons, 5 per cent. The validity of this survey is open to question; by providing a check list, the authors guided the respondents in directions they might not have taken had they been asked to come up with choices on their own. Nevertheless, the high percentage of "communications" and the low percentage of "bad" medicine answers is impressive, and probably is generally an accurate reflection of the average doctor's view that it is not medical error but less personally blameworthy factors that get him in trouble.

Be that as it may, the existence of a communications problem was verified by an HEW study[52] which took a different approach; rather than asking doctors about their troubles with patients, it asked patients about their troubles with doctors. For its purposes, more than 1,000 interviews were conducted with respondents, selected on a random basis, each asked about their dealings with doctors over the prior ten years. Of them, about two of every five recalled a "negative" experience, with almost half of the disaffected (or 20 per cent of the total) saying their displeasure was caused by the doctor's failure to cure them of what ailed them. Other than that, dissatisfaction responses were heavily oriented toward communications difficulties. Of the sample, 78 per cent said that the treatment failed to produce the results they had been led to expect. (The interviewees were allowed to give more than one reason for their unhappiness.) Another 23 per cent complained that their doctors never told them what was wrong with them, and 23 per cent also said the doctor didn't warn them in advance of adverse reactions they might expect from drugs and tests.[53] The large number of negative communications responses doesn't necessarily indicate that the doctors in question didn't try to impart information, but rather that if they did, they failed to do so in a way the patient understood.

The HEW survey also approached the communications problem another way by seeking to find the degree of expectation of cure which patients have when they visit a doctor. The results were surprising. Despite the widely heralded miracle advances in medical and drug technology, most patients felt their doctors were neither more nor less competent than they had been twenty years earlier,[54] with only a little more than one in every five[55] saying they believed their physicians were better trained or more knowledgeable than in the past. This finding argues against the AMA's pet theory[56] and that of other observers including HEW itself[57] (which apparently doesn't believe its own statistics) that the malpractice problem is brought about in large part from the public's unrealistic expectations of what medicine can accomplish. If anything, according to this study, the expectation level is too low. (This finding does not, however, mean that expectations will be equal across the board. The expectation of the specialist will be higher than of the GP, but, if the study is correct, *unrealistic* expectation is not common in any medical contact.)

In another phase of its study, HEW attempted to determine if any deterioration had taken place in the doctor's attitude toward patients, as perceived by the patients themselves. As a result, respondents were asked a number of questions about today's doctor compared with the doctor of twenty years earlier. The phrasing of this question casts limits on the response credibility, since people generally tend to think the past is better than the present, and so it is very possible that if the survey had been taken twenty years earlier it would have come up with the same answers about doctors twenty years before that time. Nevertheless, the study has impressionistic value, with the answers indicating a serious lowering of public faith in the physician. (The discrepancy was a statistically significant .77.[58]) The respondents, whether or not they'd had a negative medical experience, generally believed that today's doctor spends less time with them than his predecessor, that he is less likely to explain symptoms or treatments proposed, that he is less sympathetic, and much more money-grubbing. Only 19 per cent of the respondents believed the doctor's dedication to his work has improved over the twenty years, while 35 per cent said it had deteriorated, with the remainder seeing no difference or not venturing an opinion. (Even so, doctors made out better than "people in general"; the respondents thought only 12 per cent of them had increased their dedication to work, while 54 per cent thought dedication had decreased.[59])

The study made an attempt to establish a relationship between "negative" medical experiences and the likelihood of subsequent malpractice litigation. Of the more than four hundred people who mentioned a negative event, 8 per cent said they had "thought" about filing a suit but only 1 per cent (four individuals) did so. Since few of those with negative experiences were actually injured by them (and thus had the rudiments for a malpractice claim), the 1 per cent suit figure seems large, and may indicate that personal animosity toward a doctor may be a contributory factor in the decision to sue. Indeed, 53 per cent of those who thought about taking legal action mentioned as one of their reasons their desire to "cause the [doctor(s)] involved to be held up to public notice."[60] However, pecuniary reasons, most notably to recover medical expenses or lost income, were of the greatest importance to all respondents.[61] Such figures, based as they are on a meager statistical sample (37 peo- who thought about taking action) must be treated with caution.

Some students of the malpractice problem believe that failures in communication are not, by themselves, important causes of malpractice suits save in the sense that they exhibit personality traits in the doctor that make him vulnerable to suit for other reasons as well. These observers identify two somewhat overlapping types of suit-prone doctors. One might be called the Schneider Variation, almost invariably surgeons who have been attracted to their speciality in part because it allows them to deal with some broken part of a body rather than the human being for whom the body is the container. To their patients, these doctors come across as patronizing and cold-blooded, or as one attorney who has prosecuted many of them says: "They may be great doctors, but in their personal relationships they are unmitigated bastards. They're the doctors who talk about the 'broken pelvis in Room 14' not 'Mrs. Jones in Room 14.' They virtually ask to get sued, and when they do they make wonderful defendants. From my point of view."[62] Not too different in content was the assessment made by a defense attorney: "The incompetent ones bury their mistakes," he says. "It's the arrogant ones who call attention to them. There's something about a patient that brings out the worst in that kind of doctor. It's as if he never heard of the Golden Rule. I am firmly convinced that were medical schools to spend one quarter of the time teaching students how to relate to patients that they now spend teaching them how to cure a backache, then malpractice suits would be reduced by at least that much, and maybe more."[63]

Ego problems appear to be the genesis of the suit-proneness in a second type of doctor. These are individuals who have entered the medical profession because of a psychic need to hold a superior position to those with whom they deal. (Lawyering is another profession catering to the same need.) The problems engendered by the medical superiority complex were recognized as long ago as 1957 in a paper entitled *The Psychology of Malpractice Suits*, published by the California Medical Association. This study, according to a summary of it by the HEW Malpractice Commission,[64] characterized "the suit-prone physician as one who cannot admit to himself his own limitations of training and experience, and who, when confronted with a dissatisfied patient, often responds to the situation by neglecting the patient or dismissing his complaints as trivial. Instead of finding out how to make the patient feel less angry, less afraid, or less depressed, he is more pre-occupied with his own image. More often than not, he tends to regard the patient [who doesn't respond to treatment] as a symbol of his own failure, and unconsciously punishes him by an indifference that amounts to rejection." Such a doctor is also likely to overestimate his own abilities[65] and will attempt complex medical or surgical procedures which in terms of his training he should avoid. Because he doesn't want his expertise challenged, he will rarely voluntarily consult with colleagues about a difficult medical problem, fearing a blow to his carefully cultivated sense of omnipotence should they disagree with him. Such a doctor will also frequently discourage his patients from seeking a second opinion on their own and will reject these opinions (and sometimes the patient) if they disagree with his own findings. Doctors of this calibre have been known to order X rays and then not bother to look at them, so confident are they of their diagnostic abilities or perhaps secretly fearful that the X-ray evidence will contradict them and put them in the (to them) embarrassing position of having to tell the patient that the original diagnosis was wrong.

Fascinating as these psychological profiles may be, they do not take us very far in understanding claims-proneness. While it seems reasonable to assume that a doctor with a "bad" personality like Schneider will be more claims prone than one with a "good" personality like Robinson we may, in fact, by such analyses, be dealing with self-fulfilling prophecies. To the patient he helps, after all, Schneider's personality will be no bar; on the contrary, the patient is likely to have a high opinion of Schneider, seeing him much the way Schneider sees himself, perhaps reticent but certainly objective—the latter a quality that can generate great confidence in a patient. It is only when Schneider hurts the patient that his "bad" characteristics become significant. By the same reasoning, Robinson's warm personality is fine as long as he doesn't hurt anyone, but when he does, that warmth will now likely be perceived by the patient as "phoniness" and Robinson as a "personality boy" who covers up his incompetence with a smile. Therefore, both of them, to the plaintiff's attorney who sees them through the eyes of his client, become "unmitigated bastards." The defense attorney too may seek out personality flaws in his client. Because he wants to show that his client wasn't negligent, it is convenient for him, perhaps unconsciously, to view the client as one who got into trouble because of his poor attitude toward his patients, not because of his incompetence.

This is not to say that there aren't many doctors who are arrogant or neurotic, covering their lack of ego with a superiority complex, or to suggest that such doctors don't harm their patients because of their personality defects. At times, the harmful effects can be subtle ones: Some patients, because of their own emotional problems, are poor risks at following pre- and postoperative instructions. A patient-sensitive doctor is likely to catch such warning signs and take appropriate steps, while an "objective" doctor like Schneider, with his single-minded concentration on the patient's physical condition, will not perceive them and the patient will suffer as a consequence.

On balance, however, the relationship of a doctor's personality or his failure to "communicate" to suit-proneness appears easily overstated. Injury remains the key factor.

IV

Poor provision of medical care, however, is not the sole province of the doctors. They, after all, make up only 10 per cent of the four million people employed by the American health care industry,[66] with the majority of the remainder also involved in direct patient services and thus capable themselves of causing incompetent and legally negligent care. Their numbers include (as of 1975) 935,000 registered nurses, 370,000 practical nurses, 219,000 health aides, and 1,001,000 nursing aides, orderlies, and attendants.[67] (The remainder fill such categories as pharmacists, hospital administrators, clerical positions, dieticians, and technicians.)

The amount of work performed by non-physician hospital personnel has increased since 1960 at a pace considerably swifter than the patient admission rate, the increment probably largely related to changes in the type as well as the quantity of treatment offered patients, both those who are hospitalized and those who use outpatient facilities. As a consequence, the number of attendants per hospitalized patient rose from about two in 1960 to more than three in 1975 and is likely to reach four by 1980 or a little later.[68] Increasing the number of attendants per patient, however, does not necessarily improve the quality of care offered them; the opposite, in fact, may be more often the case.

The precipitant in the declining care is the changing role of the nurse. If the registered nurse is the non-doctor person capable of giving the best patient care, the statistics initially don't look unpromising. Between 1960 and 1975, the population of registered nurses increased by 86 per cent,[69] only a slightly lesser rate than the growth in inpatient and outpatient hospital services. However, during the same period, the personnel with the lowest degree of training (nursing aides, orderlies, and attendants) grew by 170 per cent.[70] *This means that the hospitalized patient of the 1970s is about twice as likely as the patient of the 1960s to receive some significant portion of her care from people with poor or non-existent health-provision abilities.* Expected to supervise this growing army of the unskilled is the nurse who, as a result, spends ever larger amounts of her time on administrative duties and decreasing amounts doing what she was trained to do—providing direct care to sick people.[71]

Given the rise in hospitalization (including the millions of patients admitted for unnecessary surgery) hospital administrators may well be faced with an insuperable personnel problem and must, therefore, hire people whose ability to handle the sick and whose interest in their welfare is minimal. For the patients, however, in terms of competent care, the result is not a happy one.

Hospitals, however, can do much to reduce the patient injury problem and, along with it, the hospital's suit proneness. That some hospitals are capable of doing just that is indicated by an HEW study of hospital claims-proneness in which it was observed: "The statistics disclose an entirely different picture than what has generally been assumed. Taken in the aggregate, one might expect the average hospital in the United States to be sued twice in any one year (1.9 claims)"—these figures are based on a 1970 study; today they would be considerably higher—"but a breakdown of hospital claims experience reveals that some hospitals have much better records than others. If incidences which give rise to malpractice claims occurred randomly, 33% of the nation's hospitals could be expected to have no claims filed against them during the year. The actual rate [of non-claims], distributed over all sizes of hospitals, was 68% [with] *[f]ifteen hospitals [accounting] for more than half of the claims.* If this small number could improve their claims experience, the total number of claims could be lowered substantially."[72]

Some reservations, however, must be noted about the HEW study. It does not make clear which hospitals, in terms of size and services offered, were claims-prone. Neither does the study reveal the economic status of patients in claims-prone hospitals, which may be important if, as some of our other evidence indicates, the typical malpractice claimant is middle class and possessing some degree of knowledge of the law. A 1976 study of malpractice suits ready for trial against hospitals in Philadelphia[73] showed that one hospital with a largely middle-class clientele had far many more suits filed against it than several larger hospitals with mixed clientele. The Philadelphia study, however, contains its own variables which limit its value. For example, the insurers for the large hospitals may have been more likely to settle suits before they reached the trial stage than was the insurer for the much-sued hospital. Also, the sued hospital's exposure was probably less reflective of the litigious nature of its patients than it was its failure to introduce the kind of risk management system that the HEW study suggests would have cut down on claims.

It is in risk management that the hospital administrator plays the key role either in allowing malpractice-type situations to develop or in taking steps to prevent them. The good administrator realizes that every contact between a health-care provider and a patient carries the risk that the patient will be injured. He further realizes that these risks cannot be entirely eliminated; he cannot, for instance, stop the surgeon's knife from slipping or the anesthesiologist from giving too much or not enough gas or prevent adverse reactions to drugs or halt misprescriptions that cause some of the reactions. Within his own domain, however, even if the job market limits him in the quality of people he can hire, there is much he can do.

To begin with, the wise administrator will always see to it that transit premises are uncluttered and made safe by skidproof floors, ramps, and stairways. He will also maintain constant vigilance over the safety of hospital medical equipment and make sure that accepted laboratory examination and reporting techniques are followed. He will determine that all doctors who use the hospital's facilities have the credentials they claim to have and that review panels operate meaningfully to assess the adequacy of the performance of staff surgeons and physicians. He will try to find ways to encourage doctors to continue their medical education as well as attend sessions in which methods of risk reduction in surgery and postoperative care are outlined. He will want to make sure that all doctor and nurse notes on patient condition are kept accurately and fully and that a fail-safe system exists for transfer of records when a patient moves from one part of the hospital to another (i.e., from intensive to room care.) He'll want to know that a tracing system exists, assuring that other interdepartmental transfers of records proceed in a timely and complete fashion. He'll encourage the filing of "incident" reports of mishaps to patients, which may or may not be caused by negligence, but which, if properly analyzed, can lead to the reduction of such accidents in the future. Partly in response to these injuries when they occur, but also to deal with other patient problems (such as complaints about the hospital's billing system, the quality of its food, the attitude of the personnel, and so on), the administrator will probably also want to establish an active grievance mechanism, so that patient complaints can be aired at the time they occur and not fester, establishing the basis for later lawsuits or refusals to pay bills.[74]

As apparent as is the need for good risk-management systems, unfortunately relatively few hospitals have instituted them in any sophisticated form[75] and most don't even have them rudimentarily. As a 1975 HEW study pointed out, to hospitals "the concept of risk management is largely unfamiliar, misunderstood or but dimly appreciated . . .[76] That appreciation, nevertheless, does appear to be growing, not out of any objective concern for the patient's welfare, but apparently in direct response to the increasing number of malpractice claims filed against hospitals. To the extent that malpractice litigation forces better risk management, the benefactions for all hospital patients will be notable.

CHAPTER ELEVEN

"They Could Not Help But Win"

I

The relationship between a doctor and his malpractice insurer is a contractual one. The doctor pays a premium, typically due in full at the beginning of each year, in return for which the insurer makes two guarantees: First, should a claim be lodged against the doctor, the insurer will investigate the claim and provide an attorney to defend the doctor at no cost to him. Second, should the claim result in payment to the plaintiff, the insurer covers the amount assessed up to the face value of the policy.

That amount varies. At one time, when malpractice claims were rarities, most doctors took out $5,000/$15,000 policies.[1] Under them, the insurer agreed to pay $5,000 per claim but no more than $15,000 in the course of a year. Today, it is a rare doctor who carries only that small an amount of insurance. The norm policy is $100,000 per claim and $300,000 total in one year.[2] It is, however, possible to purchase malpractice insurance in much larger amounts, and many doctors do so, with $1,000,000/$3,000,000 policies increasingly common,[3] especially in the surgical specialties. Almost all hospitals carry at least that amount.

Ordinarily, however, the $100,000 policy offers a physician or a surgeon ample protection. No more than 2 per cent of all claims against doctors result in awards larger than that, and even in those cases, there is usually more than one defendant to share the costs.[4] In any event, regardless of the size of the verdict, the insurance company pays all the investigating and legal costs in defending the claim.

A doctor's malpractice insurance rate depends not just on the amount of his coverage. Different companies charge different fees for the same coverage. This is true not only of commercial companies like Aetna and Travelers, but also of those operated by state governments and the growing number of self-insurance mutuals that have been organized by medical societies and hospitals.[5]

The amount a doctor pays for his policy, however, is less affected by the company he buys it from than by his specialty "rating." Rating customers by risk is an old idea in insurance but a relatively new one as applied to doctors. Until the 1950s each company charged all its medical clients a flat rate.[6] At that time, because malpractice claims were beginning to inch upward, insurers began to study the demographics of the problem, discovering that not only were surgeons the doctors most likely to get sued but also the ones who caused the highest average payout per claim. As a result, by 1960[7] surgeons were already paying 2.5 times the amount charged non-surgeons. (Insurance company income that year from surgeons was $19.7 million, from all other doctors, $7.6 million.[8]) The gap widened rapidly. By 1966 surgeons were paying quadruple,[9] and by 1975, in some cases, twenty-five times the rates charged non-surgeons.[10]

In the mid-1960s, another change was also instituted in the rating system. As the growing number of claims added to their knowledge of liability patterns, the insurers recognized that some doctors who performed surgery were more likely to get sued than others. Therefore, using specialty classifications established by the American Medical Association,[11] doctors were divided into five rating classifications as follows:[12]

CLASS ONE: Physicians Who Perform No Surgery.
E.g., allergists, dermatologists, internists, neurologists, pathologists, pediatricians, psychiatrists, and some general practitioners. (Nationally, in 1977 the average Class One doctor paid approximately $1,000 per year for his malpractice coverage.)[13]

CLASS TWO: Physicians Performing Minor Surgery or Assisting in Major Surgery on Own Patients.
Into this group falls the general practitioner who may set uncomplicated fractures, perform wart removals, and the like. (Average, 1977, $1,800.)

CLASS THREE: Doctors Who Perform Some Major Surgery.
Includes general practitioners not primarily engaged in major surgery, but who will perform appendectomies, tonsillectomies, deliver babies, etc. Also, ophthalmologists and proctologists. (Average, 1977, $3,700.)

CLASS FOUR: Surgical Specialists Performing Operations of Substantial Risk.
E.g., cardiac surgeons, otolaryngologists, general surgeons, thoracic surgeons, urologists, vascular surgeons. (Average, 1977, $11,500.)

CLASS FIVE: Surgical Specialists Performing Operations of the Highest Risk.
E.g., neurosurgeons, obstetrician/gynecologists, orthopedists, plastic surgeons, and anesthesiologists. Although anesthesiologists are not surgeons, their duties are performed during operations and are, therefore, considered part of the surgical function. (Average, 1977, $18,500.)

(Almost all dentists also carry malpractice insurance coverage, with oral surgeons paying the highest rates. Dentists, however, are relatively rarely sued, and when they are almost always for lesser amounts than the average claim against a medical doctor or an osteopath.[14] As a result, their rates, on the average, are lower even than most Class One physicians. Other health-care practitioners, such as chiropractors, chiropodists, podiatrists, and naturopaths can also obtain malpractice insurance, usually at very modest rates. Whatever the real value may be of the services they offer, they are unlikely to injure a patient in a way that provides grounds for a viable malpractice claim—what, for example, is the standard of care to which a chiropractor can be held?—and many of them attract customers whose faith in their techniques is so unquestioning that they are virtually immune from suit.[15])

II

In several ways, geographical considerations also play a role in determining how much a doctor will pay for insurance. Regardless of specialty, doctors working in metropolitan areas pay higher rates than do those who practice in more rural sections and who therefore are less likely to be sued. For example, in California doctors practicing in the counties of Alameda, Contra Costa, Los Angeles, Marin, San Diego, San Francisco, San Mateo, and Santa Clara pay higher rates than do doctors situated elsewhere in the state. Similarly, in New York, doctors practicing in New York City as well as the counties of Delaware, Nassau, Orange, Rockland, Suffolk, Sullivan, Ulster, and Westchester pay surcharges because of their metropolitan location.[16]

The premium a doctor pays is also determined by the state in which he lives. The single most expensive state in terms of malpractice insurance is California because, even though it contains only 10 per cent of the nation's population, it produces 20 per cent of all claims each year.[17] California's unenviable number-one standing is of no recent vintage. As long ago as the 1930s, when it was only seventh in population, instead of first as it now is, it also led the way.[18] Why California should create such a disproportionately high number of claims each year is unclear. Those who hew to the theory that claims rates are directly related to patient/doctor relationships will observe that California has a much more transient population than most other states, making such close relationships less frequent there than elsewhere. Others point out, however, that California courts traditionally have been consumer-oriented, making them likely to side with injured plaintiffs. Knowing that, California attorneys are eager to pursue malpractice cases, accepting even doubtful ones, because they know their chances of winning are good. A snowballing effect may be also visible in California. A state with many claims is likely to get more of them as the public reads about large verdicts and learns how easy it is to sue a doctor. Without discounting these factors, it is also possible that California, for recondite sociological reasons, may attract more than its share of incompetent doctors. The state seems, year after year, to proffer an extraordinarily high percentage of cases in which patient injuries are of a particularly hideous nature, as is observable from a number of the case histories described earlier. In addition to California, the states of New York, Florida, Pennsylvania, and Illinois each have a significantly higher percentage of malpractice claims annually than their percentage of the national population would predict. Together, these five states, all highly urbanized, make up only about a third of the national population but nearly half its annual malpractice claims total. At the other end of the spectrum, we find that states in the South (except Florida) and in the West (except the three Pacific Coast states) generally have lower-than-average claims frequencies. This is also true of the New England states.[19]

Thus, the more ruralized and lacking in major urban centers a state is, the lower its claims rate. There are, however, too many anomolies to accept that theory completely. In New England, the states of New Hampshire, Vermont, and Maine (which, by one computation, has the lowest claims rate of all[20]) fit that rural description, yet Massachusetts, the single most urbanized state in the nation and one which, therefore, can be expected, by insurance company theories, to have a high claims rate actually has one of the lowest,[21] as does its urbanized neighbor, Connecticut. Moving a little further south, we find that urbanized New Jersey has a much lower rate than either of its two high-claims neighbors, New York and Pennsylvania. Moreover, three other states with major urban centers—Michigan, Ohio, and Texas—also have lower-than-average rates.[22] Therefore, while *many* rural states have low claims rates, urbanization is not a necessary indicator of a high rate.

The amount a hospital pays for its malpractice coverage is charged on a per bed basis. Its insurance is also affected by geographic factors, with big city hospitals typically paying more than rural ones. Frequently, teaching hospitals (those associated with a medical college) pay the highest rates of all because they have the best equipment and the best doctors. On the face of it, this sounds illogical, but to insurance companies it makes good sense: The better the doctors and the more sophisticated the equipment of the hospital, the larger the number of difficult operations will be attempted each year, everyone of which, if something goes wrong, can lead to a major suit, such as the one Dr. Schneider and his hospital faced.

III

By 1970 malpractice premium income for the insurance industry was about quadruple the 1960 level. Nevertheless, the progress of the rate increases was uneven, with several of the highest claims states enjoying relatively low rates. In New York, for example, it wasn't until 1968 that the major malpractice insurer there first received a sizable increase in his rate structure,[23] while in California, increases were inconsiderable well into the early 1970s.[24] It can be said, therefore that while the malpractice problem was one of growing concern to insurers from the Sixties onward, the worry was hardly uniformly expressed, nor was there, in the first years of the 1970s, any evidence of the "crisis" in insurance cost and availability that was to engulf doctors and hospitals by 1974 and 1975. Indeed, in 1973, the HEW Malpractice Commission reported: "Recently [insurers have shown] renewed interest in the field caused by at least three factors: *the prevailing level of premium rates is regarded [by them] as adequate*; an increased awareness among providers of the steps that can be taken to avoid unwarranted claims has made carriers more willing to offer coverage; and health-care providers have begun to shop around for competitive sources of coverage, thereby inducing new carriers to enter the field.[25] (Italics added.)

Ironically, the HEW Malpractice Commission itself helped precipitate the insurance availability crisis. Its discovery that millions of iatrogenic injuries occur each year for the first time gave the insurers an awareness that the 10–15 per cent claims rise they had been seeing might be nothing more than the tip of the iceberg. This year, next year, or the one after that, could see claims rise by 100 per cent or 200 per cent or some incalculable per cent, causing the industry to face billions of dollars in claims payments at a time when it was earning premiums only in the hundreds of millions.

Faced with this grim prospect, many insurers jumped ship. Between 1973 and 1975, the number of companies writing statistically significant amounts of malpractice declined from twenty-five[26] to no more than twelve.[27]

At the same time, both those who stayed and those who soon were to leave demanded and received rate increases that would bring the insurers one billion dollars annually in new premium income over a two-year period. (See Table H below.) The need for the high rates was proven, it appeared, by statistics showing that company after company was suffering large underwriting losses. The number one company in total underwriting volume, St. Paul, told a United States Senate Committee that its losses between 1970 and 1974 reached $55 million.[35] Even more grim was the experience of Argonaut Insurance Company which stated its 1971–75 losses at $214,321,721.[36] Employers of Wausau described losses of more than $20 million annually in a number of the last years it sold coverage in New York.[37] An analysis by the Western Insurance Information Service found

TABLE H

Estimates of Malpractice Insurance Premiums Paid by Physicians, Surgeons, and Hospitals

YEAR	VOLUME
1960	$61,000,000 (a)
1965	$90,500,000 (a)
1970	$250,000,000 (b)
1973	$400,000,000 (c)
1974	$5–$600,000,000 (d)
1975	$1,000,000,000 (d) / $1,250,000,000 (e)
1976	$1,500,000,000 (d)
1980	$3,700,000,000 (f)

(a) HEW estimate, as published in the Malpractice Commission Report.[28]
(b) The HEW estimate for this year was $370.6 million. Retrospectively, however, this figure appears on the high side, especially since HEW[29] itself observed that its survey of 31 sizable malpractice insurers active in 1970 produced a volume of only $205.4 million. It seems unlikely that the remaining 30 insignificant insurers could have accounted for another $165 million, and HEW implicitly queries the accuracy of its own figures.[30] The estimate above, extrapolated from other sources, is probably more nearly accurate, though possibly conservative.
(c) Projection based on 1970 and 1975 estimates.
(d) HEW estimate presented to the United States Senate, December 1975.[31]
(e) Estimate supplied by General Reinsurance Company.[32]
(f) Estimate based on insurance industry statements of 24–30% increases in malpractice rates needed annually from 1976 onward.[33] It should be noted, however, that the major malpractice insurer, St. Paul Fire & Marine, does not believe "large increases" will be necessary, suggesting the 1980 estimate may be on the high side.[34]

that malpractice insurers for California, until they started raising rates in the mid-1970s, were paying out $180 on each $100 in premiums collected,[38] with Travelers Insurance telling the Senate Committee that it lost $20 million in California in 1974.[39]

Not everyone accepted these tales of woe. Some doctors expressed their disbelief by threatening or carrying out the strikes mentioned earlier. These efforts, however, were few, with most doctors content to blame the patients who were suing for the rise in rates, not the insurance companies which were getting the revenue. Consumer lobbying groups,[40] knowing that costs would be passed onto the public, occasionally also raised questions about the validity of the rate increases, but in no substantial way and with little success.

More serious opposition to the insurers came from other quarters, including spokesmen for the attorneys who represented plaintiffs[41] and some government officials. They argued that the only time the insurers had told the truth about the malpractice problem was in 1973 when they advised the HEW that rates were adequate; in the years that followed nothing had happened in terms of actual claims increases as against feared ones to suggest that the rate changes that took place were valid. The insurers, in this view, had seized on a legitimate problem that was expressing itself in manageable terms and had exploited it into a crisis, as a result reaping excess profits for themselves and simultaneously furthering other long-range insurance industry goals.[42] One prominent analyst who held such a view was the man who had served as the HEW's Malpractice Commission executive director, attorney Eli Bernzweig, himself a former executive with Argonaut.[43] Another, in a position to be equally knowledgeable, was the Insurance Administrator of the United States, J. Robert Hunter, as the following exchange during a December 1975 United States Senate investigation into malpractice insurance rates makes clear:

Senator LAXALT. Is malpractice always a loser as far as carriers are concerned?

Mr. HUNTER. If they charge these rates, they could not help but win.[44]

Should the critics be correct, then the insurance industry is guilty of "malpractice" against both doctors and the public. However, if, in fact, claims frequency and cost has run amok, as the insurers allege, then a radical overhaul of the entire health-care system or the litigation system or both will be required to prevent a catastrophe. As can be projected from Table H, by the late 1980s, if not sooner, should the existent trends in insurance cost continue, the *average* doctor will have to pay more than $50,000 annually for his malpractice coverage, which means that most high-risk specialists will have premium rates in the $150,000 to $200,000 range. Manifestly, neither doctors nor the public could afford to pay that kind of bill—not even half that amount.

The question to be answered, therefore, is: Are the insurers telling the truth when they allege losses, present and future, from malpractice underwriting?

IV

Insurance companies make money two ways. First, they profit when income from premium is larger than the sum of their claims payments plus administrative expenses, with insurers hoping to make a 5 per cent profit in this fashion.[45] (Theoretically, the 5 per cent also acts as a hedge against unexpected losses.[46]) Secondly, profit is derived by investing premium income. Investments cover a wide range. Conservative companies largely limit theirs to municipal bonds, U. S. Treasury notes, and like purchases in which the yield may not be high but on which the return is guaranteed. Other companies, while they make some of these gilt-edged investments, also take risks. They play the stock market, speculate in real estate, or buy other companies, which may or may not be in the insurance field, but which appear to have a high profit potential.[47]

Two types of insurance companies deal with the public; the life insurers, who generate the most premiums, and the casualty insurers. Casualty companies reimburse property owners from losses due to accidents (e.g., fire, auto collisions) and also insure individuals and businessmen from costs arising from injuries they do others. This latter coverage, in which medical malpractice policies are included, is known as liability insurance.

A third kind of insurance company is the reinsurer which doesn't deal with the public but rather with other insurance companies. It acts for a public insurer as a lay-off does for a bookie. When a bookie has too much action on a horse, he will turn to a "banker" who agrees to pay anything the bookie can't cover in return for part of the bookie's take. Similarly, a reinsurer, in return for a fee, accepts part of the public insurer's risk. Sometimes the arrangement calls for the reinsurer to cover a constant percentage of all policies written by the company, regardless of face value. More commonly, the reinsurer accepts losses only above a certain limit. For example, if a doctor has a $100,000 malpractice insurance policy, the reinsurer may agree to take on any losses above $75,000. Thus, if the doctor has a $90,000 verdict against him, the underwriting company pays $75,000 and the reinsurer $15,000. Because of reinsurance, the original company (just like the bookie with his banker) knows in advance the maximum it can lose on any policy it writes.[48] According to industry sources,[49] payments covered by reinsurance are *not* included in a company's statement of underwriting losses.

In deciding whether or not to write a line of insurance, a company is less concerned about the total amount of dollars it will have to pay out than the accuracy with which claims volume can be predicted. For most lines of insurance, predictor factors are developed with precision. Life insurance companies, for example, have actuarial tables to tell them how many people will die at what age, and even more detailed figures allow them to predict a person's life expectancy from the age at which the policy is written, as well as those showing longevity based on sex and occupation. The casualty industry has similar integers; the auto insurers know the likelihood of automobile accidents by age, sex, occupation, and neighborhood; the fire insurers the likelihood of fire, and so on. With such sophistication are these figures drawn that they ordinarily have the capacity of taking into account trends as they are developing, so that these can be immediately incorporated into the next year's premium charge. In the casualty industry, according to its spokesmen, companies look for trend predictors that will allow them to write policies at a 72:100 ratio, i.e., the company will make 5 per cent profit on premium if its payout is no more than $.72 on every $1.00 it takes in. The remaining $.23 goes to administrative expenses including overhead, agent commissions, taxes, etc.[50]

Therefore, if an insurer is hit by an onslaught of claims he had not trended in his rate-making process, he can be left with sizable indemnity losses that will eat into and may be greater than his investment earnings. Failures in trending are most likely to occur in an insurance pool in which there are few customers (e.g., 350,000 doctors) than in a large one (e.g., 46 million homeowners.[51]). There are several reasons for this. First, the more people there are in a pool, statistically the more likely they are to produce claims in an orderly fashion. Secondly, even if a large pool does suddenly become very volatile in claims frequency, the new pass-on cost per customer is not large (e.g., $5 million in new claims in a field in which the company has one million customers leads to a $5.00 per annum pass-on), and therefore the company is not likely to be hurt competitively when it raises rates. Finally, because the insurer already knows a lot about his large pool, the unexpected rise in claims is readily assimilated into future trending patterns.

The opposite is true in the small pool. Because it has never produced a sizable amount of his business, the insurer has never studied it as he has the large pool; moreover, faced with sudden claims acceleration, his pass-on per customer rapidly becomes large and possibly competitively prohibitive (e.g., $5 million in untrended claims for an insurer with 10,000 customs will result in a $500 pass-on per customer). Finally, both because of his previous lack of knowledge and because of the small number of customers, he lacks sufficient indices to determine whether the sudden volatility in the field is temporary, permanent at the new level, or may go much higher.

As a result, the small pool is attractive to the insurer only so long as it is quiescent (and he doesn't have to worry about rating it properly) and often not worth the bother when it begins to act aberrantly. For the small-pool customer, this means he has no trouble getting insurance when he has little need for it, but encounters great difficulty once claims volatility has made his need imperative.

As gloomy as the picture of the effects of claims volatility in the small customer pool may be, it does not mean that any of the twenty-five companies that wrote malpractice insurance in 1973 were in danger of going out of business when volatility hit them. With one exception, Medical Protective of Indiana (of which more later), the companies were multiline insurers for whom malpractice produced only a tiny amount of their annual premium volume. Even St. Paul did only 10 per cent of its business in the field (as of 1975[52]) while the giant Aetna, another sizable malpractice carrier, gained only 4/10 of 1 per cent of its casualty premium revenue from malpractice.[53] As long as profits were maintained for the dominant lines, they would swallow any losses caused by the one small line.

Total profits, however, do not make companies necessarily willing to suffer losses in the one line simply because, by so doing, they are providing a service their customers need. The sole reason for any insurance company's existence is to provide dividends for its stockholders who rightly become concerned when they see that their income would become greater if management disbanded underwriting in the losing line. The intriguing aspect of the malpractice insurer flight, therefore, is not that so many companies left the field, but that as many stayed in it as did in view of the large and unpredictable claims cost crisis they said they were undergoing.

Claims volatility was not the only disturbing aspect of malpractice underwriting for its insurers. All along, the line had carried with it the so-called "long tail" factor,[54] presenting a problem the dimensions of which grew as the number of claims increased. The "tail" in an insurance sense is the delay period between the time an accident occurs and the time a claim is asserted. In life insurance, there's rarely a "tail." When somebody dies, the company is almost always informed immediately. Similarly, people who suffer losses from fire put their claims in quickly, usually before the smoke has cleared. Even automobile insurers know that if an accident claim hasn't been made within six months, the odds are overwhelming it won't be brought at all. Medical malpractice insurers, however, principally because of the slowness with which some injuries reveal themselves, learn of only 52 per cent of the claims against their clients within one year of the accident, and even after four years, 4 per cent are still to be heard from.[55] Consequently, the malpractice insurer, unlike other underwriters, has no substantive knowledge of his total claims liability when projecting the rates he must charge for the next year. The most he can do is estimate the dollars these unknown claims will cost him; he calls this calculation his IBNR (incurred but not reported) loss figure.

Regardless of the delay in its inception, once a malpractice suit has begun it requires no longer for resolution than does any other liability claim. Variations occur from state to state, with New York having the longest delay,[56] but nationally about 90 per cent of all malpractice cases are resolved within three years,[57] a figure that compares favorably with experience in most other injury areas. (The more money that's at stake in a malpractice claim, the longer the insurer, wanting to hold onto his money, will delay settlement, but this reasoning holds true for most other injury suits as well.)

The combination of claims volatility and the long tail, each of which can lead to underpricing, has led, if the insurers are to be believed, to the gigantic losses they have suffered. There are, however, many ways in which a company's claims experience can be calculated, and not all of them result in an accurate portrayal of either its profits or its losses.

V

Every insurance company has a sum of money on its books known as its loss reserve. It represents the ultimate payments it foresees it must make for each claim file it currently has open. If the company thinks the potential from a given claim is nil, it will assign (depending on its system) either a $0.00 or $1.00 value to it. Still other claims will carry evaluations well up into the millions. The evaluation may remain the same from the day the file is opened until the day it is closed, but in many instances the figure will go up or down as new facts about the case are learned. Also included in the loss reserve is the amount the company predicts will be required to investigate and defend the claims. In this fashion, a $0.00 claim can still cost the insurer money, perhaps a sizable amount of it in legal fees, should the claimant bring a suit.

Loss reserves have great financial significance to an insurance company. The amount of business it is permitted to do is statutorially determined by the size of its surplus. Hence, every premium dollar that goes into the loss reserve inhibits income production. For this reason, a company with a large loss reserve, even though it may have sizable amounts of cash on hand, gives the appearance of unprofitability, making its stockholders unhappy and prospective investors wary. To avoid this negative impact, some companies underreserve, placing artificially low dollar values on the claims open against them. This is easily enough done; all the company has to do is tell its claims managers what it wants done. Deceptive underreserving, however, is a difficult trick to pull off over an extended period of time. It can be discovered by regulatory agencies, and if not by them, it will come to light when the time comes to pay off the claims that have been undervalued. This practice does not appear to be endemic to the malpractice insurance field.

According to some critics of the industry, however, its opposite, overreserving, may be.[58] Since loss reserves are liabilities and not assets, they are not taxable.[59] Hence, the more that goes into the loss reserve, the less tax the company pays. Moreover, since companies are permitted to use loss reserves for interest-earning purposes, the more that is put into them, the larger the company's source of tax-free investment capital.

Inflating the loss reserve also has another value for an insurance company. Whenever it is seeking a rate increase before a state insurance commission, it is permitted to prove its need not only in terms of actual payments to claimants but also by the amount that has been set aside for future payments. If this figure is exaggerated, the company's claims position looks worse than it is, and it is more likely to get the change it wants than if it had presented a truthful picture. Once the rate increase is obtained, the company can then re-reserve accurately, shifting money in this fashion back into surplus.

The casualty industry denies that overreserving occurs at all, much less in the malpractice field. As St. Paul explains it: "An insurer's financial records are an open book to fifty state regulators, the examining team of the National Association of Insurance Commissioners, the Internal Revenue Service, the outside auditing firm, and, in the case of St. Paul, an audit team of outside directors."[60] This may well be true of St. Paul, which is regarded as an excellently managed firm.[61] St. Paul's explanation, however, as a defense of the entire industry, is something less than convincing. The various state insurance commissioners, who make up the National Association of Insurance Commissioners, in most instances come to their jobs directly from the insurance industry, and some of them are not as vigilant about company practices as the public might hope. But even if they were all zealots in that regard, the chances they would ferret out wrongdoing are not great; the majority[62] do not even have actuarial staffs of their own to provide independent evaluations of rate requests, leaving these commissioners largely dependent on the statistics provided them by the insurers. Finally, although the Internal Revenue Service does indeed audit loss reserves to make sure an insurer isn't dodging taxes by overestimating them, IRS practices leave a lot to be desired. According to a spokesman[63] for the Insurance Services Office, a statistical arm of the insurance industry, IRS generally permits overreserving up to 15 per cent, which can come to quite a tidy sum when it is considered that loss reserves will easily reach the hundreds of millions of dollars for even a medium-sized company and the billions for a big one.

More importantly, it appears[64] that the IRS only looks for total overreserving and not overreserving by single lines of insurance. This makes it possible for insurers to estimate losses within acceptable limits when *company-wide* underwriting volume is considered, yet to overestimate them in the individual categories in which they are seeking their rate increases. Medical malpractice insurance, considering that it makes up only 1.5 per cent of the business the casualty industry writes (out of a total of $85 billion in 1975[65], is particularly susceptible to this kind of pinpointed overreserving, the existence of which is nearly impossible to discover unless the insurance commissioner from whom the rate increase is being sought is on the look-out for it, and then has the actuarial expertise to recognize it when he sees it.

Just because it is easy to do something, however, doesn't necessarily mean that it is done. While not deigning to defend its own reserving policies, St. Paul dealt with overreserving allegations by industry critics when it quoted the May 1975 issue of what it described as the "reputable and independent" *Professional Liability Newsletter.*[66] This publication, in the process of analyzing malpractice loss-reserve practices by Hartford Insurance Company in California, observed: "It is not difficult to evaluate reserving methods . . . once enough time has elapsed." (Time, however, is something that insurance commissioners often don't have when a demand for an immediate rate increase is before them.) "It is only necessary to take the closed claims and compare reserves on these claims against the actual amounts paid out. The first twelve months of Hartford's experience [in the early 1970s] has, by now"—i.e., 1975—"provided a substantial number of closed claims, and the losses compare favorably with the reserves."

Using that as a criteria, it is revelatory to turn to the experience of Argonaut Insurance as the official malpractice underwriter for the Pennsylvania Medical Society. By mid-1975, Argonaut had received a series of large rate increases; the most recent a whopping one of more than 200 per cent which the Society had not fought.[67] A group of surgeons did, however, when subsequent rate increases were demanded. As part of their brief, they submitted an analysis of Argonaut's loss reserves prepared by the St. Louis actuary firm of Nelson & Warren. The study found that Argonaut had overreserved—by 100 per cent—137 of 139 consecutive claims closed between May 1975 and March 1976, with the exaggerated figure one that Argonaut had included as a proof of loss when it sought its earlier rate increases. In total, Argonaut had set aside $2,049,000 to pay for these claims but actually paid out only $1,084,573. The study also noted that Argonaut had overreserved expense funds for handling the 139 claims at an even greater percentage variance. The loss reserve for this purpose was $509,280, yet actual expenses were only $148,891.[68]

The Nelson & Warren study subsequently came under attack by Argonaut which, according to a spokesman for its Pennsylvania agent, said the sample was too small.[69] The sample, of course, was exactly the kind the *Professional Liability Newsletter*, quoted with approval by St. Paul, said was ideal for determining whether or not a company was overreserving, and based on it, the Pennsylvania insurance commissioner rejected the Argonaut rate demand.

While it doesn't necessarily follow from the Nelson & Warren study that all of Argonaut's Pennsylvania claims are similarly overstated, or that the 139 claims are proof of any national policy on the part of Argonaut, it is evident that if the overreserving findings were true nationally, then rather than having lost $214 million (as the company told the Senate it had between 1971 and 1975), Argonaut would have netted at least $40 million, a figure that excludes earnings on investments.

Arguing against this profit theory is the fact that Argonaut, since 1975, has drastically cut down on its malpractice volume and apparently will be out of the field entirely when its contract with the Pennsylvania Medical Society expires. The reasons for any of Argonaut's underwriting decisions, however, are always difficult to figure. The company is controlled by a giant holding corporation, Teledyne, which at one point required Argonaut to turn $21 million over to it for purposes that had nothing to do with insurance but met Teledyne's other cash-flow problems.[70] (Best's Reports, the authoritative rating service of insurance companies, gives Argonaut a "deferred" status,[71] indicating the company did not supply sufficient or reliable information about its operation to allow Best's to recommend it for policy purchase or investment. By comparison, most of the other companies writing malpractice received an "A" for "Excellent" rating.) However, during the time Argonaut was demanding and receiving large increases to meet its supposed malpractice losses, the company was suffering sharp reversals in its substantial Workmen's Compensation insurance line, a field in which rate increases (at least of the size of the malpractice variety) are hard to come by.[72]

The important point, however, about the Argonaut findings is the evidence they provide to back the fundamental assertion by insurance industry critics that it is easy for a multiline company to produce phony losses by overreserving whenever it is to its interest. In this case, significantly enough, it was not any regulatory body (the kind in which St. Paul has such touching faith) or even the Medical Society, which had the contract with Argonaut, that discovered what was going on, but rather a group of maverick doctors who were lucky enough to get good legal advice and then had the kind of independent research done that brought the facts to light.

A second way in which a malpractice insurer can overestimate underwriting losses is to assign monetary values to incidents in which the patient has not asserted a claim. Under the terms of his policy, every customer is required to report to his insurer (though many of them don't[73]) any incident he thinks may subsequently lead to a suit. The insurance company investigates this information and will sometimes open a claim file, to which a dollar value may or may not be assigned. In its study of malpractice, *HEW discovered that approximately 40 per cent of all these reported incidents never result in any effort by the injured person to seek damages.*[74] Therefore, to the extent these non-asserted claims are assigned dollar values, the company doing so is showing losses on its books that it never incurs, and at the same time is showing a seriously inflated picture to the public of the actual frequency at which malpractice claims occur.

Although the dollar values assigned non-asserted claims are central to the entire issue of whether or not insurers are making a profit on malpractice underwriting, very little concrete information about the extensiveness of the practice is available. Insurance companies themselves never address this issue when they are describing losses, nor do insurance commissioners (despite the HEW finding) apparently ever bother to ask them about it. One insurance executive[75] has said that in his experience it is rare for a non-asserted claim to be assigned a dollar value, and that it is done only when it is "obvious" that a claim is about to be filed by the injured party. However, another executive in the same firm on the same day[76] said that assignment of dollar values to non-asserted claims was commonplace, a statement that was backed by a former insurance executive.[77] The one source that had this information available to it, the National Association of Insurance Commissioners, managed to avoid the subject in its four-volume study of the problem, and has since refused to answer questions raised on the issue.[78] This silence is in line with the NAIC's general perception of its responsibilities. Correspondence between it and HEW in 1975 and 1976 displays a consistent unwillingness by the NAIC to share with the federal government unpublished statistical information it had compiled.[79] It is as if the commissioners consider themselves members of a private club and not the tax-supported public servants they are.

Thus, until further studies are made—or information is revealed by those who know—it is impossible to estimate the impact the dollar valuations placed on non-asserted claims has in falsely swelling asserted insurance industry losses. However, some insurance companies are far more likely to open such claims than are others. As ISO noted: "Some companies may set up a claim file on the basis of only preliminary information relative to the case at hand and often incidents are closed quickly with no payment made. Other insurers may only establish claims files once fairly complete information is received."[80]

Relevant to the ISO observation is one set of statistics published by the NAIC. It purported to show, by company, how many claims result in payment to plaintiffs. The industry-wide average was 36 per cent, but with an extraordinary variation from company to company. For instance, St. Paul, according to the table, made payments on only 28 per cent of the claims raised against its customers; Travelers an astoundingly low 13 per cent. Yet, Medical Protective of Indiana was shown making payments on 60 per cent of the claims raised against it.[81] Taken at face value, it would appear that any doctor lucky enough to be insured by Travelers or St. Paul has a zealous guardian who will fight every claim tooth and nail, while the poor unfortunate covered by Medical Protective has a lax protector indeed.

The only trouble in coming to this conclusion is that it makes no sense at all. Medical Protective is the only insurance company in the nation that writes malpractice coverage exclusively, and were it an easy mark for claimants, it could not stay in business. Yet Medical Protective, far from going out of business, says that it is making a profit, just about the only company in the field that admits to so roseate a state of affairs.[82] (Medical Protective's profit possibilities are inherently better than most other companies since it largely limits its customer roster to low-risk doctors and to dentists who rarely get sued—and when they do only for small amounts.)

Then why does Medical Protective appear to be an easy mark for claims payments compared to all other companies? The only possible answer is that it, unlike the others, does not open a claims file until a claim is actually asserted. Precisely because its only source of premium income is from malpractice policies, it has a strong motive *not* to overreserve, because if it did, its surplus would be comparably reduced and with it the amount of business it would be permitted to write. The multiline companies, on the other hand, for whom malpractice is only a tiny part of their business, need have no such compunctions. They can open non-asserted claims at whatever rate and to whatever dollar amount is to their interest. In an entirely different context, St. Paul itself admitted that "nearly 50 per cent of every hundred claims are settled out of court as the result of negotiations with plaintiffs,"[83] indicating that its claims payment percentage on *asserted* claims is nearly double the figure reported to the NAIC. Incidentally, this figure doesn't even include those claims made against St. Paul customers that result in a jury verdict for the plaintiff. Therefore, if the non-asserted claims (some unknown percentage of which carry ghost loss-reserve figures) were deducted from the NAIC table, then most of the companies would be in line with the 60 per cent figure shown by Medical Protective. (But 60 per cent isn't correct either, as we shall see later.)

VI

In 1975 the casualty insurance industry attempted to refute allegations by its critics that, far from losing money in underwriting medical malpractice, it was not only making profits but exorbitant ones. In December of that year, an All-Industry Medical Malpractice Insurance Industry Committee submitted its official position to the United States Senate in a document entitled, "The Problems of Insuring Medical Malpractice."[84] Included on the committee were representatives from Aetna, St. Paul, Chubb & Sons, and Employers of Wausau insurance companies, along with the American Insurance Association (the lobbying body of the industry) and its two statistical arms, the Insurance Services Office and the American Mutual Insurance Alliance.

The keystone piece of evidence offered to prove the losses the industry was undergoing was the following:

TABLE I

Physicians and Surgeons Professional Liability Insurance Countrywide

(1) Policy Year Ending	(2) Total Premium Earned	(3) Total Claims and Claims Exp. Incurred	(4) Ratio of Claims to Premiums	(5) Expenses other than for Claims	(6) Ratio of Claims & All Expenses to Premiums
12/31/69	$20,545,602	$ 39,525,555	1.924	$ 6,225,317	2.227
12/31/70	32,804,038	51,776,375	1.578	9,939,626	1.881
12/31/71	49,514,002	72,141,183	1.457	15,002,743	1.760
12/31/72	67,575,119	109,444,032	1.620	20,475,261	1.922
12/31/73	75,877,678	158,711,822	2.092	22,941,299	2.394
Total	$246,316,439	$431,598,967	1.752	$74,584,246	2.055

TOTAL NET DEFICIT: ($246,316,439 – ($431,598,967 + $74,584,246)] – $259,866,774

Source: Insurance Services Office

The table is puzzling in a number of respects. It shows a premium volume of $32 million for 1970, yet HEW's survey of insurers (see Table H) discovered a minimal premium volume of $250 million for the same year, of which $170 million was accounted for by the physicians and surgeons who are the subject of Table I. Therefore, although it doesn't admit as much, the so-called "All-Industry" figures actually account for only one of every five dollars malpractice insurers took in that year from doctors. Further evidence is found when we turn to the year 1972. The All-Industry table shows $67 million in premium income for the entire country whereas a HEW count of premium volume from insurers in *just seven states* for the same year was $80 million.[85]

That the All-Industry Committee, in a document intended to influence the United States Senate, would fail to reveal the narrowness of its statistical base is disturbing. Nevertheless, Table I may still be credible as long as the 20 per cent representation accurately reflects industry income and expenditure on a national basis. But this is apparently not true either. Since the ISO was the statistical source of Table I, inquiry was made as to which companies and which states were incorporated in the published figures, and although ISO has generally been co-operative in aiding research in connection with this book, no response to that question was forthcoming.[86] However,

Federal Insurance Administrator Hunter estimates that no more than 25 per cent of all insurance companies writing malpractice coverage report to ISO,[87]—nor are the reporting companies representative geographically. For example, one company, which ISO has admitted elsewhere does not submit statistics to it,[88] is Employers of Wausau, even though it is represented on the All-Industry Committee. The absence of Employers' figures is relevant because during the entire period covered by the table, Employers was the official insurer for the New York State Medical Society,[89] indicating that Table I, by omitting Employers' figures, omits virtually all malpractice insurance information from the nation's second largest state, which produces 10 per cent of all its claims annually.[90] Moreover, another table in the All-Industry Report[91] indicates that St. Paul, which at the time was writing 15 per cent of the national malpractice insurance business, contributed as much as 50 per cent of the information that went into Table I. The table, therefore, appears to be askew geographically and is non-representative of the vast majority of the nation's malpractice insurers for the time period it covers.

However, even if we ignore that problem and accept Table I at face value, other problems in credibility arise.

For example, the table purports to show a net deficit from underwriting malpractice of nearly $260 million for the five years, which, assuming the table accounts for only 20–25 per cent of all claims during that period, suggests at least a $1 billion net loss for the industry. Yet the $260 million is not a real loss figure. It includes not only actual claims, claims expenses paid, and loss reserves (which, as we have seen can be inflated) but also IBNR's (incurred but not reported), those mysterious claims that companies say they *think* will be made but of which they have, as yet, no knowledge. That IBNR's, as with loss reserves, can be exaggerated is gleaned from another set of figures, ones submitted by Employers of Wausau to the New York State Insurance Commission.[92] In 1971 they showed an IBNR figure of $36 million for business written the previous policy year. Just one year later, however, after Employers had received a large rate increase from the Insurance Commission, the IBNR figure for 1970 marvelously shrank to less than $18 million, with only $6 million of the difference accountable by transfers to claims paid and loss reserves. The other $12 million in losses simply never occurred, and other evidence from the same statistics suggests that the loss reserves themselves may have been overestimated by as much as 25 per cent.[93]

Although it didn't deter them from using them, apparently the authors of the All-Industry Report were aware they were open to criticism by incorporating IBNR's in a net loss figure. As a consequence, they noted: "Eliminating reserves for claims not yet reported, the total of $431,598,967 for Column (3) would be reduced to approximately $200,000,000. The net deficit would then become approximately $30,000,000,"[94] a remarkable drop from the announced net loss of $259,866,774. This explanation raises the question of how a figure that includes unknown losses on unknown claims could be so specific ($431,598,967) and yet when it excludes them can only be expressed in "approximate" terms. In the face of this waffling, it is difficult to come to any conclusion other than that the IBNR's (which most state insurance departments won't accept as proof of loss[95]) were included in the report solely as a means of exaggerating loss in order to obtain favorable legislative consideration. When the significance of the IBNR's is appreciated, it becomes clear that the supposedly authoritative All-Industry Report is actually admitting that it doesn't know the industry's loss experience, that it could be anywhere from $30 million to $260 million, or if the loss reserves and the IBNR's have both been jacked up, the industry—or at least that quarter of it reflected in the table—may have made a profit. There is simply no way of knowing from the statistics offered.

Another problem with Table I is that it doesn't include any money the insurers earned on investing their malpractice premiums. Aware of this omission, twelve pages further on into the report, the authors state: "We now address a misunderstanding often voiced by some critics of the insurance industry, the fallacy that medical malpractice insurance is really profitable if one takes into consideration all of the investment income earned on the premiums that may be held for as long as ten years before losses are settled."[96] The report then goes on to conclude that the actual interest *earned on loss reserves* during the five-year period beginning in 1969 was 2.5 per cent, based on an assertion that claims payments ate up reserves before investment income could be realized.[97] However, in computing returns, the authors instead use a higher rate of return based on "actual returns on assets of 4.57% realized by the insurance business for 1971–73 [which produces a theoretical] average return on premium of 12.96% after taxes."[98] (The "after taxes" refers to taxes paid on interest earnings, since the loss reserves themselves are not taxable.)

Using the 12.96 per cent plus a figure of less than 1 per cent for investment income on "unearned premium reserve"—premiums are earned on a monthly basis on an annual policy; thus, after one month, a company has "earned" 1/12, and so on, but it can invest all of it—the report comes to the conclusion that the 1969–73 premiums earned $33,745,000 over the five-year period, leaving a net deficit, including IBNR's, of $226 million.[99]

There are a number of problems with this method of computing earnings, but the principal one is that the 12.96 per cent which the report says is a "healthy earning, certainly" may be nothing of the kind; rather, it appears to be grossly on the low side. Philipp Stern, actuary for the New Jersey Insurance Department, says that a realistic but still conservative estimate for that five-year period would be 19.2 per cent[100] while Federal Insurance Administrator Hunter observes that the 12.96 per cent fails to reflect compounded interest;[101] in his view, a 7 per cent per annum rate, or 35 per cent for the five years covered by the report, would be more fairly representative of the industry's actual earnings. Without calculating compound interest, it is apparent, therefore, that if Stern is correct, the investment earnings for 1969–73 actually came to $47 million, not $33 million, while if Hunter is right, the earnings reached about $91 million.

The problems with this report, however, go much deeper than just its inadequate statistical base, its misleading inclusion of IBNR losses, and its remarkable way of stating interest earnings. The real problem derives from the fact that the report, dated December 1975, confines all its statistics to premium years 1969–73 (i.e., calendar years 1968–72), and thus manages to ignore in its entirety, the rate increases the industry received during calendar years 1974 and 1975, a period during which, to use the industry's own estimates,[102] claims frequency rose by 30 per cent maximum while the industry's premium income doubled. It is evident, therefore, that if we extend Table I to 1974–75, a profit rather than a loss figure is discernible from it. Because of the inherent inadequacies of the table, however, such a calculation is of as limited value in defining profit as it is in proving loss.

CHAPTER TWELVE

They Won

I

To determine whether or not malpractice underwriting is profitable, it is necessary to measure premium income against costs over a meaningful time period. Choosing the proper elements for comparison, however, presents problems. As Table H in Chapter Eleven showed, the premium volume for any given year is a matter of dispute, while claims frequency, the basis for computing claims expenses, offers an equally confusing array of statistics; in Chapter Two, for example, we saw how apparently reputable sources quoted wildly disparate claims figures for the same year. Moreover, the All-Industry Report exhibits how losses can be maximized by choosing figures from a time span when income is rising less rapidly than claims.

The period between 1970 and 1976 offers a more relevant testing period. Unlike the All-Industry Report, it contains both the period during which the insurance industry was telling HEW that rates were adequate and the years in which the insurers sought and obtained their largest increases. Figures for 1977–78, however, cannot be incorporated. For them, the only available statistics are derived from insurance company statements about *required* income (see Table H), a goal that may or may not have been met. In the latter years of the 1970s, also, state-operated insurance funds and self-insurance mutuals played an increasingly large role in the malpractice insurance configuration, and no reliable statistics exist to permit any kind of breakdown of relative cash flows from the various sources. By limiting ourselves to 1970–76, therefore, we can concentrate only on those years in which more than 90 per cent of all premium income and expense dollars were in the control of the commercial underwriters.[1]

To estimate insurance industry income and expense between 1970 and 1976, we should select figures—based on adequate statistical sampling—that tend to favor the industry's contention that it is losing money, i.e., adopting conservative estimates for income and liberal ones for costs. By so doing, if the figures show that the industry is, despite its allegations to the contrary, making money, then there is no need to look at alternate hypotheses since they will only develop higher profits. By the same reasoning, if our "favorable" figures back the industry's loss contention, it is pointless to investigate further since we have no way of proving that the "unfavorable" figures we could select are any more reliable than the "favorable" ones. Consequently, in developing insurance company income for 1970, we will use Table H's conservative estimate rather than the much higher figure HEW developed. Similarly, for 1975 we will select the $1 billion rather than the $1.25 billion alternate estimate.

Based on that criteria, Table H is restated as follows:

YEAR	PREMIUM VOLUME
1970	$250,000,000
1971	$300,000,000
1972	$350,000,000
1973	$400,000,000
1974	$500,000,000
1975	$1,000,000,000
1976	$1,500,000,000
TOTAL	$4,300,000,000

To establish claims frequency, a number of options are open to us, all of which should lead to the same result in dollar terms. We can, for example, as the AMA has done,[2] create a very high figure by using total number of defendants, i.e., 2.1 defendants per claim.[3] Or we could concern ourselves solely with the number of claims that result in an effort by the injured party to gain payment, giving us a much lower figure. Finally, we can select claims incidents, i.e., events that led an insurer to open a file regardless of whether or not a claim was subsequently asserted. On balance, although it is misleading as to the size of real-claims volume, the last choice is the preferred one since it is congruent with the base used by the three most important studies of the problem, those of HEW, NAIC, and ISO.

But once we have selected our basis, we still have problems as to which numbers to use, although clearly whichever ones we select should come from the insurance industry itself since it is its assertions on losses we are testing. For that, we have two sets of figures available. A number of insurance sources, including ISO,[4] have stated that 6,000 claims files were opened in 1966 and that the number has increased at a 10–15 per cent rate every year since then. This would mean that in 1975 about 20,000 files were opened, a figure, incidentally, that has been quoted by Melvin L. Stark, executive vice-president of the American Insurance Association, a body hardly likely to indulge in underestimations.[5] The second set of figures was published by HEW,[6] based on statistics submitted to it by insurance companies. It showed 14,500 claims for the year 1970 which, if correct, means the 6,000 figure for 1966 is on the low side and so, therefore, will be the 20,000 for 1975. For our purposes, we will accept the HEW figures since they will produce a large claims volume, a figure again favorable to the industry's assertion that it is losing money. For the annual growth rate, we will adopt 12.5 per cent, the midway figure between the 10–15 per cent usually quoted by industry sources:

TABLE J

NUMBERS OF MEDICAL INJURIES LEADING TO THE OPENING OF MALPRACTICE CLAIMS FILES

YEAR	NUMBER OF INCIDENTS
1970	14,500
1971	16,313
1972	18,362
1973	20,657
1974	23,239
1975	26,144
1976	29,412
TOTAL	148,627

With claims volume known, we now only need obtain the average payment per claim to develop the seven-year claims cost total. The multiplier figure is available through the NAIC study, which—using

21,000 files closed between July 1, 1975, and June 30, 1976,[7]—discovered that when claims that led to payment and those that did not were taken together, the average payment per claim was $10,756.[8] In addition, the NAIC reported that expenses directly related to claims handling—principally for investigation and payment of defense attorney fees—was $1,879,[9] creating a total average cost of $12,634 per claim file. Because of inflationary factors, this figure, accurate for 1975–76, is probably somewhat high for the years preceding, but is sufficient for our purposes since any skewing is favorable to the insurance companies.

Carrying out this formula, we find that insurance claims payments and associated expenses for the period came to $1,877,753,518. To this total, it is necessary to add administrative expenses including commissions to agents. According to the insurance industry,[10] these expenses average 30 per cent of total premium volume, a percentage some critics argue[11] is on the high side, but which we will accept as asserted—thereby establishing a $1,290,000,000 for that category.

When these two figures are added together, we see that between 1970 and 1976, total malpractice insurance expenses reached slightly over $3.16 billion ($3,167, 753, 518) during a time in which insurance industry income was $4.30 billion. If we assume that the commercial companies were responsible for only 90 per cent of the volume (in both income and expenses), the *industry profits still reached over $1 billion* in the seven-year period or almost 30 per cent on premium income compared to the 5 per cent profit margin the industry itself says it tries to maintain.

The NAIC report provides evidence suggesting that, if anything, this projected profit figure is on the low side. The 21,000 claims it studied produced total payments of $224 million during a twelve-month period in which insurance company income exceeded $1 billion.[12]

Moreover, a study of Best's Insurance Guide indicates that for the year 1976 alone, the profit on malpractice underwriting was approximately 50 per cent.[13] These profit projections consider only premium income. They do not take into consideration all the additional profits insurers earn by investing their income.

Therefore, the best evidence available, indicates that malpractice underwriting is profitable for the insurance industry, highly so and that the public and the medical profession are victims of flimflammery when they are led to believe it is not.

II

This finding, however, cannot be taken to mean that the companies that left the field in the 1973–75 period gratuitously shoved profits overboard. It is evident, rather, from our analysis that it was only following the 1975–76 rate increases that underwriting profits reached the 30 per cent level. Prior to that time, although underwriting seems to have been profitable overall, the level was minimal, and it is highly likely that some individual companies were writing at rates that produced underwriting losses. (As we shall see, they may have had good reason for doing so.)

Based on this consideration, the flight of the insurers following the HEW iatrogenesis report is expicable for the reasons given in the previous chapter. There does appear, however, to be a subcurrent involved which shows that insurance industry executives, like ordinary mortals, don't always make their decisions on the basis of pure reason. What happened unfolded in this fashion: First, there was the group of companies, many of which had dangerously small malpractice customer pools, that dropped the line immediately following the HEW revelation. Then, in 1974 the second shoe dropped when Lloyds of London, a company with a legendary reputation of insuring risks that no one else would accept, created panic in the industry by announcing that it too was dropping malpractice. According to Federal Insurance Administrator Hunter,[14] Lloyds was responding to the exodus of the first group of American companies, figuring they must know something it didn't know. As soon as Lloyds got out, still other American companies, figuring Lloyds knew something *they* didn't know, decided it was time for them to leave.

Meanwhile, several of the companies that didn't quit began to limit their customer rolls, usually by dumping their high-risk customers on the newly formed state-operated insurance funds created for that purpose. All this ferment gave the survivors the best of all possible worlds: They were able to get rid of their most suit-prone doctors to the state funds, thereby increasing their profits even further, and at the same time, because so many companies had left the field, they had next to no competition to drive down rates wherever they decided to continue to sell policies. Since the shakeout of the mid-1970s, in fact, the exodus of the commercial insurers has nearly ceased, with Argonaut the only announced defector since that time. That these companies, including such large ones as Aetna, Hartford, Travelers, and St. Paul, have stayed is just one more indication that the profit potential from malpractice underwriting is excellent. (St. Paul has dropped many customers for other reasons which will be discussed later.)

If this synopsis were the complete explanation of what occurred in the malpractice field between 1973 and the present, it would then appear that we are dealing essentially with a series of benign factors by which a reasonable fear of unlimited claims growth gave way to panic, which led to high rates and limited insurance availability, which, in turn, accidentally benefited the companies that decided to tough it out.

There was, however, another crisis also at work that had nothing to do with malpractice claims per se and may have provided an even more significant reason for the flight of some companies and the concomitant demand for rate increases, both on the part of the companies that stayed and those who sought them even as they were making plans to leave. This crisis had its origin in the investment policies common to the casualty industry throughout the 1960s and into the mid-1970s. As the business publication *Forbes Magazine* explained it in an April 1976 article: "It was normal practice for these [casualty] companies to invest an amount equivalent to their legal surpluses in common stocks—figuring that if they could just break even on underwriting, a rising stock market would give them a nice profit. This encouraged a rather greedy attitude: Why not shave rates to generate more premiums to invest in the market? Who needed underwriting profits when the stock market was certain to keep going up? As the growth-stock mania spread in the late Sixties, many insurance companies went in deeper and deeper. By 1971, some companies owned stock worth 1.6 times their legal reserves."[15]

A. Addison Roberts, chairman of the board of the Reliance Insurance Companies, spoke in 1975 on the same subject: "As an industry we were blinded by a cash-flow theory that rested solely on a rising stock market and the investment income that would offset our underwriting losses. Hence, you saw companies 'buying' business, quoting rates everybody knew they couldn't make money on. But the stock market beckoned for still more and more cash to earn us more and more income and increase our surplus. It was an irresistible temptation. The chance to overcome cyclicality. To avoid tough, unpopular decisions. To ride *with* the current. At any rate, paraphrasing Shakespeare, competition made cowards of us all, and in the name of flowing cash and investment income, we wrote at rates that could have come out of *Alice in Wonderland*."[16]

While Roberts' fascinating mixture of literary allusions may overstate the case somewhat, he is correct that "buying" business occurred, and in the medical malpractice field it ordinarily took the form of a contract with a state or local medical society.

These contracts were highly lucrative as cash-flow producers. For example, let us suppose that a medical society has 10,000 members who are paying, on the average, $3,000 a year for their malpractice insurance, each premium payable at the beginning of the year. By obtaining a contract with that society, the lucky insurer, if he brings all the members on board, takes in $30 million in cash in one swoop to be used to make money on the stock market. To obtain that amount of revenue elsewhere, the same insurer might have to sell as many as 100,000 automobile-owner policies, spread across the nation, with the premiums payable at different times. So attractive was the medical society business that some insurers,[17] including Argonaut,[18] offered a 1 per cent kickback to the contractee medical society on each premium written in order to encourage the society to propagandize its members to join up with the favored insurer. This ploy was necessary because there was no legal way the society could force its members to switch from their old company to the contract insurer if they didn't want to.

Such contracts were not without their risks. By their terms, the contractor was required to accept every doctor who wanted to join. He could usually subsequently drop a claims-prone doctor, although, in some circumstances, the doctor had the right to appeal through the medical society, which, if successful, could force the insurer to continue to carry him. Since low-risk doctors often stayed with their old insurer, which might offer competitive rates to keep them, the result was the contractor was likely to pick up a disproportionately large number of the high-risk ones who turned to it when their existent insurer either dropped them or raised their rates. However, as long as the emphasis was on obtaining the quick-cash fix for stock market gambling, the risks were generally ignored.

Instructive are some events that occurred in California. For many years, the Southern California Medical Association (SCMA) had its members covered by the relatively small Nettleship Company.[19] In

1970 Nettleship, noting a sharp rise in claims frequency, asked for a rate increase. The 9,000 doctors covered by the contract[20] objected. At that point, the giant Hartford Company entered the picture, telling the SCMA that it would insure its members without a rate increase[21] if it became the contractor, and the happy doctors agreed. A couple of years passed and Hartford now began to demand large rate increases,[22] and this time it was another giant, Travelers, that rode to the rescue, again promising to hold the line on rates[23] if the SCMA would join with it. They did so. Meanwhile, the Northern California Medical Association had signed a similar highly favorable contract with Argonaut. Then the turn-about occurred. In 1975, just a year after its bargain with the SCMA was struck, Travelers filed rate increases which upped premiums by 25 per cent; six months later, it demanded still another rate hike, this one of more than 100 per cent in most categories, and just six months after that still another increase of 200–300 per cent in all categories.[24] The result was the 1975 antirate strike by the California doctors.

Eventually Travelers remained in California[25] even though it didn't get all it had demanded (suggesting that what it got was sufficient); Argonaut, on the other hand, was alleged by the North California Association to have breached its contract[26] beginning a lengthy period of acrimonious litigation.

As the California situation was developing, Argonaut also worked to break similar contracts in New York, Florida, and Pennsylvania.[27] In Pennsylvania, where, it will be recalled, the medical society was getting a 1 per cent kickback, it only opposed Argonaut reneging on the contract and did not fight the rate increase demanded as a condition for staying.[28] This approach left the Pennsylvania Insurance Commissioner, in his own mind, with no choice but to approve the rate demand, even though in so doing he described Argonaut's tactics as reminiscent of a "protection racket"[29] (pay us what we demand or else we will hurt you, in this instance by leaving the members uninsured). It was only subsequent to that rate increase that the maverick group of surgeons produced the Nelson & Warren study with its evidence that Argonaut had misstated its Pennsylvania losses through overreserving.

As this history makes clear, first Hartford and then Travelers and Argonaut had been "buying" business in California, just as Roberts said was happening, to get money for the stock market. The subsequent frenzied activity that occurred in California and elsewhere to break the contracts, or to force the members to want to break them when confiscatory rate increases were announced, meant that these contracts (and similar low rate offers elsewhere throughout the casualty industry) had suddenly no longer become desirable. The bubble, in fact, had burst. The stock market, for which the money was to be used, instead of continuing to go up and up and up, had suddenly gone down and down and down.

By early 1974 the Dow Jones average—which had jumped over the magic mark of 1,000 in 1972—had dropped to the low 800's. Worse was to come. In the third quarter of 1974, investor panic reached near 1929 proportions when the average skidded further to 607.[30] By that time, the stock market decline had caused some casualty insurers *losses that reached 80 per cent of their surplus.*[31]

Troubles rarely come singly, and so it was for the casualty industry. Simultaneous with the collapse of the market was a dizzying upward spiral in inflation, which reached a 15 per cent rate in the 1972–74 period,[32] causing a serious impact on the cost of doing business. To overcome this, the insurers sought across-the-board rate increases in all fields, but not invariably successfully because the public was under the same inflationary crunch, and their elected representatives, pressed by consumer lobbies, felt obliged to hold the line if they wanted to get re-elected. Adding further to the insurer distress was the mounting number of claims in many lines in addition to malpractice. Product liability suits, for example, were being filed at a record rate, presenting a much more serious problem than malpractice since product insurance accounted for fifteen per cent of all liability underwriting[33] compared to the 1.5 per cent for malpractice. During this period a number of auto insurers were hit by claims demands brought on by the passage of no-fault auto laws in about twenty states.[34] Although none of the big companies were affected by this, a number of the small ones, already suffering the effects of stock market losses and inflation, couldn't stand the gaff and went bankrupt. One such company left its stockholders with losses exceeding $30 million and policyholders in three states with worthless insurance on which they had spent $50 million.[35]

In 1974 the combination of rising claims and inflation caused casualty underwriting losses estimated at $1.8 billion,[36] a situation made desperate by the fact that the stock market losses for that year alone reached $3.3 billion.[37] As a result, the insurers began to sell off their stock holdings for whatever they could get in an effort to achieve cash balances for their upcoming annual statements, in that way hopefully keeping stockholders unaware of the real size of the losses that were being sustained.[38] Unfortunately for them, their largest scale selling occurred at the very bottom of the market. Had they held out a few months more, they would have made money. As it was, the casualty industry ultimately suffered a net stock market loss of $10 billion.[39]

Among those hardest hit were insurers in the malpractice business. One of the first to "throw in the towel on stocks," *Forbes* reported, was St. Paul. A billion dollar company in premium volume[40] St. Paul had a "shrinkage of $104 million after taxes in portfolio value in 1973 and another $108 million in 1974 . . . [Even so o]n December 31, 1974, it was still sitting with common stocks that had cost it $116 million but [now] had a market value of only $61 million . . . This vast shrinkage had left St. Paul badly exposed. Its premiums now amounted to 5.4 times remaining policyholder surplus. Since then it has returned to 4.6"[41] (A 4:1 ratio is considered safe; some experts prefer 2:1.[42])

Also hard hit were such major malpractice insurers as Aetna, Hartford and Travelers.[43] A. M. Best & Co., the insurance industry rating service, confirmed the *Forbes* analysis. Aetna's problems, Best found, had been particularly severe. Referring to Aetna Casualty & Surety (the Aetna corporation that handles its malpractice underwriting), Best noted that the company's net surplus at the end of 1972 had been $535,011,000; however, "substantial depreciation on the market value of security holdings during 1973 and 1974, coupled with a sizable underwriting loss in 1974, caused shrinkage in such sources of $217,230,000 by December 31, 1974, [even though] in that year the parent holding company made a surplus contribution of 50 million."[44] Travelers had similar problems. Its policyholder surplus shrank from $403 million in 1972 to $303 million in 1974 with "[t]he major portion of the . . . losses occur[ing] in 1974 as management philosophy calls [*sic*] for a reduction in equities holdings . . . with regard to the securities market and net resources."[45] In other words, when Best's gobbledegook prose is scraped clean, most of their loss was due to the stock market collapse.[46] As for St. Paul: "Policyholders' surplus and special reserve funds at the close of 1975 were $184,721,000 as compared to $142,887,000 possessed a year earlier . . ." which sounds good until one notes the $339,168,000 which the company had at the end of 1972. "Shrinkage," says Best of St. Paul, "in net resources during 1973 and 1974 mainly reflected realized capital losses of approximately $58 million and depreciation in the market of security holdings of about $218 million."[47] So it went throughout almost all the rest of the industry to one degree or another.

It was during the year that the stock market crisis was at its worst that malpractice premium income rose from $500 million to $1 billion, and in the year following climbed another $500 million. Was there a connection?

Not at all, if we believe most of the malpractice insurers. Senator Edward Kennedy of Massachusetts asked them that question as part of a 1975 investigation of the malpractice crisis.[48] Of all the companies questioned only Argonaut admitted: "Investment income is frequently taken into consideration for ratemaking." Aetna on the same subject: "In most companies, actuaries are responsible for developing appropriate rates. Investment Departments are responsible for investments. Actuaries do not change their methodology to reflect current stock market conditions . . . In other words, the operations are separate and each department will meet its own responsibilities. The only impact that stock market losses will have on our operation would be to reduce our capacity to assume risks."[49]

Aetna, therefore, is saying that stock market losses might cause a company to cut back or eliminate its malpractice underwriting (the path some companies took) if it considered it to be too risky in view of reduced surplus, but that it would never ever *raise* rates to recoup money the company had lost on stock market gambling. Travelers hewed even more vigorously to the same line: "The formal rate-making process," it told Kennedy, "and the judgmental factors included therein are in no way linked to a particular company's stock market results. Capital gains or losses reflecting the outcome of a company's investment operations, as with its underwriting results, may affect corporate management decisions on general risk-taking philosophy but have no place in individual account pricing."[50]

St. Paul agreed. "Stock market losses," it said, "reduce capital and surplus, but have no effect on the rate-making process . . . However, the reduction of capital and surplus can reduce a company's ability to keep up with an increasing need for insurance. Rates for malpractice insurance, as for other coverages, are based on claims experience and claims trends. Reserves for claims to be paid are liabilities, not assets, and stock market losses affect assets, not liabilities."[51] True enough, but a sizable portion of the money lost on the stock market came from loss reserves, thereby having a direct effect on assets. In another document submitted to the Kennedy committee, St. Paul capped its argument by observing: ". . . there is no way insurance department regulators would permit insurance companies to recover stock market losses through boosting insurance rates."[52]

This statement is not credible. Since, as was noted earlier, relatively few insurance commissions had their own actuaries, they lacked any independent avenue by which they could assess whether or not demanded rate increases related to stock market losses. Indeed, until 1976 or 1977, it was almost unheard of for insurance commissioners to inquire into investment earnings of a company seeking a rate increase,[53] and to do so now is hardly uniform practice. (Thus, for example, an insurance company will show a commissioner that it is losing 5 per cent at its current underwriting rates, but neither it nor the insurance commissioner will develop the fact that the company may be earning 10 per cent on its investments, giving it a 5 per cent net profit without the rate increase.) Even more pertinently, insurance commissioners aren't in business to punish carriers when they lose money on their investments. On the contrary, the whole reason for the existence of an insurance commission, no matter how poorly it may perform that function, is to protect its citizens who are policyholders of the company. Therefore, when an insurance company, which is otherwise well managed, is temporarily threatened with insolvency because of investment losses, an insurance commissioner is likely to be sympathetic and grant the recoupment rate increases because he doesn't want to drive the company out of business, and thus cause the policyholders in his state to lose the money they have paid out and the protection they receive from their policies.

Moreover, if recoupment of stock market rather than underwriting losses was the main purpose for increasing rates, malpractice offered a particularly easy way to get the money needed. In the mid-1970s insurance commissioners' ignorance of the intricacies of malpractice underwriting was nearly absolute. It wasn't, in fact, until 1975[54] that most commissions began to require underwriters to submit current information on malpractice claims experience. As a consequence, the commissions had no background to go by when the underwriters coupled their demands for rate increases with a threat to leave doctors uninsured if they didn't get what they wanted. The capitulations that occurred provided the casualty insurers who wrote malpractice with a billion dollar booster shot at exactly the time their stock market losses made that infusion necessary.

There was one malpractice insurer that didn't ask for big rate increases between 1974 and 1976, and its non-action stands as testimony to the relationship between the market losses and the rate increases received by the other companies. The holdout was Medical Protective, the only company that writes only malpractice and the only company to admit it makes a profit doing so. Medical Protective, unlike its giant cousins in the malpractice field, had conservative investment policies and therefore took no bath in the stock market and had no losses it had to recoup. As a result, between 1974 and 1976, its rate requests were both few and in keeping with actual perceived increases in claims liability.

In short, the gamblers, having dissipated their money, demanded that the people who had given them the money in the first place now not only make good their losses but guarantee them a profit in the future.

III

One final question remains unanswered: Why, if malpractice underwriting is now profitable, have the companies that left the field not gotten back into it?

There can be several reasons. One is a wait-and-see attitude. Many companies want to watch the progress of the various state-operated insurance funds in order to get a free informational ride about claims trending before making any decision. Still others are unwilling to get back in because they fear they might find themselves stuck, at least initially, with dangerously small pools of high-risk doctors.

A third reason, has its origin in the experience gained from the stock market crash. Because of it, the casualty insurers realized they could no longer, with any confidence, consider their premium dollars as so many gambling chips. Rather, to assure maximum corporate profitability, it was now imperative to value premium volume as the prime profit maker, which meant finding ways to build volume through rate increases and decrease the money going out the back door in the form of claims payments. In order to accomplish this, pressures had to be developed to force legislators to take actions favorable to the casualty insurers. Enlightened self-interest, therefore, dictated that it didn't make sense to re-enter a field like malpractice, thereby renewing competition and driving the artificial high rates downward. On the contrary, as long as malpractice remained difficult to obtain and required the continued existence of state-supported funds, the crisis went on and so did the leverage to get the reforms the insurers wanted. (One lawsuit, still unresolved, filed in Rhode Island, charged that something more than enlightened self-interest was involved; it averred the existence of an antitrust conspiracy entered into by St. Paul and several other companies by which St. Paul was guaranteed it would have no competition in the market.[55])

There are, of course, many ways in which insurers can bring about reduced claims payments, thereby, theoretically anyway, assuaging their lust for higher rates. For one thing, they can mount campaigns to force their customers to adopt accident-prevention measures. Automobile insurers, for instance, could get behind consumer efforts to require manufacturers to produce safer cars; they could further back legislation to penalize food, clothing, and other product manufacturers who place dangerous items on the market; and they could work with doctors and hospitals to institute risk-management systems to reduce liability in that area. Although occasionally insurers pay lip service to this kind of strategy, and in the case of some of the malpractice insurers something more than that,[56] for the most part the lobbying effort and the lobbying dollars have gone in a different direction. The priorities of this campaign were well described in 1975 by A. Addison Roberts, the chief executive of Reliance Insurance, one of the nation's largest casualty companies. In a speech, apparently not intended for public consumption, delivered to a convention of insurance agents meeting in Bermuda, Roberts, whose company has had little involvement in medical malpractice, used that field to explain what the problem was and how he and his colleagues were going to go about solving it. "In the past six years," Roberts stated, "it's estimated the number of physicians' and surgeons' malpractice claims has soared 1,000%." (ISO, in fact, estimates 90 per cent.[57]) "Million dollar awards are not unusual." (NAIC, in fact, discovered ten cases of 20,800 nationwide or 4/100 of 1 per cent in which $1 million or more was awarded.[58]) "In California, last year the awards to 74 plaintiffs who won their cases averaged $133,817."[59] (NAIC, in fact, found that the average indemnity paid to a winning plaintiff in California at that time was $31,407.[60])

Having proven, in this fashion, the desperate nature of the problem, Roberts then pointed out that in spite of the large rate increases that had taken place, "there are indications that malpractice insurers may still sustain $300 of ultimate losses for each $100 they collect in premiums. So these insurers must either raise their rates to cover these incredible [*sic*] losses, or withdraw from the field. But if they withdraw, what physicians could continue to practice?"[61] Proceeding from that vantage point of public service, Roberts observed that insurance companies are nothing if not socially responsible and therefore should be freed of any regulations of the rates they charge: "One thing [we] must continue to work for is . . . the enactment of open rating laws," he declared. ". . . In those states where there is a long history of pricing freedom, such as California, there is no evidence that the consumer has been charged excessive rates." (This will come as a surprise to the California doctors.) "The very fact that there are hundreds of insurance companies competing under a free-pricing mechanism is, in itself, just about a guarantee against excessive profits."[62]

As important as removing government regulation of rates might be, it's tort reform that, as Roberts sees it, is the key to the malpractice solution. "Daily," he declared, "we read that the various legislatures are considering a wide range of proposals for solving the current medical malpractice crisis. Unfortunately, many of the proposed approaches are not designed to provide an economically sound, long-range solution to the problem . . . For example, the joint underwriting association approach [i.e., government-operated emergency insurance funds] which spreads the risk among all liability underwriters is not in itself an adequate or sound solution. This type of transfer remedy merely shifts one of the problems of the medical profession onto unrelated groups, and unjustly places the burden on liability underwriters." (While it is difficult to understand on whom the burden should be placed if not liability underwriters, most joint underwriting associations, *remove* that burden and place it squarely on the medical profession.) However, says Roberts: "Perhaps we should consider a trade-off of sorts, in which we accept a joint underwriting association or pool approach for a specified period (say, one year, or three years) with the understanding that the necessary legal and medical reforms will be made during that period. But we should do so *only* if it is clearly agreed that the essential reforms will be effected by that time."[63] Otherwise, the insurance companies should pull out of malpractice entirely.

While it is this sort of blackjacking approach that has, no doubt erroneously, caused some people to think the insurance industry's interest in the public welfare is dim indeed, not all insurance sources agree with Roberts. They would go further. One or two spokesmen[64] have advocated that doctors be relieved of the necessity of carrying malpractice insurance at all and the burden be placed instead on the patients who, to have any chance of recovering damages, would have to buy a malpractice-injury policy upon entering the hospital, presumably out of a slot machine such as those patronized by catastrophe-fearing airlines passengers. When one thinks of the 25,000 or so claims arising from hospital accidents each year and posits that against 40 million hospital admissions, it is apparent that the insurance company profits from that reform would beggar even those now obtained from insuring the medical providers. Still other industry spokesmen would no longer allow the public to get before a jury with a malpractice claim, forcing them to pursue their case against a doctor before a panel of his fellow doctors.[65] That, it is suspected, will considerably cut down on plaintiff verdicts.

Almost without exception, these proposals aim either to remove or limit plaintiffs' access to the courts for redress of injury or to reduce the amount insurers have to pay out, under any circumstances, when a claim is made against them.

To ask people to accept such changes, which on the face of them seem against their interest, is not an easy task, but it can be accomplished. A case in point is the history of no-fault automobile insurance, a reform desired by the major insurers in that field.[66] Propaganda emanating from them was designed to lead people to believe that rising costs in automobile insurance coverage was related to a stupendous increase in claims brought about by those who faked injury (the "whiplash" syndrome) and by clever and greedy lawyers who found ways to get their clients more money than they deserved. The onslaught of phony and doubtful claims, it was pointed out, resulted in such crowding of the court calendars that payment to those who were genuinely injured was delayed for years. No-fault, it was argued, would speed payment to the deserving (one benefit) and, by reducing the number of non-meritorious and expensive law suits, cause a reduction in rates (another benefit). To accomplish this great good, all the public had to do was give up its unlimited right to sue.

Agreeing with this reasoning were many consumer groups as well as such individual articulate spokesmen as Pennsylvania's then insurance commissioner Herbert Denenberg who had gained a national reputation as an insurance industry critic. The emergence of allies such as these was ideal for the insurers who could now stand behind them, nearly invisible. After all, would consumer advocates lie to consumers about what was good for them? The advocates certainly didn't intend to, but, once no-fault was passed, the insurers were able to point with alarm to a new rise in claims (predictable all along) which gave them an excuse to demand exorbitantly high rate increases,[67] while, at the same time, their cost per claim was reduced. (The initial rise of claims in the no-fault states also had the subsidiary value of helping force out of business some of the big insurers' marginal competitors.) Although some insurers had long perceived the desirability of auto no-fault, the big push for it chronologically coincided with the $10 billion stock market debacle, with the increases in rates that were forthcoming arriving exactly at the time the insurers needed the money the most, just as had occurred for the malpractice insurers.

Medical malpractice, in fact, offered an even better launching pad for tort reforms than did the automobile no-fault campaign. Auto insurance, after all, was a major profit item for many companies, and consequently a certain amount of circumspection was required in their dealings with insurance commissions and legislators. Not so with medical malpractice; it was such a miniscule part of the industry's total annual volume that its loss was well worth the sacrifice if gains were to be forthcoming by doing so. Therefore, realistic threats, of the sort advocated by Roberts, could be made. If they didn't work in a certain state, then the insurers would simply walk out as they said they would, forcing the state to find other ways to provide insurance to its doctors, until such time that the insurance companies, at their leisure, might decide to re-enter the state. However, if the threats did work and favorable legislation was passed as a result, then the insurers had gained not only laws likely to make their malpractice underwritings more profitable but had also created laws that could readily be extended to other fields of insurance—like products liability—in which their financial stake was much greater. It was the kind of situation insurance companies like best: no-risk.

Every bit as much to their liking in the malpractice equation was the quality of allies they attracted, the doctors. Unlike manufacturers of faulty products, who enjoy precious little public sympathy, the medical profession had always held widespread respect and was likely to be believed when it talked about "litigious" patients with "unrealistic expectations" who forced doctors to practice "defensive medicine," defined as a bad thing. The growth in malpractice litigation, therefore, could be presented as a danger to the quality of medical care that people received, a frightening prospect. Moreover, as the malpractice rates went up, the doctors were quick, as we shall see, to point out to their patients that it was they who were ultimately shouldering the financial burden in the form of higher fees, in that way enlisting grass-roots support for changes to reduce those costs, the same siren song that had been sung with automobile no-fault.

The same villains were found, too. Strategically, as with no-fault, it was unwise to blame the public as a whole for the problem, since its support was required to get the desired legislation passed. Hence, the enemy had to be perceived as individual greedy patients (analogous to the whiplash litigants in automobile accident cases) and (as *Medical Opinion* magazine defined them) their "aggressive" lawyers, who, as one insurance industry analyst put it, had turned the tort system into a "giant lottery."[68] Since without a lawyer, an injured patient, greedy or otherwise, wouldn't get far in pursuing a claim, the most fruitful line of attack was the one aimed at the lawyers. Making large sums of money out of malpractice cases, any response they made to criticisms leveled against them could be easily dismissed by the (self-interested) doctors and the (self-interested) insurance companies as self-interested.

CHAPTER THIRTEEN

Justice Not Served

I

The legal professon has never enjoyed the veneration accorded the medical. Although doctors seem to strike a warm shamanistic chord in the human psyche, lawyers are seen as the couriers of power, binding people, not with thongs, but with words. "The first thing let's do, we'll kill all the lawyers," said Shakespeare in *Henry VI*, a thought no doubt as welcome by the groundlings of our day as of his.

Not all lawyers, however, are held in equal public disesteem. Many a prosecuting attorney has become a public hero, as has an occasional criminal lawyer as long as his clients, like Perry Mason's, are white, middle class, and therefore not dangerous whatever they do. Perhaps held in highest regard of all is the corporation lawyer; moving in the best of social circles, he rarely sullies himself by entering a courtroom, and when he does he comports himself as a gentleman in a manner befitting the capitalist system he represents. John Mitchell and Richard Nixon are examples.

At the lowest end of the scale are the negligence lawyers, the ones who represent malpractice clients. The common view held of them was expressed by Senator Claiborne Pell of Rhode Island, a legislator whose mastery of syntax matches his contributions to the public weal:

Senator PELL. (Speaking at 1975 malpractice hearings presided over by Senator Edward Kennedy.) I have heard that in Massachusetts, the chairman's state, that when they outlawed no-fault [he means when they passed no-fault] then there was the class of lawyers that were interested in that kind of work, and moved into the field, and the result was malpractice suits jumped up substantially; is that a correct statement?

Mr. Hunter. The timing of the jump might indicate that would be so, but I really have no direct knowledge of that.

Senator Pell. Is there any experience in other states showing when you rule out no-fault that the *ambulance-chasing lawyers* move into this field?[1] (Italics added.)

Hunter said no, but Pell's description lingers. Ambulance chasing means solicitation of clients, a practice considered unethical by the American Bar Association when negligence lawyers, many of whom are Jewish, do it among the poor, but proper when blue-blood attorneys do it on a country club golf course. The phrase itself (like *Medical Opinion*'s use of the anti-Semitic code word "aggressive") is designed to make people wary of the lawyers they would otherwise go to when they have been injured. To the extent they fear falling into the hands of the ambulance-chasers, their claims are not pursued, a matter of no small financial benefit to business interests having spokesmen such as Senator Pell.

Ambulance chasing, often charged but rarely proven, is not the only allegation made against the negligence lawyer. Ethically an attorney is not supposed to accept a tort case unless there are legal grounds by which the plaintiff has a right to recovery. Yet the negligence lawyer often violates that principle, according to his critics. Because he works on a contingency fee he collects only if he wins, and then only if he can collect what he has won. Therefore, it does him little good to sue an impecunious defendant, since neither he nor his client will get a penny out of such a victory no matter how well-merited.

Defendants who carry insurance are another matter entirely. They are said, in lawyer jargon, to have "deep pockets,"[2] meaning they have the money (through their insurance) to pay for verdicts against them. As a result, it is believed, negligence lawyers will often accept "deep pocket" cases lacking in legal merit, not only because they can collect if they win, but also because they believe that juries are more likely to return a verdict against a defendant who carries insurance—a business firm, an automobile driver, a doctor—than one who does not. Jurors, according to this folklore, don't consider insurance company money "real" money and are happy to grab some out of the company's deep pocket and give it to the plaintiff, at which point, presumably, it becomes "real." It is, therefore, primarily the insurer's ability to pay, not the negligence of his clients, that has created the rash of injury claims pocking the court calendars in recent years. Of all these deep-pocket cases, malpractice is supposedly among the most attractive to the negligence lawyer because of its potential for very large verdicts. A person who receives a broken leg in an automobile accident may collect only $3,000 and his lawyer $1,000, but the person who is lucky enough, from the lawyer's point of view, to have been crippled by the doctor who treated the broken leg might well win $50,000 to several hundred thousand dollars (see Chapter Five). The lawyer thereby earns himself a fee of anywhere from $17,000 to $100,000 depending on his contingency percentage arrangement with the client.

The assertion that the non-meritorious case is commonplace in malpractice litigation comes from both insurance and medical sources. The Insurance Information Institute,[3] has stated that "slightly more" than half of all malpractice claims are found to be without merit, a belief concurred in by Dr. Norman Blackman in a 1975 statement made when he was president of the King's County (N.Y.) Medical Society. According to Blackman, a substantial majority of malpractice suits "have no merit . . . the best doctors have the most malpractice suits brought against them because they do the riskiest procedures that require the greatest skills . . ."[4] Or as an AMA spokesman put it: "You end up with a situation where every time medical care doesn't effect a cure, there's a law suit filed."[5] The same reasoning was expressed by Dr. George Northrup, president of the American Osteopathic Association and a member of the HEW Malpractice Commission: "It is my opinion that if . . . bad health-care providers were removed from the medical community overnight, the malpractice problem, or better stated the professional liability problem, would remain," since lawyers would continue to bring lucrative non-meritorious suits.[6] Dr. Charles A. Hoffman of West Virginia, a former president of the American Medical Association and also a member of the HEW Malpractice Commission, was even more specific: "Of the many injuries to patients which occur every year," he declared, "only a small percentage are caused by substandard performance or misconduct of providers of health care. Only this small proportion of injuries are legally compensable. Nevertheless, where an injury is permanent or severe, a claim for legal compensation is likely to arise regardless of how the injury was caused . . . [because] it is likely that the amount of compensation would be very substantial if liability can be established. In these circumstances, the lawyer is more likely to agree to representation, even though the issue of liability may be very doubtful. With the anticipation of a large percentage legal fee, the lawyer is more likely to take a chance that he will be able to find some basis for liability . . ."[7]

The ideal basis for the non-meritorious suit, it is frequently observed, is the "sympathetic" plaintiff, one who has been hideously scarred, crippled, blinded, or brain-damaged, best of all a child who can then be paraded in front of the jury. Swayed by the medical tragedy it sees before it, the jurors ignore evidence showing that negligence played no part in the injury, and teary-eyed dip deep into the deep pocket of the (insurance company) defendant.

Malpractice lawyers, however, are accused not only of bringing non-meritorious suits to win a big verdict, and a big fee for themselves, but also of burdening insurance companies and luckless doctor defendants with marginal small claims or "nuisance suits" as they are usually called. In them, the insurance company pays the claimant a few hundred or a few thousand dollars solely to get rid of a case that isn't worth the time and effort it would take to defend. According to the ISO study,[8] the nuisance settlement (defined by it as one in which the payment is $5,000 or less) accounts for slightly over half of all claims paid but only 1 per cent of the money paid. The blame for nuisance claims, however, can hardly be placed entirely on the lawyers. Quite often, payment is initiated by the insurance company dealing directly with a patient who doesn't have an attorney and who, in return for several hundred dollars, signs a waiver agreeing she won't subsequently sue. In at least some of these instances, and maybe the majority, the company knows the injury is one that might open them to considerable liability if the patient did go to an attorney who would recognize the true recovery possibilities.

Plaintiff lawyers have also allegedly added to the cost of the malpractice problem another way. As Dr. Hoffman of the AMA sees it: "The real core of medical malpractice problems . . . derives from the attempt of the legal profession to deal with the much larger and more complex problems of the financial needs of injured patients." (I.e., the lawyers argue that their clients are entitled to recovery not only for their medical bills and lost income, which few would deny, but also for speculative loss of future income, as well as such essentially indefinable elements as pain and suffering, mental anguish, "gross" negligence and so on.) "It is, of course, the professional duty of a lawyer," Hoffman generously adds, "to do his very best, within the law, to solve the problems of his client . . . If a lawyer can obtain compensation for an injured patient by persuadng a court to adopt new legal rules of procedure, evidence, or liability . . . the lawyer has a duty to do so. In changng legal rules, the court should give careful consideration to their effect on the public welfare. Most often, however, there is no one before the court to speak for the interest of public welfare, and there is not an adequate opportunity for the court to investigate the impact of legal rules on public welfare."[9] While there will be many who will disagree with Dr. Hoffman's analysis of the proper role of a trial court, and still others who will wonder whose public welfare he has in mind, his thesis leads to a conclusion that has been adopted by the insurance industry: "Where the court fails to protect public welfare in establishing new legal rules," says Hoffman, "it then becomes the responsibility of the legislature to act in the public interest by correcting the rules established by the court."[10]

II

The personal-injury lawyers, it will come as no surprise, disagree with the charges made against them. During the course of the malpractice crisis, their most active spokesman has been the 25,000 member[11] Association of Trial Lawyers of America (ATLA), a group that has lobbied both at the federal and state level against the reforms sought by the insurers and their medical allies.

The ATLA perceives the role of lawyers, and therefore of the malpractice suit, as a positive force for the same public welfare that Hoffman thinks they violate. As former ATLA president Robert A. Cartwright has expressed it: "Successful medical cases have caused hospitals and doctors to utilize such safety techniques and procedures as sponge counts, instrument counts, electrical grounding of anesthesia machines, padding of shoulder bars on operating tables, the avoidance of colorless sterilization solutions in spinal anesthesia counts, and colored bandages. In the . . . John Nork case in California"—see Case Thirty-two—"we have a specific example of a trial lawyer's intense digging, studying, and investigating to expose the doctor's drug addiction and unnecessary operations to raise money for his drug habit—all performed while the medical profession closed its eyes . . . This case's therapeutic and prophylactic effect was to create demands for 'peer reviews,' give justice to the injured patients, and perhaps stop hundreds of unnecessary operations."[12]

A study, which in large part supported Cartwright's position, was conducted among four thousand practicing physicians.[13] It found that 80 per cent of the doctors interviewed could name at least one precautionary step they were now taking that they hadn't taken in the past because of their fear of a malpractice suit. Of them, forty-eight per cent said they were ordering more diagnostic tests; forty-four per cent were keeping more detailed patient records; forty-four per cent were explaining procedural risks to their patients more carefully; forty per cent were more likely than before to consult with another physician when in doubt about their diagnosis or the proper medical procedure to adopt; thirty-seven per cent were allowing fewer prescription refills without a new examination; and thirty-one per cent were less free about giving medical advice over the phone to patients they hadn't examined. While, no doubt, all the extra diagnostic tests aren't necessary and some—those involving X rays particularly—may themselves be dangerous to patients, the list, nevertheless, is quite a catalogue of changes in the interest of patient health.

Cartwright is not alone in his view of the social welfare role of the lawyer. Just as many doctors find that healing the sick provides a satisfaction that transcends the income it provides, so are there large numbers of lawyers who are fulfilled by helping the legally ill and trying to make society work better for everyone. Though none denied the importance of earning a good income, virtually every attorney interviewed in connection with this book struck the public service theme. As one man, for whom malpractice cases are only an inconsiderable part of his practice, observed: "You must remember that most of the work lawyers do is boring and inconsequential: Property settlements, wills, contracts, all kinds of minor civil litigation that are important to the people involved but have no wider meaning. Malpractice cases, on the other hand, are inherently interesting and bring out the best in you as a person. What you see is some poor patient who has been victimized by the negligence of a doctor they trusted. You want to help that person and at the same time expose the negligence that occurred in the hope that the medical profession will say to itself, 'Hey, this is the kind of thing we've got to stop doing; it costs us money.' You can't be a crusader often in the law, no matter what you might think from television shows, but with the malpractice case you sometimes can be, and it makes you feel good."[14] Even attorneys for the doctor defendants don't disagree. Says one: "Most attorneys went into law in the first place because they saw it, no matter how dimly, as a force for change in the society. The malpractice case appeals to them for that reason."[15]

A variation on this theme was stated by several attorneys who largely handle minor personal injury cases. Because, as one pointed out, millions of people over the years have been injured when they fall on someone's icy sidewalk or break a leg as a result of an automobile accident, the tort actions that arise from these accidents have a choreographed quality. The plaintiff's lawyer interviews the witnesses, files the papers, the defense lawyer objects, the defense lawyer delays, an offer is made, an offer is rejected, and eventually—several years down the pike—the case is settled for almost exactly the amount both sides knew would be the final figure the day each opened a file on the case. (The reason for this ritual dance, most often, is the insurance company's desire to keep earning interest on its loss reserve for as long as possible.) Not so with the malpractice case. For it, from beginning to end, the result is not known, and the plaintiff lawyer knows that his chance of winning (or, at least, winning a sizable amount) is almost entirely dependent on his skill in questioning witnesses, grasping medical concepts, and then discovering legal theories that best fit the often very complex information he has obtained. The game is afoot, the chase an exciting one.

Nevertheless, the very reasons that make malpractice cases attractive to some lawyers also cause others to shy away from them, or so says the ATLA. Responding to the allegation that lawyers seize on malpractice cases with glee because of the large verdicts obtainable from deep-pocket defendants, the ATLA says, on the contrary,[16] "Most lawyers are reluctant to undertake medical professional liability cases, since (a) their complexity requires a very high degree of skill and effort, (b) relatively substantial expenses are incurred . . . (c) the defense wins a high proportion of the cases adjudicated, (d) experience has shown that very few of these cases can be settled before suit, (e) experience demonstrates that an unusually large portion of the cases are actually tried rather than being settled before trial, and (f) the lawyer handling such a case antagonizes members of the medical community who are important witnesses for him in other personal litigation."

While this argumentation would be more impressive if there were any substantiating evidence that the malpractice victim with the right kind of injury (see below) has any difficulty getting a lawyer, it is not entirely without its merit. Although the ATLA fudges, what it is really saying is that many high-volume negligence lawyers avoid malpractice cases because of the amount of time they take. Such lawyers prefer fifty broken-leg suits, which they know will produce $150,000 in damages and anywhere from $50,000 to $60,000 for themselves, rather than one malpractice case, which *might* produce twice that amount. According to one study,[17] the average malpractice case requires 3.5 times more hours of lawyer time than the average automobile case. For the high-volume lawyer, therefore, the double earning power that the malpractice case could have is of little moment when he considers the quadrupling of time that's also involved and the likelihood, untrue in almost all his other cases, that he might not win anything. This reasoning does not necessarily stop the high-volume lawyer from accepting malpractice cases, but it may cause him to act on them in ways that are not always to his client's interest, and are sometimes in the defense's interest, a possibility that will be discussed later in this chapter.

In addition to the high-volume negligence lawyer, two other types of attorneys handle malpractice cases. One is the generalist, usually either a solo practitioner or a member of a small law firm, who takes on almost every kind of case, criminal or civil, that comes in the front door. The other is the major case specialist. He is to personal injury cases what Perry Mason is to the criminal bar. Almost invariably highly personable, extraordinarily adept in the area of his specialty, and with forensic abilities that make him a formidable opponent in any courtroom situation, his philosophy is directly the opposite of the volume lawyer. Rather than accepting dozens of humdrum suits at one time, he concentrates on the zesty handful in which the potential recovery is high. Because of his skills, he often becomes very rich indeed.

Quite apparently, the malpractice victim is best off if she can obtain one of these top-flight specialists to handle her case. Unfortunately, there's a great likelihood that even if she finds her way to one, her case will be rejected by him. Robert Begam of Arizona, a personal-injury specialist and also a former ATLA president, has said that he rejects eleven of every twelve malpractice suits offered him,[18] while S. Gerald Litvin, one of the foremost personal-injury attorneys on the East Coast, estimates his rejection rate at eight of ten,[19] a figure concurred in by another equally highly regarded specialist, James Beasley, whose firm prosecuted the case that identified the cancer-causing proclivities of chloramphenicol.[20] Still other studies have placed the rejection rate at anywhere from 50 per cent to 71 per cent,[21] with the wide range probably explainable by variations in defining who is and isn't a specialist.[22]

Attorneys, specialist or not, turn down cases for many reasons. Some would-be clients lack even the rudiments of a suit, having incurred no physical injury. (It usually turns out that these people want to sue just because they're angry at their doctor.) For a lawyer to accept such a case is foolish; the defense will be able to get it dismissed by a judge at an early stage. But it is the lawyer's perception of time as money that is usually the imperative factor. True, an injury that is trivial but in which negligence is apparent will sometimes be pursued at least through the claims stage, with the aim of getting a quick settlement, which the insurance company will label a nuisance one. On the other hand, if the injury is trivial *and* the negligence issue doubtful or difficult legally, few lawyers will want to be bothered with it at all. "Trivial," however, is a word that is defined differently by different lawyers. One study suggests that a bottom recovery figure of $10,000 must exist before an attorney will take any malpractice claim into the suit stage,[23] while the specialist often won't accept any case in which the potential recovery is less than $50,000.[24] Thus, in malpractice cases, as in other branches of the law, the wealthy client gets the best legal services; the only difference is that the wealthy malpractice client is one who is "rich" in terms of injury, not cash in the bank.

Whenever a lawyer weeds out a meritorious case because it doesn't serve his economic needs, he inadvertently also serves the interests of the insurance companies. The putative client who is rejected by the specialist because her case is worth only $40,000 often becomes discouraged at that point and doesn't go to a lesser lawyer for whom the case would be a bonanza. Similarly, the complex case that has a $5,000 value is $5,000 the insuance company saves because it is not worth the time of any lawyer to handle it. Therefore, if it is fair to accuse lawyers of sometimes litigating non-meritorious cases, then it is also appropriate to commend them (although their opponents rarely do so) for the role they play in preventing clients with good cases from ever getting their day in court.

But is the "non-meritorious" accusation itself a fair one? Are such suits as rare in their occurrence as the lawyers say or as commonplace as the doctors and insurers think? The question is not easily answered. Merit is essentially a subjective term. Lawyers think of it one way, doctors another.

When a lawyer is presented with a malpractice case, before going ahead with it he will almost invariably submit the known facts to a doctor with knowledge of the medical field in which the accident occurred. This doctor may be a personal friend of the lawyer, although more often there is a business arrangement involved. The lawyer, for example, in return for getting his cases evaluated may perform routine legal work free of charge for his stable of medical advisors. More often, the lawyer hires an individual doctor or one of the medical consulting firms that have sprung up in recent years as the number of malpractice claims have increased. Typically, these firms evaluate medical information not only for plaintiffs but for defendants as well.

As a result of the consultation, the plaintiff lawyer may become convinced that no viable suit exists, and that is the end of the matter. However, the true purpose of the consultation is not to find a definitive answer to the negligence question. While it would be nice for the lawyer to hear from his medical expert that his client was victimized by a clear-cut case of malpractice, the lawyer will be satisfied if the medical data can be interpreted in such a way that a reasonable hypothesis (i.e., a legally arguable case) exists which suggests that malpractice *may* have occurred.

Once this much is established, the lawyer is ready to go ahead, seeing that, as an advocate, his duty now is to develop the evidence in ways that are most favorable to his client's contention. This intellectual leap on the lawyer's part—that since something may have happened, it should be argued as if it did happen—is a difficult one for many doctors to accept. As one thoughtful commentator, Dr. Norman W. Frink, has analyzed it: "The doctor, by training and expectation, seeks truth. The lawyer knows that absolute truth is rarely, if ever, found and is satisfied to look for probability."[25] The philosophic wedge between the two professions, therefore, is a substantial one. As the lawyer weaves his theory of what may have happened, the doctor defendant—who may *know* he did nothing wrong—perceives the lawyer as calculatedly pursuing a non-meritorious case, motivated by greed and a desire to twist facts to fit a self-satisfying conclusion. The lawyer, however, who wasn't there when the injury happened, sees his case has "merit" because it carries with it, as Dr. Frink points out, the *probability* it could have happened the way he argues it did.

Although undoubtedly some malpractice cases are litigated and even won that are motivated by greed—on the client's part or the lawyer's—the accusation that non-meritorious cases are commonplace can be accepted only if we assume that a doctor's definition of merit, ethically and legally, is superior to that of an attorney's. If we accept that premise, then we also have to believe that a plaintiff doesn't have the right to have her case argued "on its merits" if the doctor denies the accusation.

III

Even if she is rich in terms of her injury, the malpractice victim, once she decides she wants a lawyer, will often have trouble, not in finding one, but finding the right one. One way she might try is through one of the referral services run by bar associations throughout the nation. A call to these associations will result in the name of a lawyer who will handle her case. Unluckily for clients, most of these services exist largely to drum up business for lawyers; when they receive an inquiry, they refer the caller to the attorney whose name is next on their rotation list regardless of whether or not he has any experience in the caller's area of legal concern. Exceptions are the referral services in St. Louis and Philadelphia; they catalogue their attorneys by specialty and also offer free or virtually free legal advice.[26] But even the best of them may be of minimal help to the person who needs expert legal advice, principally because the attorneys who join them are usually young and relatively inexperienced. Thus, the malpractice specialist or even the high-volume negligence lawyer cannot ordinarily be located through such a device.

There are other ways to get a lawyer, and although perhaps not typical, the experience of some of the people whose problems were recounted in earlier chapters is enlightening in depicting the almost accidental way in which the individuals involved got legal help that ranged from the mediocre to the outstanding.

The Lazzeri family had no problems with lawyers because they never sought one, having accepted the version of Lillian's death given by the hospital officials.

Tommy Manning's parents were also, for some time, unaware that malpractice may have been the cause of his paralysis. Indeed, for several months after her son was wounded, Mrs. Manning spent most of her time fruitlessly trying to get the police to arrest gang members who she and Tommy thought were responsible. It wasn't until almost a year after the shooting that the malpractice issue was raised. At that time, Tommy was being attended to by a woman physical therapist at the same hospital which employed Dr. Kane. (The hospital was not offering this service free; the bills were paid by Medicaid.) On this particular day, the therapist took Mrs. Manning aside and told her it had always seemed odd to her that the doctor in charge had not tried to remove the bullet when Tommy first arrived at the hospital; apparently this thought had been weighing on her mind for some time, much as Rose Turner had been troubled about Lillian Lazzeri's death.

According to a number of plaintiff attorneys, non-doctor hospital personnel, usually nurses, are the ones most likely to advise patients they have been injured negligently. When they do so, they are taking a step that requires considerable courage because they know that a hospital will likely get rid of any employee who, it believes, has helped instigate a malpractice suit. The firing rarely directly follows the incident and may not even involve a formal dismissal. Instead, the suspected nurse (and often the hospital has nothing more than suspicion to go on) will suddenly find her performance rating has declined and that she is now drawing bad hours and the most onerous kind of work. Realizing what is happening, should she try to get a job at another hospital, the poor evaluation will follow her, often accompanied by a phone call, as a result of which her would-be new employer learns she is a "trouble maker." In effect, she has been blackballed in her profession. (This can be compared to what happens when the same hospital gives the doctor who caused the accident a good reference when he agrees to leave its staff and join another hospital.)

In the Manning case, the therapist refused to add to her original comment, but what she had said was sufficient to plant the seed of suspicion in Mrs. Manning's mind. The next day she called the city's Community Legal Services which had earlier provided aid to a neighborhood housing group in which she was active. The attorney to whom she spoke told her he wasn't permitted to handle private cases, but gave her the name of a young friend of his who had done some personal-injury work. This attorney accepted the case and appeared to be genuinely outraged by it. As he said later: "Here we had a child paralyzed for life because some stupid doctor didn't bother to take an X ray, just put a Band-Aid on a goddamn bullet wound, for Christ's sake." When, however, the hospital established its array of experts to testify that Tommy would have been paralyzed regardless of anything Dr. Kane failed to do, the Manning lawyer, as limited in funds as was his client, lacked the wherewithal to hire medical experts of his own (even if he had known where to find them) to testify to the contrary. Even so, he thought of going to trial. "Here we had this boy, life ruined, never walk again. He should be very sympathetic to a jury. Ordinarily. The only trouble was he was a black kid and juries expect black kids to get shot. They would have figured he was in a gang war and got what he deserved, even though that wasn't true." The insurance company, which may not have been so sure of a favorable verdict as it appeared to be, offered the Mannings $15,000 to settle the case. The young attorney recommended they accept the offer and they did. "I felt lousy," he recalled. "I felt so bad for them I didn't even take a fee." As far as the Mannings were concerned, he might as well have taken the entire $15,000, for, as soon as Medicaid learned of the award, it suspended payments for Tommy's care until the money was used up.

Like the Mannings, Martha Anderson's cousin, on her own, probably would not have known how to find a good attorney. But the bank, which was the executor of the estate, did. After reading the suspicious autopsy report, bank officials assigned the case to a law firm which frequently handled litigation work for them. There, the case was handled by a partner who, while not a specialist, had a good working knowledge of malpractice law. Even so, thanks to delaying tactics on the part of the hospital, more than two years passed before the lawyer was able to obtain an accurate chronology of the case, and even then it appeared that some records were still missing as was the doctor who administered the barium enema. By that time, the firm had put out several thousand dollars in deposition and investigation costs and several thousand dollars more in lawyers' time, an expenditure which a small practice attorney, such as the one the Mannings had, would never have been able to afford. Even after the evidence was put together, the case remained stalled, apparently usually by delaying tactics on the part of the defense. Not until the eve of the trial, almost ten years after Miss Anderson's death, did the defendants make a settlement offer of approximately $20,000. Because of Miss Anderson's short life expectancy, her non-existent earning capacity, and the fact that she had no one who depended on her for financial support, it seemed unlikely any jury would award more than that, regardless of how horrendous the negligence may have been. The offer was refused. As it turned out, the plaintiff's lawyer had not been idle all those years. In studying the case, he noted that the doctors who attended Miss Anderson after her collapse had never been told that it had been caused by the barium enema perforating her vaginal wall. With that information in mind, he began to contact specialists in barium-type injuries and was able to introduce evidence at the trial which showed that if the doctors attending Miss Anderson had been informed, she could have been operated upon and would have had nearly a 50 per cent chance of recovery. By not informing the attending physicians, the laboratory people had effectively sentenced the old lady to death. Shortly after this testimony was introduced, the defense made and the plaintiffs accepted a settlement offer "in excess of $70,000."

Only the Hadleys, whose daughter incurred brain damage in the operation in which Dr. Schneider was the surgeon, ended with a lawyer who specialized in personal-injury cases. The Hadleys didn't know, any more than did the Mannings or Martha Anderson's niece, that such specialists existed. However, the Hadleys did have a lawyer who handled the legal affairs of three small dry cleaning shops they owned, and it was to him they turned for help. Sufficiently knowledgeable to recognize the case as one that might carry a large verdict if it could be won, but also sufficiently aware of his own limitations not to want to take it on himself, this lawyer set up a meeting for the Hadleys with the specialist.

Once this new attorney agreed to represent the Hadleys, as far as they were concerned their business lawyer was no longer involved in the case. Unknown to them, however, he had made an arrangement with the specialist who agreed to pay him one third of any money he earned on the case as a referral fee. Such agreements, according to the American Bar Association (ABA), are unethical, and any lawyer who engages in them is subject to censure and eventually, under some circumstances, to disbarment. The danger of the referral fee is that the lawyer who is paying it will add it to the amount he charges his client, and the ABA, of course, would never want to see the public overcharged. Rather, it piously points out, any attorney who lacks the expertise to handle a case has the obligation to refer it without remuneration to a qualified attorney.

This regulation, however, is easily side-stepped, as it was in the Hadley case, by not calling the referral fee a referral fee. Instead, the Hadley's business lawyer was named "co-counsel" on the case, a practice which is perfectly acceptable to the ABA even though there is not a scintilla of difference between it and the referral fee. By whatever name it is called, the referral fee is a commonplace of the legal profession. One study[27] revealed that 95 per cent of all personal injury specialists said they would name the referring attorney as "co-counsel," with the one-third kickback the almost universally mentioned percentage. For its co-counsel, the Hadley case turned out to be quite productive. It produced a $200,000 award; after $10,000, in round figures, was deducted for legal expenses, the specialist took one third of the remainder for himself and sent one third of that, or $21,000, back to the Hadley's business attorney who had spent two hours of work on the case.

The one third the specialist charged the Hadleys is the norm fee in negligence cases with 58 per cent of all lawyers, according to a 1971 investigation, working on that percentage.[28] Another 15 per cent of lawyers, the study found, charge malpractice clients 40 per cent, with one in every five charging 50 per cent. The remaining lawyers in the study worked on a sliding scale, sometimes to the advantage of the client and sometimes not. With certain of these lawyers, if a case could be settled prior to trial, their charge was 25 per cent, one third if carried through trial, 40 per cent if appeals work was necessary. However, the sliding scale could also start at one third through the settlement stage and reach 50 per cent at the appeals level. Although these fee variations show that some lawyers are more money-hungry (to the point of rapaciousness) than others, the role played by the co-counsel fee appears a major factor in driving contingency percentages upward and plaintiff net recoveries downward.

Whatever its evils may be, the referral system can work to the client's advantage. Did it not exist, many plaintiffs would never get to the best lawyer to handle their claim. In the Hadley case, for example, had their business lawyer not been able to make his deal with the specialist, he likely would have kept the suit for himself, and because he wasn't as skillful as the specialist, the Hadleys almost certainly would have ended with a lesser net than they got, and considering the legal difficulties of their case, they might not have gotten anything at all.

Once a malpractice client gets a lawyer, of one degree of ability or another, to take her claim, a number of events are immediately set in motion. As part of the contingency fee arrangement, the new client gives the attorney the authority to obtain all the medical records pertaining to the accident. When the lawyer writes for them, the doctor involved then informs his insurance company (if he didn't do so when the accident occurred), thereby causing the insurer not only to open a claim file but also to assign the case to a defense attorney. This man is almost never on the payroll of the insurance company, but rather is a member of a firm that specializes in negligence defense in the city or state in which the accident occurred. Unlike the plaintiff's lawyer, he works on an hourly fee basis. Should the plaintiff's attorney send letters to more than one party (e.g., a hospital as well as a surgeon), the result will be that the case gets a claim file in the offices of as many insurance companies as become involved, each of which hires its own defense attorney.

After the plaintiff's lawyer receives the medical records, which may or may not be complete and which in some cases will have been altered,[29] the attorney may decide, perhaps because his medical expert says so, that the case which looked so promising when the client told him about it, is in fact a weak one. At that point, however, the attorney is not ordinarily going to pick up the phone and tell the other side he has decided not to sue. Instead, he sits back and waits to see if the defense comes up with an offer or some other indication they are worried about the case. Should that happen, it's a signal—or should be—to the lawyer that he and his expert may have missed something and the case deserves a fresh look. (It was this signal the Manning lawyer failed to recognize; while a $15,000 offer was minimal in terms of Tommy's injury, it was suspiciously large if the defense had in reality as little to worry about as they said they did.)

Should the lawyer decide he has a meritorious case, in the probability sense described above, he will then begin to move to enter suit, though usually only after a series of pre-suit settlement discussions with the various attorneys for the defense. This is good strategy on the plaintiff lawyer's part. He knows that the actual threat to enter the suit may scare a concrete offer out of the other side. That the offer will almost always be unacceptably low is unimportant; it's the multiplication that can be done from it that counts. For example, if the defense offers $10,000 "to get the case off our books," as it is often phrased, the plaintiff's lawyer can assume the case is valued by the company at five to ten times that amount. As a result, he has gained a major bargaining insight that will be useful to him as negotiations mature between the time of filing the suit and the date of trial.

Once the determination to begin litigation has been made, the plaintiff's attorney must be careful about whom he sues. In a 1973 case, for example, a patient died on the operating table apparently a the result of an anesthesia accident. The family hired an attorney who named as defendants the surgeon, the anesthesiologist and the hospital that employed the anesthesiologist. The defense refused to settle. At trial, the attorney for the hospital produced evidence that pointed to a failure in the anesthesia equipment as the real cause of the patient's death. The jury accepted this argument and exonerated the defendants. By that time, the statute of limitations prevented the plaintiff's attorney from suing the equipment manufacturer on product liability grounds. The family of the dead patient, however, had no such statutory problems; they could sue their lawyer and did, charging him with legal malpractice for his negligent failure to name the equipment manufacturer as a defendant when the suit was filed. The lawyer's insurance company paid the family $50,000 to settle the case before trial.[30] An attorney's fear that he can become the subject of suit himself if he fails to name the right defendant is one reason doctors sometimes find themselves in suits in which their involvement with the injury was peripheral or non-existent. As such doctors see it, their inclusion respresents outrageous conduct on the part of a greedy lawyer.

A doctor, however, must not only fear that a plaintiff's lawyer will name him in a malpractice suit; he sometimes has even greater reason to fear he will be named as an additional defendant by those who have already been sued.[31] For example, let us suppose that the plaintiff has sued a surgeon and an anesthesiologist, neither of whom is a hospital employee. Since, we will assume, each of these doctors has a different insurer, immediately two companies are involved, two defense lawyers, and probably two sets of medical experts to examine the facts of the case. After that examination is complete, the insurance company lawyers decide that while a strong case can be made against their customers, it also appears that a hospital resident had a degree of culpability. As a consequence, he (i.e., his employer) is added as a defendant, bringing a third insurer, the hospital's, into the picture. Now there are not just two but three deep-pocket defendants from whom the plaintiff can collect. This is to the plaintiff's advantage and is one reason plaintiff attorneys themselves try to toss as many defendants as they can into the pot. However, the addition of the hospital also acts to the advantage of the original two insurers since they have now created a deep pocket of their own. Should the case go to trial and they lose, the jury may divide the damages to be paid among all three defendants, reducing comparably the amount paid by the first two. Similarly, should the case be settled pre-trial, three insurance companies, rather than two, are now available to divide the costs. In the example given, the agreed settlement figure, we will say, is $100,000 of which the first two companies agree to put up $40,000 each because of the admittedly greater involvement of their clients; the hospital insurance company then adds the remainder, even though it may be convinced that its client had no degree of liability. By so doing, the hospital insurer is responding to priorities more important to it than the mere guilt or innocence of its client. The company sees $20,000, in fact, as a very cheap way out of the situation in which it has found itself. It knows that if the case goes to a jury and the evidence of negligence is great, there's no guarantee the jury will come up with the same 80–20 split, and may instead dump almost all the damages on the hospital and in an amount far greater than that visualized in the settlement. (Given the choice between two individual doctors and an impersonal hospital, jurors often prefer to blame the latter.) The hospital insurer, however, may have an even more compelling reason for going along with its assigned share of the settlement. It knows that malpractice cases do not exist in isolation from one another. The same insurers and the same defense attorneys, case after case, sit down on the same side of the bargaining table. In Detroit, for example, between 1970 and 1974, ten insurer-defense firms represented two thirds of all defendants in malpractice cases,[32] while in Philadelphia, one firm[33] handles close to 50 per cent of defenses for doctors. The consequence is, as one study puts it,[34] "The system does indeed permit, if not encourage, counsel to negotiate many cases with an eye to the next one." For the hospital insurer in our example, $20,000 is a small price to pay if, by so doing, he knows that the next time a case comes along in that city in which it is his customer who is principally responsible, the other defendants will then also chip in to help take him off the hook.

This type of negotiating situation can occur in any malpractice suit in which there is more than one defendant; and for any defendant (i.e., the doctor, not the insurance company) the negotiating process can lead to wrenching decisions, as a result of which he often feels ill-used, sometimes exploited, and occasionally out of money.

The fate of Dr. Schneider is a case in point. He believed that whatever else might have happened during the Hadley operation, every action he had taken was a proper one, and he was furious at having been included in the suit. Early on in the pre-trial negotiations, Schneider's lawyer, in fact, did try to prevail on the specialist hired by the Hadleys to drop Schneider as a defendant. (The Hadley lawyer could have done this, but he would not have been permitted to drop any defendants named by the other defendants.[35]) The lawyer, however, was adamant about keeping Schneider in the case. He had developed a theory, tenuous but conceivable, that implicated Schneider in the supposed negligence. But this never seems to have been his major reason for not wanting to let Schneider out. The Hadley lawyer was an astute judge of character and recognized that the apparently arrogant and cold-blooded Schneider was just the sort of defendant a jury would enjoy finding negligent, and he further recognized, from taking Schneider's deposition, something even more important to him: So eager was Schneider to prove his innocence that as a witness on his own behalf (if the case went to trial) he was likely to give self-serving testimony that would harm the other defendants, something he would not be apt to do if he were only a witness and not a defendant. Finally, to the Hadley lawyer, Schneider should not be dropped because his doing so would cause him to lose one of the insurance companies that would otherwise contribute to the pre-trial settlement kitty.

As the evidence in the case mounted via the depositions, it became increasingly clear to the attorneys for the four defendants that not only did they have a "sympathetic" plaintiff on their hands, a brain-damaged fourteen-year-old girl, but that sufficient evidence, shaky though it might be, existed to support a jury finding for the

Hadleys. It was not, from their point of view, a good combination. At that point, negotiations, which had stalled at the $50,000 level, began in earnest. Ultimately, by the time the offer was up to $120,000, the Hadley attorney (who himself was far from sure he had enough to win) commented, "I doubt if my clients will even take $300,000." The defense took this as a signal that the Hadley attorney was really saying that $200,000 would bring the case to an end. So it turned out. The Hadleys, who had all along been told (truthfully enough) by their attorney that their chances at trial were no better than 50-50, agreed to the offer, with any hesitation they might have had removed when the attorney reminded them that even though they might win more at trial, the other side was sure to appeal, and it would be years before the family saw any money, which, by then, they desperately needed for their daughter's care. In urging them to accept the offer, the Hadley attorney could be said to be also acting in his own interest; as long as the case wended its way through the appeals process, he wouldn't see any money either. The Hadley attorney, however, had a reputation for being willing to go to trial and take as long as necessary to win an appeal. Therefore, in recommending the settlement, he appears to have been acting strictly in the Hadleys' best interest.

Once the plaintiffs, all the lawyers, and all the insurance companies had agreed to a figure, it only remained to get the hospital and the three doctor defendants to sign the settlement. After some complaining, all but Schneider did so. Since the Schneider insurance firm had agreed to put up $50,000, the pot was now short by that amount, and unless the other three insurers agreed to make up the difference, the deal might fall through. They refused, but after further negotiation, the Hadley attorney, under pressure from his client, agreed to accept the $150,000 and bring Schneider to trial separately. Whether, considering the weakness of his case against Schneider, the Hadley attorney would have followed through on that threat is uncertain, but the possibility seemed real enough to Schneider's lawyer who had the same opinion of the effect Schneider would have on a jury as did the Hadley lawyer. Moreover, with the other defendants no longer in the case to share the blame, it was at least possible the jury would focus exclusively on Schneider and conceivably award an amount that would dwarf the settlement figure. In any event, the case never came to trial because Schneider, at the last moment, changed his mind and signed the agreement. While it is unknown what caused his about-face, it is probable that he gave in to one of the ploys attorneys use on their clients when they want to avoid trial. As one defense attorney, who for reasons that will become immediately obvious desires anonymity, explained it: "Some clients don't understand their own best interest. They insist on going to trial on cases that might cost us"—he means the insurance company that pays his bill—"huge losses. When that happens, there are some things you can do. First of all, you're always sympathetic; you never tell the client you think he's a fool or that he should be found negligent. You tell him, on the contrary, that you admire his courage in standing up for what he believes is right. But then, when it's getting near to trial, you begin to lay on the pressure. You advise him to be sure not to talk to the press; that's something he's probably not thought of, but when he does he immediately visualizes headlines with his name and the word 'malpractice' coupled together in them. Then you begin to set up meetings with him to go over his testimony, during your office hours, not at his convenience. That means he's got to cancel appointments, and for the first time he really understands that it's not just the insurance company that might lose money but that he will, too. Once you've got him thinking about that, you casually mention again how much you admire his courage, that he'd be willing to sit in a courtroom for two weeks or more listening to doctors for the prosecution say what a lousy doctor he is. When he thinks about hearing his reputation smeared that way and when he thinks about losing two more weeks of income—well, that usually brings the sons-of-bitches into line."

Schneider, according to his colleague Robinson, was left embittered by the entire experience. He believed his lawyer had always been more interested in saving the insurance company money than in helping him, and he found the signing of the agreement repellent, an unwarranted admission, as he saw it, that he had been guilty of malpractice. The agreement, in fact, doesn't say that, but Schneider was correct about its implication. At least, that was the view his insurance company took. After having spent weeks pressuring him into signing, six months later the company sent him a letter telling him a five per cent surcharge had been added to his insurance premium because of his "adverse malpractice experience." At that, Schneider was fortunate: Some insurance companies surcharge or cancel customer policies solely because a malpractice claim has been lodged, regardless of whether or not the claim is ever pursued.[36]

But the doctor defendant in a malpractice case is not the only one at the mercy of his lawyer; so is the plaintiff who has sued him. Unlike the insurance company that appoints the defense lawyer and has the expertise to judge whether he is doing a good job (from its point of view), the plaintiff is usually unsophisticated in the law. Except to the extent she can measure it by her medical bills and lost wages, she has no way of knowing how much her case is worth or even whether it is strong or weak. As a consequence, when her lawyer tells her he has an offer he thinks she should accept, the chances are she will take it even if she suspects he has not gotten as much money for her as he should have. At that point, in fact, she has few real options open to her. Theoretically, she could fire the lawyer and hire another one to take on the case, but not only will that delay her suit further, but her first lawyer has no obligation to release any records to the new lawyer until the client has paid him all the money he has put up on her behalf, thousands of dollars she probably doesn't have.[37]

As any lawyer will point out, all clients are paranoid, harboring deep suspicions that their lawyer is out to cheat them. At times, however, these suspicions are merited. Should the client have wandered into a high-volume negligence firm where the emphasis is to move every case to settlement as quickly as possible to make room for the next one, she may well find herself accepting an inadequate figure.[38] And that may not be the only reason the lawyer will press the low settlement figure on her. Once she accepts it, he knows he will now recover the expense money he has put up and earn at least some fee, certitudes he doesn't enjoy should it become necessary to take a case to trial.

It is also possible, unknown to the client, that the lawyer has an unduly close relationship with the defense attorneys. This doesn't mean that anything as crass as a pay-off occurs; that simply doesn't happen. But something more subtle and as harmful to the client can. Just as defense attorneys know one another and keep an eye to future cases when deciding how much they'll contribute to the current one, so do the plaintiff and the defense attorneys know one another and understand the needs that each has. As the Michigan Physicians Crisis Committee has pointed out in its study of malpractice cases settled in Detroit, lawyers on both sides "know the other must make a living (either by satisfying an insurance company client or by earning a satisfactory contingency fee) and both . . . are fully aware that if either presses a momentary advantage too far, 'the chicken may come home to roost' in the next case where his position might not be as strong . . ."[39] Recognizing they will all be sitting down together, again and again in the future, the plaintiff's lawyer lowers his demand so that his defense attorney friend can go to his insurance company client and tell them what a fine job of negotiating he did, and similarly the defense counsel makes a decent offer to a co-operative plaintiff's lawyer so that he can earn a decent wage out of a case that perhaps should be lost, but into which his "opponent" knows he has put a lot of time. The result: One client gets less than she should, another gets more, justice isn't served for anyone. But the negotiating system has well served the uninterrupted economic well-being of the lawyers.

IV

There is, however, one oddity in all this. Considering all the negotiating that goes on, all the settlements that are made which may or may not be fair to plaintiff or defendant, all the non-meritorious suits that supposedly are filed and won each year, to say nothing of the thousands of nuisance claims that also get settled annually, despite all this, if we are to believe the doctors, the insurance companies, and even the plaintiff lawyers themselves, the plaintiff rarely wins.

The consensus view is best expressed by insurance executive Roberts: "It's . . . interesting," he says, "that, irrespective of the huge sum of money [paid out on malpractice claims], the verdict"—he apparently is referring to all claims, not just those that go to trial—"went to the plaintiff in only 34% of the cases. In 66% the medical profession was found to be innocent of the claimed injury."[40] The respected publication, *Medical World News*, has quoted the same healthy win ratio for defendants.[41] Donald Drake, one of the nation's leading medical journalists, was somewhat more conservative; he said defendants win 55 per cent of the time.[42] Other sources claim that plaintiffs "win only a small minority of cases,"[43] some say 40 per cent,[44] while even the most conservative insurance sources[45] depict a 50 per cent win rate for doctors, and none show them doing any worse than that. The ATLA apparently agrees. Its 1976–77 president, Robert Begam, says that "less than half the cases result in payouts to plaintiffs" and to prove his case, he further quotes an

NAIC finding that, he says, shows that defendants win 80 per cent of cases resolved by trial verdict.[46]

These percentages usually have their basis in reputable studies. Although it is unclear where Roberts and *Medical World News* came up with their 66 per cent, NAIC at one point shows a 64 per cent win ratio for defendants, although a few pages back[47] in the same study discovers 60 per cent, the same figure HEW arrived at, except HEW in its study also published an alternative of 55 per cent[48] which Drake used. Meanwhile, rattling about with its typical small statistical sample, ISO derived a 53 per cent defendant victory rate.[49]

Nevertheless, all these statistics, individually and taken in their entirety, present a false picture of the likelihood of a plaintiff winning a malpractice claim. By doing so, they propagate an image of the problem that importantly serves the interests of those whose economic stake in it is major and continuing. Insurers, for example, have everything going their way when they can quote one set of false figures to prove a claims crisis and then another false set to show that the plaintiff's chance of winning the claim is small. (The last thing the insurers want to create, after all, is a real claims crisis, which is what might happen if people in general thought a malpractice suit was a sure way to riches.) Doctors too are comforted by figures showing high defendant win rates, not only because they see them as deterrents to suit, but also because they tend to give credence to the profession's monomaniacal concentration on the non-meritorious suit issue, itself, as we have seen, largely a fabrication. Meanwhile, the plaintiff lawyers, who *know* how often they win, are equally happy to keep the public uninformed. If their clients ever came to believe that most malpractice suits weren't perilous adventures in which the chances of victory were small, then the clients might begin to wonder why it is they are expected to pay up to half their winnings to their lawyers.

When analyzed without bias, however, these same statistics show that while a malpractice suit is by no means an easy way to any pot of gold, the claimant, far from usually losing, wins at least some money in the large majority of cases.

Paradoxically, however, this does not mean the defendants necessarily lose more often than they win. What we are facing here, at least in some of these statistics, is the hoary problem of comparing apples with pears. Let us suppose, for example, that three doctors are named as defendants in a malpractice suit. Somewhere along the line, two of them are dropped as defendants or prevail at trial. As far as they are concerned, they have won. However, the third defendant either settles or is found liable at trial, so that—from the plaintiff's view—she has also won. The NAIC's 80 per cent win figure for defendants at trial[50] actually means that 80 per cent of the *defendants* win, not that 80 per cent of the *trials* are won. Thus, we could have trial after trial in which there are five defendants, four of whom are always exonerated by a jury, but one of whom is always found liable. The result is an 80 per cent win ratio for the defendants but a 100 per cent win ratio for the plaintiffs.

Therefore, if we define plaintiff wins in terms of defendant losses, we are going to create precisely those statistics that serve the interests of everyone except those who are interested in the truth.

But we are hardly any closer to the truth if we rely just on statistics based on claims *incidents*. As we have seen, HEW found that almost 40 per cent of them (actually 39.1 per cent[51]) never result in any legal action by the injured party. Hence, when insurers talk of 30,000 claims a year, they are really referring only to 18,000 or so incidents that were followed by an assertion of legal rights by the injured party. HEW, however, after having discovered this startling fact, then proceeded to ignore it in its calculations, and produced its comforting figure which could be publicized by doctors and insurers to show that claimants better beware filing a suit since they have only two chances in five of winning it. How a claimant can "lose" a claim of which she is unaware was left unexplained by HEW, as well as by NAIC and ISO, both of which studies completely ignored non-asserted claims in developing healthy defendant win percentages.

In order to find out how often a claimant wins, therefore, it is necessary to exclude all those incidents in which no legal action was taken.

There is, however, a problem in doing this. As noted earlier, sometimes an insurer gives an injured person money *before* she has asserted a claim. In that sense, she has "won" money, no matter how inadequate an amount, as a result of her injury. To incorporate these wins, in the following table, all claims, asserted or not, are included to show how many result in a win—even a token amount. The table is a recapitulation of the HEW analysis, including non-asserted claims, which developed the frequently quoted 60 per cent defendant win rate. The study, with its 1970 figures, is an old one, but since the 1977 NAIC study (using the same win/loss counting method) came up with almost exactly the same statistical picture, the HEW percentages apparently remained valid:

STAGE AT WHICH MEDICAL INCIDENT WAS RESOLVED	NUMBER OF INCIDENTS	PCT. OF WHOLE	PCT. WITH PAYMENT TO CLAIMANT	NUMBER OF INCIDENTS PD.
Claim Not Asserted	4,692	39.1	28	1,314
Claim Asserted, Resolved Prior to Filing of Suit	3,096	25.8	33	1,022
Suit Entered, Ended Without Trial	3,120	26.0	64	1,997
Suit Ended During Course of Trial	396	3.3	64	253
Suit Ended with Trial Verdict	696	5.8	29	202
TOTALS	12,000	100.0	39.9	4,788

With this basic calculation before us, it now becomes possible to begin to approach a true plaintiff win percentage by deducting all the non-asserted claims, but retaining those on which the insurer made a payment to get rid of the situation:

STAGE AT WHICH MEDICAL INCIDENT WAS RESOLVED	NUMBER OF INCIDENTS	PCT. OF WHOLE	PCT. WITH PAYMENT TO CLAIMANT	NUMBER OF INCIDENTS PD.
Claim Never Asserted But Payment Made	1,314	15.2	100	1,314
Claim Asserted, Resolved Prior to Filing Suit	3,096	36.0	33	1,022
Suit Entered, Ended Without Trial	3,120	36.2	64	1,997
Suit Ended During Course of Trial	396	4.6	64	253
Suit Ended with Trial Verdict	696	8.0	29	202
TOTALS	8,622	100.0	55.5	4,788

But even this table, while accurate enough, is not completely satisfactory. Claims settled pre-suit are the trivia of the malpractice problem. They develop large numbers but very few dollars, no more than

1–2 per cent of total annual payments.[52] More importantly, in legal terms it is difficult to say that a defendant or a plaintiff has "won" if a suit has never been filed. Therefore, the followng table is included to show what happens when we include only those claims that resulted in the filing of a suit:

STAGE AT WHICH MEDICAL INCIDENT WAS RESOLVED	NUMBER OF INCIDENTS	PCT. OF WHOLE	PCT. PAID TO LITIGANT	NUMBER OF INCIDENTS PD.
Suit Entered, Ended Prior to Trial	3,120	74.1	64	1,997
Suit Ended During Course of Trial	396	9.4	64	253
Suit Ended with Trial Verdict	696	16.5	29	202
TOTALS	4,212	100.0	58	2,452

Using either this table or the one preceding as our basis, therefore, it is evident that the plaintiff win ratio is actually almost the reverse of the publicized figures, i.e., it is the plaintiff who wins close to 60 per cent of the time, not the defendant.

There is, however, still one other way of defining wins and losses, and it may be the only accurate way of doing it. This picture develops when we think of litigation in its true sense as a contest between someone who wants something and someone else who doesn't want to give it. Thus, when a person asserts a claim, usually in the form of a letter for her medical records, and the insurance company, in an effort to avoid suit, pays her an agreed upon sum of money, she has won a contest, even though the legal issues haven't been formally debated. Similarly, she can win at a settlement conference or at trial. In each of these instances, she has not only asserted a claim but pursued it successfully.

In other instances, however, the injured person asserts a claim but never pursues it. The plaintiff drops the action because her lawyer tells her the case will be difficult to win, that it lacks merit, doesn't have a meaningful amount of recovery attached to it; or the plaintiff dies for reasons unrelated to the injury, moves away, loses interest, and on and on. Whenever any of these non-pursuit decisions are made, they are gratuitous on the plaintiff's side in that they are not the consequence of any positive legal action taken by the defense to win.

There are, nevertheless, steps the defense can take, once a suit is filed, that produces a win for it. For example, the defense may successfully aver in pre-trial motions that the suit wasn't filed within the statute of limitations. Or it may file motions alleging that even if everything the plaintiff says is true, no legal basis for negligence can be shown. If the judge agrees (as we have seen from our case histories that sometimes happens), the case will be dismissed. More rarely, the case may be lost because the plaintiff's action was filed in the wrong court,[53] or there may be technical failures in the plaintiff's brief that could lead to a dismissal; usually, however, the plaintiff's attorney will be able to correct these errors in time to prevent a loss.

It is difficult to estimate how often the defendant prevails on any of these grounds between the time a suit is entered and the time it goes to trial. However, based in part on the Michigan Crisis Committee study,[54] from inferences drawn from the HEW study of malpractice attorneys,[55] from interviews with plaintiff and defense attorneys,[56] and the NAIC study,[57] probably no more than 20 per cent of all suits are lost by the plaintiff prior to trial because of successful defense motions. Thus, if we *include* this kind of defense win prior to trial but *exclude* all those instances in which the plaintiff gratuitously dropped her action, we are left finally only with those cases pursued from the claims stage onward, resulting in either a plaintiff win or loss:

STAGE AT WHICH MEDICAL INCIDENT WAS RESOLVED	NUMBER OF INCIDENTS	PCT. OF WHOLE	PCT. WON BY PLAINTIFF	NUMBER OF INCIDENTS PD.
Claim Asserted and Paid Prior to Suit	1,022	23	100	1,022
Suit Entered, Pursued by Plaintiff, Case Ends Prior to Trial	2,322	52	80	1,997
Suit Entered, Ended During Course of Trial	396	9	64	263
Suit Ends with Trial Verdict	696	16	29	202
TOTALS	4,436	100.0	78.5	3,484

Other studies concur with this 78.5 per cent finding. In 1975, for example, the Michigan Physicians Crisis Committee analyzed 664 cases[58] disposed of between 1970 and 1974 in the three-county Detroit area and learned that plaintiffs received compensation in 91 per cent of them.[59] It is apparent from this study that the analysts were dealing only with pursued claims. In agreement are statements from two leading Pennsylvania defense attorneys, each of whom quote an 80–90 per cent win rate for plaintiffs when pre-trial settlement only, at the claim or suit stage, is included. Further, a 1975 study in Wisconsin, the statistical base of which is not clear, observed that 87 per cent of all claims resulted in payment to plaintiffs prior to trial, and that at trial the plaintiff won 53 per cent of the time.[60] These figures, however while representative of the states in which they occurred, may be atypical nationally when the low plaintiff-win rates in southern states are included.[61] In that context, worth noting is an HEW Malpractice Commission[62] study that incorporated ten states plus the District of Columbia; although the sample from several of these states was small, they are ones which in aggregate produce 60 per cent of all claims filed annually.[63] According to this analysis, attorneys who regularly handle malpractice cases stated they won some compensation for their clients 84 per cent of the time, while those who only occasionally handle such cases reported success 80 per cent of the time.[64] The study was published in the HEW statistical supplement but was not referred to in the major report that publicized the false 55 per cent defense win rate.

Therefore, propaganda from interested sources to the contrary, any person who files and then pursues a malpractice claim has an excellent chance of winning at least some compensation. The only question remaining is whether the compensation is usually adequate or not. That problem will be discussed in the following two chapters.

CHAPTER FOURTEEN

A Matter of Rights

I

At no other time in the history of the United States have state legislatures moved with such unanimity or with greater rapidity than they did to confront the medical malpractice problem. Between 1974 and 1976, every state in the union passed a malpractice law,[1] and while a number of these acts attempted to deal with only one or two specific issues (including statutes passed in such small states as Vermont, Montana, and Nevada), most frequently the legislation was of an omnibus nature (including laws passed in such major states as New York, California, Pennsylvania, Ohio, Indiana, Illinois, and Massachusetts[2]).

Setting the stage for all this legislative activity were the insurance companies. Coupling their demands for confiscatory rate increases with threats they would leave doctors uninsured (and the public thereby with no way to collect damages when victims of malpractice), threats which, as we have seen, they were perfectly willing to back with action, the insurers on their own created a potent pressure point on the legislators. Aetna, one of the major malpractice insurers, is not only one of the largest corporations in the United States but also one of the largest in the world. Hartford, a giant on its own, is a subsidiary of the meganational International Telephone and Telegraph. Argonaut, not large in itself, is a creature of the sprawling Teledyne empire. Travelers, relatively puny in such company, even so ranks high on the list of American multibillion-dollar corporations. When such people, owning a sizable chunk of the nation's wealth, speak individually or through a lobbying body, like the American Insurance Association, legislators rarely turn deaf ears.

Hardly less powerful was the doctors' own lobbying body, the

American Medical Association. Although the AMA realized that insurance company rate demands related directly to their gambling losses ("The twin pincers of exploding claims *and tremendous investment losses* are the fundamental cause of rising malpractice rates," says the AMA[3] [italics added]), it and related state and local medical societies throughout the country focused their criticism only occasionally on the insurers. Just as consumers bought the argument that no-fault would reduce their auto insurance rates, so did the doctors believe that tort reforms, and specifically the tort reforms the insurers wanted, would solve their malpractice problems.

They backed their belief with money. In New York, for example, according to one legislative observer,[4] the various medical societies of that state spent $3.2 million in just twelve months in an advertising and public relations campaign to get the kind of malpractice law passed they wanted, while in California, a single medical society spent $750,000 for the same purpose.[5]

As actions such as these were occurring at the state level, the AMA nationally took up the principal propagandistic burden, with one significant goal of the campaign to educate doctors and their patients about the desperate nature of the crisis. Some AMA literature[6] used scare tactics, offering misleading and exaggerated statistics to convince the average doctor that he stood in mortal peril of becoming the next malpractice defendant unless dramatic steps were taken immediately. Simultaneous efforts were engendered to convince the patients, often through leaflets doctors were to hand out to them, that their impoverished physician had no choice but to pass his rising insurance costs on to them. It was not, however, the AMA advised the doctors, a good idea to talk about pass-ons "at the same time bills are presented."[7] This might hamper the "attitude adjustment" that the public had to undergo before it understood that giving up its right to sue was for its own good.

Working in close co-operation with the American Hospital Association (AHA), the AMA developed detailed prospectuses for the strategy to be followed. In this schemata, hospital administrators were perceived as a vital link because they "have control over staff"[8] (i.e., they can fire them) and therefore can require doctors and other personnel reporting to them to get behind the lobbying effort. The main burden, however, fell on the state medical and hospital societies. They were urged to take the drafting of malpractice laws out of the hands of the legislators: "Although many state legislatures have personnel who draft bills," a joint conference of the AMA and AHA noted in July 1975, in a guideline not intended for public dissemination, "it is important that the state medical and hospital groups jointly undertake the initial responsibility . . . Each word is critical. There should be agreement on the part of all parties concerned on every word, not simply the general principles expressed. Also, alternative legislative language for use in compromise options should be developed, agreed on, and be ready well before the time when it might be used." The lawmakers themselves, however, should not be completely ignored: "Seek suggestions and advice from legislators," the AMA/AHA counseled. "Learn to listen to them, instead of simply telling them what they should do. If you let the legislator take the lead, he will be flattered and will be a more effective supporter of your campaign. Above all, be appreciative for help that is given: Legislators do not receive many thanks; express gratitude every time something positive happens. Also, appreciation can be shown at the time of the legislator's next campaign."[9] Evidently, if flattery wouldn't do the trick, buying votes would.

Despite such firm guidance, by 1977 thirty-two states[10] had authorized the formation of independent commissions to study the malpractice problem further, and the possibility that these commissions would, in fact, be independent worried the AMA/AHA strategists enormously: "Legislative strategy is a key consideration here," they noted, "because *a study commission whose members are not carefully chosen could be counter-productive* . . . there should be prior identification of the individuals to be asked to serve, and there should be some assurance that physicians and hospitals will be able to see that appropriate and competent persons are selected for the commission."[11] (Italics added.)

Within this directive, the insurance companies were seen if not always as allies, at least as a body to be protected from attack. Along this line, medical societies were warned to "anticipate that some [opponents] may attempt to obscure the problem by claiming that it is 'an insurance company-created crisis' . . ."[12] Insurance company statistics on losses, it was noted, could be offered as a useful source to frighten recalcitrant legislators into taking the desired actions.[13]

At no point in the strategy outline developed by the AMA and AHA was any suggestion made that doctors or hospitals should try to improve the quality of care they offer patients as a means of combatting the malpractice problem.

II

As the AMA and the AHA developed their strategies and the insurance companies developed theirs, state after state in domino fashion found itself facing its "crisis." In some states, like California, the problem had been serious and visible for many years, but in others the trouble seemed to arrive overnight and full-blown, but with little or no empirical evidence that any problem, much less a crisis, existed. One state suffering such an experience was Wisconsin.

In the summer of 1974 the Wisconsin legislature, aware that malpractice problems were developing elsewhere, appointed a committee of seven of its members and fifteen public representatives to study the general "health professional liability problem."[14] Although the state's medical society and the insurers presented the usual grab bag of reforms (abolish the contingency-fee system, reinstate the locality rule, etc.), generally the testimony was reassuring. According to Joseph C. Czerwinski, chairman of the Wisconsin House of Representatives Health Committee:[15] ". . . it appeared that the problem in Wisconsin was availability of malpractice insurance for podiatrists and osteopaths with some concern over *future* lack of availability of malpractice insurance for physicians. The cost of malpractice insurance was not a problem at the time . . . [and] [h]ospitals indicated . . . [they had] no difficulty in obtaining insurance either. The insurers who appeared before the Committee indicated that, although they had some concerns about the problem on a national basis, there was no intention to cease writing business in Wisconsin."[16]

Then in late October 1974 a series of situations developed simultaneously on the insurance front. St. Paul, which at that time was selling out its stock holdings at great loss, announced restrictions on accepting new business from Wisconsin physicians. Shelby Mutual, which previously had been writing policies at 20 per cent below the recommended ISO rates, brought their prices up to ISO standards, and Continental Insurance announced it would no longer write new business involving hospital emergency rooms.[17] "In none of these cases," says Czerwinski, "was there any indication that the insurance company decision was based on Wisconsin information or experience. As a matter of fact, the responses indicated that these changes reflected *national policy* . . . it appeared that Wisconsin was being affected by a national crisis which was totally unrelated to its own malpractice experience."[18]

Another Wisconsin legislator, Paul Sicula, who subsequently became chairman of the state's Malpractice Committee, agrees with Czerwinski. In 1974, Sicula says, only 250 malpractice claims were filed in the entire state. "The malpractice insurance industry," he found, "collected some $5,366,000 in insurance premiums in Wisconsin and paid out only $850,000 [that year]. Not a bad underwriting experience as far as I'm concerned."[19] St. Paul, Sicula adds, told his committee that it paid out "only about 10% to 15% of the $2.5 million it collected in Wisconsin premiums."[20] At the same time, other statistics showed that the average pre-trial settlement in a Wisconsin case was about $8,500, 20 per cent less than the national average, with only one award in 146 consecutive cases exceeding $100,000.[21]

Despite its happy experience in Wisconsin, St. Paul precipitated that state's crisis in January 1975 when it announced it would no longer write insurance policies on the traditional *occurrence* basis; if a doctor wanted St. Paul as his insurer he would have to accept the new *claims-made* system. Pioneered by Lloyds of London for certain lines of liability insurance, claims-made has the practical effect of wedding a customer to his insurance company for as long as the company wants him. Briefly, the difference between the two kinds of policies is this: Under the occurrence system, the company pays for all claims that rise *in the future* from an incident that occurred during the year the customer was covered; under claims-made, the insurer pays only for incidents reported during the year of the coverage. For example, under occurrence insurance, if a doctor is covered by Company A in 1975 and a claim is filed in 1978 for a 1975 incident, Company A pays for the claim even if the doctor is no longer its customer. Under claims-made, Company A does not pay for the 1975 incident unless the doctor is its customer the year the claim is reported.

The Wisconsin doctors were furious at the change. Under the claims-made system, a doctor, even when he retired, they pointed out, would have to keep paying malpractice premiums or else he wouldn't be covered when a late claim rose from his active days; just as bad, if he decided to switch insurers, he'd then have to buy back coverage from St. Paul or else he'd have no protection from an incident that rose from the earlier period when he was its customer. The

Wisconsin doctors were not the only ones unhappy; St. Paul had instituted its new system (which obviously it saw as highly profitable) nationally, and if doctors in a state didn't like it, St. Paul simply packed up its policies and left. Eventually, its switch to claims-made led the company to stop writing malpractice in sixteen states, according to one estimate,[22] or in nine, based on an ambiguous statement from St. Paul itself late in 1975.[23] In a number of states, it was the St. Paul departure that forced the adoption of state-operated emergency insurance funds or Joint Underwriting Associations (JUA's) as they were usually called.

So it happened in Wisconsin. When St. Paul showed no inclination to back down from its position, the legislature hastily wrote a bill establishing a JUA so that doctors would not be forced to go without insurance should St. Paul leave. In implementing the new act, however, the Wisconsin Insurance Commissioner decided that the claims-made idea was a good one and ordered that all policies written by the state be under that system.[24] The horrified Medical Society protested, and when the Insurance Commissioner refused to back down, the Society threatened a doctor work stoppage by July 1. The strike, however, wasn't tied just to the occurrence policies the doctors wanted; it also included a demand for the panoply of reforms they had been talking about a year earlier. If something wasn't done by the deadline, Wisconsin, despite absolutely no visible evidence of a malpractice problem, was about to go without medical care because of it.

In what was decidedly now a crisis atmosphere, the legislature went back to work to come up with a bill that would prevent the walkout. State Senate Bill 299, which passed by a vote of 31 to 1,[25] didn't delegalize the contingency fee but did sharply limit the percentage a lawyer could charge, in the hope that would discourage them from accepting malpractice cases. At the same time, the bill placed a cap on the amount any patient could recover. Both steps made S.B. 299 acceptable to the physicians and the remaining insurers. However, the state's House of Representatives, led by legislators like Czerwinski and Sicula, rejected this approach. Far from convinced that tort reform was necessary, their bill limited itself to establishing a JUA to issue policies on an occurrence basis and a medication panel system for claims of $10,000 or less. That bill was opposed by the Medical Society which, by now aware that the Senate bill was doomed, abruptly shifted gears and told the legislators there was, after all, no immediate crisis and they should wait a while before doing anything.[26] The House of Representatives bill was passed anyway.

As Czerwinski summarized it: "I can't help but believe that the 'crisis' in Wisconsin may have been artificially developed. The sudden momentum is highly suspect. Although the Wisconsin legislature had, as early as July of 1974, begun to address the problems relating to malpractice and was proceeding to pass legislation for the benefit of the medical community, we suddenly found ourselves faced with a 'deadline' imposed by the insurance industry and the medical profession. We were pressured to respond immediately under great pressure from all sides, including the many patients filled with anxiety by the public threats of the physicians to cease practice if the Legislature didn't enact S.B. 299. An atmosphere of confusion existed because fundamental changes in Wisconsin's tort liability system were being demanded, without providing the Legislature with the data necessary to evaluate such changes. It appears that on a national basis the insurance industry was prepared to go the final mile in developing a crisis. Perhaps they were convinced that if such a crisis could be created, legislators would respond by passing legislation which would combine the liability limitations of a 'no-fault system,' and a requirement of proof fault with changed legal doctrines to make that proof more difficult, with the result that malpractice suits would be discouraged. It appears that in some states they succeeded."[27]

They did. In Idaho, Argonaut set the crisis in action.[28] On June 1, 1974, the company, which had a year earlier turned $21 million of its surplus over to Teledyne,[29] and which was now claiming large malpractice losses as the stock market collapsed, announced it would no longer underwrite malpractice in the state, leaving 60 per cent of the state's physicians without insurance.[30] Argonaut took this step despite the fact there was no more evidence of a malpractice crisis in Idaho than there had been in Wisconsin. For example, a year later, only twenty-eight malpractice claims were settled state-wide with payment to the plaintiff; of them, only six exceeded $10,000, only one exceeding $50,000 (that for $75,000).[31] Despite this impressive track record, the Idaho legislature, under pressure from the doctors, passed two bills, one in 1975 and the other in 1976,[32] which, established a JUA, put a $150,000 cap on malpractice awards, a $60,000 ceiling on the fee a lawyer could earn, require arbitration of claims, and modify the informed-consent doctrine in the doctors' favor.[33] An Idaho court subsequently ruled this law "unconstitutional and null and void" in its entirety.[34]

In Utah, where the principal malpractice insurer was Aetna,[35] malpractice rates also took a sudden upward turn in 1974 and 1975, this time in a state that had a much lower than average malpractice claims frequency,[36] with only three claims settled in excess of $50,000 between 1975 and 1976.[37] One major medical-care provider, Intermountain Health Services, *which had never had to pay a single malpractice claim in its history,* saw its insurance canceled and only reinstated when it agreed to a new charge of $157,000 a year compared to the $27,000 it had been paying.[38] According to the Utah Medical Society's executive director, the state's doctors were told by Aetna that "we had to pursue legislative relief in terms of tort reform" or else Aetna would not guarantee extension of the Society's malpractice insurance contract beyond its 1976 expiration date.[39] How did Utah react? It did not react by protecting its citizens against apparently unjustified rate increases but instead passed a law limiting their right to recovery when injured[40]—exactly the kind of belled-sheep-type law which, as Wisconsin legislator Sicula observed,[41] could be easily extended to cover the much more important (to the insurers) product-liability exposure.

Still another western state, Colorado, paid an ironic price for a historic tightfistedness in awarding injured patients. In that state there had never been a malpractice award in excess of $100,000, and for that reason the state's principal malpractice insurer, Hartford, demanded that doctors now be required to pay rates based on *national* trends, which were, of course, much higher. As the chairperson of Colorado's Study Committee on Medical Malpractice put it: "This would seem to indicate that a particular state's success, however achieved, in keeping claims amounts down will have little benefit to that state's medical practitioners from an insurance standpoint."[42] Although to a lesser degree than either Utah or Idaho, Colorado also passed legislation limiting the right to sue[43] and also established a complex and expensive JUA in response to pressure from its medical providers.[44]

In Indiana, a state in which there was evidence of sizable increases in malpractice claims by the mid-1970s,[45] not only did premium rates escalate but some doctors (most notably orthopedic surgeons and anesthesiologists) were finding difficulty in obtaining insurance at any rates. There, as in Wisconsin, a threat existed that doctors would curtail or cease offering medical care entirely unless the government provided them with protection from suit.[46] Consequently, in January 1975 Indiana Governor Otis. T. Bowen, himself a physician, called on the legislature to enact a malpractice bill. He made it clear he favored one that had been drafted by the Indiana State Medical Association and represented the AMA's views in their most complete flowering.[47] The bill proposed to abolish the jury system and replace it with a euphemistically entitled Patients' Compensation Board consisting of two doctors, two attorneys (who might or might not be plaintiff-oriented) and two laypersons who could be expected to be swayed by the doctors on the panel. The less compensation the patient got the better Governor Bowen and the Indiana Medical Association liked it: The bill proposed that the maximum amount of recovery permitted for the negligent death of a child should be $25,000; for the death of an adult without dependents, $50,000; for anyone else who died, $100,000. In fact, the maximum award for any injury, no matter how grave or how steep the patient's medical bills was also to be $100,000. In order to discourage attorneys from taking cases, a maximum fee of $20,850 was set for them on the $100,000 case, less for lower verdicts. The bill also reduced the statute of limitations period and added other restrictions against patients' recovering anything from the Patient's Compensation Board.[48] In explaining his support for the bill, Bowen "asserted that the problem is not one of doctors, lawyers or insurance companies; rather it is a people's problem . . ."[49]

As indeed it would have been had the bill been passed in its original form. However, it ran into trouble in the State Senate and came out somewhat liberalized with a $500,000 limitation on any reward regardless of whether it involved death or injury. The final bill also permitted plaintiffs' attorneys to charge whatever they felt like up to $100,000, but only 15 per cent of any amount over that. In a fit of generosity, the State Senate also restored to the people of Indiana their right to trial by jury, but not quite; plaintiffs were required first to take their cases through the Patient's Compensation Board which now consisted of three doctors and a lawyer—although the lawyer had no vote—and whose opinion could be admitted as evidence if a plaintiff disagreed with it and decided to go to trial.[50] Despite these changes, the final bill was "lauded"[51] by the insurance industry as a step in the right direction and enjoyed the support of the Indiana

Medical Association. Perhaps its greatest benefaction, as Governor Bowen saw it, was that it proved that states can solve their own malpractice problems: "A federal malpractice effort," the Governor observed, "would require a Congressional bulldozer, where perhaps only a sensitive state hand is truly required."[52]

In the nation's two largest states, California and New York, the malpractice crisis was also instigated in the 1974–75 period following the stock market collapse. As in most other states, legislators' problems in deciding which kind of bills to pass were compounded by their exposure to inadequate, false, or misleading statistics on the numbers of claims and payouts, as well as the failure by most concerned parties to dinstinguish between actual payments, loss reserves, and IBNR's. In New York, for example, in June 1975 at the height of the crisis, the ISO filed a recommendation with the insurance commissioner that hospital rates be increased by 194.6 per cent, this coming on top of a 65.6 per cent that had been authorized just six months earlier.[53] It turned out that ISO's evidence to back the rate increase was either non-existent or erroneous;[54] among other things, ISO, it was discovered, had added to hospital malpractice costs payments made by these institutions for litigation that had no connection to malpractice whatsoever. Based on this disquieting information—after all, if the insurance industry's statistical arm couldn't be trusted to come up with accurate figures, why should any individual insurer be believed?—the New York Insurance Department stated, ". . . we find that the proposed rate filing of Insurance Services Office has no validity" and disapproved it.[55]

In both states, strikes by the doctors and their threats to renew them at a moment's notice proved valuable to their cause. In California, the Keene Bill, named after the assemblyman who introduced it,[56] was passed, containing many of the tort-reform elements demanded by the California Medical Association.[57] Negligence attorneys predictably opposed the bill on the grounds that it gave doctors favored treatment when they injured someone, which was true enough, although the California bill, on the whole, was considerably less severe than the one passed in Indiana. In California, for example, no limitation was placed on the amount a patient could recover in medical bills and wage losses; the only ceiling established was on recovery for pain and suffering and that was placed at a liberal $250,000. The California law, however, was somewhat stiffer than Indiana's on attorney fees, confining them to one third of the first

$200,000 and 10 per cent on any amount over that. This codicil also brought cries of anguish from the negligence lawyers who now saw themselves making only $200,000 on a million-dollar verdict instead of $400,000 as had been common before.[58]

In New York, using not only the strike but newspaper ads and radio commercials[59] as their principal propagandizing weapons, the physicians also made substantial legislative gains, although many of the doctors themselves did not see it that way. The history of the New York malpractice crisis, indeed, is inordinately complex. Some of the time, the insurers were in agreement with the doctors; other times, the two groups were fighting with one another; in still other instances, the doctors and the insurers agreed to favor one element of legislation and then a few months later opposed the same proposal. In the end, New York came out with a JUA plus a plan that allowed doctors to form their own insurance companies; in the line of tort reform, the statute of limitations was reduced and a three-member medical malpractice commission (consisting of one doctor, one lawyer, and one judge) was established to hear all cases. Its decisions are appealable but, as in Indiana, admissible as evidence in any trials that followed. The new law also set up a medical-conduct review board. Control of physician discipline, however, remained in the hands of the medical profession,[60] and since the bill's enactment the staff has been kept sufficiently small as to make serious inquiries into medical incompetence impossible. The baby teeth California added to the gummy surface of its medical-discipline system looked incisor-sharp by comparison.

Nationally, by the beginning of 1977 the picture on malpractice legislation looked something like this: Thirty-five states had instituted a Joint Underwriting Association, and several others had developed comparable plans; on the line of tort reform, 27 states had acted to abolish the *ad damnum* clause (that's the system whereby a plaintiff states in the lawsuit the amount of damages demanded, and which often leads to headlines like "Doctor Sued for $10 Million" even though the ultimate result may be a settlement for $10,000); 11 states had enacted laws to replace, in part, the jury system with arbitration; attorney fees had been regulated downward in 17 states; a collateral source rule (see below) had been adopted in 16 states; the *res ipsa loquitur* doctrine (see below) had been abolished in 17 states; the informed consent doctrine had been changed in the physicians' favor in 21 states; the amount of money a patient could recover in a malpractice suit had been reduced in 10 states; pre-trial mediation panels had been established in 25 states, in 19 of them on a mandatory basis (including Illinois in which the law was subsequently declared unconstitutional in its entirety); standard-of-care evidence admissibility—usually with the intent of reinstituting the locality rule—had been changed in 16 states; 36 states had passed laws shortening the statute of limitations period; and the burden of proof on the plaintiff had been stiffened in 16 states. Also, 42 states had granted immunity to various medical peer-review systems so that doctors could not be sued by other doctors when carrying out their monitoring duties; 30 states, including most of those that granted immunity, had added provisions forbading plaintiffs access to any medical testimony developed during the reviews; 30 states had passed laws (like those in New York and California), that were intended to help the medical profession rid itself of its incompetents; and just 9 states had passed laws requiring continuing education for doctors.[61]

The fate of some of these statutes remains unclear. By early 1978, in addition to the Illinois and Utah laws, those passed in Kentucky and Ohio were declared unconstitutional in key provisions[62] with others under similar attack. Still others, however, including those passed in New York and Florida,[63] have survived legal challenges at least at the state level. The United States Supreme Court will be the final arbiter, with the most serious Constitutional issue raised by provisions that permit juries to hear (and possibly be prejudiced by) the recommendations handed down by the arbitration panels.

Unconstitutional or not, this catalogue of laws, when taken in its entirety, probably accurately depicts the national consensus on the malpractice problem. The public, to the extent it was aware of the issues—and it was highly aware in those states in which doctor strikes were threatened or carried out—generally supported the laws; in some states, including California,[64] consumer groups, fearful of loss of medical services, actually backed the worst anti-consumer aspects of the legislation, apparently accepting the thesis that the problem was one drummed up by the greedy patients and their lawyers. Organized opposition, in fact, was almost universally limited to the plaintiff attorneys, who in their isolation were easily dismissed by their victorious opponents as money-grubbing and self-interested. Except in Wisconsin and one or two other places, the anti-tort bills, as a result, passed by wide margins and were endorsed, or at least accepted, by the governors who signed them into law.

Taken as a whole, the legislation gave voice to three concerns: First, it was perceived everywhere that medical providers must continue to carry malpractice insurance, not only for their own protection against judgments but also to insure money being available to pay winning plaintiffs. Second, there was in most places at least some recognition that not all malpractice suits were frivolous, that some doctors did negligently hurt their patients, and the thought was that since most doctors weren't negligent, they should be given the legislative tools to help them police their own system and get rid of their own incompetents. Third, it was widely concluded (Wisconsin again an exception) that the existent tort system required some prohibitive tinkering. This conclusion, at the legislative level, was most articulately stated by Assemblyman Keene, author of the California bill. Pointing out that the high cost of malpractice insurance threatened some California citizens with loss of health care, he observed: "It was our argument that these reforms fall within the legitimate health, safety and police authority of the state. It is our duty [as legislators] to balance the needs of the individual against the public good in general. There is an analogous argument in the area of defamation cases . . . The argument [concerning them] is that free speech is so important that society does not want any undue burden placed upon it. In our view, health care and access to it is also so essential that steps must be taken to assure its continued availability.[65]

II

The Joint Underwriting Association, which was the step most commonly taken first by legislators, varied somewhat from state to state, and in a few instances[66] was enacted on a stand-by rather than an operative basis. Structurally, however, all JUA's had much in common. Doctors who couldn't get insurance elsewhere (or who for some reason wanted to use the JUA rather than a commercial source) were able to buy policies in whatever amount they wanted and could not be rejected because of their previous malpractice-suit experience. Theoretically, all loss risk associated with a JUA was to be underwritten, as Roberts said, by the casualty insurers, regardless of whether they presently or in the past had offered malpractice insurance. Cooperation from them was to be obtained by forbidding a casualty company from selling its profitable policies in the state if it refused to support this one supposedly unprofitable line, with the insurers required to pay the difference any time that premium payments didn't match claims costs.

It was for them a liability that was never likely to occur. Although the JUA's acted as a dumping ground for the highest risk doctors and therefore were likely to be susceptible to large claims, this danger was compensated for by rates that typically were far in excess of even those assessed by the commercial companies. The Rhode Island JUA, for example, levied charges on its customers quadruple the commercial rate,[67] while in Texas they were about double.[68] In Pennsylvania, the JUA charged rates about 30 per cent higher than that of the most expensive commercial carrier, Argonaut, and in that state, as well as in some others, an additional financial backup was created in the form of a Catastrophe Fund.[69] Under its terms, every doctor and hospital in the state, whether covered by the JUA or not, was required to pay a 10 per cent malpractice surcharge, and it was this fund that would be dipped into before the casualty companies were required to put up a penny. The Catastrophe Fund in Pennsylvania was also to be used to pay the amount by which any malpractice verdict exceeded $100,000; by putting that maximum on the amount a commercial underwriter had to pay out, the Catastrophe Fund acted, at the doctors' expense, as a free-of-charge reinsurance system for the commercial companies. At the same time, the Fund paid 100 per cent of the costs of any case in which the accident was four years old or more when the suit was entered, thereby eliminating for the commercial companies their "long tail" problem.

Meanwhile, in Utah,[70] a "stabilization reserve fund" was enacted that ultimately permitted any insurer who was cost money by the JUA to deduct that amount from past or future taxes due the state on premium income. If this wasn't enough assurance for the commercial companies, in most states the JUA was permitted to raise its rates, based not only on actual losses and loss reserves, but on IBNR estimates as well. Since the operation of the JUA typically was under the guidance or administration of the commercial companies, it was susceptible to maneuvering to establish whatever income was necessary to protect the companies from having to dip into their own tills.

In general, the JUA's provide an example of what can happen

when outside forces induce a panic condition: the remedial legislation that is passed is more likely to benefit the perpetrators of the crisis than their victims. Thus, while the JUA's met the prime "crisis" goal of providing insurance coverage for everyone who needed it, they also served the interests of the insurers. In an immediate sense, the presence of the JUA's eased the way for the insurers to get rid of doctors who were the most likely to cause them claims, since these doctors now had an alternate source of coverage which the insurance company, as a matter of public relations, could argue it was helping to support. Simultaneously, the high cost of the JUA's tended to take the focus off the somewhat lower rates the commercial companies were charging and seemed to give credence to their assertion that their own high rates did not represent profiteering.

But that wasn't all. By their very existence, the high-cost JUA's perpetuated the insurance crisis, making it likely that doctors, even though they were now guaranteed coverage, would continue to campaign for the tort reforms the insurers wanted, the enactment of which the doctors were led to believe would decrease their premiums. Finally, the JUA's, again because of the rates they charged, were not competitive to the commercial companies. On the contrary, should a commercial company decide to open its rolls to some JUA doctors, these doctors would flock to it because of the relatively low charges that would be offered to them. Such an opening of enrollment was a real possibility since far from all the JUA doctors were high-risk surgeons. Many were general practitioners or other low-risk doctors who had found it necessary to turn to the JUA when their underwriter quit the state.

III

Turning to the merits of the tort reforms which have either been legislated or proposed, Assemblyman Keene's analogy between malpractice and free-speech protections is at the root of most of them. As Keene sees it, because we consider free speech important we have made it difficult for plaintiffs to win defamation cases, and since health is equally important, we should similarly restrict malpractice plaintiffs in winning their cases. If we don't, the cost of malpractice verdicts will continue to escalate, insurance costs continue to rise, and doctors, as a result, cut back on services or go on strike, creating a danger to everybody's health. There are some difficulties with Keene's analogy. Concepts of freedom of speech, in fact, play only a peripheral role in defamation cases involving private individuals. For these actions, the same tort rules apply as in malpractice litigation, with the defamation suit the more difficult to win principally because injury to reputation is not as easily provable as physical injury. Keene, however, was probably thinking about libel suits in which a public official or public figure asserts he was harmed by a story in a newspaper or other medium. In these cases, the courts have generally ruled that such a person, to win, must show the story was written with a reckless and malicious disregard for the truth. The judicial thinking here is that the public person—because he can use his position to harm the common good—must be open to nearly unfettered criticism by the news media. The public person, therefore, does have a more difficult task winning a libel case than does the private individual, so Keene is right in saying that freedom of speech (in the sense of freedom of the press) is specially protected. However, that protection was not extended because newspapers threatened they would cease publication if they did not have it. Doctors in California and elsewhere did make threats, and when Keene, and others who think like him, urge that doctors—because they threaten—be given special protection from malpractice suits and the resultant rise in insurance rates, he is really urging that the public give in to medical blackmail, to say nothing of the blackmail perpetrated by the insurance companies when they threaten they will leave doctors uninsured if they don't get the legislative reforms they want. It is hard to see how capitulation to such threats protects health, much less freedom.

Free speech and access to the courts do have an important attribute in common. They are both civil rights, ones which the nation has spent two hundred years developing and protecting. Neither should be given up easily, yet each is most likely to be abridged when the society, correctly or not, perceives a crisis situation. In Assemblyman Keene's own state such a crisis was espied following the bombing of Pearl Harbor in 1941, with the result that Americans of Japanese descent were herded into internment camps. The crisis-tort reforms engendered by the AMA, the AHA, and the insurance companies similarly herd the public away from the courts and the exercise of their liberty to pursue those who have performed tortious acts against them.

This does not mean that all the tort reforms proposed for malpractice adversely affect plaintiff rights. Indeed, *ad damnum* clauses, because they often tend to defame the defendant through the "doctor-sued-for-$10-million" type of publicity, impinge on the rights of the accused not the accuser. Neither is it easy to feel any sense of sympathy (or even any sense of credibility) when plaintiff attorneys complain that a reasonable ceiling on the contingency fee will cause them not to accept malpractice cases. Not only do they win too many of them for that to be a factor, but no lawyer will refuse a million-dollar malpractice case because he can now earn only $200,000 instead of the $400,000 he could have earned before. Exorbitant contingency fees, in other words, are open to *prescriptive* remedy, and as we shall see, there are ways to assure that plaintiffs will get an equitable recovery without, at the same time, discouraging attorneys from accepting their cases. The danger, rather, is the *proscriptive* remedy, which has been attempted in some states, by which the contingency fee is so curtailed that the plaintiff's access to competent counsel is meaningfully abridged and with it the accompanying civil right.

Other reforms proposed by the AMA and its allies also represent serious attacks on the public. These include the efforts to re-establish the locality rule, abolish the informed-consent doctrine, abolish *res ipsa loquitur*, and to place ceilings on the amount of awards a plaintiff can receive.

There was a time in the United States when the locality rule had a reasonable basis. Those days, however, have long since passed. The nation is now three-quarters urbanized, with improvements in transportation and communications systems not only giving most patients quick accessibility to qualified medical care, but also bringing their providers within the same orbit. Although some rural doctors and hospitals in emergency situations will lack proper equipment, and allowances must continue to be made for them, accreditation procedures for hospitals and the almost universal dissemination of medical libraries,[71] as well as the imposition of federal standards on medical care via Medicare/Medicaid provisions,[72] have made archaic the belief that one community's standard of medical practice should differ from another's. Therefore, the only purpose for the reinstitution of the locality rule is to deny plaintiffs access to expert witnesses, a violation of their rights.

The informed-consent doctrine raises a more difficult issue of right and wrong. It is likely, as the doctors maintain, that the necessity of obtaining an informed consent sometimes forces them (if they don't want to get sued later) into a posture of giving a patient information that may frighten her into rejecting the best treatment for her condition. To the extent such events occur, they are deplorable. The informed-consent doctrine, however, is not intended to be applied to critical or emergency situations in which an immediate life-or-death decision must be made. Its purpose, rather, as applied not only to doctors but to all other professionals, is to assure the patient or client will be given meaningful information about the options open to her before deciding on any elective course of action. Thus, while it is apparent from our earlier discussions that significant problems surround the *definition* of informed consent and the *boundaries* of the situations in which it is applicable, nevertheless, as an extension of the concept of civil rights the doctrine is inherently sound; patients, as well as lawyers' clients, and so on, will be more harmed by its absence than the provider is by its presence. On balance, the prudent way to establish the perimeters of the medical informed-consent doctrine is not through legislative fiat but to continue to do so through the courts, permitting them to develop meaningful precedents as real situations manifest themselves from case to case.

Despite its Latin name, *res ipsa loquitur* has its roots in the old English common law, and literally interpreted means "the thing speaks for itself." As a doctrine, when it is applied by a judge in a negligence case, almost always on the request of the plaintiff's attorney, the plaintiff has removed from her the usual burden of proving that her accident was caused by someone's carelessness or incompetence. To use first a non-medical example of a *res ipsa* situation, let us suppose a man is walking down the street and a bag of cement left on a third floor window ledge is knocked over, falls on him, and kills him. In the tort action that arises from the accident, the *res ipsa* doctrine will be applied since common sense dictates that a bag of cement should never be left on a window ledge; the negligence speaks for itself. In medical malpractice cases, the same concept holds true. In one case,[73] a freezing device was used on a patient undergoing a kidney operation. During the course of the surgery, the machine malfunctioned causing death of tissues in the patient's buttocks, legs, and feet, necessitating amputations. The judged ruled the accident could not have occurred without negligence, thereby removing from the defense arsenal one of its strongest arguments in most cases, namely, that the injury was purely iatrogenic, not negligent. With negligence established through *res ipsa,* the only legal question remaining was who caused the accident: Was it the anesthesiologist who operated the freezing machine, the hospital which failed to maintain it in working order, or the manufacturer of it? (The jury found against the latter two.) To the doctors and the insurers who defend them, *res ipsa* is an onerous doctrine because in removing the defense that negligence did not occur, it usually creates, in effect, a directed verdict against least one defendant. To the malpractice plaintiff, however, *res ipsa* offers a means of achieving legal equity she might not otherwise have. Of all accident victims, her position is often the most difficult; usually unconscious when the mal-event occurs to her, she, unlike the auto victim who may find objective witnesses on her behalf, has as her only witnesses those in whose interest it is not to tell the truth. In those extraordinary situations, therefore, in which the presence of negligence is self-evident but not susceptible of legal proof (i.e., those who know the truth can defeat the case by remaining silent), *res ipsa* appears to be a legitimate method of providing proper protection to the plaintiff. That it is subject to mishandling by a judge who improperly imposes it is undeniable, but that's why we have appeals courts. That its abolition would be a convenience to the defense is also undeniable, but that is not a good reason to do away with it. (Despite the high priority which *res ipsa* holds on the list of tort reforms desired by doctors and insurers, the issue is raised in only 8 per cent of all malpractice cases at trial;[74] the number of times the judge then agrees to impose it is unknown, but the frequency will obviously be considerably less than the number of times it is demanded, with one study of approximately three hundred malpractice trials observing its imposition in less than 2 per cent of the cases.[75])

The tort system change, however, which has been most zealously pressed by both medical providers and insurers is the demand to place a limitation on the amount of money that can be awarded any victim of medical negligence. Under this scheme, those with relatively minor economic losses are permitted full recovery since their costs fall under the ceiling, while those whose losses exceed the ceiling are not. The proponents of award limitations ignore this inherent injustice in their plan. Instead, they focus on the frequency of excessive awards made by juries.[76] The insurance magazine *Perspective,* for example, has stated that "the average jury award has shot up more than 500 per cent—from $62,000 in 1965 to $350,000 today, according to national insurance figures."[77] It is not known which "national insurance figures" *Perspective* is quoting, but the NAIC in 1977 found that the average award from a trial verdict was $26,786,[78] not $350,000, and even the insurance industry's own statistical arm, ISO, came up with a jury award average of only $44,351.[79] Startling if apparently false figures such as the ones quoted by *Perspective* have helped propagate the theory that unless legal limitations are placed on jury awards, there will be no way of combating the runaway costs of malpractice verdicts. By placing a cap on awards—the theory concludes on a familiar refrain—insurers will now have to pay out less money, will pass their savings on to doctors who, in turn, will pass them on to their patients in the form of lower fees.

To believe this argument, it is necessary: (1) to grant that juries regularly do make excessive awards, though perhaps not to the gaudy extremes of the *Perspective* quotation; (2) to believe that large jury awards significantly effect the cost of malpractice insurance; and (3) to believe that either insurers or doctors will pass their savings on to anyone. The last point is a matter of speculation, but the first two premises can be tested. If either is to be found false, then there may be reasons for award limitations that are not immediately evident.

In validating the second premise, we can assume that any verdict of more than $500,000 is definably excessive to those who advocate award limitations, since that is the amount that has been set in every state in which their efforts have been successful, except Virginia, where it is $750,000.[80] The NAIC study shows that of all cases resulting in payment to the plaintiff, only ½ of 1 per cent fell into the $500,000 and up category.[81] Although the study did not show how many of these awards resulted from a trial verdict and how many from a settlement, so-called excessive award is, therefore, a statistical rarity. However, the same study showed that these large awards accounted for 14 per cent of all payment dollars made by insurance companies.[82] Consequently, the insurers' assertion that large verdicts cost them a disproportionate amount of their claims cost is a correct one.

It cannot be assumed from that, however, that the few large awards are excessive. For that contention to be true, it is necessary to develop evidence showing either that juries are incapable of understanding the complex issues raised in malpractice cases and therefore make senseless awards, or else that the size of the award is affected by misguided sympathy for the plaintiff. Although juries have inherent problems in coming to an equitable award figure, neither of these premises appears to have any general validity. To begin with, medical defendants win the majority of all jury verdicts, which doesn't exactly suggest that jurors, as a whole, have any undue sympathy toward plaintiffs. A study undertaken by HEW[83] came to the same conclusion. In it, both defense and plaintiff attorneys were asked about jury bias. Among the plaintiff attorneys, 30 per cent said they believed juries tended to be biased in favor of the doctor, 4 per cent thought against the doctor, with the remaining 66 per cent detecting no bias at all. Even more impressive was the response from the defense attorneys, since they, if anyone, could be expected to detect bias against their clients, yet they noted even less prejudice than did the plaintiff attorneys. Just 7 per cent of the defense lawyers thought juries were biased for the doctor, 11 per cent against, while 82 per cent found no bias. However, 44 per cent of the defense attorneys thought juries were likely to be influenced by the demonstrability of injury in a case or by a medical "horror" story, as maybe they should be, with 34 per cent of the plaintiff attorneys feeling the same way. Both sides of the bar also had a high opinion of the average juror's ability to understand the facts of a case. On medical issues, 94 per cent of the plaintiff attorneys and 97 per cent of the defense attorneys agreed that juries were capable of following the testimony, while the same percentage of defense attorneys and 91 per cent of the plaintiff attorneys said jurors were able to grasp legal issues.

While these statistics, by themselves, neither prove nor disprove the existence of an occasional run-away verdict by an overly sympathetic jury, they do indicate that those who are in the best position to know (the lawyers who try these cases) believe overwhelmingly that juries do understand them, do treat them on their facts, and by and large are not biased.

A second test of the "jumbo" verdict theory is derived by studying the nature of the injuries associated with them. In earlier chapters, we described three cases that resulted in awards of one million dollars or more: in one, a previously healthy person became a human vegetable as a result of a negligent mistake made during minor surgery; in another, a healthy boy became a quadraplegic because a hospital clerk refused to let a doctor treat him; in still another, an unnecessary operation, one of a series by the same doctor, left the patient in physical agony and with a significantly shortened life span. It is difficult to say that any of these cases resulted in "windfalls" of money[84] for the plaintiff.

The NAIC's study provides confirmation of the conclusion suggested by this handful of case histories. It discovered just ten incidents in which the award exceeded one million dollars.[85] The average severity of injury in these cases, *as identified by the insurers themselves*, was "grave," a term defined by the NAIC as incorporating such injuries as "quadraplegia, severe brain damage, lifelong care or fatal prognosis."[86] The average severity of *all awards in excess of $100,000* was depicted as "major," a category that included "paraplegia, blindness, loss of two limbs, and [lesser] brain damage."[87] That's a tough way for any patient to get a "windfall" of money.

The NAIC also attempted to determine whether malpractice defendants tended to be overcompensated or undercompensated in terms of economic loss. Although recognizing that its study proceeded from a somewhat narrow statistical base, NAIC nevertheless concluded: "Incidents associated with small amounts of economic loss are generally overcompensated, while *incidents with very large amounts of economic loss are often "undercompensated."*[88] (Italics added.) For example, successful plaintiffs with losses between $1,000 and $2,000 were paid an average indemnity of $12,000. Yet, those whose losses were between $500,000 and $999,999 received an average payment of $271,517 while those with losses of $1 million or more, received an average award of $474,297. The ISO closed-claims survey, using a much smaller sample and apparently a different method for calculating loss, come to the conclusion preferred by the insurers;[89] it found that small claims are usually underpaid, large ones overpaid. But even ISO observed that when *all* claims were considered, plaintiffs were undercompensated by an average of $7,000 per claim.[90] Moreover, neither study deducted the amount plaintiffs pay for attorney fees and other legal expenses. When these are considered, the true economic degree of loss per compensated patient is anywhere from one-third to one-half greater than the figures show.

From this analysis, we can state that the third premise is false and that the so-called "runaway" verdict resulting in a "windfall" for the plaintiff is of such rarity as to have no statistical impact on the problem, and that to place a limitation on plaintiff awards serves only to worsen a system that doesn't compensate with justice without the limitation.

Although the medical profession may, from ignorance, sincerely believe in the reality of the runaway verdict, the statistics showing the opposite all emanate from the insurance industry, so that its advocacy of award limitations must be perceived as based on a knowing misrepresentation of the facts.

The campaign to place a cap on awards, in fact, probably has nothing to do with the occasional large award itself. Indeed, the $500,000 cap that has been enacted in a number of states is meaningless statistically when we consider that the average state has less than one such award a year.[91] The real frequency is even less than that, since about a quarter of all awards of $500,000 and up occur in a single state, California.[92] Placing an awards cap, however, is valuable to the insurers because it has the effect of depressing the size of award made to everyone who is injured. If the quadraplegic plaintiff who used to be able to get a million dollar award now can get only $500,000, then it follows that the paraplegic who used to get $500,000 will only get $250,000 and so on down the line. In this fashion, the proclivities of a system that already undercompensates the most gravely injured is extended to all categories, and the insurance industry, at the expense of the injured, has increased its profits comparably.

Related to the awards-limitation plan are two other ideas promoted by insurers and their medical allies. One is the collateral-source rule, the other the accrual-payment plan. Each also has as its intent to prevent "windfall" awards for lucky (quadraplegic, brain-damaged) patients who win the tort "lottery" described by insurance company spokesmen.

To illustrate the collateral-source rule, let us suppose a malpractice plaintiff is out of work for a protracted time because of her injury, forcing her to go on welfare; or, alternatively, let us suppose she has bought income protection insurance that pays for lost wages due to injury or illness. Traditionally, when she receives a malpractice award, the insurer is not permitted to deduct from it any compensation she received separately. The result is the plaintiff may be paid twice for her wage losses. (However, she will have to reimburse any medical insurance plan she has, such as Blue Cross or Blue Shield, for any payments they made on her behalf out of her suit winnings.) When a collateral-source rule is adopted, the insurer deducts from his payment to the plaintiff all money she received for her injury that she herself doesn't have to pay back to someone else. The result is the plaintiff no longer gets a "windfall" in the form of duplicated payment, but the insurer, who now pays out less, does. As a matter of fairness, if anyone should get a "windfall" out of an injury, it should be the person who was negligently harmed, not the one whose customer did the harm. But the insurance companies don't see it that way.

The accrual-payment plan likewise usually acts to reduce insurance company costs. As explained by Grant Miller, counsel for Employers of Wausau: "Plaintiffs' lawyers have had great success in achieving relatively large verdicts based on evidence and jury arguments relating to damages to be expected in the future, that is to say, damages from loss of wages and necessity of future medical care and custodial treatment. Juries award verdicts for these damages based on evidence as to the plaintiff's life expectancy and other elements relating to future events which cannot now be known . . . In other words, if an award of future damages is based on a life expectancy of, say, 35 years and the plaintiff actually only lives 15 years, the original award was obviously much too large. [Delayed payment] laws would permit a defendant, through a funding arrangement, to pay for future damages only as they actually accrue. Obviously, such an agreement would do much to reduce the size of jumbo verdicts."[93]

Unlike the collateral-source rule, the accrual system is not without its merit for the plaintiff. In order to see what can happen, let us consider a case which, under the lump-sum payment system, results in a million-dollar verdict to a patient with a life-expectancy of thirty-five years and annual medical bills of $30,000. When attorney fees, legal costs, and pre-existent medical bills are deducted, the hypothetical patient nets $300,000. To make maximum use of it, we will assume that the plaintiff, or her family if she is unable to care for herself, invests the money in Treasury notes paying 8 per cent annum, in this fashion earning $24,000 the first year. Since, however, the medical expenses are $30,000, the fund is depleted by $6,000 that year and diminishes ever more rapidly in succeeding years, so that by the end of the nineteenth year, the fund is depleted, leaving the patient possibly with sixteen years or more of medical expenses and no money to pay for them. It is evident, therefore, that unless the patient has the good grace to die early, her family gets no "windfall" verdict, and if they eventually are faced with paying out $30,000 a year for her care, they will end up in penury or on the dole. The accrual system avoids this grim result since it guarantees payment of all medical expenses whether the plaintiff lives one year or fifty.

The insurance company, however, can also benefit. Typically, under the accrual system, since there is no lump payment to the plaintiff, the insurer is required initially to pay the victim's legal fees and other existent expenses. Following that, the company only pays the annual medical costs, and thereby continues to keep and earn interest on money that otherwise would have gone to the plaintiff. Should the plaintiff's costs be less than the company earns on the amount it would otherwise have had to pay out, it has made a profit on that residue. Similarly, if the patient dies earlier than predicted, the insurance company's medical payout will be proportionately insignificant. (In our example, if the patient dies after one year, the company has saved $294,000.) In that sense, under the accrual system, as under the collateral-source rule, the party liable for the negligent act is permitted to profit from it.

This does not mean the accrual system should not be adopted. For the patient with major and unending medical expenses, its value is considerable. To assure equity, however, a trustee system, under court supervision, should be developed by which if there is any net on principal or interest, the amount goes to the plaintiff or the plaintiff's estate rather than to the insurance company whose client did the damage.[94]

CHAPTER FIFTEEN

Nobody's Fault

I

With inconsequential exceptions, the malpractice legislation passed during the mid-1970s tried to solve the problem it faced within the framework of existent systems and did not consider that the systems themselves might be at the root of the problem. Typical were the medical review panels established in a number of states. Their purpose was to help doctors police their profession; they did not address the possibility that there might be no desire on the part of the doctors to do that policing. Similarly, the legislation that created the JUA's had as its sole purpose to offer an alternative source for insurance coverage, and as a result succeeded only in replicating rate-making procedures that were guaranteed to increase costs. Neither did the tort changes, no matter how far reaching they might be, move away from the fundamental assumption that litigation was the proper way to resolve disputes between patient and medical provider.

There are reformers, however, who believe that the tinkering that has taken place is at best an inadequate response to the problem, and probably one which will worsen it. In the view of some, the lawsuit, at least as far as malpractice is concerned, has outlived any usefulness it may have had and should be replaced by another, more equitable, compensation method. Still others agree with former ATLA president Cartwright that the only cause of the malpractice problem is malpractice and that as long as the medical profession is allowed to continue certain of its practices undeterred, the problem will grow in seriousness, no matter what nostrums are offered at other places along the line.

One of those who argues against a retention of the tort system for resolving malpractice disputes is Eli Bernzweig, the HEW Malpractice Commission's executive director. "The health-care consumer," he says, "is failed by the present [tort] system which makes it economically impractical to process small claims, inordinately expensive to process slightly larger claims, and extremely uncertain to process the large claims. The courts are burdened by the litigation, and huge amounts of money are spent in determining whether or not, under the circumstances, it is more reasonable for the doctor (i.e., his insurance carrier) to bear the burden of the loss instead of the patient. Results in litigated cases with similar disabilities and similar acts of alleged negligence vary widely . . . If the patient has a bad result, the factors on which compensation will turn are extremely arbitrary . . . One plaintiff will receive a small verdict as a result of jury compromise. A second plaintiff will receive a very large verdict . . . Those who receive nothing generally become burdens upon their families or upon society as a whole. In addition, large sums and much valuable time has been spent in determining that they are not to be paid."[1]

According to this reasoning, the tort system can be seen as one that at its rare best provides a means of effective compensation only for those patients who can construct a legally viable theory that they were injured by negligence, meanwhile leaving unattended the equally serious financial problems befalling millions of people injured by their medical care but not because of negligence. For example, let us suppose we have two patients each of whom has suffered massive brain damage as a result of a medical accident; the one patient's injury is caused by negligence, the other's by an unpredictable reaction to anesthesia. Neither did anything to bring about their own tragedies, yet one has a chance for compensation from the courts but the other does not. Is this equitable? asks Bernzweig.

The belief that victims of injury should *not* have to prove negligence to gain reparations has gradually been gaining acceptance in the United States. The proposition was stated as long ago as 1921 by the distinguished jurist Roscoe Pound who, in his *Spirit of the Common Law*, observed that increasingly the question courts will have to decide in injury litigation is not who was culpable but "who can best bear the loss."[2] The same thought, more than fifty years later, was echoed in a malpractice case by Justice Tobriner of the California Supreme Court in a suit involving an inexplicable operating room accident. Finding for the plaintiff, the judge expressed his displeasure with "the largely fictitious and often futile search for fault which characterizes medical injury litigation." In cases in which negligence cannot be clearly established, he commented, the responsibility for the cost of the injury should be "shifted to the parties best able to protect against [loss] through insurance . . ."[3]

Both Workmen's Compensation and no-fault automobile insurance laws are based on the belief that it is existence of the injury, not any precipitating negligence, that should be the guide in compensation. A variation of the same reasoning holds true in most jurisdictions for product-liability cases, which have generally held that the injured consumer need not prove the manufacturer was negligent in his manufacturing techniques before recovery is possible. The landmark decision in this field occurred in 1962, also in a California case: "The purpose of [setting] such [strict standards of manufacturer] liability is to insure," said the judge, "that the cost of injuries resulting from defective products are borne by the manufacturers who put such products on the market rather than the injured persons who are powerless to protect themselves . . ."[4] This thinking has found still another expression in recent years as a number of states have enacted laws to compensate victims of crime for their losses. As insurance executive Miller puts it: "Our people . . . have embraced the doctrine that it is the responsibility of the state or at least of someone other than themselves to provide them with security and minister to their needs and comfort."[5]

Medical no-fault, or "patient compensation" as Bernzweig prefers to call it,[6] therefore, represents thinking with an ample base both in the law and in evolving social policy. Precedence also exists for an insurance system to support it. Just as drivers do under automobile no-fault, doctors, under medical no-fault, would continue to pay annual premiums to commercial underwriters (or possibly to JUA's) who would be responsible for making claims payments. The difference is that claims, instead of being decided on a determination of negligence, now become payable on proof of *any* iatrogenic injury. From the doctor's view, this means he no longer gets sued; for him, the ugly word "malpractice" passes out of the language. Because of this happy consequence, no-fault has gained support in some medical circles.[7]

No-fault thinking, however, made no headway at the state level during the malpractice insurance availability crisis of 1974–76. Legislators, already under pressure to limit access to the courts via the tort system, were hardly in the mood to introduce an entirely new compensation system. Neither was the timing propitious for no-fault medical thinking. The sharp rate increases that had followed the enactment of automobile no-fault in many states a year or so earlier had given the word itself a bad odor both in the public's and the legislators' minds.

More importantly, the insurers were not ready to back medical no-fault as they had automotive. In the automobile field, they had a large universe of insureds who acted in a predictable way. In malpractice, to adopt no-fault, as they saw it, meant dropping one volatile claims universe (i.e., allegations of *negligent* injury) and replacing it with a much larger and even more volatile universe (i.e., allegations of injury *regardless* of negligence).

The possible financial dimensions of a no-fault system are visible when we recall that at least five million people each year are injured by their medical treatment, all of whom have grounds for recovery when negligence is no longer the criterion. While there is no way of projecting how many of these people will take advantage of a no-fault system, we can assume the number will be far larger than the less than 1 per cent of the injured who presently file a malpractice claim. Moreover, based on the experience of the tort system, we can also assume that those who are most seriously injured will be the ones most likely to seek no-fault reparations. At present, these relatively seriously injured people, whether they win their claim or not, have an average monetary loss of $15,239.[8] Should the number of injury claims at this loss level increase only ten-fold under no fault, the reparations cost becomes $45 *billion* annually, compared to the $200 million paid out each year under the tort system. And this calculation doesn't take into account the hundreds of thousands and possibly millions of small claims that aren't asserted under the tort formula but that might be in a system in which there is no need to prove fault.

Considering these ominous statistics, it is apparent that to make medical no-fault practicable, we must satisfy ourselves with compensating very many people very inadequately. Bernzweig himself recognizes this necessity when he refers to establishing a "comprehensive injury reparations system providing prompt though *limited* compensation . . ."[9] (Italics added.) Another no-fault proponent, Professor Jeffrey O'Connell, professor of insurance at the University of Illinois, has advocated that the no-fault system "pay [only] for out-of-pocket loss that the patient was put to . . ."[10]

Yet if that out-of-pocket loss doesn't include lost income, and it appears that O'Connell wishes to exclude it, at least in the sense of *future* loss of income, then the no-fault system simply replicates the worst aspects of the fault system, namely, those with the most severe losses are the ones most likely to be severely undercompensated. The NAIC, for instance, found that the average person who received a $12,000 malpractice award had only $171 in lost wages, but that the person who received a $200,000 award lost $400,000 in income, actual and prospective.[11] The $171 person, under O'Connell's approach, will probably get his money back, but the family that has been left without a breadwinner because of a medical accident gets nothing except its out-of-pocket costs.

Speculations about how to implement a no-fault system, however, may all be idle unless they meet the needs of the insurers and the doctors. Yet these are the two groups that bewail the claims-cost crisis they say already exists under the tort system, demanding that herculean and draconian efforts be made to bring it under control. It is unimaginable, therefore, that either the doctors or the insurers will accept any no-fault program unless it *reduces* the amount they are already paying.

One ingenious theory, developed by two professors at Duke University, will, if applied diligently, meet the cost-reduction goal by combining the worst aspects of both the tort and the no-fault system. To understand the beauty of this idea, it's first necessary to look at another difficulty endemic to the no-fault approach and that is the problem of how to identify and trace the cause of an iatrogenic injury.

In an earlier chapter, we saw that patients often find it difficult to know they have incurred an iatrogenic injury because they may mistake its symptoms as part of the normal progress of the disease for which they are being treated. Because of their frequent hidden nature, therefore, many of these injuries will go unnoticed and not result in a no-fault claim, just as many viable negligence claims are presently lost in the same way. But even when the patient recognizes the presence of injury and is prepared to assert a claim under no-fault, it is still necessary to identify its origin so that it can be determined which insurance company is responsible for paying for it. This can lead to complex questions. As Dr. William B. Schwartz, senior professor at Tufts University Medical College has pointed out: "If we have someone, say, who had transfusions and developed hepatitis, the question then is going to be which of the blood transfusions given by which doctor caused the hepatitis? And did he develop it so many weeks after the transfusion so that we wonder if it could be due to the transfusion, or is it due to something else? And if the patient is taking a drug for some other purpose which causes liver damage, could it be that, rather than the blood, that caused the problem?[12]

Dr. Schwartz's example could be multiplied almost endlessly: Was it the surgeon or the anesthesiologist whose action caused iatrogenic injury, and therefore should the surgeon's or the anesthesiologist's insurer pay the no-fault claim? Or was it perhaps a nurse, and therefore the hospital which should pay; yet maybe the nurse, at that moment, was acting under the control of the surgeon, so is it not his company's duty to pay? In short, we are back to exactly the same situation we faced when we were trying to determine fault under the tort system; the only difference is that we are now dealing with the much larger universe of iatrogenic injury. As a result, lawyers gain a comparably larger trough to feed at than they had under the malpractice system. Defense lawyers for one insurance company will dispute with lawyers from another company as to who should pay the claim. Doctors, although they will no longer have to worry about going to trial in a negligence suit, will find themselves appearing before compensation boards to explain[13] why it wasn't they who caused the iatrogenic injury, a shifting of responsibility they will quickly find a wise strategy to adopt since it is certain that any doctor with a significant number of iatrogenic claims against him is going to pay a hefty surcharge on his no-fault insurance and maybe lose it altogether just as he did in the bad old negligence days (when he had a 99 per cent chance that no matter what he did bad, nobody would notice it). Patients will have their problems, too. The insurance company, wherever possible, will take the position that no iatrogenic injury occurred, or if it did, its cost (which has to be separated from the cost of the patient's original illness) is nowhere near what the patient says it is. The patient with the no-fault claim will find it wise, in most circumstances, to hire a lawyer to represent her just as was true in the discarded system. Without such advocacy, she may find she gets nothing.

Purporting to have as its purpose to clear away part of this disputation is the "medical adversity" theory propounded by the two Duke University professors, Clark Havighurst and Laurence R. Tancredi,[14] and supported by Professor O'Connell of the University of Illinois.[15] Under their formula, the no-fault system will recompense only such "adverse" medical results as are always (or almost invariably) the consequence of iatrogenesis, as identified by a panel of medical experts. When these injuries occur, there is no longer any question that the patient will be compensated, although the problem of paid by whom remains. "At least initially," say professors Havighurst and Tancredi,[16] "only [those identified] events . . . could be made compensable, the remainder being left for adjudication under traditional principles," i.e., the tort system. It is difficult to guess which medical events the expert panel will decide are always iatrogenic, but it is apparent by the nature of the premise of the theory, that at least the most obvious and the most serious injuries (brain damage, quadraplegia, paraplegia, blindness, etc.) will be moved over to no-fault. Since, however, no-fault under all its constructs is intended only to provide "limited out-of-pocket" damages, the underlying thrust of the medical adversity theory is to forbid access to the tort system to people with the most severe injuries, whose cases ordinarily produce the largest verdicts. Remaining in the tort system, meanwhile, are cases that involve lesser injuries and those that are the most difficult to prove, and whose victims, gain no access to even the limited payments no-fault provides. Adoption of the Havighurst/Tancredi plan creates a mechanism for reduced payment for the insurers; the medical adversity is the patients'.

No matter how it is applied, one principal consequence of no-fault is to remove from the doctor's shoulders most of his legal responsibilities to his patient. While the AMA and various medical societies clearly believe that is the direction in which the law should go, it is not a view universally held within the medical profession. Dr. Schwartz, who in addition to serving as a professor of medicine works as a practicing physician, is one who worries about the consequences of removing that responsibility. Speaking in December 1976,[17] he noted: "I'm on rounds this month. I'm looking after about—between fifteen and twenty very sick patients each day. And I know, as I go into each room and look at each record, that I am far more sensitive today to the question of the care that I'm exerting and the quality of the care that I'm providing than I was five years ago.

"Now I hasten to say, I think that I've provided good quality care, but I think that I'm just a little bit more careful. I'm sensitive to the fact there is a potential for suit.

"And in talking to my colleagues, every physician that I speak to . . . indicates that they are responding to the larger number of suits and the increased size of awards with a greater degree of care. In other words, I would suggest—and I'm not the first to suggest this—that the malpractice system has, one of its major purposes, a mechanism for quality of care control, a mechanism for improving quality of care.

"Now the concept that the major purpose of liability coverage . . . is not to compensate the patient . . . goes back to Oliver Wendell Holmes nearly one hundred years ago. He pointed out that there are other ways that victims of accidents could protect themselves; for example, by buying insurance.

"And he expressed serious doubt that the compensation of the individual was the key to the purpose of the liability system. And many legal scholars have pursued that theme and most of the people who thought hard about this recently, as far as I can tell, feel that the major purpose of the system is to send a signal to the provider to keep them careful and keep the standard of care that he's providing at an appropriate level.

"According to that view, then, it is important that the plaintiff be compensated because we need an incentive to each injured party to sue the offending individual, and we also need the doctor or whoever the provider is to pay the plaintiff so that he gets the signal he must be careful . . .

"Theoretically, in a perfectly functioning system, we would like to have every major malpractice incident result in a claim. This is from a public policy point of view. Only then would a physician—myself, as I go on ward rounds—know that a lapse from the appropriate standard of care is likely to cost me something in both embarrassment, time and money . . .

"So I would like to raise the totally heretical point of view that the increase in the number of claims may not be appropriate; that, in fact, what we may be doing is seeing a better signal to physicians, to me, to be more careful than in the past, and that before we tinker too much with the system, we'd better understand its implications for quality of care."

Schwartz sees one other fault in the no-fault approach. Recognizing that a doctor with too many no-fault claims against him will begin to run into the same insurance problems as the malpractice-suit-prone doctor, Schwartz points out that when the doctor's no-fault rate begins to go up, he "simply starts avoiding doing those things which throw him into your no-fault category in which he knows there is going to be a high incidence of untoward results over which he has no control, because they're non-negligent, but which he has to pay for under a no-fault system. So, you're caught on the horns of a terrible dilemma. Either you remove the deterrent aspect, in which case no-fault allows a doctor to do what he wants without any concern, or you force him to pay even for those incidents for which he's not responsible, in terms of negligence, in which case he starts being seriously influenced in his decisions and choice of patients and procedures because he doesn't feel that he should be burdened with a cost that is unrelated to the quality of his performance."[18]

In substantial agreement with Schwartz is another physician, Sidney Wolfe, director of Ralph Nader's Public Citizen Health Research Group. "The main problem with the present [tort] malpractice system," Wolfe says, "is that not enough 'fault' is discovered, pursued, and corrected. Whether the fault be in technical incompetence, poor judgment, or poor doctor-patient relationships, those who cause it need to be identified, urged to change their ways, and disciplined. No-fault . . . insurance guarantees that this central problem of failure to differentiate those hospitals and doctors who cause malpractice incidents from those who don't will worsen rather than improve. What is needed is more-fault, not no-fault."[19]

Despite this gloomy analysis of the no-fault proposal, its underlying philosophy addresses a significant question of justice. If it is true, as Schwartz and Wolfe believe, that the deterrence signal is paramount, it is also true, as Bernzweig understands, that it is unfair to compensate only the patient injured by negligent injury and force the person equally injured by non-negligence to fend for herself. It may be, therefore, as Havighurst and Tancredi propose, a no-fault system should be adopted without completely abandoning the tort system. But such a system should not, as medical adversity does, act for the benefit of the insurers. More appropriate is a system in which the patient is permitted a free choice between a no-fault and a fault claim. Such a proposal was embodied in a bill introduced in the United States Senate by Senators Kennedy of Massachusetts and Inouye of Hawaii.[20]

Under its guidelines, any medically injured patient may use the tort system but has the alternative of applying for no-fault benefits. The no-fault portion, under this bill, is funded by insurance premiums paid by medical providers which go directly to the federal government with the program administered by HEW: "The Secretary shall determine the amount of . . . benefits through an administrative procedure . . . [with benefits including] all medical expenses, all vocational rehabilitation expenses . . . lost earnings or cost of hiring a substitute up to $2,000 per month, and traditional general damages up to $2,000 per month—but with no provision for punitive damages. The no-fault benefits are payable only to the extent that the losses are not covered by other governmental or private disability or health insurance (except life insurance)."[21] The bill is not without its problems. It is most pertinently questionable, for the reason Dr. Schwartz gives, to ever require doctors to pay premiums for injuries that result from non-negligent care. More properly, the no-fault aspect of the plan, which could be quite expensive, should be paid from taxpayer funds, based on the assumption that it is in the public's interest to compensate those who have been injured medically through no fault of their own. Nevertheless, the Kennedy-Inouye bill represents a real and enlightened concern for the plight of the medically injured, which may be the reason it was never passed into law.

II

Impatient with all such reforms are the critics of the medical delivery system. Says Dr. Wolfe: "No amount of self-insurance, instead of commercial insurance, no-fault instead of fault, or abolishing contingency fees is going to improve the quality or accountability of the American health care system. Those who pretend that it will are deceiving the public." Rather than such "diversionary tactics," Wolfe says, we should face the only real question: "Do we want to institute systems to ensure better quality of care now or not?"[22]

Since no one wants to institute a worse quality of care, Wolfe's rhetoric, while stirring, avoids the difficult question of which systems should be inaugurated to force better care. To that, there is no easy answer. Several ways have been tried. Of them all, the deterrent lawsuit system, for the reasons praised by Wolfe, Schwartz, and others, including the ATLA which is well served by it, has probably been the most successful in forcing hospitals and doctors to initiate risk-management systems. Looked at that way, our legislative goal in handling the malpractice problem, therefore, should be to find ways to encourage people to file suits and to extend the situations in which providers can be found liable, rather than taking the opposite tack as has been done.

Unfortunately, the value of the lawsuit as a means of remedying the quality-of-care problem is sharply limited by its fortuitous nature. Its existence depends on the occurrence of an injury that is evident to a patient who then also has the legal knowledge and the willingness to do something about it. As a result, the malpractice suit is always reflective of the complex set of circumstances surrounding it, and while it may also reflect a serious medical delivery system problem, no inherent reason exists why it should. There is, for example, very little in the annals of malpractice literature suggesting that the cases that get litigated bear any positive relationship to the most serious systemic flaws, i.e., the prevalence of unnecessary surgery, of improper prescriptions, and the failure to solve the incompetent doctor problem. We have, therefore, no reason to expect that if we encouraged suits and as a result saw their numbers double or triple, their deterrent effects would be any more substantial than they are at present. But even if we were to assume the contrary and believe that by multiplying the frequency of suit we will also begin to focus on the more important problems, we must still consider that the plaintiff has no interest in establishing social policy but rather, quite properly, only in recovering damages. She and her lawyer, perceiving that as their goal, will continue to place their heaviest reliance on settlement negotiations and will want to avoid trial, the forum that is necessary if legal precedents of a meaningful nature are to be established.

If the lawsuit has its limitations as a deterrence weapon, the only significant alternative—monitoring systems—have an even less encouraging history.

One of the earliest was instituted in 1949 by the American College of Surgeons.[23] Concerned at that time about the prevalence of improper surgery, the College called for the establishment of "tissue" committees in hospitals around the country, their purpose to determine whether or not each operation that took place was a justified one. Theoretically, a surgeon who developed a track record of bad performance was subject to discipline by the committee and might lose his operating-room privileges or his position on the staff. Although some surgeons no doubt have been disciplined in that fashion since the committees were formed, and although there is no question that the committees act as a good teaching device by which young doctors learn which operations should be performed and which not, the effectiveness of the committees as deterrents to bad surgery can be gauged by the fact that twenty-eight years after their formation, the same College of Surgeons issued another report decrying, in exactly the same way, the high incidence of improper surgery.

In 1953 a second major monitoring step was taken when the Joint Commission on Accreditation of Hospitals (JCAH)[24] instituted a medical audit guideline which hospitals were supposed to adopt as a means of measuring the quality of care their patients received. One JCAH-approved hospital, which had a full-blown medical audit procedure, was the one in which Dr. John Nork performed his disastrous back operations. The hospital, however, despite its monitoring never had a glimmer of an idea of what Nork was doing, and the reason was, according to Judge B. Abbott Goldberg who rendered the decision in the case,[25] that the JCAH procedures "were predicated on the assumption that a doctor was reporting honestly [to the audit committee] and that [his] records were truthful and accurate." As Goldberg noted, this was an assumption that defeated the whole purpose of any audit and left patients totally unprotected when the assumption proved incorrect. But that wasn't the only problem the judge found with the JCAH procedures as followed in this hospital. "The required clinical review," he observed, "was subjective according to the personal standards of the reviewer. The [analysis of it done on behalf of the court by Dr. Reid M. Nesbit, a surgeon and himself a deputy director of the JCAH] show[s] that such a subjective review will not disclose known deficiencies . . ." Further: "The review [system in effect at Nork's hospital] was random. Therefore, bad cases were picked up only by chance [and it was] infrequent . . . casual, uncritical, and sandwiched between the doctors' other work . . ." Even common sense wasn't followed: "The review did not include a comparison of the doctor's progress notes and the nurses' notes . . . No protocol, profile or record was made of [a] doctor's deficiency so that there was no common fund of knowledge available to the hospital . . . It takes," the judge concluded, "no great ingenuity of medical knowledge to compare nurses' notes with doctors' progress notes. It is no triumph of intellect to record a doctor's deficiencies. Omission of such precaution cannot be excused, because they are imperative to patient care."

In 1974, perhaps in response to cases like the Nork one and at a time when the malpractice crisis was at its most visible, the JCAH announced stiffened auditing procedures to be followed by any hospital wanting to obtain or retain accreditation. As praiseworthy as this effort was, it was not a complete success. A case in point was that involving twin brothers, Drs. Cyril and Stewart Marcus of New York City: Despite substantial evidence of the deterioration of the skills of both men due to barbituate addiction, the JCAH-approved hospital in which they practiced failed to withdraw their staff privileges until just a few days before the brothers died, the one an apparent suicide, the other from the effects of drug withdrawal.[26]

But the College of Surgeons and the JCAH are not the only ones who have had indifferent success in attempting to force private hospitals and doctors to offer their patients better and safer care. The federal government has taken its unlucky stab, too. Its involvement began in 1965 following the passage of the Medicare/Medicaid Act. The government feared, with some prescience as it turned out, that hospitals would be tempted to overhospitalize eligible patients in order to enrich themselves on federal government payments. To assure this wouldn't happen, the Social Security Administration, in a marvelous flash of bureaucratic wisdom, required participating hospitals to established so-called Utilization Review Committees, thus putting in the hands of those who stood to profit from excessive hospitalization the job of seeing to it that it didn't happen. As HEW subsequently dryly noted: "Utilization Review Committees . . . generally have been ineffective."[27]

In 1972 changes in the Medicare/Medicaid Act gave the federal government a new means of controlling both the cost and the quality of medical care for patients covered by the Act. By terms of one amendment, Professional Standard Review Organizations (PSRO's) were established in each of the 203 medical districts into which the country was divided. Funding of the PSRO's came from HEW with their activities subject to review both by state and national administrative superstructures. The job of the PSRO, its membership made up of practicing physicians in the district, was to determine which services provided to Medicare/Medicaid patients were necessary and reimbursable and which were not.[28] In order to accomplish this, each

PSRO was to draw up standard procedural guidelines "to be followed for various diagnoses with various types of patients. It is recognized that there will be instances where a physician's clinical judgment will require him to deviate from the established standards and criteria, and, if the judgment is sound, the PSRO will not object to the deviation. If the PSRO should disapprove of a proposed procedure or service . . . the government would not pay . . ." although the physician or institution so rebuked has the right to appeal to the statewide PSRO.[29] The district PSRO's are also expected to "compile up-to-date profiles on individual physicians to spot doctors who overprescribe certain drugs, overutilize certain procedures, or otherwise fail to meet stipulated guidelines."[30]

This might be considered monitoring with a vengeance, and some doctors fear that will be the result of it. To them, the PSRO smacks of Big Brotherism by which elitist physicians powerful in the local medical society are empowered to snoop into their affairs and establish standards of care that may be idiosyncratic to the committee members themselves.

Unquestionably, the possibility for the vendetta against the unpopular or maverick doctor exists in the PSRO structure, which leads to the possibility that the immunity from legal action now widely enjoyed by these committees under state legislation may be used exploitively rather than in the patient's interest.

It can also be feared that, despite the wording of the law, PSRO standards, no matter how well-intentioned, at times will inhibit innovative treatment of the sort that in the past has led to important advances in medical science. With the threat of malpractice suits always lurking, doctors may become increasingly conservative, fearing to deviate from the PSRO dictates—even when they are not treating Medicare/Medicaid patients—because they reasonably expect that judges will use PSRO guidelines as a general handy means to define acceptable professional standards of care for every patient.

Whether any or all of this will happen is hard to say. As of January 1978,[31] despite the 1972 law requiring their formation, only 120 districts of 203 nationally had received conditional federal approval for their PSRO's. Sixty-three were still moseying through the planning stage, while the remainder, located in three states—Texas, Georgia, and Nebraska—didn't even exist on paper. Of the 120 in operation, not a single one had moved beyond the setting of guidelines for short-term hospital care, something most people thought had long since been established by JCAH, Tissue Committees, and Utilization Review standards. The possibility that the PSRO's will be too vigorous, therefore, is at least matched by the possibility that they will never do anything at all.

In any event, as with all previous review systems, PSRO's are predicated on the belief that the medical profession is capable of policing itself and that it has the collective will to do so. That such a premise is questionable is suggested by the bizarre history of still another peer review system that existed in Philadelphia from the early 1960s until 1974.

This committee came into existence when the doctor who was then the city's medical examiner (the same office that is coroner in other jurisdictions) noted a growing number of deaths that he attributed to medical negligence. Once having made this determination, he seems to have been puzzled as to what to do about it. (The doctor has since died, so his motivations are a matter of speculation.) One thing he determined *not* to do was to inform the survivors of the dead patients that their relatives would still be alive if they hadn't run into medical incompetence. In order to forefend this possibility, on his autopsy reports, instead of listing the cause of death as "medical negligence," he called it "therapeutic misadventure" which could, to a layman, mean almost anything—or, most likely, nothing. He seems, in any case, to have been uneasy about keeping his knowledge of the deaths to himself, either out of ethical concerns or possibly a suspicion that his silence might leave him exposed to legal problems in some instances. In the long run, he decided the best way to get the problem off his shoulders was to turn his reports over to the Philadelphia Medical Society, which, on his urging, formed a special committee to investigate them.

From the beginning of its existence until the end, the Committee always operated in secrecy,[32] its existence revealed only when an enterprising reporter for the Philadelphia *Bulletin* uncovered its doings two years after its demise. No records were ever kept. One *Bulletin* story quoted a former chairman of the committee as saying, "We were afraid to keep anything around, to be honest with you."[33] Exactly what the committee did do is unclear. Admittedly it, like the medical examiner, never informed families of the dead patients about the apparent malpractice: "The only concrete value in giving that information to the family," observed the president of the Medical Society, "would be that that would instigate a suit for dollar damages . . . It is not in the best interests of the consumer for the Society to function as the instigator of potential suits."[34] Nor did the committee ever turn the results of its investigations over to the appropriate state agency for possible disciplinary action against the doctors involved.[35]

Dr. Marvin Aronson, the man who succeeded the founder of the committee as medical examiner, was asked by a reporter what happened to a case after it reached the committee: "I'd ask what happened to it," Aronson recalled, "and was told it was under advisement . . . The best they would say would be, 'Well, we need a little more information on this as to why the physician did this or that.' I never saw any physician around to explain the situation, and I never saw anything done to a physician who failed to come."[36] The *Bulletin* then asked the former committee chairman if the body ever communicated with the doctors who were responsible for the alleged malpractice deaths. His response: ". . . there must have been occasions when I wrote to physicians asking them to elucidate or provide additional information. Now I don't remember whether we ever gave a verdict to them." He was also asked if the committee reported its findings to the hospital in which a death had taken place: "The chief of staff or the chief of the department was . . . Now I don't know what we did really. I mean, you've got me over a barrel. I think there were times when we asked the chief, the professor, the head of the department, to comment on the case and he was aware of what went on in his hospital. Now what he did about it I have no idea."[37]

Nobody, as far as is known, did anything. However, the *Bulletin* revelations caused a sufficient scandal that the Pennsylvania Board of Medical Education and Licensure—a body famed for its inertia in a field in which glacierlike stillness is the norm—to appoint a special committee to investigate eighty of the cases which had slithered through the hands of the Philadelphia Medical Society committee. After ten months of investigation, the special committee reported, to no one's particular surprise, that the medical examiner had been wrong in alleging malpractice in sixty-six of the eighty deaths.[38] The nature of the fourteen cases in which malpractice apparently did take place can be glimpsed by the summaries of the circumstances of some of the cases which, in the words of the special committee, the medical care offered was within "standards of acceptable care."[39] They included: a forty-year-old woman who died when the left ventricle of her heart was torn during surgery; a forty-two-year-old man who died when his liver was lacerated during the course of obtaining a routine tissue sample; a sixty-year-old man who died when his heart was punctured by a needle; a fifty-five-year-old man who died when his rectum was punctured during the administration of an enema; a twenty-eight-year-old woman who died of a heart laceration which occurred during routine tests; a seventy-six-year-old woman who died following an exploratory laparotomy, apparently because the hospital laboratory delayed six hours in sending its findings to the surgeon; a fifty-two-year-old woman who died following a routine hysterectomy and appendectomy (exactly the kind of death the American College of Surgeons says cannot occur unless there is improper care); a sixty-five-year-old woman who died following a routine hysterectomy following a liver biopsy; a fifty-nine-year-old woman who died during an operation when forceps lacerated her pulmonary artery; and a twenty-seven-year-old woman who died following a biopsy on her bronchial tubes.[40]

But it doesn't always take a special committee or a peer review body to cover up the evidence of a suspicious medical death. Government agencies do their part, too. A case in point is the aftermath of the Lillian Lazzeri death, which also occurred in Philadelphia, about a year after the Medical Society committee disbanded its activities, such as they were. Several months after Mrs. Lazzeri's death, an informant, not Rose Turner, revealed the entire history of the case to a consumer ombudsperson employed by the Pennsylvania Department of Health. This woman, an attorney, turned the case over to her superior, who, in turn, shifted the case to the Philadelphia Department of Health which, he noted, was required by law to investigate all questionable maternal deaths. (The state's health department, however, had had the legal right to conduct the investigation itself.) The Philadelphia Department of Health received the case either in August or September 1975; six months later, a reporter contacted the physician in charge to learn the status of the investigation. She said the records she had received so far were "incomplete" and she was waiting for additional information before proceeding further. The reporter, who knew that witnesses at the hospital would testify if they were approached by a government agency, then asked the Health Department doctor if anyone at the hospital had been interviewed about the circumstances surrounding Mrs. Lazzeri's death. Her reply: "Conducting interviews with witnesses who would know the facts of a case is against Health Department policy."

Startled by the existence of this novel investigative technique, the reporter turned to the state health department superviser, who admitted he had been "remiss" in not following through on the case but said he would get right on it and let the reporter know everything he had uncovered by the end of the month. He did not do so. The reporter called him. The call was not returned. Finally the reporter reached the ombudsperson who learned that the Philadelphia Health Department had now decided—after sitting on the case for nine months—that it had no jurisdiction to investigate it. A month or so later, a spokesman for the Pennsylvania Health Department, under pressure from the ombudsperson, said it was going to conduct a full-scale investigation of the case. The investigation never took place. As a source in the Health Department told the reporter: "Don't expect anything to happen. The state office always tells the Philadelphia office to lay off investigations of hospitals. There's always somebody politically important who has to be protected."[41]

Since only those medical cover-ups that fail are revealed, there is no way of knowing how often families like the Lazzeris aren't told the truth about a medical fatality, nor of how often peer review committees and related government agencies see as their duty to protect not the public but the doctors from the consequences of their misdoings. Revelatory, however, is a HEW study. In it, plaintiff and defense attorneys were asked which factors in a malpractice case were most likely to influence a jury's decision. The response that came second in frequency only to "demonstrability of the injury" was "evidence of record falsification," with "about one fourth of plaintiff and defense attorneys both [mentioning it.]"[42] As the HEW commented: "What is surprising is not that record alteration influenced jurors, but that it was mentioned with sufficient frequency to suggest it is not a rare practice among defendants accused of an act of medical malpractice."[43] Armed with this disturbing piece of information, the HEW Malpractice Commission made no further investigation of it, and the subject has generally also been ignored by others who have researched the malpractice problem.

Regardless of its frequency, the cover-up, whether it takes the form of lying to patients or altering or destroying incriminating records, points up the inherent difficulty of asking the medical profession to monitor its own activities in such ways that its misdoings become public knowledge. To expect that is to expect people to act in ways that they conceive to be against their own interest. Not much more can be expected from relevant government agencies. Like the two health departments involved in the Lazzeri case, they too are usually controlled by doctors who tend to protect other doctors. But even when this isn't the case, they perceive—as public officials—that their principal duty is to provide a co-operative atmosphere with the physicians and hospitals they regulate, and not to develop information which will cause that co-operation to disintegrate or make people in general fearful of using medical services.

There is another problem inherent to the medical system that makes monitoring it especially difficult, whether done internally or by an outside agency. This problem relates to the psychology of the average physician. Because of it, support for significant efforts to analyze and improve systemic weaknesses at best tends to be spasmodic, and most often non-existent, and without support by the people who run the system, no reforms will ever get far. As one noted American surgeon[44] has analyzed the problem: "The doctor['s] . . . education, while prolonged and intensive, is rather structured and narrow . . . In a way, a set of blinders is put on him at the outset. In the environment in which he leads his professional life, other people wait upon him. His authority and knowledge are rarely questioned. He is resentful if they are. Every day he must make decisions that can have far-reaching effects upon the lives of his patients; he often must make those decisions immediately. Usually, his work totally consumes his available time and energy. He is not much given to philosophical meditation. But, headiest of all, is the total control he has over those patients who come to him. Life, health and well-being are things that people value greatly, and they entrust them all to the doctor. Is it any wonder that he sometimes develops a sort of 'God complex?' It is a difficult thing to resist or even avoid. In time, this can make the admission of fallibility very awkward indeed." If the kind of mind-set that this portrait develops is accurate, it then follows that not only will the doctor be reluctant to admit his own mistakes, but he will perceive his medical environment as an extension of his own infallibility, so that anything that others perceive as wrong within it is viewed by him as an attack on him personally. At the same time, and perhaps more importantly, because of his concentration on the small universe of patients in which he rules as king, he has little time or interest to devote to the consideration of medical delivery problems that don't affect him personally.

It may be, therefore, that the doctor's absorption in his patients, a positive characteristic to possess, as far as their welfare is concerned, illuminates the underlying reason why, nearly thirty years after their institution, the tissue committees were found by the American College of Surgeons to have had little effect on the reduction of bad surgery, why the hospital in the Nork case paid no attention to what Nork was doing despite the JCAH guidelines, and why monitoring systems in general have failed: Nobody has the time to watch, nobody has the interest to watch. The result is that those who would circumvent the guidelines or who find it to their interest to lie to patients and to alter records, only rarely will find anyone to say them nay.

To reach such a conclusion, however, does not mean that peer review systems should be discouraged. It is, rather, that we should be realistic in our expectations of what they can accomplish. To the extent the peer reviews, whether they are PSRO's or JCAH guidelines or tissue committees, act within the profession itself to improve quality of care, to that extent they are likely to reduce the amount of patient injury occuring each year, deterring the situations that lead to malpractice suits.

However, when we consider the millions of patient injuries that occur annually as against the 30–40,000 malpractice claims asserted, it is evident that many decades will pass before a declining injury rate developed by the best internal monitoring begins to affect the claims rate. In the meanwhile, we are still faced with how to prevent medical negligence cover-ups from succeeding, how to weed out the incompetent doctors left untouched by either monitoring or lawsuits, how to decide who is to be compensated and for how much, and finally how we go about changing the insurance system so that the doctors and their patients are no longer financially exploited by it.

CHAPTER SIXTEEN

Some Answers

I

"Publicity," Judge Learned Hand once said, "is the evil enemy of truth." The validity of his observation can be seen in the history of the malpractice crisis. Between 1974 and 1976 publicity caused legislators across the land to enact laws based on false and misleading statistics, which eroded citizens' rights by responding to insurance company profit priorities and to the medical establishment's factually unfounded assertion that the only way to solve the crisis was to make it difficult for people to sue and limit the amounts of money they could win.

But publicity, when it is used to create a crisis, not only causes people to make wrong decisions, but also makes them lose sight of how much or how little they actually know about the problem they are facing. As a consequence, when a crisis atmosphere develops a future is predicted on the basis of the crisis, not on the problem that was the lever to bring the crisis into existence. Futures based on crisis presumptions, as a result, often don't occur. The student protests of the 1960s, for example, seemed to assure a youth in permanent rebellion against authority; the students of the 1970s belie that prediction. The black militancy of the same earlier period, in the minds of many,[1] ushered in a period of violent racial confrontation that was certain to continue for decades; that didn't occur either.

In each instance, the prediction was wrong because it was founded on the manifestation of the problem, not on the problem itself. The student rebellion ended when students no longer faced the possibility of having to fight a war. The racial violence faded away because the essence of the black protest had always been political and economic, not racial, and as responses were made, the presumed racial confrontations disappeared along with them. The adverse result was that in neither case did the underlying problem get solved: blacks remain largely poor and relatively powerless politically, while the ideological issue of the abuse of Presidential power in an unjust war was avoided in its entirety. The essential trade-off, therefore, was to solve the crisis in order to prevent the bad future but not to solve the problem. Malpractice legislation has accepted the same trade-off.

If we assume, however, that it is better to solve problems than crises, our results might be different. In that case, our remedying job has as its goal not to prevent or fulfill a predicted future, but rather to understand symptoms and find ways to alleviate those that should be alleviated and encourage those that should be encouraged. To do that, the first task is to find out what we know about our problem, not just what we guess about it.

Unfortunately, despite or because of the plethora of statistical studies that have been done by interested parties, our reliable information about the malpractice problem is rather scant. We do know, with a considerable degree of certitude, although the subject has been largely ignored since HEW discerned it in 1972, that of the five million or more patients injured each year by their medical treatment, upward of one million injuries have a sufficient base in negligence that a viable lawsuit could be forthcoming from them. Our deterrents against that occurring, however, are almost entirely fortuitous, having their origin in patient ignorance, the difficulty of learning of injury, and the self-interested activities of the legal practitioners in making their decisions about which cases to accept and which to reject. The second fact, in which all sources appear in agreement, is that the malpractice claims rate began to rise at about a 10–15 per cent rate annually in the mid-1960s and has continued at that pace ever since. This is an interesting and perhaps crucial fact. The interest lies not in the rate increase itself—there have been many reasons for that which have been discussed earlier—but that it appears to have been largely unaffected by outside events. When we have claims rising at a 10–15 per cent rate in 1967, when malpractice hardly loomed large in the public consciousness, it should be expected that the percentage increase would be much larger or much smaller in 1977 when the crisis situation, the tort reforms, and all the attendant publicity about it were at work. Yet that did not happen. Since it appears, therefore, that the rate increase is not affected by crisis atmosphere, it is very possible that it represents the single most ominous integer in our problem, suggesting that no matter what we do (in a crisis-solution way) the 10–15 per cent rate will remain. If it does, within not many years the annual true claims rate will hit the 100,000 level and, by mathematical progression, in fewer years after that, reach 200,000, at which point we will have a real cost crisis on our hands. (By inference, this suggests that any no-fault intervention will simply hasten the crisis.) However, it may be that we cannot properly assume that claims will continue to rise at the existent pace. Ten years is a relatively brief trending period. What we may be undergoing, instead, is a period of upward adjustment that will be followed by a leveling off period, no matter what we do or don't do. With these considerations in mind, it is apparent that our second fact—the claims-rate increase—is difficult to interpret and dangerous to act upon precipitately. What it principally points up is the considerable need we have for additional causal data, unprejudiced as to source and free of the mysterious non-asserted claims factor, before we can properly use this fact to make any recommendations.

Consequently, any remedy programs that can be recommended must include those that permit, and quickly, the obtainment of objective and publicly accessible data about the types of situations leading to negligent injury, the profiles of offending doctors and hospitals, and so on. However, our remedy posture cannot simply be one of research. We may not have, at the moment, a genuine crisis on our hands, but we do have a serious problem, which has its real victims with real needs whose legitimate rights must be guaranteed. Those victims do not include the AMA, the insurance companies, or the lawyers, but do include individual doctors, who are required to pay exorbitant insurance fees, and the patients, who have been harmed by the medical treatment they have received.

The following suggestions, therefore, are not intended as a "solution" to the malpractice problem, but rather approaches which, if adopted, are most likely to create a manageable, non-crisis atmosphere in which final judgments can rise from reason rather than from panic.

Before considering these suggestions, it should be noted that they are all predicated on the assumption that the tort system will continue to be the prime patient-recovery vehicle. If, however, a no-fault approach is to be adopted, it should retain free access to the tort system along the lines proposed by the Kennedy-Inouye bill described in the last chapter.

II

1. *Institute non-binding arbitration for resolution of malpractice disputes.*

As of 1977, twenty-five states had established some form of malpractice arbitration,[2] with the concept endorsed, at least in principle, by the AMA,[3] the AHA,[4] a number of major insurers (including St. Paul,[5] Travelers,[6] and Aetna[7]), as well as by the Association of Trial Lawyers[8] and, with grave reservations, by the Defense Research Institute,[9] which includes among its members, attorneys who represent doctors in malpractice suits.

That the endorsements should be forthcoming is not surprising. In recent years, arbitration has become an increasingly popular tool for the pre-trial settlement of many types of tort disputes other than malpractice. Although they vary in structure and function from jurisdiction to jurisdiction, the non-malpractice arbitration panels typically consist of three lawyers who, in return for a token fee, listen to the facts in a dispute, then make a ruling on its merits which, when appropriate, includes a recommendation for an amount to be paid the plaintiff. If both sides agree to the ruling, that is the end of the case. If either side disagrees, the case then goes onto a trial docket. In many of the jurisdictions, panels hear only cases in which the amount in dispute is relatively small, with the ceiling on award frequently set at $10,000; any suit in which the plaintiff demands more than that is considered a trial case. The history of these panels is that, although their decisions are not binding on the participants, their recommendations are frequently accepted or at least become the basis from which a somewhat later pre-trial settlement is derived.

The arbitration (or "mediation" or "pre-trial panel") system's great attraction lies in the speedy resolution it permits of cases. Suits that used to have to wait five to ten years before coming to trial, because of overcrowded court calendars, are likely to reach an arbitration panel in six months to one year. For a malpractice plaintiff who may have tens of thousands of dollars in existent medical bills and lost wages, and may well have continuing costs, this virtue of the arbitration system is so considerable that it outweighs any of its drawbacks and is the principal reason its universal adoption is recommended here.

To work most effectively, the arbitration process should be mandatory. This means that if the disputants haven't been able to settle the case among themselves within a defined time period (in Pennsylvania, it's six months from the time the suit is filed[10]), the panel comes into existence automatically. Setting a near-future time limit has two virtues. First, it forces lawyers to get to work on the case immediately and not put it off until it fits their convenience, which usually has nothing to do with the convenience of the plaintiff or the defendant. Second, knowing that the arbitration panel comes into existence automatically and quickly, lawyers on both sides have an impetus to arrive at a satisfactory settlement among themselves because each realizes the panel may come up with a recommendation not to their liking. The speeding of the negotiating process will more often benefit the plaintiff than the defendant insurer since its recalcitrance to settle a good claim is based principally on its desire to keep its loss-reserve money earning interest as long as possible. However, protracted delays are sometimes improperly instigated by the plaintiff's lawyer who figures if he can just keep the case going, the other side will eventually make some kind of offer to end it. This is most likely to occur if the negotiating time begins to run up large defense legal bills, which, if they continue, will approach or surpass the amount that will get rid of the claim.

The great danger of any malpractice-arbitration system is that it will be rigged to favor the medical defendants and their insurers. There are two problem areas in this regard, one dealing with the composition of the panel, the other with the weight to be given its findings.

Looking at the composition problem first, we find that most of the arbitration systems initiated during the malpractice crisis have included doctors as members of the panel. In Indiana, for example, the voting board consists entirely of medical practitioners;[11] in New York, one doctor, one lawyer, one judge;[12] in Pennsylvania, two doctors, two lawyers, and three laypersons.[13] Logically, however, there seems no reason that malpractice panels should contain either doctors or laypersons. The whole point of any arbitration system for tort cases is to bring those with *legal* skills into the picture so they can use their abilities to help bring about a settlement when the disputants can't. That purpose is defeated when the arbiters brought on board are other than lawyers. Since we don't want lawyers to perform as doctors, it's unclear why we should want doctors performing as lawyers. It cannot be argued that doctors are needed for such panels because only they are capable of understanding medical problems. Lay juries, as we have seen from the HEW study, are almost universally believed by the lawyers who try these cases to be capable of understanding them, a view in which the doctors must concur since juries most often acquit them, and there seems no reason to think that an arbitration panel consisting of lawyers should be any the less bright in its verdict-rendering than one consisting of lay jurors.

Not that the advice of doctors should be ignored; if needed, they can be called as witnesses just as they would at a trial. However, to include them on the panel ineluctably suggests it is then necessary to have automobile manufacturers serving on arbitration panels involving automobile accidents, owners of buildings on panels involving falls, and so on. However, even were we to assume for the moment that doctors should be included for their expertise, then by what rationale are laypersons included? By their very nature, they are nonexperts, which is why we ask them to serve on trial juries, an altogether different function from serving on a dispute-settlement panel where they do not even have the neutral guidance of a judge to steer them through the legal shoals.

Since the placement of individuals other than lawyers on arbitration panels makes no reasoned sense, the probable real purpose for their incorporation, as Dr. James W. Bush, a director of the University of California Medical School at San Diego has observed, is to create "a systematic prejudice for providers, especially if the experts are selected from lists nominated by hospitals and medical societies." (This is precisely what occurs in most states.) "Even where their technical competence to rule on a particular case is no greater than that of a jury's . . . providers can expect greater 'understanding'" from their fellow doctors on an arbitration panel than they would from lawyers. "For professionals contributing their time to serve as arbitrators," Dr. Bush adds, "problems of wealth, motivation, and social class are likely to create further distortions."[14]

The inclusion of the laypersons furthers the same distortion goal since it can be expected (and it was apparently the hope of the medical societies which urged their inclusion[15]) that their judgment will be most influenced by the doctor members of the panel.

The defense bias that is created by an arbitration panel that includes doctors has its maximum impact if the panel's decision is binding, i.e., neither litigant has a right to trial if dissatisfied.

A number of the major malpractice insurers, including St. Paul and Aetna,[16] prefer the binding system, as do a number of major medical providers. Among the latter, the Kaiser Health Plan, for one, notes: ". . . a binding arbitration provision [is included] in our membership contracts in four of our operating Regions. By accepting [Kaiser] Health Plan coverage, the subscriber and his dependents agree to binding arbitration of any subsequent professional liability claims. The purpose is to reduce legal fees"—this will happen, suggesting the real reason that many defense attorneys dislike arbitration, binding or otherwise—"and administrative costs by simplifying and speeding up the hearing process, and to limit the distress of physicians involved in the claim."[17]

The great virtue of binding arbitration, however, as most of its advocates see it, is that it removes malpractice suits from the uncertainty of the jury process. Irving Ladimer, director of health services and medical malpractice programs for the American Arbitration Association, notes: "Arbitration . . . offers a fairer, less emotional atmosphere [than a jury trial]. In a complex case where, for example, the main defense is causation rather than negligence, the jury might be impressed by a dramatic plea that if an operation had been performed or treatment given earlier, death or injury would have been averted. A neutral arbitrator, better able to sort out the issues and distinguish negligence from cause, might conclude that regardless of negligence, there was no causal relationship . . . But," Ladimer is quick to add, "arbitration is not stacked against a plaintiff because the panelists are better equipped [than a jury] to comprehend facts and weigh evidence. They can also consider textbook testimony and see through objections that often prevent the plaintiff-litigant from getting to the heart of his case."[18]

The crowning argument in favor of binding arbitration, however, say its advocates, is that the public wants it. As proof, they point out, that hospitals that ask entering patients to voluntarily sign agreements to waive a jury trial in case of a malpractice claim and accept binding arbitration in its place, find that 99 per cent of all patients agree to do so. The University of California's Dr. Bush believes that the conclusion to be drawn from this statistic is the converse of its intent. Patients entering hospitals, he points out, usually "are hardly aware of their acceptance [of the binding arbitration].

Many think it is a routine (even required) part of the admissions process. Many are too sick and worried . . . to consider it thoroughly. Others, not understanding its significance, trust the hospital . . . But [even] among patients who understand the disadvantages [of binding arbitration] thoroughly, many agree to satisfy the hospital and physicians on whom they depend for medical care. The agreements, signed or unsigned, are placed on the [patients'] charts. The whole staff can know the decisions and patients fear they may be marked [if they don't sign] . . . Ninety-nine per cent conformity suggests ignorance and coercion not freedom . . ."[19]

As Dr. Bush summaries it: "For the negligently injured patient, binding arbitration piles poor legal care on top of poor medical care,"[20] and the evidence is persuasive that he is correct, particularly when the panels include or, more often, are dominated by doctors who have every reason to find in favor of their colleagues in their desperate effort to cut down on the frequency and cost of malpractice litigation. The right to trial by jury has been one of the most hard won of all human endeavors in history; it should not be given up to serve those who find that the binding system serves their financial interests best.

As noted earlier, a variation on the non-binding process has been introduced in several major states (including New York, Indiana, and Pennsylvania[21]) by which the arbitration panel's decision is admissible as evidence should the case eventually go to trial. This codicil is analogous to permitting a second trial for a criminal defendant who has been convicted at his first trial but then allowing the jury at the second trial to know he was convicted the first time around. The result is inherently prejudicial and quite possibly unconstitutional and should not be permitted in malpractice trials anymore than it is in criminal trials.

The plaintiffs bar, via the ATLA, has come up with its own variation on the malpractice arbitration system. It recommends that only those cases in which the damages demanded by the plaintiff do not exceed $25,000 should be subject to arbitration. In so doing, the proposal adheres to the rationale of other arbitration systems namely to mediate only minor disputes so that the courts aren't stuck with them and can bring the serious cases to trial without long delay.

Although the ATLA position is not without its theoretical attractions, it does not, despite its espousal by plaintiff attorneys, act in the best interest of those plaintiffs who have suffered the most serious injuries and who, as a consequence, are the ones needing financial relief the most desperately. It is these plaintiffs, not those with minor injuries, who should have first access to some award system. They need not agree with the award, in which event they can enter into further negotiations and perhaps ultimately trial. They should, however, have the opportunity to gain quick redress in a non-binding situation before an all-lawyer panel.

A second reform of the settlement process should also be considered; it can be used either in an arbitration or a trial context and will add to both the speed and the justice of the suit's resolution for both sides:

2. *Provide free medical evaluations in a malpractice dispute.*

The cost of pursuing malpractice litigation from the plaintiff attorney's view can be substantial. These costs—the most important of which are pre-trial consultation fees with medical evaluators and expert witness fees—can easily run between $5,000 and $10,000. Although the plaintiff is technically liable for the payment of these costs, win or lose, the attorney knows from experience that if he does lose, he also loses the money he has put out—unless he wants to sue a client who has, most likely, no money to begin with because of her medical injuries—a realization that marvelously discourages him from accepting all but those cases in which the likelihood for a big win is great. Insurers have similar expenses. Not only must they find their own expert witnesses for a trial, but they too require medical advice at the onset of a case to determine how great is their possible exposure to loss—knowledge that will play a meaningful role in their subsequent negotiating posture.

By permitting free medical advice to both plaintiff and defense prior to the filing of suit, much of this expense for both sides is eliminated. More importantly, for the cause of justice, if the system is properly administered, it acts to remove from the litigational process cases that should not be pursued, and provides quick settlement for those that are merited.

An experiment along this line was conducted in Montana in the early 1970s[22] but fell into disuse because it was laxly organized, but more importantly because it met with the opposition of the state's principal insurer,[23] an indication of one problem area in the idea, but also perhaps an indication it has merit. Without noting the details of the Montana plan, the recommended program is as follows:

A person who believes she has been injured by malpractice is permitted to write a letter (in practice, the letter will usually be written by her attorney) to the State Medical Board, announcing she has filed a malpractice claim. In response, the Board provides her with the names of three to five physicians, all of whom have agreed to serve as examiners with their fee paid by the state, and all of whom are specialists in the area of medicine in which the injury occurred. The plaintiff selects one of these experts and gives him permission to perform a detailed examination of the medical circumstances of her injury. His opinion, whether for or against the plaintiff, is admissible as evidence in any subsequent arbitration hearing or trial. The defense, similarly, is provided a specialist of its choosing, and that opinion, pro or con the defendant, is likewise admissible. Either side in a claim may invoke the process, and once the one side does, the other must agree to it, as long as one of the doctors recommended is acceptable. If neither side initiates, then the normal tort process obtains and the state and its experts remain uninvolved.

There is always the possibility, as Dr. Bush points out in his critique of arbitration panels, that the medical experts will be unduly defense oriented. Should this situation develop, plaintiff attorneys will refuse to use the system, and it will quickly fall into disuse. This does not, however, appear to have been a problem in Montana, and the great likelihood is that, just as plaintiff attorneys have been able to find doctors who will evaluate cases objectively for them for a fee under the existent system, similar cadres of objective doctors can be developed (and maybe more easily) who are paid by the state. A fail safe, in any event, exists since the plaintiff can stop the process if none of the doctors are acceptable to her (as, for that matter, can the defense).

This caveat to one side, the system generally should help resolve claims in an equitable and speedy manner. For example, let us suppose that both the outside expert chosen by the plaintiff and the one chosen by the defense agree that the plaintiff has a legitimate cause for action. Knowing that these opinions are admissible at trial, it is a foolhardy insurance company that will not then move vigorously to settle the case before trial. Similarly, if both experts agree there is no malpractice, few plaintiffs will want to continue what will now almost certainly be a losing claim. Finally, if the two experts disagree with one another, no one is worse off than they were at the beginning, and both sides have obtained expert testimony at no cost to themselves.

An objection that might be raised to this proposal is that it requires the public to underwrite the cost of the advice. However, the public is already underwriting the cost of the malpractice problem every time it pays a medical bill, with part of that payment going to cover the fees of the medical experts the insurers hire. In that sense, the only extra cost to the public is that of the advice given the plaintiff. But even this cost add-on becomes insignificant if the consequence of the system is to speed the resolution of meritorious cases and eliminate some which should be eliminated, in both events cutting down on the amount of money it takes to operate not only the malpractice insurance system but the judicial system as well, for which the public also pays.

III

The next reform is intended to remove an important inequity in the jury award system.

At present only about 3 per cent of all medical injuries that lead to the opening of a claim file[24] eventually result in a trial. Of these, it is unknown how many are heard before a jury and in how many the right to jury was waived so that the decision was made exclusively by a judge; however, a jury probably is empaneled in approximately three quarters of all trial cases.[25]

Despite the rarity of the jury trial, its impact on the malpractice problem is a significant one. Although defendants win most of them, trial awards, even so, make up about 10 per cent of all money awarded plaintiffs annually.[26] This largely comes about because it is only the most serious cases that normally go to trial, those in which both the prospective damages are the greatest and the legal issues the thorniest, and which can't, as a result, be settled at the pre-trial stage. The job of the malpractice jury, simply in reaching a decision, therefore, is a difficult one.

Once that decision is made, and if the jury has decided to make an award to the plaintiff, it then enters into a whole new area of difficulty. Its duty at that point, as the judge will explain to it, is to make the plaintiff "whole," i.e., award her such an amount as equals her costs plus the value of any pain and suffering the jury decides she underwent. The only exception occurs in those jurisdictions that permit comparative awards based on contributory negligence, i.e., the plaintiff is made whole less any amount by which the jury believes she brought her woes on herself. (The decision-making process in many jurisdictions is bifurcated: The jury first decides the merit of the case and then, if it finds one or more defendants liable, listens to additional testimony on damages issues, after which it retires a second time to consider how much to award. Where this system doesn't apply, the jury decides liability and makes any award in one sitting.)

At the best of times, determining the amount to be given can offer a Solomon-like problem. Although the jury will know from the damages testimony the amount of the plaintiff's expenses, it still must decide if it wants to make the pain and suffering award and, if so, find a way of putting a dollar value on that. Moreover, if the jury believes the defendant was grossly negligent, it knows it can also make a punitive damages award; should that be $1.00 or $1 million? Such determinations, based on the jury's own sense of values, are fundamental to all award situations. But their problems can sometimes be much more complex than that. For example, if the plaintiff's loss is a continuing one, necessitating future medical expenses and future loss of income, the jury must attempt to decide the amount of that, pondering such problems as the likelihood of the plaintiff's eventual recovery from the injury, the number of years she may live, the effect of future inflation on the award, and so on. If the case involves a person who has died as a result of medical negligence, the jury then has to consider how much longer that person normally would have lived and her likely earnings, or if the deceased was an unemployed housewife the value of the loss of her services to her husband and children. Such considerations are particularly difficult if the decedent was a child since the jury has no way of knowing the occupation that person would have chosen and thus the earnings that were lost.

As difficult as it may be to come to an equitable decision on these problems, the jury at least, has gathered *some* information about them. On other important matters, however, it receives no information whatsoever, either through the trial testimony or from the judge in his instructions.

In most jurisdictions, for example, neither the judge nor the attorneys for either side are permitted to tell the jury to what degree the plaintiff's medical expenses were covered by a private insurance plan such as Blue Cross. The jury's ignorance of this can sometimes cause it to harm the plaintiff. Knowing from their own experience that most people have private hospitalization coverage, the jurors may decide that this plaintiff probably did also and so deducts some arbitrary figure to cover that amount, unaware that the plaintiff is obliged to pay back to the medical plan all it paid out in her behalf.

However, the most important fact about which the jury is kept in ignorance everywhere is the financial arrangement between the plaintiff and her attorney. (As a matter of law in the United States, fee arrangements between attorneys and clients are privileged and may not be revealed to a jury.[27]) The jury's dilemma here is a real one. It has decided the plaintiff should be made whole, but it has no way of doing so, even assuming it can resolve all its other difficulties, as long as it doesn't know how much of the money the lawyer will get.

As an illustration, let us assume a jury decides that a plaintiff deserves $100,000. It makes its award in that amount and lets it go at that. Under those circumstances, it has failed the plaintiff because, depending on her arrangements with her lawyer, she nets only $50,000 to $67,000 after his contingency fee is deducted. The jury, therefore, has made her only 50 per cent to two-thirds whole. Often, however, juries will consider lawyer fees, even though the judge hasn't mentioned them in his instructions. As realistic people, the jurors know that lawyers cost money, and probably one or more of them will also know[28] that attorneys in negligence cases work on a percentage basis. No one on the jury, however, will probably have any way of knowing the exact percentage. One member may have heard that the norm is 40 per cent, but if the jury, as a result, decides to simply add $40,000 to the $100,000 it wants the plaintiff to have, it still hasn't accomplished its purpose, since 40 per cent of $140,000 is $56,000, leaving the plaintiff with $86,000 instead of the desired $100,000. Or, the jury may have a better mathematician in its midst than that, who will realize that it's necessary to raise the award to approximately $167,250 to reach a nearly equitable figure. But what if the jury is wrong about its 40 per cent assumption? The lawyer's fee may be 50 per cent which means the plaintiff has again been undercompensated, or it may be one third, which means the plaintiff is overcompensated and the defense has to pay more than the jury intended it should. The possibilities of making a mistake with this guesswork system are almost endless, and the larger the award the wider the discrepancies become. (Under the example given, if the award is $1 million instead of $100,000, the plaintiff might be undercompensated by as much as $500,000, as frequently happens,[29] or overcompensated by $100,000 or an even larger amount.)

In order to relieve this inequitable situation, it is recommended that:

3. *The attorney's contingency fee become an add-on to the jury's award.*

The jury, under this reform, is specifically advised by the judge that they should not consider legal fees in their deliberations; the fee will be added automatically to any award they make.

Through the agency of this simple change, the jury for the first time has the capacity to properly fulfill its duty to make the plaintiff whole, and the plaintiff for the first time is assured she will actually receive the amount of money the jury intends her to have. Further, because the plaintiff now gets the proper amount, the defense also, for the first time, knows it is required to pay the proper amount and no more.

To illustrate what happens in dollar terms, let's turn again to the jury that wanted the plaintiff to have $100,000. For simplicity's sake, we'll further suppose they guess correctly that the lawyer's fee is one third. Therefore, if they make the add-on, it's necessary for them to award the plaintiff $150,000 so that she gets her $100,000. Her lawyer, by this process, gets not his agreed-upon one third but a 50 per cent fee ($50,000 compared to $100,000.) However, when it is the judge making the add-on, he just adds one third to $100,000, or $33,333.33. The savings to the defense is almost $17,000. The larger the award, the larger the savings to the defense, e.g., the jury, under the existing system, wants the plaintiff to have $600,000. To do so, if they make the add-on, they have to give her $900,000; if the judge makes the add-on, the lawyer's fee is $200,000, a savings to the defense of $100,000.

Although the plaintiff's bar, which is well aware of how nicely the jury add-on system usually works to its financial benefit, will no doubt object to this change, the equity it creates is a compelling reason for its adoption. To assure that attorneys won't try to get around the new system by the expediency of raising their percentages, it would be wise to legislate the one-third fee as the maximum any attorney can receive for handling a malpractice case. This is a sufficiently large amount, even under the judge add-on, for malpractice cases to remain attractive to them, but moves away from the exorbitant fees that frequently occur now. For very large verdicts, it may be appropriate to limit the attorney's fee even further, e.g., one third up to $500,000, 25 per cent of any amount over that. However, this kind of dickering with percentage points is much less significant, both in terms of equity and of dollars, than taking the fundamental step of seeing to it that the plaintiff gets what the jury wants her to have.

The plaintiff, however, still doesn't get what the jury wants her to have if she is obliged to pay from her winnings the cost of witnesses, depositions, and other associated expenses. Since it was the defendants' negligence that put her in the position of having to sue, it seems appropriate (except possibly in some contributory negligence cases) that the defense be required to pay these amounts as well. On the other hand, to require unsuccessful plaintiffs to pay defense costs, as some have urged and as is now the rule in England,[30] is not equitable. Most plaintiffs, as it is, can't afford to pay their own costs if they lose, much less the defense's; to require the unsuccessful plaintiff to do so (and open her to suit by the defendant's insurer if she doesn't) will act to frighten people from entering legitimate suits when they know the great financial risk they run if they lose. This creates a chilling effect on the justice system which should not be countenanced.

The one ground on which the plaintiff and her attorney should be liable occurs in situations in which it can be shown that the malpractice suit was motivated, on the part of either, by malice or fraud. Such suits against plaintiffs and their attorneys have been filed in recent years by successful malpractice defendants, and some of them have been won.[31] It should, however, be noted that the successful defendants could themselves be open to countersuit by the original plaintiff and attorney if it can be proven they were motivated by malice in their countersuit. So it goes in the justice system.

A problem more difficult to resolve than that presented by attorney fees and trial costs is that created by the impact of the defendant's insurance on the size of jury verdicts. As we have seen, insurance executives believe juries often adhere to the "deep pocket" theory and make unduly large awards because they assume the insurance company can afford it. Although this situation may occur more frequently in fancy than in fact, to the extent it is a reality, it is unjust to insurance companies and can be even more unjust to a doctor defendant if the jury, thinking insurance covers everything, makes an award beyond the limits of his coverage. The converse can also happen. A jury that's not conversant with malpractice insurance may make a small award in a serious case because it doesn't want to harm a defendant who, it is convinced, did something wrong but not to the extent he should be bankrupted because of it. It is difficult, however, to recommend that juries be given information about the extent of the defendants' insurance coverage since it is possible they might take that as a signal from the judge as to the amount they should award. There seems no easy answer to this problem, and it is one which deserves more study.

IV

The next two reforms deal with insurance. For purposes of discussion, they are considered separately, but each will work better if adopted in conjunction with the other.

4. *Provide malpractice insurance to all providers on a flat-rate basis.*

As was discussed earlier, until the 1950s the flat-rate system was universal. Rates differed from company to company, but not from specialty to specialty, nor was there any rate separatism on a geographic basis. The categorical system that was instituted to meet climbing claims rates seemed to offer at least a rough measure of fairness, both in terms of risk and of ability to pay. The doctors who were the most likely to cause the most serious injuries—surgeons—also earned the most money; the same was true geographically, with the higher rated city doctors, who are somewhat more likely to get sued regardless of specialty than rural ones, typically also earning more money than their rural cousins.

Rather early on, however, some observers became uneasy about the categorical structuring. The HEW Malpractice Commission, for one, expressed concern that steeply rising premiums in certain categories might cause "physicians in some high-risk fields to change specialties or retire early. High rates may also have a bearing on a young doctor's decision to enter one specialty rather than another. If physicians avoid certain specialties because of high malpractice insurance premiums, the result could adversely affect patient care . . ."[32] The Commission went on to note that the AMA and other "*health-care providers by encouraging numerous specialty rating classifications have contributed to the establishment of a rating classification program which may be inequitable to some practitioners and which . . . may adversely affect the cost and availability of professional liability insurance.*"[33] (Italics in original.) As a result, the Commission urged the AMA, the AHA, and other professional bodies to meet with the insurers "to study alternative methods to classifying individuals and institutions for rate-making purposes . . ."[34] This was never done and shortly afterward came the skyrocketing of malpractice rates with the largest increments concentrated in the highest-risk fields.

As its ambiguous wording suggests, the HEW Commission was unclear[35] about which kinds of rating reforms should be instituted, but it never directly questioned the fundamental propriety of the categorical system. In so doing, it was following mainstream thinking about insurance, which recognizes that all rating systems are discriminatory but not to be discarded for that reason. For example, the careful eighteen-year-old driver unfairly pays more for his automobile insurance than does the careless twenty-eight-year-old, because nationally there are more careless eighteen-year-olds than twenty-eight-year-olds. Similarly, the forty-year-old man in excellent health buying a life insurance policy unfairly pays more than the twenty-year-old whose health may not be so good. The only alternative to the categorical system, however, it is perceived, is to rate each person individually, which would be so prohibitively expensive to accomplish that everyone would pay higher rates as a result. Moreover, because only adverse results are knowable (the customer who is claims-free today may have one lodged against him tomorrow), when insurance companies do individualize rates they do it punitively, as when one twenty-eight-year-old driver's rates become higher than another's because of his bad driving record; or when one doctor pays more than another because of his bad claims record.

Most categorical systems, including medical malpractice ratings, are further based on the theory of self-ending responsibility. This means that although one customer may pay $300 rather than $200 because of the risk group or groups to which he actuarially belongs, any claims made against his policy are perceived as originating and ending with him, i.e., it is his house that burned down, his icy sidewalk on which someone slipped. Whatever the merits of this philosophy may be as applied to most lines of insurance, it is far from clear that it can be properly applied to medical malpractice. To accept it there is to assume that the doctors in the so-called "low risk" categories perform their services in orbits discontinuous from the "high risk" categories. This, however, is not the case. Rather, medical care, and quite properly so, is provided on both a discrete and an interrelated basis. A general practitioner, for instance, treats *some* of his patients from the beginning to the end of their illnesses, but there are others he refers on to specialists who are more qualified to help them. In that sense, the specialist is but the final link in an ongoing chain of treatment. When the specialist's knife slips and severs the nerve, he is not, therefore, analogous to the householder who negligently failed to clear his sidewalk and whose neighbors are *not* responsible for his carelessness; instead, his knife never would have been there to slip had it not been for the general practitioner who sent the unfortunate patient to him in the first place.

This is not to suggest that doctors should be held legally responsible for the negligence of other doctors to whom they refer patients (although, in fact, general practitioners are being named in increasing numbers in malpractice suits[36] based at least in part on that theory). To accept such a legal hypothesis is highly debatable because it may discourage doctors from referring patients when they should do so. The pertinent question, rather, is should specialists pay the highest rates when the bulk of their practice is derived from providing care to patients whose difficult problems cannot be helped by lesser-trained doctors? Since the treatment burden is a dispersed one, it is at least arguable that the rate burden should be equally dispersed.

Categorization of risk based on geographic location is even more questionable. Theoretically, the system has one prospective virtue; it may encourage doctors—especially young ones who can't afford to pay high malpractice rates—to set up practice in rural areas. But even if we assume that it's a good idea to have insurance companies, in effect, decide (by their rate structures) where doctors practice, many of them, in reality, don't have any choice about where they set up their practice; rather, by the nature of their work they require close-at-hand well-equipped hospitals and laboratories with highly trained staffs of the kind that can usually only be found in the large cities and their suburbs. The specialist, therefore, typically is susceptible to a double insurance charge. He pays a high rate to begin with because he is a specialist and then pays a surcharge because the nature of his specialty requires him to perform his services in the "high risk" areas that are created by the fact of him and his facilities being there.

Geographic ratings also at times create unfair competitive burdens for doctors. For example, since New York City and a number of its surrounding counties are identified by insurers as a "high risk" area, all doctors who practice within the boundary pay higher rates than do doctors in immediately adjoining counties. As a consequence, we could have two surgeons, one just within the "high risk" area and the other just outside it, both using the same hospital to perform their operations, both drawing their patients from the same general neighborhood, yet the one outside the "high risk" area can charge his patients less than the other solely because his malpractice rates are lower. If the "outside" surgeon isn't as good as the "inside" surgeon but gets more patients because his rates are lower, not only does the "inside" surgeon unjustly lose income, but because of the insurance rating system patients end up in the hands of a doctor less well qualified to help them.

This, however, is not the only way nor the most serious one by which patients are adversely affected by the categorical rating system. Unlike self-ending systems, the malpractice categories create inequitable economic burdens for those patients who can afford them the least.

To illustrate, consider two doctors, one a general practitioner, the other a neurosurgeon. Under the categorical system, the GP, let us assume, pays $2,000 for his malpractice insurance; the neurosurgeon $20,000. Since even a moderately busy GP will see 3,000 patients a year, in order to recoup his malpractice insurance costs he need pass on only $.67 per patient. The surgeon, however, performs only 200 operations a year, which means for him to recoup he must pass on $100 per patient. But who are the surgeon's patients? Because they require surgery, they have medical bills much higher initially than the patient who has her minor ailments treated by the GP. But it is not only the surgeon's fees such patients face. Unlike the GP's patients, they have hospital bills necessitated by the surgery (bills that include the hospital's malpractice pass-on), and even if the patient has private hospital insurance (the cost of which also includes a malpractice pass-on), her surgery-related costs may still amount to thousands of dollars, leaving her in penury. Yet it is surgical patients, needing financial relief the most, who are, because of the categorical system, required to pay the largest percentage of the malpractice insurance bill. Therefore, the fact that higher-income doctors generally pay higher insurance rates, in effect, only means that their patients pay higher insurance rates.

By abandoning the categorical system and replacing it with the old flat-rate system, as has been urged by the ATLA[37] and by Senator Gaylord Nelson of Wisconsin in his national health insurance proposal,[38] a substantial measure of fairness is restored to the insurance system for patients and for doctors.

For example, at the beginning of 1978 there were approximately 350,000 doctors in the United States who could be covered by individual malpractice insurance policies.[39] (This figure does not include doctors whose premiums are paid by a hospital employer.) For the private-practice doctors, the estimated bill for the year is $1.4 billion.[40] On a flat-rate basis, therefore, each doctor would pay approximately $4,000 in 1978 for malpractice coverage. (We are not, at this moment, considering that the insurance charges are exorbitantly high to begin with.)

Under this reform then, the rates for general practitioners and other low-risk doctors rise considerably, but not to prohibitive heights, no more than doubling in most instances, while, at the same time, rates for the highest-risk doctors are reduced by 75 per cent or more. Offhand, this seems an inequitable result for the low-risk doctors, and it would be if they, in fact, were absorbing rather than passing on their costs. Because they do pass them on, however, the ultimate bearer of the burden, the patient, moves into an equitable position. The GP of our example, as a result of his increase, now passes on $1.33 per patient rather than $.67 as before, hardly an insuperable cost to place on his clientele. On the other hand, the surgeon, whose rate is reduced from $20,000 to $4,000, now has to pass on only $20 per patient rather than $100, providing greatest relief for those who need it most.

Whether, in fact, surgeons will voluntarily reduce their rates accordingly is an imponderable, although if the public is properly made aware of the new rating system, pressure will develop on the surgeons to make downward adjustments, and this might well be a requisite legislatively. In any event, at the minimum, the reform will act as a brake on further increases in fees to surgical patients based on insurance costs.

Because of the simplicity it reintroduces to ratings, the flat charge system is also amenable to ancillary restructuring that is difficult to administer within the complex categorical system. For example, it might be appropriately decided that young doctors just starting out in practice should pay a lesser flat rate than doctors with larger patient rolls, and similarly older doctors slowing down on their practice might have their flat rate reduced comparably.

More importantly, inauguration of the flat-rate system should encourage at least some specialists to set up practice in low-income or rural areas where their services are badly needed because they will now know they don't have to churn up $20–$30,000 in income each year just to pay their insurance. To the extent this occurs, an inestimable benefit has evolved within the medical delivery system.

From the doctors' view, however, probably the single greatest value of the flat rate is the surcease it provides against sudden gigantic increases in their malpractice premiums. Let us suppose, for example, that one year the cost of handling malpractice claims escalates by $100,000,000. Under the categorical system, this means that certain specialists in certain geographic locations would be faced with increments of $5,000 to $10,000. The immediate out-of-pocket cost to the affected doctors is severe and might cause them (as has happened in the past) to threaten to go out on strike if the rate increase is not rescinded, thereby creating adverse effects in the quality of medical care. Under the flat system, the $100,000,000 can be covered by increasing each doctor's premium by less than $300, a sum that can readily be passed on to patients or absorbed by the doctor himself.

Although the flat system distributes the malpractice insurance burden more fairly, it does not deal with our conclusion that the cost as it exists is excessive. The following proposal seeks to create a malpractice insurance system that not only is accurately priced, but also contains deterrent provisions and supplies the much needed statistical data on the malpractice problem.

5. *Malpractice insurance for doctors and hospitals should be written by a national company operating under federal guidelines.*

Immediately prior to the 1974 malpractice insurance crisis, there were perhaps thirty companies competing for business in the field.[41] By the end of 1977, that number had much more than doubled, including, along with the remaining commercial companies, a growing assortment of self-insurance mutuals and the dozens of state-operated JUA's. Because the number of underwriting sources increased, the number of customers available to each decreased, so that the pool of insureds, small to begin with and already riddled by claims volatility, was now seriously fractionalized, thereby increasing the solvency risk for each source should it be hit by a rash of random claims. To meet this danger, rates—already at confiscatory levels because insurance commissions had capitulated to commercial carrier demands—continued to escalate.

But that wasn't the only way the new insurance outlets added to the national malpractice cost. Each new company, JUA or self-insurance mutual, also brought into existence its own set of expenses: the cost of hiring high-priced legal counsel, actuaries, claims investigators, clerks and so on, as well as paying for office space and other overhead charges. Moreover, some JUA's were managed by commercial companies which charged the JUA a commission—sometimes as high as 20 per cent[42]—for each new customer it signed. It is difficult to imagine a solution to the cost of the malpractice-insurance problem that was better designed to worsen it.

The opposite tack could have been taken. Rather than caving into insurance company pressure and passing panic legislation, the affected state governments could have told the companies to get out if they couldn't provide insurance at a reasonable cost, and then used their very considerable lobbying powers to demand that the federal government immediately establish a new malpractice insurance system designed to work in the interest of both doctors and the public.

That can still be done, and should be.

Such an insurance system can be administered by the federal government, by the medical profession, or by a single commercial insurance company.[43] The first two alternatives, however, are not to be recommended. The federal government has shown scant ability to serve the public well in controlling costs and creating benefits under Medicaid, and its track record on Medicare is not much better. The thought, therefore, of establishing a federal bureaucracy to run a malpractice insurance company is hardly cause for optimism. Similarly, an insurance company operated by the AMA is not likely, given the medical profession's shoddy history of monitoring itself, to develop safeguards that are necessary for the public's benefit. By retaining management in the private sector, we doubtlessly run other risks; however, a commercial company's profit motive can be exploited in such a way that it will find it to its interest to carry out properly the enabling legislation.

For clarity's sake, in the discussion that follows we will assume there will be just one national company, keeping in mind that the system can work equally well with several companies as long as each operates in regions separate from the others and under identical federal controls. Further, we will assume that the company is not a new one but an independent division within an existent company, operating the malpractice-insurance program on a renewable contract basis with the federal government. Finally, we will assume the enabling legislation mandates that all doctors, osteopaths, hospitals, and other institutional health-care providers must buy their coverage from the contractor company. (Excepted would be dentists, chiropractors, chiropodists, podiatrists, and the like, who rarely get sued and will continue to obtain their low-price insurance from normal commercial insurance outlets.)

Under the national system, rate regulation is removed from the province of state insurance commissions and turned over to the Federal Insurance Administration or a similar body established for that purpose under HEW auspices.

Within the rate structure, a sum is set aside to pay the company a management fee. Since the aim of the system is to peg rates at the lowest level that is fiscally sound—as determined by the regulatory agency—the company should be given a profit incentive in that direction. Thus, its management fee might be $1 million as long as it is necessary to charge customers a billion dollars or more in premiums, but increases .5 per cent at each $100 million drop below a billion. At the $600 million (or pre-1975) level, the company, therefore, earns a $3 million fee. The company is also permitted to invest a percentage of premium volume for its own benefit using the same de-escalation system, i.e., it might be permitted to invest 10 per cent of $1 billion but 50 per cent of $600 million.[44] The balance the company is not permitted to invest is invested by it for the benefit of policyholders, to help bring down rates in that fashion.) Under this formula, the management-company profits increase to the extent it operates efficiently and is successful in keeping claims costs down.

IBNR estimates and inflated loss reserves become a thing of the past. Instead, each customer is billed exclusively on actual—not predicted—loss experience. Let us suppose, for example, in its first year of existence, the regulatory agency determines that the national company shall take in $1.5 billion in premiums.[45] At the end of that year, it is learned that actual expenses (claims payments, overhead, attorney fees, management fee, etc.) is $1 billion. Based on this experience, rates for the following year are reduced by a third. The company, however, doesn't disperse the $500 million differential back to its customers but rather holds it as the basis for later payments for that and succeeding years. Should its loss reserve, developed in this fashion, in the future fall below a level deemed safe by the Insurance Administrator, rather than increasing rates, the Administrator has the option of invoking reinsurance treaties. The reinsurance may be provided by commercial companies or by a federal reinsurance system, such as that proposed by Senator Nelson.[46] The same reinsurance provision makes it feasible to establish a *maximum* loss reserve; any time it is exceeded, once again insurance rates are comparably reduced. Consequently, at no time under the national insurance plan will medical providers find their rates raised to make up for past losses, nor will they any longer be supporting, with their premium payments, projected losses that may never occur. They pay only in terms of current experience, not past, not future. (Neither, of course, do they pay for any investment losses the national company may suffer; that's entirely its risk.)

The savings in premium payments by the medical profession should be sizable. Laying aside the question of whether all providers should now pay the same flat rate or still be assessed under the existent categorical method, an immediate rate reduction of 25–30 per cent (based on the analysis in Chapter Twelve) is a reasonable expectation. The reduction could be even higher, when we recall the analysis of Best's 1976 statistics, suggesting that commercial insurers that year were enjoying an underwriting profit of approximately 50 per cent. It is difficult, however, to make precise predictions on rates because of the variables. Continued escalations in claims frequency will adversely affect them as will ongoing inflationary trends, to say nothing of the monetary impact that liberalized court rulings might have on cases yet to be decided.

For the national company, the deal is a good one. It not only has a guaranteed annual profit from the management fee, but—assuming it can earn 10 per cent on investments—might well make an additional $10–$30 million annually that way. As a consequence, it will not wish to see its franchise turned over to a rival company when its contract comes up for renewal, and will find it advisable to enforce diligently various public interest regulations:

Under the existent system, as we have seen, doctors and hospitals are supposed to advise their insurer of any injury that seems likely to lead to the filing of a malpractice claim. As we have also seen, however, most doctors and hospitals don't do this because they fear the insurer will use the report as grounds for raising their rate or revoking their policy. The enabling legislation for the replacement system will require the contract insurer to obtain incident reports from all customers. Because rates will no longer be raised on the basis of an incident report, there should be a high rate of compliance with the regulation. By adopting this procedure, the federal regulatory agency can use the incident reports to develop statistical information about medical injury patterns that then become available to all medical providers to help them institute internal programs designed to reduce the frequency of both iatrogenic and negligent injury situations.

Incident reports, however, create a problem in dissemination. Under the existent system, insurance companies consider them private property (unlike the patient's medical records) and will not ordinarily release them to a plaintiff for fear of giving her evidence that will help her win her claim. The national insurance company will take the same view, since the size of its profits to a large extent depend on its ability to hold down claims payments. From the public's view, this is a desirable trait for the company to have, since it is the public, after all, that ultimately pays for the cost of the system. Nevertheless, since patients are members of that paying public, it is equitable that they have access to information about any medical injuries they may have received. On balance, therefore, incident reports should be made available from the regulatory agency to any patient who requests them. If a provider fails to make an incident report when he should have done so, under circumstances defined in his policy, he is a subject to a fine by the insurance company. If the provider made the report and the company hid it to avoid making it available to the plaintiff, it pays the fine.

Lack of access to these reports, however, is only one handicap—and far from the most serious one—under which the malpractice victim labors in her effort to obtain redress for her injury. When her medical providers, to escape a suit, lie to her about the cause of her injury, perhaps alter or destroy the medical charts pertaining to her care, she becomes not only the victim of malpractice but of fraud as well. Under the existent system, such deceptions are counterproductive only when the deceiver is caught in the act and a jury is informed of it; otherwise, these practices help the insurer keep money he would otherwise have had to pay out.

To mount a meaningful attack against patient deception—there is probably no way to end it completely—under the insurance model recommended here, any customer who is found to have altered or destroyed records or who can be shown to have lied to a patient (or a patient's family) about the cause of an injury for the purpose of avoiding a malpractice suit will be subject to suspension of their insurance coverage. During the suspension period, they will be held personally responsible for the cost of any malpractice suits initiated. To assure that the plaintiffs will collect what is owed them in these situations, should the provider be unable to pay, the insurance company will. Subsequently, it collects from the defendant (perhaps in the form of surcharges) as a condition for reinstatement of the insurance. Similarly, proof that the insurance company itself has collaborated with any customer in fraudulent practices will subject it to non-recoverable fines or revocation of its license.

Since the vast majority of all known incidents of destruction and alteration have occurred in hospitals, the impact of this rule would be most severe on them and should act to motivate hospital administrators to insist on maintenance of integrity of all records and to require truth telling to patients.

Initially, these deterrent protocols will increase the number of malpractice claims. If they are meritorious, however, they should be instituted. It should not, after all, be the purpose of a malpractice-insurance system to subvert justice by giving wrongdoers the maximum opportunity to hide evidence, although this is exactly what happens under the existent conditions. The purpose, rather, is to establish mechanisms that force medical providers to act in ways that prevent the kinds of situations that lead to justified claims. The proposed penalties, therefore, in the long run, will act to reduce rather than increase claims frequency.

The legislation that creates the national insurance system, however, should incorporate not only penalties but rewards as well. Doctors who remain free of a justified malpractice claim over a stated period of time should have their rates reduced by a meaningful percentage. The same holds true of hospitals. In their case, knowing their payout on premium is less when they remain suit free, they are given positive reinforcement (in addition to the negative reinforcement of the penalties) to institute meaningful risk-management systems. The alternative approach of raising rates for providers who have caused justified claims is not desirable since these doctors and hospitals will simply pass their higher rates on to their unlucky patients.

The single-company insurance system also has positive effects on the litigation process. Since there is now only one insurer—except in those instances in which an equipment manufacturer has been named a codefendant—no longer will doctors find themselves shoehorned into malpractice suits, either by plaintiffs or by other defendants, solely to bring an additional company or two into the settlement pot. No longer will decisions on one case be made with an eye to gaining co-operation from a fellow insurer on the next case. Although the doctor defendants may still sometimes find themselves signing settlement papers with which they are in disagreement, on the whole, because of the single-insurer reform, the quality of defense they get will be more vigorous and certainly more unified.

By establishing a national insurance company, we have also eliminated most of our problems in obtaining accurate information about the malpractice problem. Since there is only one company, there will be only one way of counting claims; neither will national statistics any longer be biased, as they are at present, by the shifting about of IBNR's and loss reserves to meet the exigencies of different corporate policies. The information that the regulatory agency receives from the national company, rather, is relatively pristine and considerably more simple to analyze accurately than is possible now. Not only will the universal availability of the incident reports help provide valuable guidelines for establishing sophisticated risk-management systems, but—from these figures and others provided to the agency from the company—we will also learn a great deal we don't know now about the people who do the suing and, more pertinently, the malpractice proneness of individual doctors and hospitals, making it possible to single out in a non-haphazard way those providers whose practices fall below acceptable standards. To the extent this kind of information is productively used, the most important of all public goals has been met—the improvement of medical care.

Bibliography

Three major statistical surveys of the malpractice problem were consulted in the writing of this book. Pre-eminent in terms of thoroughness and general objectivity is the *Report of the Secretary's Commission on Medical Malpractice*, Department of Health, Education and Welfare, Government Printing Office, Washington, D.C., 1973. The report appears in two volumes, the first a 146-page summary of the Commission's principal findings. The second volume, and the more valuable, is an 870-page supplement consisting of statistical analyses and problem-area studies directed by the Commission staff. In the footnotes, references to material from the findings referred to as *HEW Report*, and material from the supplement as *HEW Appendix*.

The second principal statistical source is *NAIC Malpractice Claims*, a study of some 20,000 incidents resolved between July 1, 1975, and June 30, 1976, compiled and published by the National Association of Insurance Commissioners, 633 W. Wisconsin Avenue, Milwaukee, Wisconsin 53203. Unlike the HEW study, which is, for the most part, lucidly written, the NAIC study is often ambiguously worded in a prose that can be described, generously, as turgid. The study's fundamental statistical base is flawed by inclusion of medical incidents that never led to the assertion of a claim. Nevertheless, within its limitations this study is quite valuable, and is especially noteworthy for its detailed documentation of medical events leading to malpractice incidents, as well as for certain of its tables on claims payments in aggregate and by state.

The third statistical source is the *1974 Closed Claims Survey*, prepared by the Insurance Services Office, copyright 1975 by the American Insurance Association, and available through ISO, 160 Water Street, New York, New York 10038. It also was published in two volumes, and in the footnotes, material from the original report is described as *ISO Report*, with the more detailed analysis of the same material, published a year later, described as *ISO Appendix*. The prose style in this effort makes the NAIC's appear sparkling, with certain descriptive choices that may strike the lay reader as macabre; for example, at one point, the study presents a category it calls "death with no other disability." Some of the weaknesses of this study have been described in the preceding text. It is particularly worth noting that the narrow statistical base, just eleven companies, may be significantly misbalanced by an overrepresentation of figures from the small Medical Protective Company, and similarly underrepresented by the omission of figures from such insurers as Employers of Wausau and Argonaut. Further, many of the tables are beyond any objective evaluation because of the omission of explanatory keys. In the text, this study was relied upon only when information on the subject at hand was not available from more reliable sources.

Three other publications provide excellent sources of malpractice case histories. One ongoing source is the bi-monthly publication, *Citation*, American Medical Association, 535 N. Dearborn Street, Chicago, Illinois 60610. The histories are written in precise, expository prose and are models of clarity for the lay reader. The publication regularly also contains valuable articles on judicial decisions on malpractice legislation.

The second major source for case histories was published in 1975 by *Trial Magazine*, Association of Trial Lawyers of America, 20 Garden Street, Cambridge, Massachusetts 02138. Unfortunately, the material in this mimeographed study is poorly organized, written in legalese, and, for that reason, difficult for laypersons or indeed literate lawyers to follow. (In a couple instances, histories are cut off in midsentence.) However, the material is well annotated and appears to be objective in its presentation. The reader, nevertheless, should keep in mind that this source represents the interests of plaintiff attorneys and as a consequence emphasizes those legal issues that have proven successful in prosecuting malpractice cases, not those that proved good for the defense.

A third case history source is *Physician's Liability to Third Parties —A Kaleidoscopic View* by Harold L. Hirsh, M.D., J.D., published by the Pittsburgh Institute of Legal Medicine, 1417 Frick Building, Pittsburgh, Pennsylvania 15219; Cyril H. Wecht, M.D., J.D., Director. This study is highly informative, well written, and well annotated.

The following publications were also of value as source material for the writing of this book: *Trends Affecting the U. S. Health Care System*, prepared by Cambridge Research Institute for HEW, Publication No. HRA 76-14503, 1975, Government Printing Office, Washington, D.C. It is referred to as *Trends* in the footnotes. Also, *Continuing Medical Malpractice Insurance Crisis*, 1975-6, hearings before the Subcommittee on Health of the Committee on Labor and Public Welfare, United States Senate, Government Printing Office, Washington, D.C. It is referred to as "United States Senate Hearings" in the footnotes.

Also, *Intermountain Medical Malpractice Seminar*, HEW Publication (HRA) 76-3150, National Center for Health Services Research, referred to in the footnotes as "Intermountain"; *A Legislator's Guide to the Medical Malpractice Issue*, copyright 1976 by the Health Policy Center, Graduate School, Georgetown University, Washington, D.C., available through the National Conference of State Legislatures, 1150 17th Street, NW, Washington, D.C. 20036. (It is referred to in the footnotes as *Legislator's Guide* and is especially valuable for the reports it contains from various legislators describing how the burgeoning medical malpractice crisis hit their states and what they did about it.)

Also, *Malpractice in Focus*, American Medical Association, prepared by the editors of the AMA's *Prism* magazine staff. (It is referred to in the footnotes as "AMA.") Also, *Malpractice Digest*, published bi-monthly for distribution to its doctor customers by St. Paul Fire & Marine Insurance Company, 385 Washington Street, St. Paul, Minnesota 55102. Also, *Court Docket Survey*, 1975, Physicians Crisis Committee, 1930 Buhl Building, Detroit, Michigan 48226.

Valuable as basic statistical sources for general health delivery information, other than malpractice information, are the *Statistical Abstract of the United States*, 1976, Goverment Printing Office; and *Health in the United States, A Chartbook*, available from the National Center for Health Statistics, Health Resources Administration, Rockville, Maryland.

Other sources consulted in the writing of this book include: Bulletins of American Hospital Association; a California Hospital Association study of malpractice insurance rates; a 1976 New York *Times* study of incompetent medical care in the United States; *Queuing of*

Malpractice Claims by Judith K. Mann, assistant professor of Econonics, University of California, San Diego; *The Economics of Medical Malpractice Claims, Awards and Defensive Medicine* by Marnie Mueller, professor, Wesleyan University, a paper presented to the American Economic Association, September 1976; *Medical Malpractice and the Cost of Doctors' Services* by Professor Mueller and others; two seminar papers by Eli Bernzweig, "The Malpractice Equation: A Conceptual Tool for Analyzing the Problem," published in the *Journal of Legal Medicine*, February 1976; and an unpublished paper, "The Need for a National Policy on Injury Reparations," December 1976. Also, minutes of the meetings of the American Enterprise Institute for Public Policy Research, December 14–15, 1976; *Medical Injury Compensation: Comments and Suggestions for Altering the Present System*, Kaiser Health Plan, Inc., 1972; also, "Is Arbitration the Answer to Malpractice Disputes?" by Irving Ladimer and James W. Bush, M.D., *Medical World News*, January 26, 1976; *Legislative Index*, Medical Liability Commission, Suite 215, Palmer House, Chicago, Illinois 60690, dated December 31, 1976. Also, *Home Birth Versus Hospital Birth* by Lewis E. Mehl, M.D., and others, Departments of Psychiatry and Pediatrics, University of Wisconsin, Madison, Wisconsin and Department of Gynecology and Obstetrics, Stanford University School of Medicine, Stanford, California; and *The Prevention of Birth Trauma and Injury Through Education* by Doris B. Haire; and by the same author (see acknowledgments), *Cultural Warping of Childbirth*, American Foundation for Maternal and Child Health, Inc., 30 Beekman Place, New York, New York 10022; State of New York Insurance Department, "In the Matter of Medical Malpractice Insurance Association (MMIA)"; Statement by James J. Sheeran, Insurance Commissioner of New Jersey, March 10, 1977; a Nelson & Warren study of Consecutive Closed Claims of the Argonaut Insurance Company in Pennsylvania; Commonwealth of Pennsylvania Insurance Department "In the Matter of Request by David S. Masland and the Pennsylvania Medical Society;" *Attorney General vs. Commissioner of Insurance*, J. Kaplan (Massachusetts); the National Association of Blue Shield Plans, economic report September 1976; *Remarks of A. Addison Roberts*, Reliance Insurance Companies, Bermuda, 1975; *Medical Malpractice, A Selected Annotated Bibliography*, Division of Health Care Systems, Inc., Office of Assistant Secretary for Health, HEW, prepared by Macro Systems, Inc.; *Legislative Briefs*,

National Center for Health Services Research, Rockville, Maryland; *Sources for Malpractice Information*, periodic listings by National Center for Health Services Research, Rockville, Maryland; "A Position of Responsibility," Association of Trial Lawyers of America; and *Classification for Physicians and Surgeons by Specialty, by Geographic Location*, ISO. See also footnotes for other sources.

Note also that in the footnotes that follow, certain references are listed as "Author's Notes." They generally refer to interviews conducted during the course of research for this book; when appropriate, the interviewee is named. In other instances, as noted in the acknowledgment section, certain comments were made on a "not for attribution" basis, but came from sources the author has found to be reputable.

Notes

CHAPTER ONE

1. United States Senate Hearing, December 3, 1975, pp. 154, 220 (for further description of this source, see Bibliography); *Medical Economics Magazine*, September 29, 1975; *All-Industry Medical Malpractice Insurance Committee Report* quoting ISO statistics, p. 20. (Hereafter referred to as *All-Industry Report*.)
2. *Report of the Secretary's Commission on Medical Malpractice, Appendix*, p. 664. Dept. of HEW, 1973. For further description of this study, see Bibliography. (Hereafter referred to as *HEW Appendix*.)
3. *All-Industry Report*, op. cit., p. 1.
4. Tarky Lombardi, Jr., "New York's Medical Malpractice Crisis," *Legislator's Guide to the Medical Malpractice Issue*, pp. 44ff. (Hereafter referred to as *Legislator's Guide*.) For a description of this publication, see Bibliography. (Mr. Lombardi was chairman of the New York State Senate Health Committee at the time of the passage of its malpractice bill.)
5. Barry Keene, "California's Medical Malpractice Crisis," *Legislator's Guide*, p. 27. (Mr. Keene was chairman of the Health Committee of the California Assembly and is the principal author of that state's malpractice bill.)
6. Joseph C. Czerwinski, "Wisconsin's Medical Malpractice Crisis," *Legislator's Guide*, pp. 49ff. (Mr. Czerwinski was chairman of the Wisconsin House of Representatives Health Committee at the time of the passage of its medical malpractice bill.)
7. American Hospital Association, interoffice memo report dated October 10, 1975, directed to Allied Hospital Association Executives, summarizing strategy meetings of the National Invitational Conference on Professional Liability jointly held by the AHA and the AMA, July 28, 1975, pp. 19–36. (Hereafter referred to as *AMA/AHA Memo*.)
8. Melvin L. Stark, "Medical Malpractice: An Insurance Industry Representative's View," *Legislator's Guide*, p. 66.
9. U. S. Senate Hearing, op. cit., p. 186.
10. "Malpractice in Focus, An AMA Source Document," published by the American Medical Association, prepared by the editors of *Prism* magazine, August 1975, p. 12. (Hereafter referred to as "AMA.")

11. U. S. Senate Hearing, op. cit., p. 321.
12. Ibid., pp. 6–7.
13. Sidney M. Wolfe, M.D., "Medical Malpractice: A Consumer Representative's View," *Legislator's Guide*, p. 75.
14. Ibid., p. 73.
15. Robert E. Cartwright, "Medical Malpractice: A Trial Lawyer's View," *Legislator's Guide*, p. 61.
16. AMA, op. cit., p. 14. Also, *Report of the Secretary's Commission on Medical Malpractice, Findings*, p. 3, 113ff, dissenting statement to the Commission's findings by Charles A. Hoffman, M.D., then president of the AMA. (Hereafter referred to as *HEW Report.*)
17. *HEW Report*, p. 3.
18. New York *Times*, quoting president of Kings County Medical Society, May 29, 1975.
19. *All-Industry Report*, op. cit., p. 1.
20. Insurance Services Office, "Special Malpractice Review: 1974 Closed Claim Survey Preliminary Analysis of Survey Results," December 1975, p. 33. (Hereafter referred to as *ISO Report.*) Also, Insurance Services Office, "Special Malpractice Review: 1974 Closed Claim Survey, Technical Analysis of Survey Results," December 1976, pp. 43–44. (Hereafter referred to as *ISO Appendix.*)
21. *HEW Report*, loc cit.
22. *Trends Affecting the U. S. Health Care System*, prepared by Cambridge Research Institute for HEW, January 1976, p. 284, quoting U. S. Senate Special Committee on Aging, March 1975. (Hereafter referred to as *Trends.*) Also see, in general, Mary Adelaide Mendelson, *Tender Loving Greed* (New York: Alfred A. Knopf, Inc.), 1974.
23. *NAIC Malpractice Claims*, No. 4, p. 1. For further description see Bibliography. (Hereafter referred to as "NAIC.")
24. Ibid., pp. 65–69; No. 3, pp. 27–36.
25. Ibid., see esp. p. 32.
26. *Statistical Abstract of the United States*, 1976, by projection from Table 28, p. 27. The median age in the United States is 28.
27. NAIC, No. 4, op. cit., p. 77.
28. *HEW Report*, op. cit., p. 11.
29. NAIC, No. 4, loc cit.; *HEW Appendix*, op. cit., p. 12.
30. *Statistical Abstract*, loc. cit.
31. *Health in the United States, 1975, A Chartbook*, U. S. Department of Health, Education and Welfare, National Center for Health Statistics, Pub. No. (HRA) 76-1233, p. 58. (Hereafter referred to as *Health in U.S.*)
32. Ibid., p. 56.
33. Ibid., p. 32.
34. Ibid., p. 36.
35. Ibid.
36. *Statistical Abstract*, op. cit., p. 25.
37. NAIC, No. 4, loc. cit.; *HEW Appendix*, loc. cit.
38. NAIC, ibid.

39. *Statistical Abstract*, op. cit., p. 27.
40. *HEW Appendix*, loc. cit.; *ISO Appendix*, op. cit., p. 27.
41. *Statistical Abstract*, op. cit., p. 78.
42. Ibid., p. 166.
43. *ISO Report*, op. cit., p. 21.
44. *ISO Appendix*, op. cit., pp. 26–27, quoting *National Health Insurance Resource Book*, 1972 data.
45. *HEW Appendix*, loc. cit.
46. *Statistical Abstract*, op. cit., p. 27.
47. *HEW Appendix*, loc. cit.
48. *ISO Appendix*, op. cit., p. 29.
49. *ISO Report*, op. cit., p. 23.
50. Author's interviews, 1976–77.

CHAPTER TWO

1. U. S. Senate Hearing, op. cit., pp. 6, 152; *American Hospital Review*, July 1975. Projections based on known and estimated 1975 figures.
2. *HEW Appendix*, op. cit., p. 509.
3. U. S. Senate Hearing, loc. cit., *American Hospital Review*, loc. cit.; *Modern Health Care*, June 1975.
4. *Statistical Abstract*, op. cit., pp. 77, 79.
5. Based on statistics released by HEW, July 24, 1977.
6. *Blue Shield News* (monthly publication of National Association of Blue Shield Plans), December 1976, p. 3.
7. AMA, op. cit., p. 21.
8. U. S. Senate Hearing, op. cit., p. 130; California Hospital Association, memo, October 13, 1975, unpaged table.
9. *Washington Developments*, (publication of the American Hospital Association), January 31, 1975.
10. *Journal of the American Medical Association*, May 1, 1975.
11. Ibid.
12. John Guinther, "Take Two Affidavits and Call Me in the Morning," *Philadelphia Magazine*, May 1976. (Hereafter referred to as "Guinther.")
13. Ibid.
14. California Hospital Association, loc. cit.
15. *U. S. News & World Report*, May 26, 1975.
16. Senator Gaylord Nelson (D., Wisc.), "Mushrooming Malpractice," *Trial Magazine*, May/June 1975, p. 19.
17. Bruce C. N. Greenwald, Marnie W. Mueller, and Alan Marcus, *Medical Malpractice and the Cost of Doctors Services*, an economic analysis available through National Center for Health Statistics (see Bibliography) passim, see esp. pp. 13, 16, 25; AMA, op. cit., p. 21, "Burden of Bigger Payments Falls on Patients."

18. Greenwald *et al.*, ibid.
19. Ibid.
20. U. S. Senate Hearing, op. cit., p. 330.
21. Author's interviews.
22. *Blue Shield News*, loc. cit.
23. U. S. Senate Hearing, op. cit., p. 7, statement of Dr. Roger Egeberg, special assistant to Secretary for Health Policy, HEW; also, Egeberg and Senator Edward F. Kennedy quoting Casper Weinberger, then Secretary of HEW; *U. S. News & World Report*, loc. cit.; Dr. Sidney Wolfe, op. cit., p. 75.
24. Marnie Mueller, *The Economics of Medical Malpractice: Claims, Awards, and Defensive Medicine*, pp. 8–9.
25. Ibid., pp. 15–18; also quoted by *Blue Shield News*, op. cit., p. 4.
26. Ibid., p. 8.
27. *Trends*, op. cit., pp. 123, 127–29, 132.
28. *HEW Report*, op. cit., p. 14.
29. Ibid.

CHAPTER THREE

1. *Black's Law Dictionary*; St. Paul, Minn: West Publishing Co., 1933.
2. Killey Estate, 326 Atlantic 2nd, 372 (1974).
3. Francis J. McCarthy, General Counsel, Travelers Insurance Co., speech to American Bar Association, New York, N.Y., May 5, 1977.
4. *The Wall Street Journal*, February 3, 1976. For discussion in general of higher degree of expertise demanded of legal specialists, see *Restatement of Torts*, ※299A, comment c; St. Paul, Minnesota: American Law Institute; also, "Legal Effects of Attorney Specialization," 30 *Albany Law Review* 282 (1966), quoted by Benedict A. Casey, Esq. in "Malpractice Liability of Lawyers," Philadelphia, Pa., 1977.
5. *Cobbs v. Grant*, quoted in William J. Curran and George B. Moseley III, "The Malpractice Experience of Health Maintenance Organizations," *Northwestern University Law Review*, Vol. 70, No. 1, March/April 1975, p. 76.
6. *Canterbury v. Spence*, 464 F. 2nd, 772 (D. C. Circuit, 1972.)
7. In most instances, decisions rendered in one court are advisory rather than binding on another court. However, the lower courts of a state are bound by decisions promulgated by the highest court in that state as well as by decisions of the United States Supreme Court either as they affect the law of the particular state or in those decisions that define the meaning of the Constitution in all states.
8. Speech by Thomas Uehlin, risk management officer of St. Paul Fire & Marine Insurance Company, May 13, 1975.
9. *HEW Appendix*, op. cit., p. 114.
10. Norman W. Frink, M.D., "The Twain Must Meet or . . ." *Trial Magazine*, May/June 1975, p. 32. (Dr. Frink is Chief of Surgery

Emeritus and one of the founders of the Kaiser Permanente Clinic, Portland, Oregon.)

11. This phrase is used by many of sources, or "conspiracy of silence." See esp. *Preserving a Medical Malpractice Insurance Marketplace*, St. Paul Fire & Marine Insurance Co., p. 9.
12. Author's interview with plaintiff attorney, J. Gerald Litvin.
13. *HEW Appendix*, op. cit., p. 498.
14. Ibid.
15. Ibid.

CHAPTER FOUR

1. E. Stewart Taylor, *Obstetrics*, condensed from Beck's *Obstetrical Practice*, 9th Ed. (Baltimore: Williams & Wilkins), 1972.
2. Ibid., p. 234.
3. Ibid., p. 234.
4. NAIC, No. 4, op. cit., p. 49.
5. No reliable statistics are available to suggest how often an equipment manufacturer or supplier is named as a defendant. The three major surveys concentrate solely on medical providers. It should be noted, however, that when a manufacturer or supplier is included as a defendant, that company is not technically a *malpractice* defendant in a professional liability sense; it is named as a codefendant with medical providers as having participated in the civil trespass against the plaintiff. In some cases, the manufacturer is the sole defendant. Such suits are products-liability cases, and the discussion of them is, except as noted later in the text, beyond the scope of this book.
6. St. Paul Fire & Marine Insurance Co., *Malpractice Digest*, March/April 1974.
7. NAIC, No. 3, op. cit., pp. 4–5.
8. American Medical Association, *The Citation, a Medicolegal Digest for Physicians*, prepared by the General Counsel of the American Medical Association, Vol. 33, No. 9, August 15, 1975. (Hereafter referred to as *Citation.*)
9. Ibid., Vol. 34, No. 4, December 1, 1976.
10. Association of Trial Lawyers of America, *Trial Magazine*, March 1973. (Hereafter referred to as *Trial Magazine.*)
11. Ibid., March 1971.
12. *Citation*, op. cit., Vol. 32, No. 4, December 1, 1975.
13. Ibid., Vol. 30, No. 7, January 15, 1975.
14. Ibid., Vol. 34, No. 10, March 1, 1977.
15. *Trial Magazine*, op. cit., November 1972.
16. *Citation*, op. cit., Vol. 30, No. 7, January 1, 1975.
17. Ibid.
18. *Trial Magazine*, op. cit., December 1973.
19. *Citation*, op. cit., Vol. 32, No. 3, November 15, 1975.

20. Ibid., Vol. 32, No. 9, February 15, 1976.
21. Ibid., Vol. 31, No. 8, August 1, 1975.
22. Ibid., Vol. 33, No. 12, October 1, 1976.
23. Ibid., Vol. 33, No. 4, December 1, 1976.

CHAPTER FIVE

1. NAIC, No. 4, op. cit., p. 65.
2. *Citation*, op. cit., Vol. 31, No. 2, May 1, 1975.
3. Ibid., Vol. 34, No. 4, December 1, 1976; deposition, *Fillinger v. Fitzgerald Mercy Hospital*, passim.
4. Philadelphia *Inquirer*, May 29, 1975.
5. *Trial Magazine*, op. cit., December 1971.
6. New York *Times*, January 27, 1976. See also discussion of elective surgery, Chapter Nine.
7. *Citation*, op. cit., Vol. 31, No. 5, June 15, 1976.
8. *Trial Magazine*, op. cit., December 1971.
9. *Citation*, op. cit., Vol. 33, No. 12, October 1, 1976.
10. Ibid., Vol. 32, No. 6, January 1, 1976.
11. Ibid., Vol. 32, No. 12, October 1, 1976.
12. *Trial Magazine*, op. cit., August 1974.
13. *Citation*, op. cit., Vol. 30, No. 7, January 15, 1975.
14. *Trial Magazine*, op. cit., February 1971; New York *Post*, October 23, 1970.
15. *Citation*, op. cit., Vol. 34, No. 9, February 15, 1977.
16. Ibid., Vol. 34, No. 5, December 15, 1976.
17. *Trial Magazine*, op. cit., December 1971. The legal arguments described in connection with this case have been fictionalized to encompass the legal issues presented, in general, in continuous care cases.
18. The large majority of malpractice cases are heard in state courts. Cases heard in federal court include those in which a federal medical facility or a federally employed physician is involved, as well as those in which there is diversity of jurisdiction. Diversity occurs when a patient lives in one state but is treated by a doctor or a facility in another state.
19. Interview with David Shrager, an attorney who specializes in personal injury cases.
20. In Maryland, for example, the statute of limitations is five years; in Florida, four years. (*Medical Economics*, September 29, 1975.)
21. *Citation*, op. cit., Vol. 34, No. 4, December 1, 1976.
22. Various sources, but see esp. *Trial Magazine*, op. cit., May 1971, May 1973, August 1971, April 1971, November 1971, December 1972, for discussion of applicable cases. Also, *Citation*, op. cit., various cases, but see esp. discussion of *Hardin v. Farris*, Vol. 31, No. 4, June 1, 1975.

23. For frequency of this type of injury, see U. S. Senate Hearing, op. cit., pp. 435–69. Also, NAIC, No. 4, op. cit., p. 43.
24. *Citation,* op. cit., Vol. 34, No. 4, December 1, 1976.
25. Ibid., Vol. 34, No. 8, February 1, 1977.
26. *Trends,* op. cit., p. 41.
27. Ibid.
28. *Citation,* op. cit., Vol. 34, No. 3, November 15, 1976; and Vol. 34, No. 8, February 1, 1977.
29. *Trial Magazine,* op. cit., October 1971.
30. Ibid., June 1973.
31. *Citation,* op. cit., Vol. 34, No. 4, December 1, 1976
32. *Trial Magazine,* op. cit., October 1974.
33. Ibid., January 1973.
34. *Citation,* op. cit., Vol. 34, No. 12, April 1, 1977.
35. Ibid.
36. Ibid., Vol. 34, No. 10, March 1, 1977.
37. Author's notes.
38. Ward Wagner, Jr., "At the Core: The Patient," *Trial Magazine,* op. cit., May/June 1975. (Mr. Wagner is a former president of the Association of Trial Lawyers of America.)
39. Author's interview with Jeffrey Stopford, attorney for the plaintiff in the case.
40. *Citation,* op. cit., Vol. 34, No. 4, December 1, 1976.
41. Wagner, loc. cit.

CHAPTER SIX

1. NAIC, No. 4, op. cit., p. 93.
2. *Citation,* op. cit., Vol. 34, No. 1, October 15, 1976.
3. Philadelphia *Evening Bulletin,* October 1, 1977.
4. *Citation,* op. cit., Vol. 35, No. 5, June 15, 1977.
5. *Trial Magazine,* op. cit., February 1974, August 1974; *Perspective Magazine,* 2nd Quarter, 1975; *Journal of Legal Medicine,* July/August 1974.
6. *Journal of Legal Medicine,* loc. cit.
7. *Trial Magazine,* op. cit., February 1974.
8. Ibid.
9. *Citation,* op. cit., Vol. 34, No. 2, November 1, 1976.
10. Guinther, loc. cit.
11. *Citation,* op. cit., Vol. 34, No. 2, November 1, 1976. The narrative of this case is as reported. However, note that the later description of plaintiff and defense arguments on the issues raised relate not only to this case but are typical of arguments raised in similar cases.
12. Ibid., Vol. 29, No. 10, July 5, 1974; also, *Trial Magazine,* op. cit., March 1972.

13. *Trial Magazine*, op. cit., February 1973.
14. Ibid.
15. *Cobbs v. Grant*, op. cit.; *Canterbury v. Spence*, op. cit.; *Holland v. Sisters of St. Joseph of Peace*, 522 P. 2d208 (Ore. En Banc, 1974); *Getchell v. Mansfield*, 489 P. 2d953, 1971.
16. *Citation*, op. cit., Vol. 34, No. 8, February 1, 1977. In this case, a doctor took a dying patient's photograph for his medical records without the permission of the patient or his family. The case was dismissed at the lower court level but reinstated for trial on the grounds that the patient had been subject to an invasion of privacy, a tort, by the photography session, the tort arising from the doctor's failure to obtain consent.
17. *Trial Magazine*, op. cit., March 1975.
18. CBS News, "Sixty Minutes," February 27, 1977.
19. Author's notes.
20. *Citation*, op. cit., Vol. 34, No. 5, December 15, 1976.
21. Ibid., Vol. 32, No. 6, January 1, 1976.
22. Harold L. Hirsh, M.D., J.D., *Physician's Liability to Third Parties—A Kaleidoscopic View*, Pittsburgh Institute of Legal Medicine. (See Bibliography. Hereafter referred to as "Hirsh.")
23. Ibid.
24. Ibid.
25. Ibid.
26. Ibid.
27. Ibid.
28. Ibid.
29. *Trial Magazine*, op. cit., October 1973.

CHAPTER SEVEN

1. Sir Henry Maine, *The Ancient Law*, 1890, quoted in *Trial Magazine*, May/June 1975.
2. *Citation*, op. cit., Vol. 30, No. 12, April 1, 1974; also, Hirsh, op. cit.
3. Ibid., Vol. 34, No. 1, October 15, 1976; Hirsh, op. cit.
4. Ibid., Vol. 34, No. 10, March 1, 1977.
5. *Trends*, op. cit., pp. 357–66, quoting studies by the American Medical Association, HEW statistical studies, among others.
6. *Citation*, op. cit., Vol. 32, No. 9, February 15, 1975.
7. Although the available information on this case is not clear on this point.
8. *Journal of Legal Medicine*, op. cit., September/October 1974; *Trial Magazine*, op. cit., May 1974.
9. Ibid.; ibid.
10. For the full text of this decision, see *Helling v. Carey et al.*, 519, P. 2d, 981 Wash. No. 42775, March 14, 1974.

CHAPTER EIGHT

1. *Trends*, op. cit., p. 40.
2. Ibid.
3. Ibid., p. 38–39.
4. *Statistical Abstract*, op. cit., p. 5.
5. Bureau of Census, preliminary statistics, 1977.
6. *Statistical Abstract*, op. cit., p. 60.
7. Ibid.
8. *HEW Report*, op. cit., p. 2.
9. *Health in U.S.*, op. cit., p. 50.
10. ISO statistics, supplied to author.
11. *HEW Appendix*, op. cit., pp. 637–44.
12. *Statistical Abstract*, op. cit., p. 373.
13. Malpractice insurance rates for lawyers began to rise noticeably around 1972, a dozen years after such trends were noted in medical liability cases.
14. *Trends*, op. cit., p. 2.
15. Ibid., p. 60.
16. Ibid.
17. *Statistical Abstract*, op. cit., pp. 6–7.
18. *Health in U.S.*, op. cit., p. 58.
19. Ibid.
20. Author's notes.
21. *Trends*, op. cit., p. 16; *Statistical Abstract*, op. cit., p. 42.
22. Ibid., p. 15.
23. *Trends*, op. cit., pp. 13–14, 64–65.
24. *Statistical Abstract*, op. cit., p. 65.
25. Ibid., p. 91.
26. *Trends*, op. cit., p. 61.
27. Ibid., p. 16.
28. Ibid.
29. *Statistical Abstract*, op. cit., p. 86.
30. *Trends*, op. cit., p. 361.
31. Ibid., p. 117.
32. *Statistical Abstract*, op. cit., p. 311. The development of employer-paid health plans during this same period also encouraged workers to make greater use of medical services, adding further to the annual income of doctors.
33. *Trends*, op. cit., p. 117.
34. Ibid., p. 128.
35. Ibid., p. 120.
36. Ibid., p. 124.
37. Ibid. Changes in the act passed in 1974 make comparisons for more recent years misleading.

38. Ibid., p. 123.
39. Ibid., pp. 131, 266–67.
40. Ibid., p. 283.
41. *Health in U.S.*, op. cit., p. 7.
42. Ibid.
43. *Trends*, op. cit., p. 283.
44. Ibid., p. 284.
45. Mary Mendelson, op. cit., passim.
46. *Health in U.S.*, op. cit., pp. 56, 58.
47. U. S. Senate Hearing, op. cit., p. 311; *All-Industry Report*, "The Problems of Insuring Medical Malpractice," p. 20; statement by General Reinsurance Corporation, U. S. Senate Hearing, op. cit., p. 220; ISO, as supplied to author; *Medical Economics Magazine*, loc. cit.
48. *HEW Appendix*, op. cit., p. 48.
49. NAIC, No. 4, op. cit., p. 40.
50. *HEW Report*, op. cit., p. 12.
51. *Statistical Abstract*, op. cit., p. 28.
52. NAIC, No. 4, op. cit., p. 129.
53. *Statistical Abstract*, op. cit., p. 28.
54. *ISO Report*, op. cit., p. 21.
55. NAIC, No. 4, op. cit., p. 77.
56. *Trends*, op. cit., p. 17.
57. *Statistical Abstract*, op. cit., p. 401.
58. Ibid., p. 10; *Health in U.S.*, op. cit., pp. 6–7.
59. *Statistical Abstract*, op. cit., p. 432.
60. *Health in U.S.*, loc. cit.
61. Ibid.
62. Ibid.
63. Ibid.
64. Ibid., p. 10.
65. *Statistical Abstract*, op. cit., p. 83; *Trends*, op. cit., p. 297.
66. Ibid.
67. NAIC, No. 4, op. cit., p. 129.
68. *Health in U.S.*, op. cit., p. 21, quoting AMA statistics.
69. Ibid.; NAIC, No. 4, op. cit., p. 129.
70. Ibid.; ibid.
71. *Health in U.S.*, loc. cit.
72. *Statistical Abstract*, op. cit., p. 84; *Trends*, op. cit., p. 361.
73. Based on ISO estimates, and other projections, see footnote 47 above.
74. *Statistical Abstract*, op. cit., p. 77.

CHAPTER NINE

1. An estimation; see discussion of claims definition in chapters Eleven, Twelve, and Thirteen. Figure includes claims in which more than one doctor was cited.

2. *Statistical Abstract*, loc. cit.; *Health in U.S.*, op. cit., p. 20.
3. Estimations of total annual number of doctor/patient contacts vary depending on the definition of "contact." Robert W. Jamplis, M.D., president, American Group Practice Association has estimated (Intermountain Medical Malpractice Seminar, August 11–12, 1975), p. 13, that 5 million such contacts occur daily, which would suggest a figure double that given. The lower figure is extrapolated from various sources, but see esp., *Health in U.S.*, op. cit., pp. 32–38. The figure quoted in the text would not include casual contacts between hospital residents and interns with patients.
4. *HEW Appendix*, op. cit., p. 52.
5. Ibid., p. 55.
6. Ibid., p. 62.
7. Eli Bernzweig, "The Malpractice Equation: A Conceptual Tool for Analyzing the Problem," *Journal of Legal Medicine*, February 1976; the same article is reprinted in the *Legislator's Guide to the Medical Malpractice Issue*, op. cit., see p. 68.
8. Author interview with Eli Bernzweig, August 1977.
9. The Hew estimate is 15 per cent. *HEW Appendix*, p. 1.
10. Ibid., p. 665.
11. Ibid.
12. Bernzweig, op. cit., p. 71 in *Legislator's Guide*.
13. "A Preliminary Assessment of Risk Management in Health Care Settings," July 1975, a report to HEW by Macro Systems, Inc., pp. 15–16.
14. Exceptions would include the occasional person who is medically injured during a routine physical examination, and women who receive injuries during child delivery.
15. The subject is discussed further in chapters Fifteen and Sixteen.
16. New York *Times*, January 27, 1976.
17. Ibid.
18. Ibid.
19. *Wall Street Journal*, May 12, 1976.
20. New York *Times*, op. cit.
21. The unnecessary surgery study was one of a five-part series on problems in the medical profession published by the New York *Times* between January 26 and January 30, 1976. The authors were Boyce Rensberger and Jane E. Brody.
22. Ibid.
23. Reported by United Press International, April 25, 1977.
24. Ibid.
25. New York *Times*., loc. cit.
26. Author's interview notes with a malpractice defense attorney.
27. *Trends*, op. cit., p. 221.
28. Ibid., p. 232, quoting *American Journal of Public Health*.
29. Ibid., p. 234.
30. Ibid.
31. Ibid.

32. Ibid., p. 223.
33. New York *Times,* loc. cit.
34. *Statistical Abstract,* op. cit., p. 79.
35. New York *Times,* loc. cit.
36. Ibid.
37. Ibid., quoting the American College of Surgeons.
38. Ibid.
39. NAIC, No. 4, op. cit., p. 29.
40. Ibid.
41. New York *Times,* loc. cit.
42. Ibid., January 28, 1976.
43. Ibid.
44. Ibid.
45. Ibid.
46. Ibid., based on the Jick and the University of Florida studies.
47. Ibid.
48. Ibid., quoting the *New England Journal of Medicine.*
49. Ibid.
50. Ibid.
51. Ibid.
52. Ibid.
53. Ibid.
54. Ibid.
55. *Incolingo v. Ewing,* Parke Davis & Co.
56. New York *Times,* loc. cit.
57. Author's interview with John Mock, M.D., a psychiatrist.
58. *Physicians Desk Reference,* page varies by edition.
59. Ibid.
60. Jerome Miller, former head of juvenile services, Massachusetts and Pennsylvania.
61. John Guinther, "A Child's Garden of Horrors," *Philadelphia Magazine,* March 1976.
62. New York *Times,* loc. cit.
63. Ibid.
64. Ibid., quoting Network of Continuing Medical Education, Columbia University.
65. Doris Haire, *The Cultural Warping of Childbirth,* International Childbirth Education Association (see Bibliography), p. 5.
66. Ibid.; *Statistical Abstract,* op. cit., p. 91; *Health in U.S.,* op. cit., p. 49.
67. Doris Haire, "The Prevention of Birth Trauma and Injury Through Education for Childbearing," paper delivered at Fourth International Congress of the International Association for the Scientific Study of Mental Deficiency, August 25, 1976, p. 6.
68. Ibid.
69. Ibid.
70. "Home Birth Versus Hospital Birth: Comparisons of Outcomes of Matched Populations," prepared by the Departments of Psychiatry

and Pediatrics, University of Wisconsin, and Departments of Gynecology Obstetrics, Stanford University School of Medicine, delivered annual meeting of American Public Health Assoc., October 20, 1976, p. 7.

71. Haire, *Prevention of . . .*, op. cit., p. 3.
72. Ibid., p. 13.
73. Ibid., pp. 15–16.

CHAPTER TEN

1. New York *Times*, op. cit., January 27, 1976.
2. Ibid., January 29, 1976.
3. *HEW Report*, op. cit., p. 53.
4. *Trends*, op. cit., p. 89.
5. Ibid.; New York *Times*, January 26, 1976.
6. New York *Times*, op. cit., loc. cit.
7. Ibid.
8. Ibid.; U. S. Senate Hearing, op. cit., p. 3, identifies Dr. Egeberg as special assistant to the Secretary for Health Policy.
9. *Health in U.S.*, op. cit., p. 20. This is a projection on 1975 figures.
10. More or less. The figure is based on the assumption that incompetent doctors see as many patients as do competent ones.
11. *HEW Report*, op. cit., p. 5.
12. New York *Times*, op. cit., January 29, 1976.
13. Ibid.
14. Ibid.
15. Ibid.
16. Ibid.
17. HEW, Office of Development and Planning, "An Analysis of State Licensing Provisions on the Disciplinary Powers of State Medical Examining Boards," pp. 4–8.
18. Ibid.
19. Interview with Eli Bernzweig, August 1977.
20. New York *Times*, loc. cit.
21. Wolfe, op. cit., p. 74.
22. *Health in U.S.*, op. cit., p. 20.
23. *Trends*, op. cit., p. 349.
24. Ibid.
25. Ibid., p. 350.
26. *Health in U.S.*, op. cit., p. 20, based on AMA statistics, 1973.
27. Ibid.
28. *Trends*, op. cit., p. 344.
29. Ibid., pp. 360–61; author's interview, American Medical Association, January 1978.
30. Author's interview, ibid.
31. Ibid.

32. *Journal of the American Medical Association*, Vol. 238, No. 26, December 26, 1977, p. 2,767.
33. *Trends*, op. cit., p. 344.
34. Author's interview, op. cit.
35. NAIC, No. 4, op. cit., p. 28.
36. *Statistical Abstract*, op. cit., p. 78.
37. *Trends*, op. cit., p. 344.
38. Ibid., p. 352.
39. Ibid., p. 355.
40. Ibid., p. 355.
41. Ibid., p. 351.
42. Ibid.
43. Author's interview notes.
44. *Trends*, op. cit., p. 348.
45. Ibid., p. 349.
46. Ibid.
47. Ibid., p. 354.
48. NAIC, No. 4, op. cit., p. 28.
49. The NAIC was the only body contacted in connection with the writing of this book that failed to respond to questions.
50. Author's interview notes.
51. *HEW Appendix*, op. cit., p. 84. The survey was conducted in December 1971.
52. Ibid., pp. 658–96.
53. Ibid., p. 672.
54. Ibid., p. 687.
55. Ibid., p. 668.
56. AMA, op. cit., p. 14.
57. *HEW Report*, op. cit., p. 70.
58. *HEW Appendix*, op. cit., p. 667.
59. Ibid.
60. Ibid., p. 674.
61. Ibid., p. 675.
62. Author's interview notes.
63. Author's interview notes.
64. *HEW Report*, op. cit., p. 68.
65. Howard Eisenberg, "New Light on the Costliest Malpractice Mistakes," *Medical Economics*, August 20, 1973.
66. *Statistical Abstract*, op. cit., p. 76.
67. Ibid.
68. Ibid.; *Health in U.S.*, op. cit., p. 28, quoting American Hospital Association statistics.
69. *Statistical Abstract*, loc. cit.; *Trends*, op. cit., p. 400.
70. Ibid.; ibid.
71. *Trends*, op. cit., p. 398.
72. *HEW Report*, op cit., p. 9.
73. 1976 computer print-out supplied author by Philadelphia Court of Common Pleas.

74. HEW, "A Preliminary Assessment of Risk Management in Health Care Settings," prepared by Macro Systems, Inc., July 1975, passim., esp. pp. 20–21; *HEW Appendix*, op. cit., pp. 758–835.
75. HEW, "A Preliminary Assessment . . ." op. cit., p. 1.
76. Ibid.

CHAPTER ELEVEN

1. *HEW Appendix*, op. cit., p. 505.
2. Ibid.
3. U. S. Senate Hearing, op. cit., p. 130; AMA, op. cit., p. 21; California Hospital Association, memo, October 13, 1975, see. esp., p. 5.
4. NAIC, No. 4, op. cit., pp. 98–99; 110–27.
5. *Medical Economics*, September 2, 1975.
6. *HEW Appendix*, op. cit., p. 509.
7. Ibid.
8. Ibid.
9. Ibid.
10. *U. S. News & World Report*, May 26, 1975.
11. *HEW Report*, op. cit., p. 43.
12. Insurance Services Office, "Corrolation—Classification & Rate Differential, Revised Physicians & Surgeons Classification vs. Present Classification," 1977, pp. 1–16. (In some parts of the country, an eight-category system applies, California Hospital Association, op. cit., unpaged table.)
13. Estimates are projected from various sources, based on 1975–76 data, averages may have an error factor of 10 per cent upward or downward.
14. Dentists accounted for 152—or 3 per cent—of 5,000 paid malpractice claims studied by NAIC. The average payment per claim was approximately one fourth that of claims against medical doctors. NAIC, No. 4, p. 32.
15. Ibid. The study discovered only one paid claim against a chiropractor, none against chiropodists, naturopaths, or podiatrists.
16. Insurance Services Office, "Territory Code—III," January 1, 1976.
17. *Statistical Abstract of the United States*, 1976, U. S. Department of Commerce, Bureau of the Census, Washington D. C., 1976, p. 11.
18. NAIC, No. 4, op. cit., p. 129.
19. *HEW Report*, op. cit., p. 3.
20. See Appendix One, Table II.
21. Ibid., Tables I and II.
22. Ibid., Table I. All three states have about average claims rates when the Table II computation method is used.
23. State of New York Insurance Department, *In the Matter of the Medical Malpractice Insurance Association and Insurance Services Office*, Exhibit D, July 27, 1976.
24. California Hospital Association, op. cit., p. 2.

25. *HEW Report*, op. cit., p. 38.
26. *Wall Street Journal*, loc. cit.
27. Estimates from various sources, including ISO; see also NAIC, No. 4, op. cit., p. 108.
28. *HEW Appendix*, op. cit., p. 509.
29. Ibid., p. 511.
30. Ibid.
31. U. S. Senate Hearing, op. cit., p. 6.
32. Ibid., p. 152
33. Ibid., pp. 316, 333.
34. Ibid., p. 288.
35. Ibid., p. 163.
36. Ibid., p. 351.
37. New York Insurance Dept., op. cit., pp. 35ff.
38. Keene, op. cit., p. 27.
39. U. S. Senate Hearing, op. cit., p. 149.
40. Wolfe, op. cit., p. 73ff.
41. Association of Trial Lawyers of America, "A Position of Responsibility." (See Bibliography.)
42. See Chapter Twelve.
43. Author interview notes.
44. U. S. Senate Hearing, op. cit., p. 141.
45. Various sources but see *All-Industry Report*, op. cit., p. 22, for official casualty industry statement.
46. Interview with Stephen Blumenkrantz, ISO.
47. *Forbes Magazine*, "A Close Call," April 15, 1976.
48. U. S. Senate Hearing, op. cit., pp. 151–53, 216–22.
49. However, although this isn't clear, it appears that reinsurance fees are.
50. Blumenkrantz, ISO. The *All-Industry Report*, p. 22, quotes 25 per cent.
51. *Statistical Abstract*, op. cit., p. 793.
52. *Best's Insurance Reports: Property & Casualty*, p. 983 (Oldwick, N.J.: A. M. Best and Co.), 1976. (Hereafter referred to as "Best's 1976.")
53. Ibid., pp. 3, 5.
54. Various sources, but see esp., *All-Industry Report*, op. cit., pp. 8–9.
55. NAIC, No. 3, op. cit., p. 7; *ISO Report*, op. cit., p. 25.
56. NAIC, No. 4, op. cit., pp. 122–24, compare with other states in same table, pp. 110–27.
57. NAIC, No. 3, loc. cit.; *ISO Report*, loc. cit.
58. St. Paul, *Malpractice Digest*, op. cit., Summer 1975, p. 3.
59. Blumenkrantz, ISO, op. cit.; Bernzweig, interview, December 1976.
60. St. Paul, loc. cit.
61. *Best's Insurance Reports: Property & Casualty*, 1977, p. 1,044. (Hereafter referred to as "Best's 1977.")
62. Bernzweig, op. cit.; Philipp Stern, actuary, New Jersey Insurance Dept., interview.

63. Blumenkrantz, op. cit.
64. Bernzweig, op. cit.; Otis Littleton, former insurance executive, interview.
65. *Forbes Magazine*, op. cit.
66. St. Paul, loc. cit.
67. Guinther, "Take Two . . . ," op. cit.
68. Commonwealth of Pennsylvania Insurance Department, *In the Matter of: Request by David S. Masland and the Pennsylvania Medical Society . . .* ; Docket No. R76-6-1.
69. Author's interview notes.
70. *Medical World News*, "Argonaut and Malpractice: A Tangled Web," July 14, 1975, p. 23.
71. Best's 1977, op. cit., pp. 144–46.
72. Ibid.; Best's 1976, op. cit., shows a healthy pure loss ratio of 40.6 per cent for Argonaut in 1975 malpractice claims payments, but 104.3 per cent claims payment ratio for Workmen's Compensation Insurance, p. 143.
73. Analysis by Van Damm Associates, 1977.
74. *HEW Appendix*, op. cit., p. 14.
75. John Smithers, Frank B. Hall Company, Philadelphia, general agent, Argonaut Insurance in Pennsylvania, author's interview.
76. William Churchman, chief executive officer, Frank B. Hall.
77. Otis Littleton, op. cit.
78. See footnote 44, Chapter Ten.
79. U. S. Senate Hearing, op. cit., pp. 60–81, 355–416. The HEW's attempts to gain co-operation from the NAIC interestingly exhibit the latter group's concept of its public responsibility.
80. *ISO Appendix*, op. cit., p. 3.
81. NAIC, No. 4, op. cit., p. 108.
82. Author's interview notes; Best's 1977, op cit. p. 727: "On only four occasions in the past quarter century were operating results on a less than profitable basis. The most recent . . . 1967."
83. St. Paul, loc. cit.
84. *All-Industry Report*, op. cit. The reproduced table appears on p. 4.
85. *HEW Appendix*, op. cit., p. 510.
86. Author's notes.
87. Interview, June 1977.
88. Nor would it. Employers is a mutual insurance company, and casualty companies in that group apparently report statistics to the American Mutual Insurance Alliance.
89. State of New York Insurance Dept., op. cit.
90. NAIC, No. 4, op. cit., p. 129.
91. *All-Industry Report*, op. cit., p. 7.
92. State of New York Insurance Dept., loc. cit.
93. Ibid., author's projection on statistical tables.
94. *All-Industry Report*, op. cit., pp. 4–5.
95. Author's interview with Mr. Stern.
96. *All-Industry Report*, op. cit., p. 26.

97. Ibid., p. 27.
98. Ibid., loc. cit.
99. Ibid., p. 28.
100. See footnote 95 above.
101. Hunter interview, December 1976.
102. Based on the industry estimate of 10–15 per cent per annum.

CHAPTER TWELVE

1. A few of the non-commercial sources began to operate in 1975, more in 1976, so that nationwide their claims experience did not begin in any significant way until 1977.
2. AMA, op. cit., p. 12.
3. NAIC, No. 4, op. cit., p. 29.
4. Blumenkrantz, op. cit.; *Hospital Medical Staff* magazine, May 1975, quoting Carl Weissberg, counsel, American Federation of Hospitals.
5. Stark, op. cit., p. 66.
6. *HEW Report*, op. cit., p. 6.
7. NAIC, No. 4, op. cit., p. 1.
8. Ibid., p. 101.
9. Ibid.
10. *All-Industry Report*, op. cit., p. 4.
11. U. S. Senate Hearing, op. cit. Senator Edward Kennedy of Massachusetts pressed this point, and got few if any direct answers to it from the malpractice underwriters, p. 253, see responses throughout.
12. NAIC, No. 4, loc. cit.
13. Based on insurance industry statistics supplied to A. M. Best and Co., as analyzed by Francis V. Reilly, Actuarial Assistant Administrator for Insurance Examination and Actuarial Services, United States Government, Insurance Administrators Office, supplied to the author and projected by him to incorporate claims and administrative expenses along with pure loss ratios; correspondence, October 20, 1977.
14. Interview, June 1977.
15. *Forbes Magazine*, loc. cit.
16. Speech at annual meeting of Connecticut Association of Independent Insurance Agents, Inc., May 18–21, Bermuda. (Hereafter referred to as "Roberts.")
17. Though not all of them. In a letter to the author, St. Paul denies it has ever engaged in this unusual policy.
18. Pennsylvania Medical Society newsletter to members.
19. U. S. Senate Hearing, op. cit., p. 170.
20. Keene, op. cit., p. 28.
21. Ibid.
22. California Hospital Association, op. cit., Table A.
23. Keene, op. cit., p. 29.
24. California Hospital Association, loc. cit.

25. U. S. Senate Hearing, loc. cit.
26. California Hospital Association, op. cit., Table C.
27. *Medical World News*, op. cit., July 14, 1975.
28. Guinther, "Take Two . . . ," op. cit.
29. Pennsylvania Insurance Commissioner William Sheppard, p. 6 of decision granting Argonaut the rate increase.
30. *Forbes Magazine*, loc. cit.
31. Ibid.
32. *Statistical Abstract*, op. cit., p. 439. By some indices, the inflationary increase was even steeper than that, see same source, pp. 430–32.
33. Interview with Steven Blumenkrantz, Insurance Services Office, October 20, 1976.
34. Roberts, op. cit., p. 8.
35. Gateway Insurance Company, Inc.: See, 1974 Annual Report, Fisco, Inc.: p. 2.
36. *Forbes Magazine*, loc. cit.
37. Ibid.
38. Ibid.
39. Ibid.
40. Ibid.
41. Ibid.
42. Ibid.
43. Ibid.
44. Best's 1976, op. cit., p. 4.
45. Ibid, 1977, op. cit., p. 1,176.
46. Ibid.
47. Ibid., 1976, op. cit., p. 983.
48. U. S. Senate Hearing, op. cit., p. 254.
49. Ibid., Argonaut's response, p. 343; Aetna, p. 326.
50. Ibid., p. 318.
51. Ibid., p. 292.
52. St. Paul, *Malpractice Digest*, loc. cit.
53. Blumenkrantz, op. cit.; Hunter, op. cit., Bernzweig, op. cit., interviews; one insurance commissioner who does is Massachusetts'; see *Attorney General vs. Commissioner of Insurance* (Mass.) in which auto insurers were not permitted rate increases until interest earnings were incorporated.
54. Best's 1976, op. cit., passim.
55. *Berry et al. v. St. Paul Fire and Marine Insurance Company et al.*, 1975. The complaint alleges federal antitrust violations and common law fraud and deceit. The basic thrust of the complaint was that the three other insurers involved in the suit agreed not to write policies for any customer who wanted to switch from St. Paul. The defendants have denied the charges, and in the words of St. Paul (in letter to author, July 26, 1977), "we . . . remain committed to energetically defending this lawsuit."
56. U. S. Senate Hearings, op. cit., pp. 297–98, 319, 327, 347.

57. Based on the ISO maximum estimate of claims frequency increase of 15 per cent per annum.
58. NAIC, No. 4, op. cit., p. 101.
59. Roberts, op. cit., p. 5.
60. NAIC, No. 4, op. cit., p. 129.
61. Roberts, op. cit., p. 6.
62. Ibid, p. 9.
63. Ibid., p. 7.
64. Author's notes.
65. See Chapter Fourteen and Chapter Sixteen.
66. Roberts, op. cit., p. 8.
67. The insurance industry denies this, but see *Attorney General vs. Commissioner of Insurance,* footnote 53.
68. Grant Miller, "Malpractice Insurance: Where We Are; Where We're Going," *National Underwriter,* December 27, 1975. (Mr. Miller is Assistant General Counsel of Employers of Wausau Insurance Co.; article is reprint of speech given to the Mutual Insurance Technical Conference.)

CHAPTER THIRTEEN

1. U. S. Senate Hearing, op. cit., p. 142.
2. Miller, loc. cit., among others. The term is widely used among negligence lawyers themselves.
3. Quoted by *Modern Health Care* magazine, June 1975.
4. New York *Times,* May 29, 1975.
5. *Business Insurance* magazine, June 2, 1975.
6. *HEW Report,* op. cit., p. 105.
7. Ibid., p. 102.
8. *ISO Report,* op. cit., p. 48.
9. *HEW Report,* op. cit., p. 121.
10. Ibid.
11. Association of Trial Lawyers, "A Position of Responsibility," p. 1. See Bibliography. (Hereafter referred to as "ATLA.")
12. *Trial Magazine,* op. cit., May/June, 1975, p. 2.
13. *Perspective,* op. cit., Second Quarter 1975, quoting *Medical Economics* magazine survey.
14. Author's interview notes.
15. Ibid.
16. ATLA, op. cit., pp. 10–11.
17. *HEW Appendix,* op. cit., p. 101.
18. Intermountain Medical Malpractice Seminar, p. 34. See also Bibliography. (Hereafter referred to as "Intermountain.")
19. Author's interview notes.
20. Ibid.
21. *HEW Appendix,* op. cit., p. 97.
22. Ibid.

23. Neil T. Shayne, "Meritless Malpractice Cases," *Trial Magazine*, op. cit., May/June 1975.
24. Author's notes.
25. Norman W. Frink, M.D., "The Twain Must Meet or . . . ," *Trial Magazine*, op. cit., May/June 1975.
26. *Consumer's Report*, June 1977.
27. *HEW Appendix*, op. cit., p. 102.
28. Ibid., p. 114.
29. See chapters Fifteen and Sixteen.
30. Author's interview notes.
31. Ibid.
32. Physicians Crisis Committee, "Court Docket Survey," 1975, p. 20. (See Bibliography.)
33. Guinther, "Take Two . . . ," op. cit.
34. Physicians Crisis Committee, op. cit., p. 557.
35. Interview, S. Gerald Litvin, personal-injury specialist.
36. Physicians Crisis Committee, op. cit., p. 14; ATLA, op. cit., p. 7; author's interview notes.
37. Author's interview notes.
38. Ibid.
39. Physicians Crisis Committee, op. cit., pp. 10, 12, for general discussions this paragraph; quotation, p. 15.
40. Roberts, op. cit., p. 5.
41. July 12, 1976 issue.
42. Philadelphia *Inquirer*, May 29, 1975.
43. Author's interview notes.
44. This is probably the figure singly most frequently quoted, perhaps because it is the one that can be interpreted as being mutually agreed upon by the NAIC and the HEW studies.
45. St. Paul, loc. cit.; Insurance Information Institute, quoted by *Modern Health Care*, op. cit., June 1975.
46. Author's interview notes.
47. E.g., p. 19.
48. *HEW Appendix*, op. cit., p. 14; *HEW Report*, op. cit., p. 50.
49. *ISO Report*, op. cit., p. 50; *ISO Appendix*, op. cit., p. 22.
50. NAIC, No. 4, op. cit., p. 94.
51. *HEW Report*, op. cit., p. 6; *HEW Appendix*, op. cit., p. 13.
52. *ISO Report*, op. cit., pp. 48–49.
53. This usually happens when the plaintiff's attorney wants to get his case into federal court, where the quality of the judiciary is usually superiority to state court. In order to establish jurisdiction, he names as guardian for the deceased victim or a minor child, someone who lives in a different state from that of the plaintiff, thereby establishing diversity. This sometimes works, but when it doesn't, the case can be lost on that basis. Also, author's interview with David Shrager Esq.
54. Physicians Crisis Committee, op. cit., pp. 23–24.
55. *HEW Appendix*, op. cit., p. 103.
56. J.G. interview notes.

57. NAIC, No. 1, op. cit., p. 48. For reasons that are unclear, the NAIC ceased publishing this useful compilation in subsequent volumes. Therefore, this figure is based on only about 4,000 claims, which was the number that had been compiled at the time volume one was published. Throughout, the NAIC study, so valuable otherwise in so many ways, avoids detailed analysis of suit resolution almost as mightily as it does the subject of non-asserted claims. That which is not pursued, is not learned to the advantage of those who want others to remain ignorant.
58. Physicians Crisis Committee, op. cit., p. 23.
59. Ibid., p. 560.
60. Czerwinski, op. cit., p. 54.
61. NAIC, No. 4, op. cit., p. 129.
62. *HEW Appendix*, op. cit., p. 104.
63. NAIC, No. 4, loc. cit.
64. *HEW Appendix*, loc. cit.

CHAPTER FOURTEEN

1. NAIC, No. 4, op. cit., pp. 131–44.
2. Ibid.; Medical Liability Commission, Suite 215, Palmer House, Chicago, Illinois, 1977, pp. 5–31; *Legislator's Guide*, op. cit., pp. 3–21.
3. AMA, op. cit., p. 23.
4. Robert E. Cartwright, "Medical Malpractice: A Trial Lawyer's View," in *Legislator's Guide*, op. cit., p. 62.
5. Frank Shields, ATLA, author's interview notes.
6. See AMA's *Malpractice in Focus*, op. cit., passim.
7. AMA/AHA memo, op. cit., p. 21.
8. Ibid.
9. Ibid, pp. 24–26.
10. NAIC, No. 4, op. cit., p. 144.
11. AMA/AHA memo, op. cit., p. 21.
12. Ibid., p. 27.
13. Ibid.
14. Czerwinski, op. cit., p. 49.
15. Ibid.
16. Ibid., p. 50.
17. Ibid., p. 51.
18. Ibid.
19. Intermountain, op. cit., p. 55.
20. Ibid., p. 56.
21. Czerwinski, op. cit., p. 54.
22. *Medical World News*, op. cit., July 12, 1975.
23. U. S. Senate Hearing, op. cit., p. 147.
24. Czerwinski, op. cit., p. 52.
25. Ibid., pp. 53–54.

26. Intermountain, op. cit., p. 59.
27. Czerwinski, op. cit., p. 55.
28. Intermountain, op. cit., p. 105.
29. See Chapter Twelve.
30. Intermountain, loc. cit.
31. NAIC, No. 4, op. cit., pp. 117, 129.
32. Medical Liability Commission, op. cit., p. 11.
33. Intermountain, op. cit., p. 106.
34. Mike Mitchell, "Idaho's Medical Malpractice Crisis," in *Legislator's Guide*, op. cit., p. 37. Mr. Mitchell is a member of the Idaho State Senate.
35. Intermountain, op. cit., p. 102.
36. NAIC, No. 4, op. cit., p. 129.
37. Ibid., p. 126.
38. Intermountain, op. cit., p. 103.
39. *Medical World News*, op. cit., January 12, 1976.
40. NAIC, No. 4, op. cit., pp. 139–40.
41. Intermountain, op. cit., p. 58.
42. Ibid., p. 100.
43. Medical Liability Commission, op. cit., p. 8.
44. *Legislator's Guide*, op. cit., pp. 4–5.
45. NAIC, No. 4, op. cit., p. 129.
46. Adam Benjamin, Jr., "Indiana's Medical Malpractice Crisis," *Legislator's Guide*, p. 38.
47. Ibid.
48. Ibid., pp. 39–40.
49. Ibid., p. 38.
50. Ibid., pp. 41–42.
51. Ibid.
52. Ibid., p. 38.
53. New York Insurance Dept., op. cit., p. 27.
54. Ibid., p. 28.
55. Ibid., p. 30.
56. Keene, op. cit., p. 30.
57. Ibid., p. 32.
58. Ob-Gyn News, September 1, 1975.
59. Lombardi, op. cit., p. 45.
60. Ibid., p. 47.
61. NAIC, No. 4, op. cit., pp. 131–44; Medical Liability Commission, op. cit., pp. 5–29.
62. NAIC, No. 4, op. cit., pp. 145–47.
63. Ibid.
64. Keene, op. cit., p. 29.
65. Ibid., p. 31.
66. *Legislator's Guide*, op. cit., pp. 4–7.
67. *Medical World News*, loc. cit.
68. National Underwriter, May 5, 1975.
69. Guinther, "Take Two . . . ," op. cit.

70. *Legislator's Guide*, op. cit., p. 5.
71. Dean Leiser, "Hospital Administrators: Passing Muster?" *Trial Magazine*, op. cit., May/June 1975.
72. Ibid.
73. Ibid., October 1973.
74. *ISO Report*, op. cit., p. 31.
75. Based on examination of *Citation* and *Trial Magazine* case histories.
76. Keene, op. cit., p. 28; U. S. Senate Hearing, op. cit., p. 39; Intermountain, op. cit., p. 11; Miller, loc. cit.; Roberts, op. cit., p. 5; American Hospital Association statement of position to U. S. House of Representatives, March 5, 1975; *Medical World News*, op. cit., January 26, 1976, p. 40.
77. *Perspective*, op. cit., p. 29.
78. NAIC, No. 4, op. cit., p. 95.
79. *ISO Report*, op. cit., p. 43.
80. Medical Liability Commission, op. cit., passim.
81. NAIC, No. 4, op. cit., pp. 101, 110–27.
82. Ibid., pp. 110–27.
83. *HEW Appendix*, op. cit., pp. 110–12.
84. Miller, loc. cit.; Keene, op. cit., p. 28.
85. NAIC, No. 4, op. cit., p. 101.
86. Ibid., p. 15.
87. Ibid., pp. 15, 101.
88. Ibid., p. 103.
89. *ISO Report*, op. cit., pp. 105–7.
90. Ibid., p. 37.
91. NAIC, No. 4, op. cit., p. 101.
92. Ibid.
93. Miller, loc. cit.
94. This could be accomplished a number of ways, but perhaps the simplest would be to establish a lump sum payment, but dole it out on the accrual system. Should the plaintiff then die before the residue is expended, her estate would receive the balance. If the plaintiff recovers and a balance is left, she receives the residue unexpended that was to cover pain and suffering costs but not the balance to cover medical costs and lost wages.

CHAPTER FIFTEEN

1. Eli Bernzweig, "Getting to the Root of the Problem," *Trial Magazine*, op. cit., May/June 1975.
2. Roscoe Pound, *Spirit of the Common Law*, p. 189. (Boston: Beacon Press.)
3. 66 Calif. 2d, 339, 426, p. 2nd, 525, 538.
4. *Greeman v. Yuba Power Products, Inc.*, 377 p. 2d 897 (Cal. 1962).
5. Miller, loc. cit.
6. Bernzweig, loc. cit.

7. See esp. Lanzone, op. cit.; David Masland, M.D., former president of the Pennsylvania Medical Society, believes Workmen's Compensation laws are the vehicles on which to model the plan; author's interview notes.
8. NAIC, No. 4, op. cit., p. 103.
9. Bernzweig, op. cit., in *Legislator's Guide*, p. 71.
10. American Economic Institute, seminar held December 1976, Washington, D.C., at a televised round-table discussion, p. 32. (Hereafter referred to as "AEI.")
11. NAIC, No. 4, op. cit., p. 103.
12. Ibid., p. 36.
13. Anthony M. Lanzone, "No-Fault Medical Malpractice: Is This Really the Answer?" *Trial Magazine*, April/May 1975.
14. Clark C. Havighurst and Laurence R. Tancredi, "Medical Adversity Insurance," *Milbank Memorial Fund Quarterly*, 51, pp. 125–68, Spring 1973.
15. AEI, op. cit., pp. 31ff.
16. Havighurst, loc. cit.
17. AEI, op. cit.
18. Ibid., pp. 6–9, 37.
19. Wolfe, op. cit., p. 75.
20. *Trial Magazine*, op. cit., May/June 1975, p. 20.
21. Ibid.
22. Wolfe, loc. cit.
23. *Trends*, op. cit., p. 131.
24. Ibid., p. 132.
25. *Trial Magazine*, op. cit., February 1974.
26. New York *Times*, op. cit., January 26, 1976.
27. *Trends*, op. cit., p. 132.
28. P.L. 92–602; Section 249F, Subsection 1152.
29. *Trends*, op. cit., pp. 132–34.
30. Ibid., p. 134.
31. Based on information provided the author by Pennsylvania Secretary of Health, Leonard Bachman, based on statistics compiled by Health Services Quality Bureau, Dept. of HEW.
32. Philadelphia *Bulletin*, October 3, 1976.
33. Ibid.
34. Ibid., October 10, 1976.
35. Ibid., October 3, 1976.
36. Ibid.
37. Ibid.
38. Ibid., July 3, 1977.
39. Ibid.
40. Ibid.
41. Guinther, "Take Two . . . ," loc. cit.
42. *HEW Appendix*, op. cit., p. 112.
43. Ibid.
44. Frink, loc. cit.

CHAPTER SIXTEEN

1. E.g., see Edward C. Banfield, *The Unheavenly City, The Nature and Future of Our Urban Crisis* (Boston: Little Brown & Co.), 1968.
2. NAIC, No. 4, op. cit., p. 137.
3. AMA, op. cit., p. 28.
4. *AHA Bulletin*, February 2, 1976.
5. U. S. Senate Hearing, op. cit., p. 304.
6. Ibid., p. 321.
7. Ibid., p. 329.
8. ATLA, op. cit., p. 2.
9. Defense Research Institute, op. cit., pp. 14–15.
10. Guinther, "Take Two . . . ," loc. cit.
11. Benjamin, op. cit., p. 42.
12. Lombardi, op. cit., pp. 46–47.
13. Guinther, loc. cit.
14. *Medical World News*, "Is Arbitration the Answer to Malpractice Disputes?" January 26, 1976, p. 51.
15. E.g., see history of Indiana malpractice law passage narrated in Chapter Fourteen.
16. U. S. Senate Hearing, loc. cit.
17. Statement submitted to the National Academy of Sciences, November 22, 1976.
18. *Medical World News*, January 26, 1976, op. cit., p. 40.
19. Ibid., p. 52.
20. Ibid., p. 38.
21. NAIC, No. 4, op. cit., p. 137.
22. Intermountain, op. cit., pp. 92–94.
23. Ibid., p. 95.
24. *ISO Appendix*, op. cit., p. 40.
25. Author's interview notes.
26. *ISO Appendix*, loc. cit.
27. Author's interview notes.
28. *HEW Appendix*, op. cit., p. 665.
29. NAIC, No. 4, op. cit., pp. 106–7.
30. S. Gerald Litvin interview.
31. Various sources, but see esp. *Citation*, op. cit., Vol. 34, No. 10, March 1, 1977.
32. *HEW Report*, op. cit., p. 43.
33. Ibid.
34. Ibid.
35. Ibid.; *HEW Appendix*, op. cit., pp. 529–35.
36. *Medical World News*, op. cit., December 1, 1976.
37. ATLA, op. cit., p. 1.
38. Gaylord Nelson, "Mushrooming Malpractice," *Trial Magazine*, op. cit., May/June 1975, see esp. p. 22.

39. *Statistical Abstract*, op. cit., p. 79.
40. See Chapter Twelve.
41. *HEW Appendix*, op. cit., p. 511.
42. Guinther, "Take Two . . . ," loc. cit.
43. A somewhat similar idea was proposed by Arthur H. Bernstein, Counsel for Kaiser Foundation Health Plan, in *Hospitals, Journal of American Hospital Association*, July 1, 1972. (In this article, Mr. Bernstein was not speaking for the Kaiser Plan.)
44. This formula is intended for illustrative purposes only. Management fees and investment percentages may either be established by legislative fiat or be worked out on a competitive basis by companies wishing to obtain the management franchise.
45. The $1.5 billion suggested here is considerably lower than the insurance industry's own current estimates of required income from malpractice customers. That estimate, however, as noted in Chapter Twelve, is almost certainly seriously inflated. But even if it were not, the estimate includes premiums from dentists and other medical providers who will not be included under the national insurance company formula. It also includes hundreds of millions of dollars presently paid to insurance agents in the states in which the commercial companies do business. Since all customers are now captive, the national company has no need for agents and that money is saved. Duplicative costs created by the multi-source system are also eliminated. Finally, the industry estimate does not include investment earnings to policyholders as visualized in the national company formula.
46. *Trial Magazine*, May/June 1975, op. cit., p. 20.

Index

JOHN GUINTHER is an award-winning investigative reporter whose articles have appeared in a number of publications. He is a contributing editor for *Philadelphia Magazine,* and has served as a visiting professor in urban affairs at Temple University. In 1973, he received the Robert F. Kennedy Memorial Award for the best article of the year on disadvantaged people. He has been cited three times by the American Bar Association for his outstanding articles on the American Justice system. In 1975, he received the National Journalism fraternity, Sigma Delta Chi, award for the best magazine article of the year. In 1976, UCLA's Gerald Loeb awards program for business and financial reporting created a special recognition award for his article "Don't Worry, It's Only Money." Mr. Guinther is also the author of *Moralists and Managers,* published by Anchor Press in 1976.